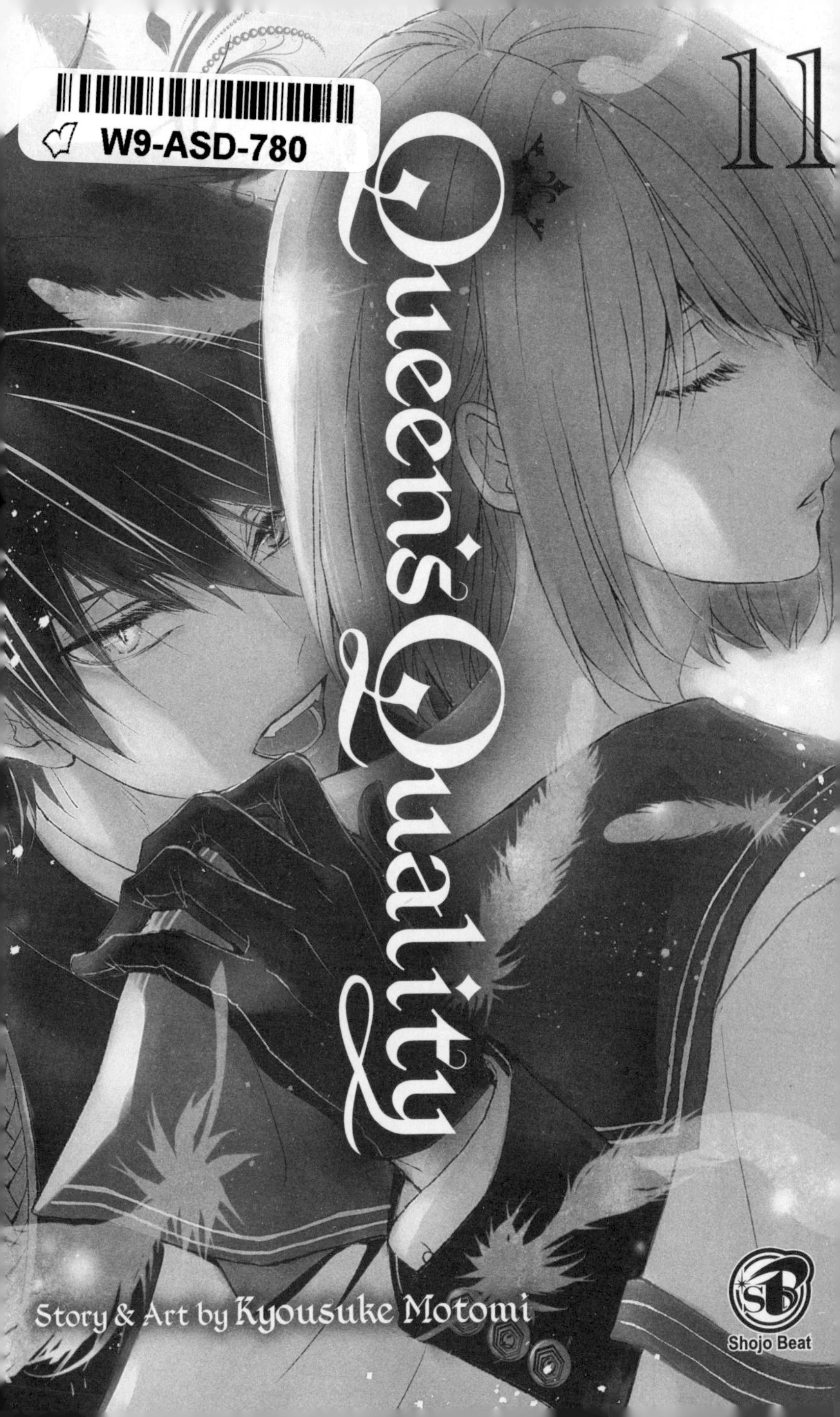

11
Queen's Quality
Story & Art by Kyousuke Motomi
Shojo Beat

Queen's Quality

CONTENTS

11

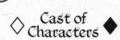

Cast of Characters

Fumi Nishioka

An apprentice Sweeper with the powers of a Queen, this second-year high school student dreams of finding her very own Prince Charming.

Kyutaro Horikita

A mind Sweeper who cleanses people's minds of dangerous impurities. Although incredibly awkward with people, he and Fumi are now dating.

Ataru Shikata

A former bug handler who uses bugs to manipulate people. Saved by Fumi and Kyutaro, he has joined the Genbu Clan.

Miyako Horikita

The prior head of the Genbu Gate Sweepers. She can be both strict and kind, and she watches over and advises Fumi.

Koichi Kitagawa

The chairman of the school Fumi and Kyutaro attend. He's a Sweeper as well as being Kyutaro's brother-in-law.

Takaya Kitahara

One of the Genbu Clan, he was originally a member of the main Byakko Clan. He's an expert with suggestive therapy and is actually Fumi's uncle.

Story Thus Far

The Horikitas are a family of Sweepers—people who cleanse impurities from human hearts. After seeing Fumi's potential, they take her on as an assistant and trainee. Within Fumi dwells the power of both the White and the Dark-Gray queens, both of whom have the ability to give people immense power.

Having both paid the compensation demanded by the White Queen and completed their training in Seichi, Fumi and Kyutaro are finally on the same page emotionally and are now in a relationship! Fumi is overjoyed, but the Horikitas are deeply worried about the presence of the snake inside Kyutaro. Now that Fumi possesses the powers of the True Queen, she and Kyutaro set out to deal with the snake within him once and for all. But when the snake begs them to spare his life, Kyutaro offers a deal…

MONTHLY BETSUCOMI SALE DATE NOTICE ON TWITTER

CHAPTER 49

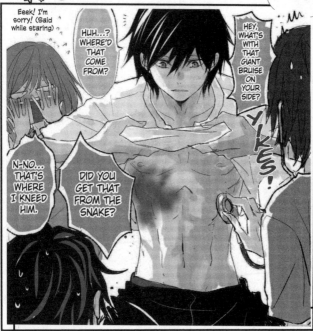

HEY, WHAT'S WITH THAT GIANT BRUISE ON YOUR SIDE?
YIKES!
HUH...? WHERE'D THAT COME FROM?
Eeek! I'm sorry! (Said while staring)
DID YOU GET THAT FROM THE SNAKE?
N-NO... THAT'S WHERE I KNEED HIM.

YOU CAN'T SHOW A WOMAN'S NIPPLES IN *BETSUCOMI*, BUT A MAN'S ARE FINE...

LET'S SEE... WHAT'S UP IN *QUEEN'S QUALITY* THIS MONTH?
(1) THIS IS THE FIRST TIME I'VE DRAWN A CHARACTER WHO'S SO FULL OF HIMSELF.
(2) SORRY... PLEASE DON'T LOOK CLOSELY AT THE DESIGN ON TAKAYA'S T-SHIRT.
(3) "OH, MY. THOSE KIDS ARE MAKING OUT AGAIN..." IS PROBABLY WHAT THE GROWN-UPS ARE THINKING.
KYUTARO SUDDENLY STRIPPED DOWN IN THIS NEW CHAPTER!

I SEND OUT TWITTER UPDATES LIKE THIS EVERY MONTH. YOU CAN READ SOME OF MY OTHER MUTTERINGS THERE TOO.

@motomikyosuke

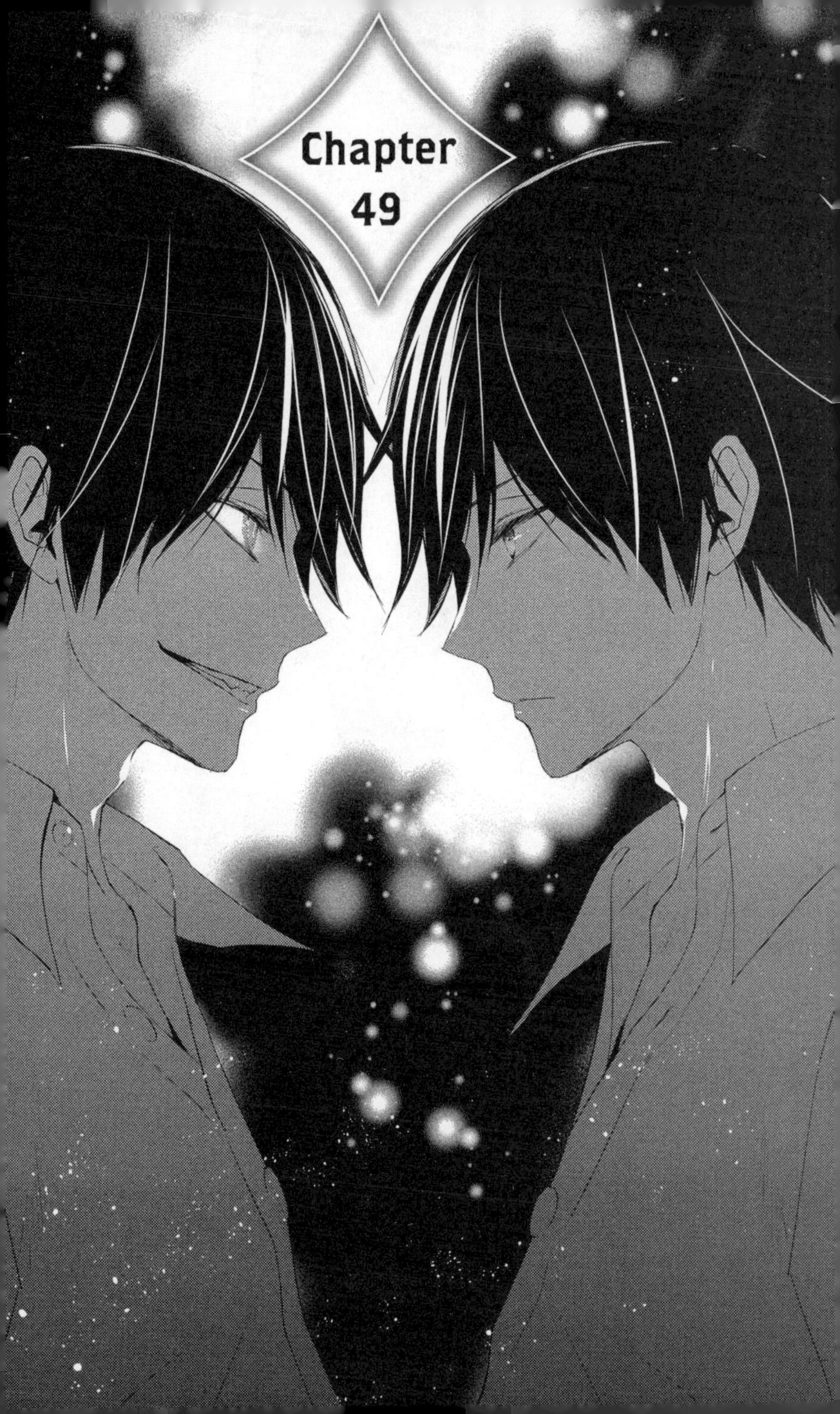
Chapter 49

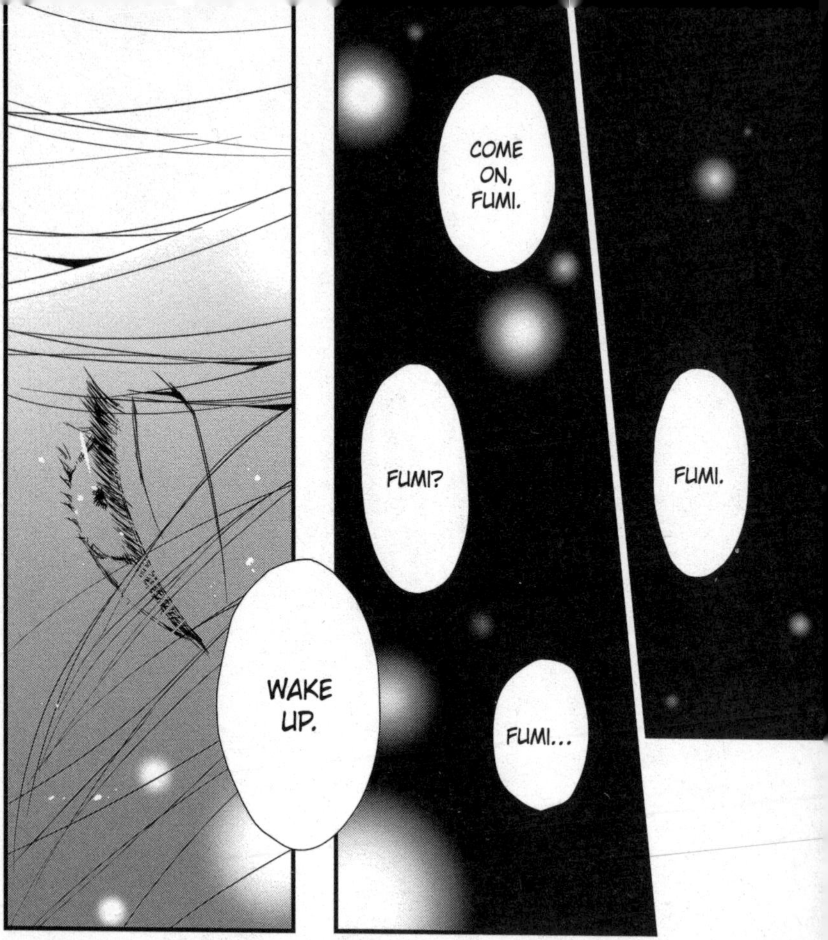
FUMI.
COME ON, FUMI.
FUMI?
FUMI...
WAKE UP.

Hello, everyone! I'm Kyousuke Motomi, and this is volume 11 of *Queen's Quality*. I'm so happy! It looks like this will bring the total number of books printed for the series to 1.8 million in Japan. (This includes the numbers for *QQ Sweeper*.) I'm so grateful to all of you!

In volume 11, we delve deeper into the Seiryu arc. I hope you enjoy it.

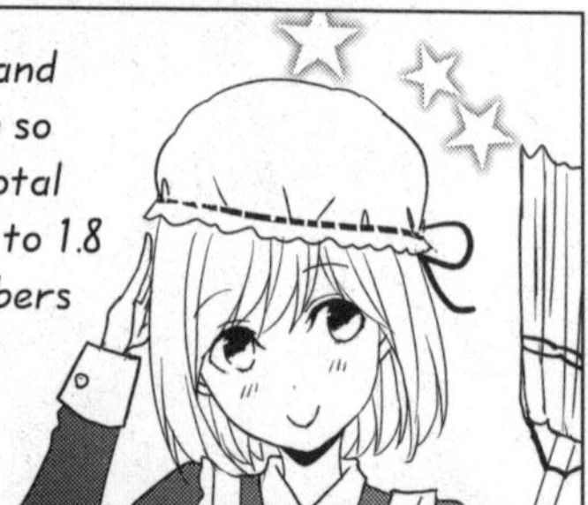

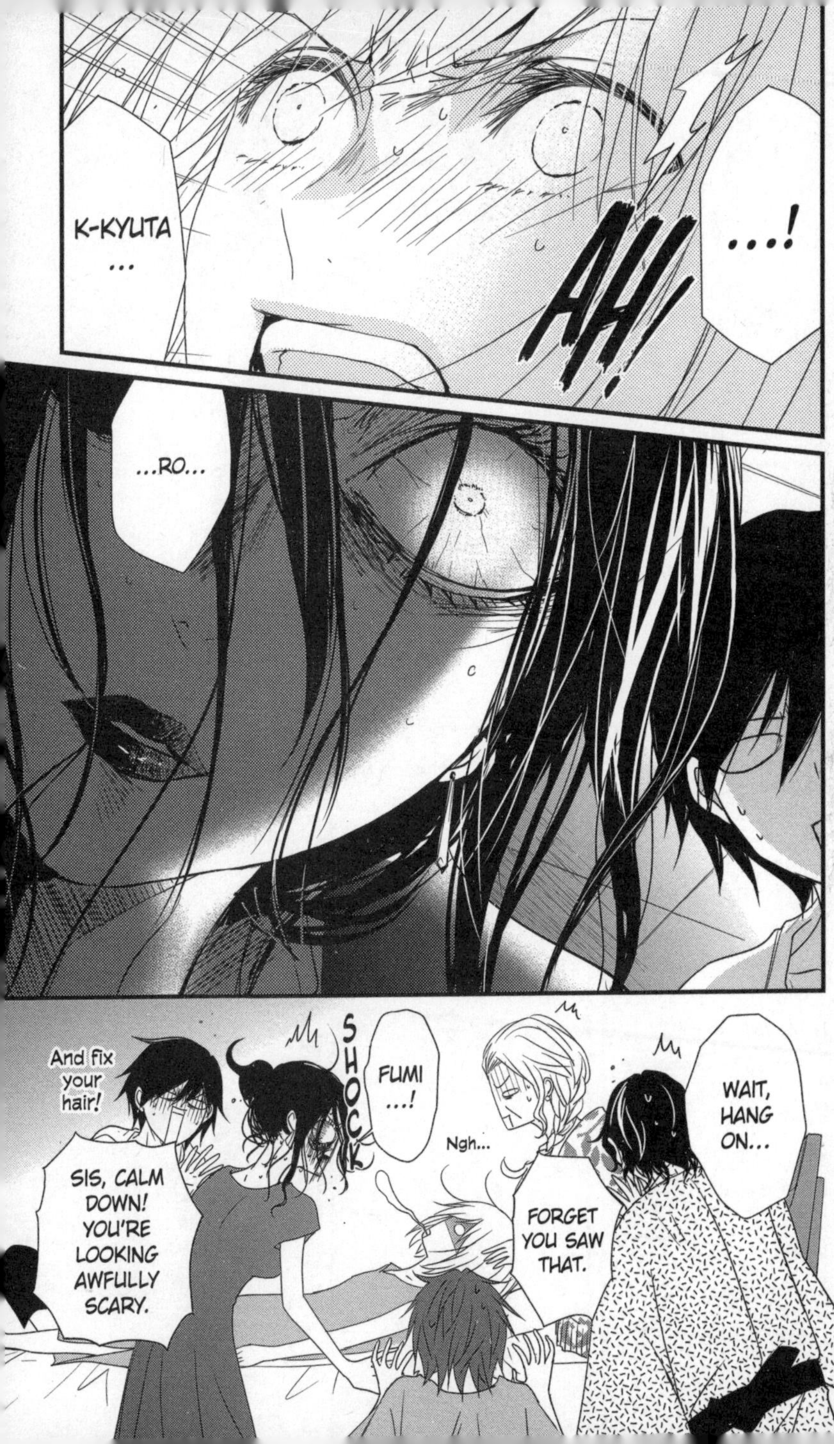
...!
AH!
K-KYUTA ...
...RO...
WAIT, HANG ON...
FORGET YOU SAW THAT.
Ngh...
FUMI ...!
SHOCK
SIS, CALM DOWN! YOU'RE LOOKING AWFULLY SCARY.
And fix your hair!

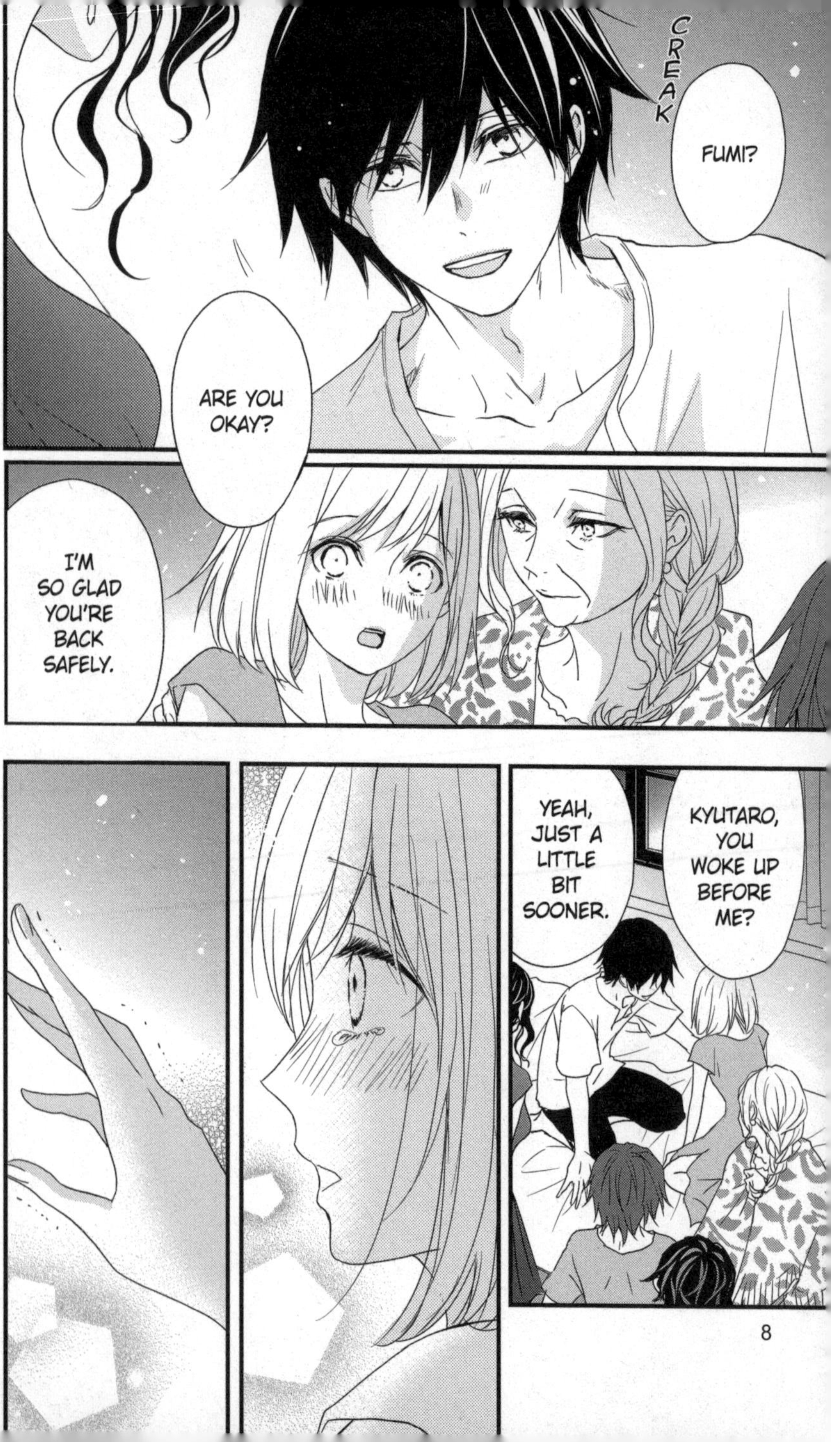
CREAK
FUMI?
ARE YOU OKAY?
I'M SO GLAD YOU'RE BACK SAFELY.
KYUTARO, YOU WOKE UP BEFORE ME?
YEAH, JUST A LITTLE BIT SOONER.

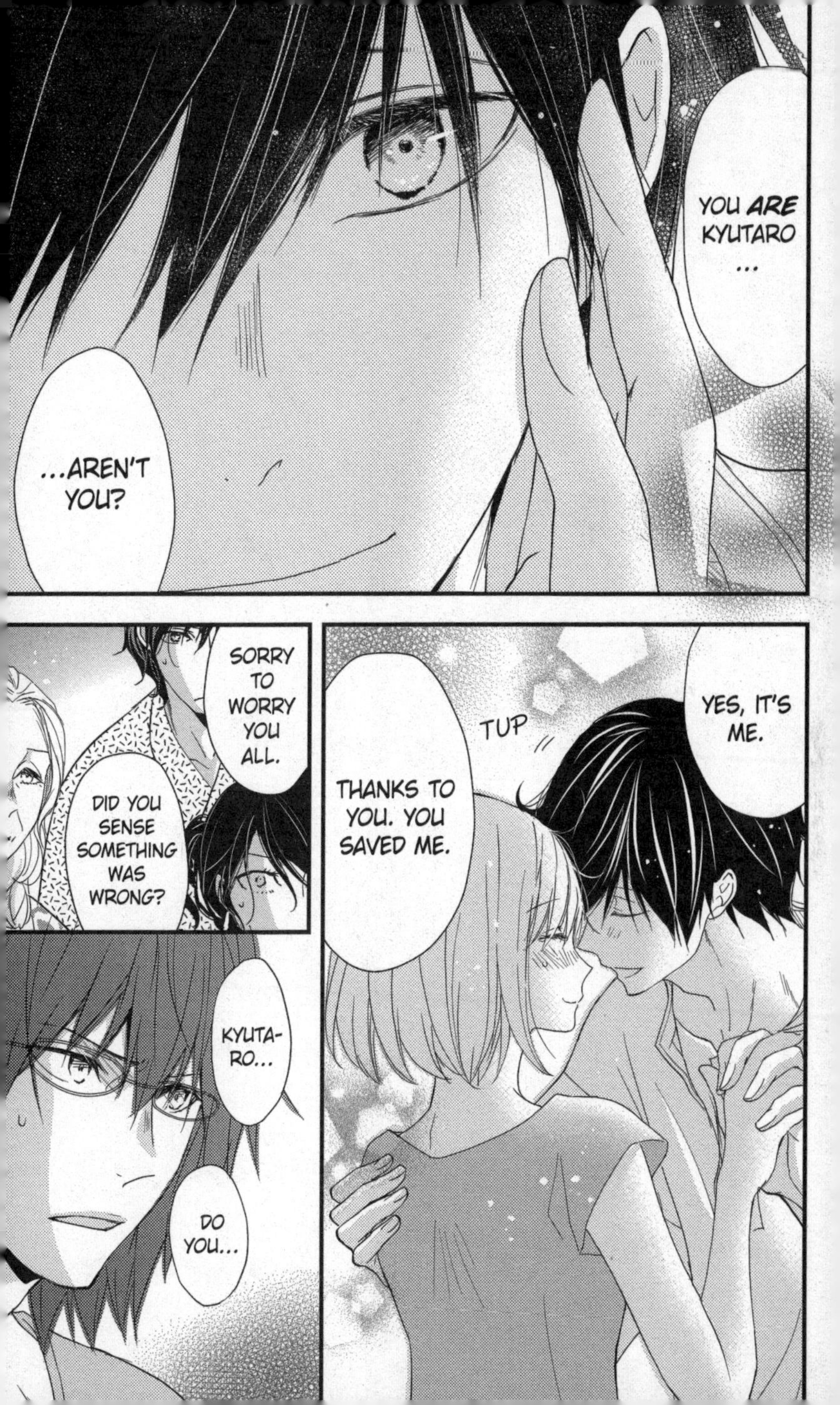
YOU **ARE** KYUTARO ...
...AREN'T YOU?
YES, IT'S ME.
TUP
THANKS TO YOU. YOU SAVED ME.
SORRY TO WORRY YOU ALL.
DID YOU SENSE SOMETHING WAS WRONG?
KYUTA-RO...
DO YOU...

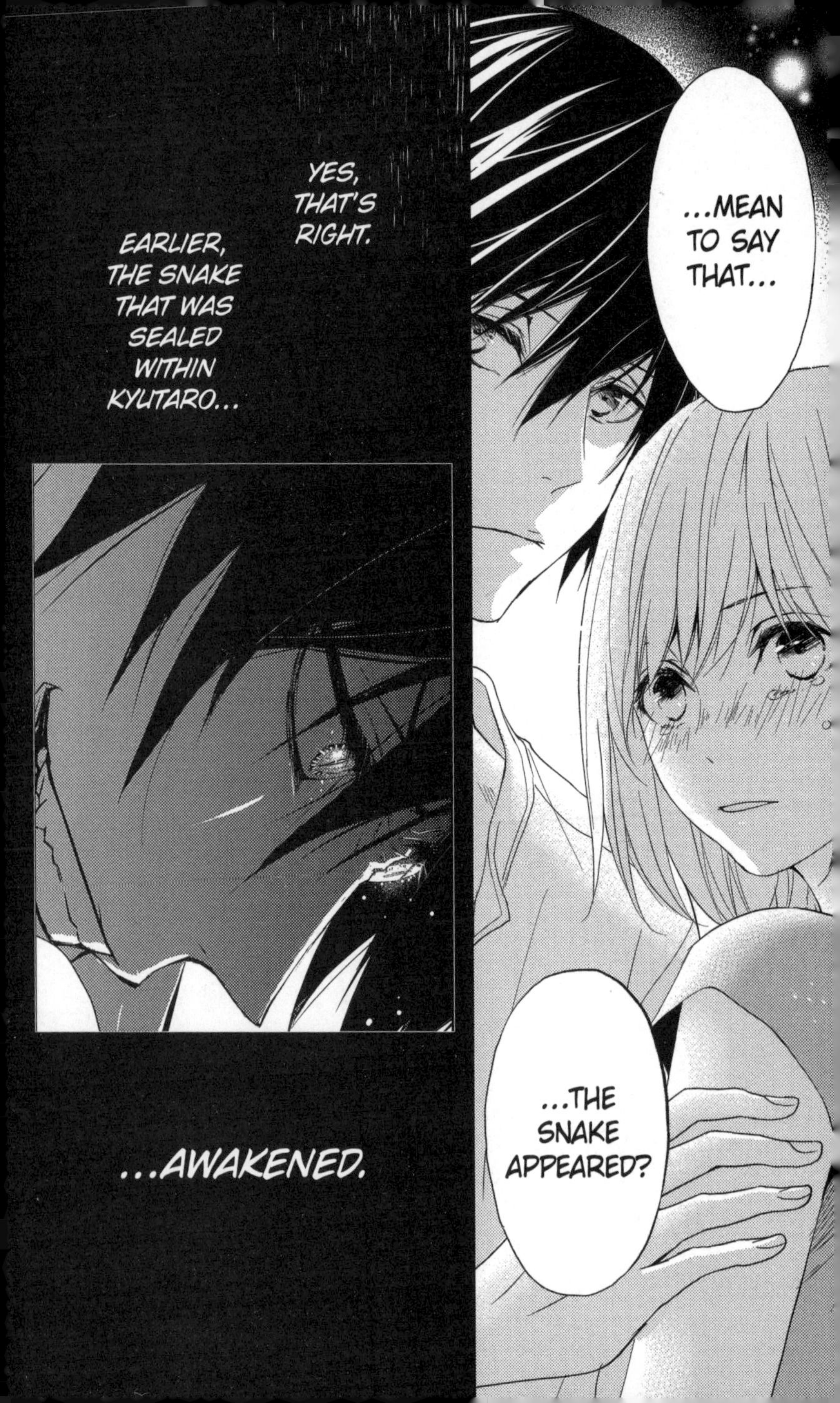
...MEAN TO SAY THAT...
...THE SNAKE APPEARED?
YES, THAT'S RIGHT.
EARLIER, THE SNAKE THAT WAS SEALED WITHIN KYUTARO...
...AWAKENED.

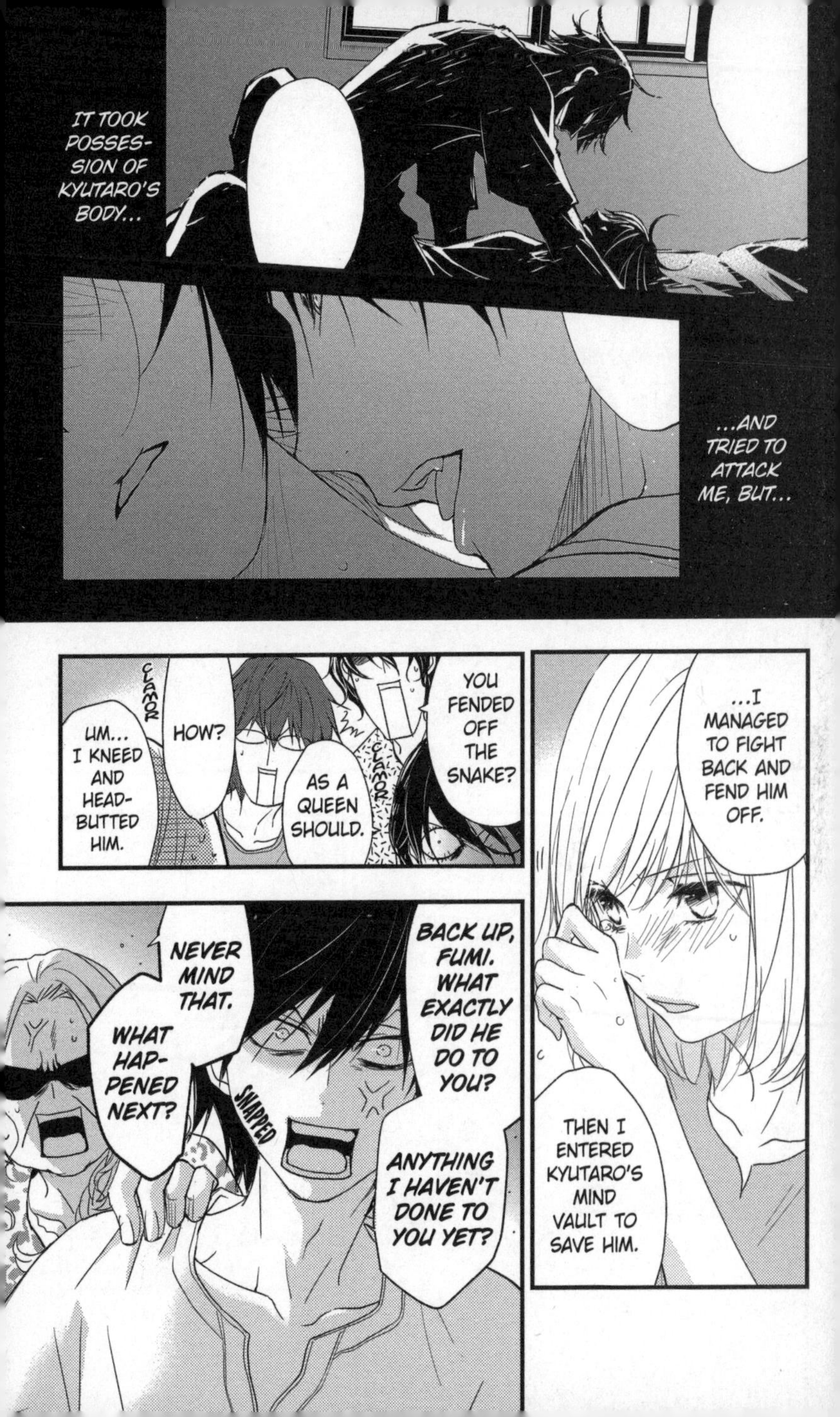
IT TOOK POSSESSION OF KYUTARO'S BODY...
...AND TRIED TO ATTACK ME, BUT...
...I MANAGED TO FIGHT BACK AND FEND HIM OFF.
THEN I ENTERED KYUTARO'S MIND VAULT TO SAVE HIM.
YOU FENDED OFF THE SNAKE?
CLAMOR
AS A QUEEN SHOULD.
HOW?
CLAMOR
UM... I KNEED AND HEAD-BUTTED HIM.
BACK UP, FUMI. WHAT EXACTLY DID HE DO TO YOU?
ANYTHING I HAVEN'T DONE TO YOU YET?
SNAPPED
NEVER MIND THAT.
WHAT HAPPENED NEXT?

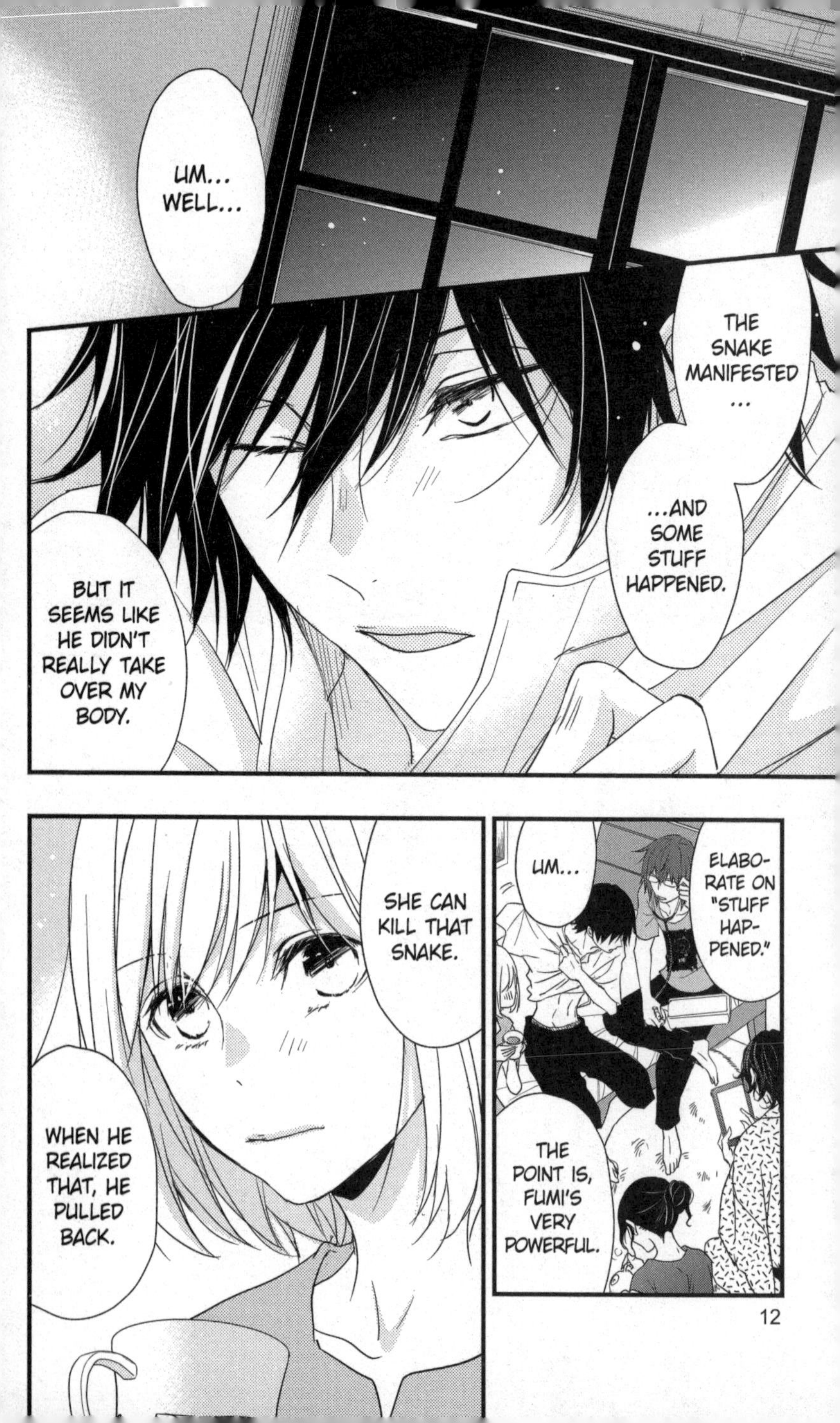
UM... WELL...
THE SNAKE MANIFESTED ...
...AND SOME STUFF HAPPENED.
BUT IT SEEMS LIKE HE DIDN'T REALLY TAKE OVER MY BODY.
ELABORATE ON "STUFF HAPPENED."
UM...
THE POINT IS, FUMI'S VERY POWERFUL.
SHE CAN KILL THAT SNAKE.
WHEN HE REALIZED THAT, HE PULLED BACK.

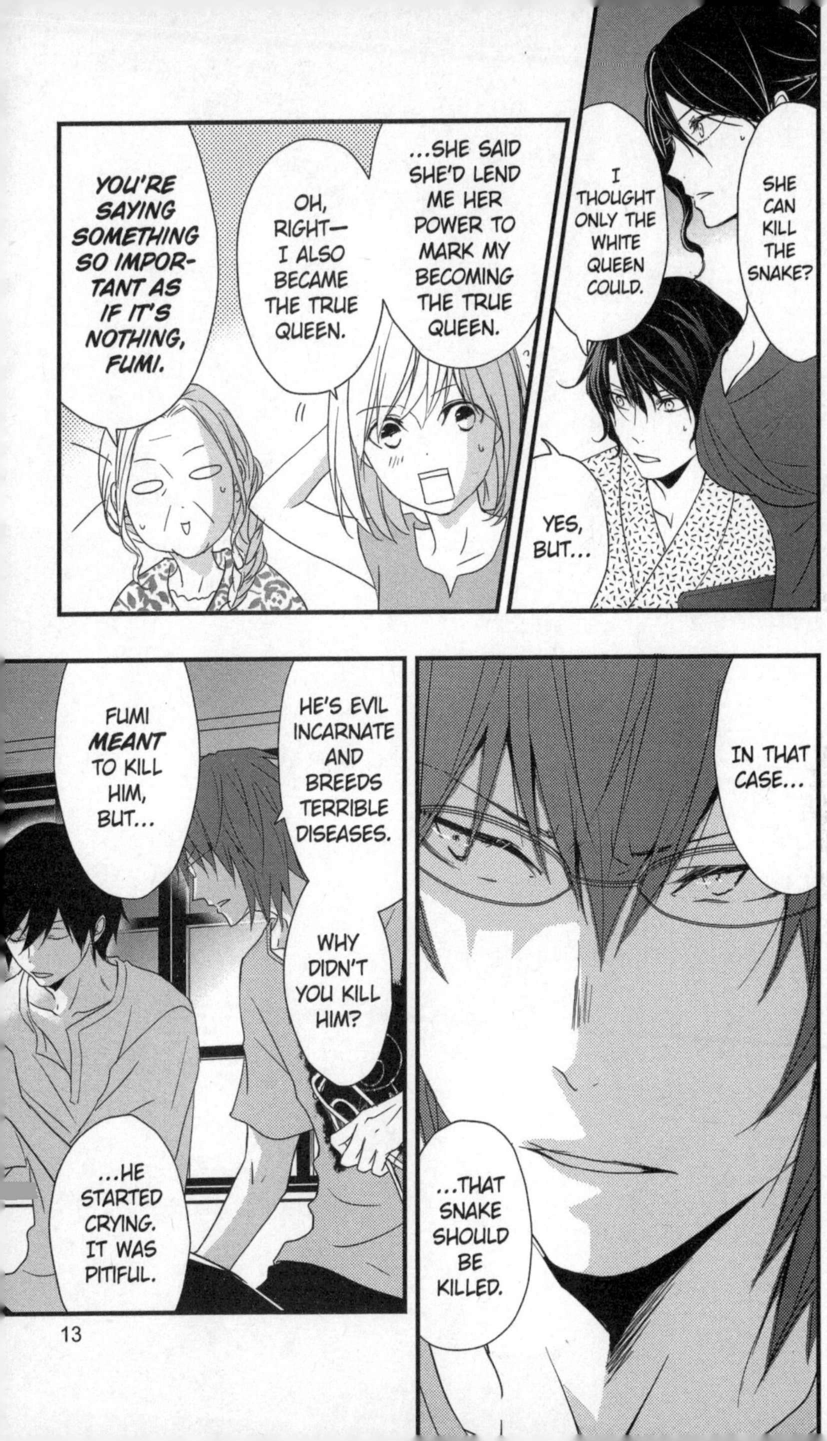
SHE CAN KILL THE SNAKE?
I THOUGHT ONLY THE WHITE QUEEN COULD.
YES, BUT...
...SHE SAID SHE'D LEND ME HER POWER TO MARK MY BECOMING THE TRUE QUEEN.
OH, RIGHT— I ALSO BECAME THE TRUE QUEEN.
YOU'RE SAYING SOMETHING SO IMPORTANT AS IF IT'S NOTHING, FUMI.
IN THAT CASE...
...THAT SNAKE SHOULD BE KILLED.
HE'S EVIL INCARNATE AND BREEDS TERRIBLE DISEASES.
WHY DIDN'T YOU KILL HIM?
FUMI *MEANT* TO KILL HIM, BUT...
...HE STARTED CRYING. IT WAS PITIFUL.

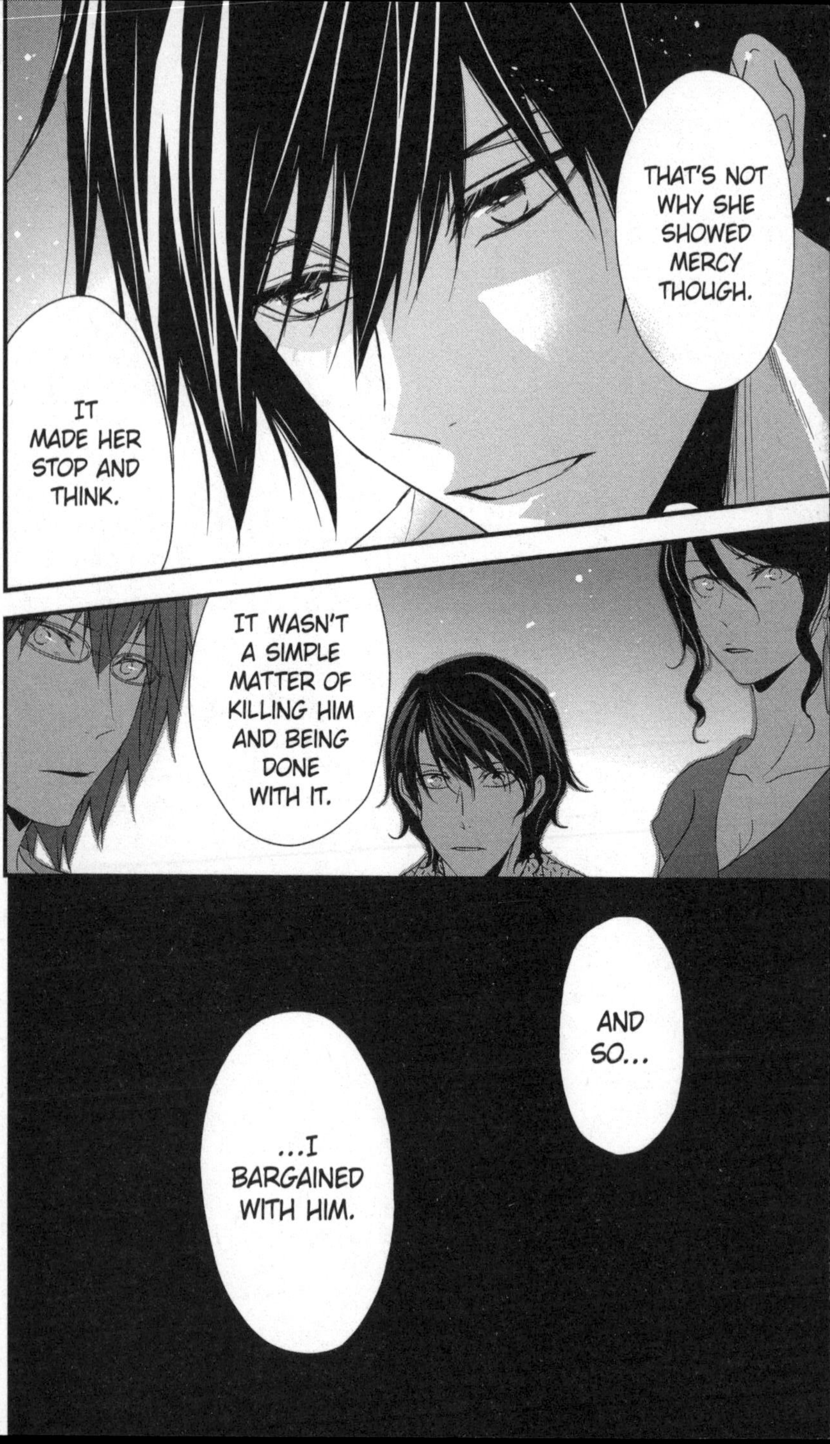
THAT'S NOT WHY SHE SHOWED MERCY THOUGH.
IT MADE HER STOP AND THINK.
IT WASN'T A SIMPLE MATTER OF KILLING HIM AND BEING DONE WITH IT.
AND SO...
...I BARGAINED WITH HIM.

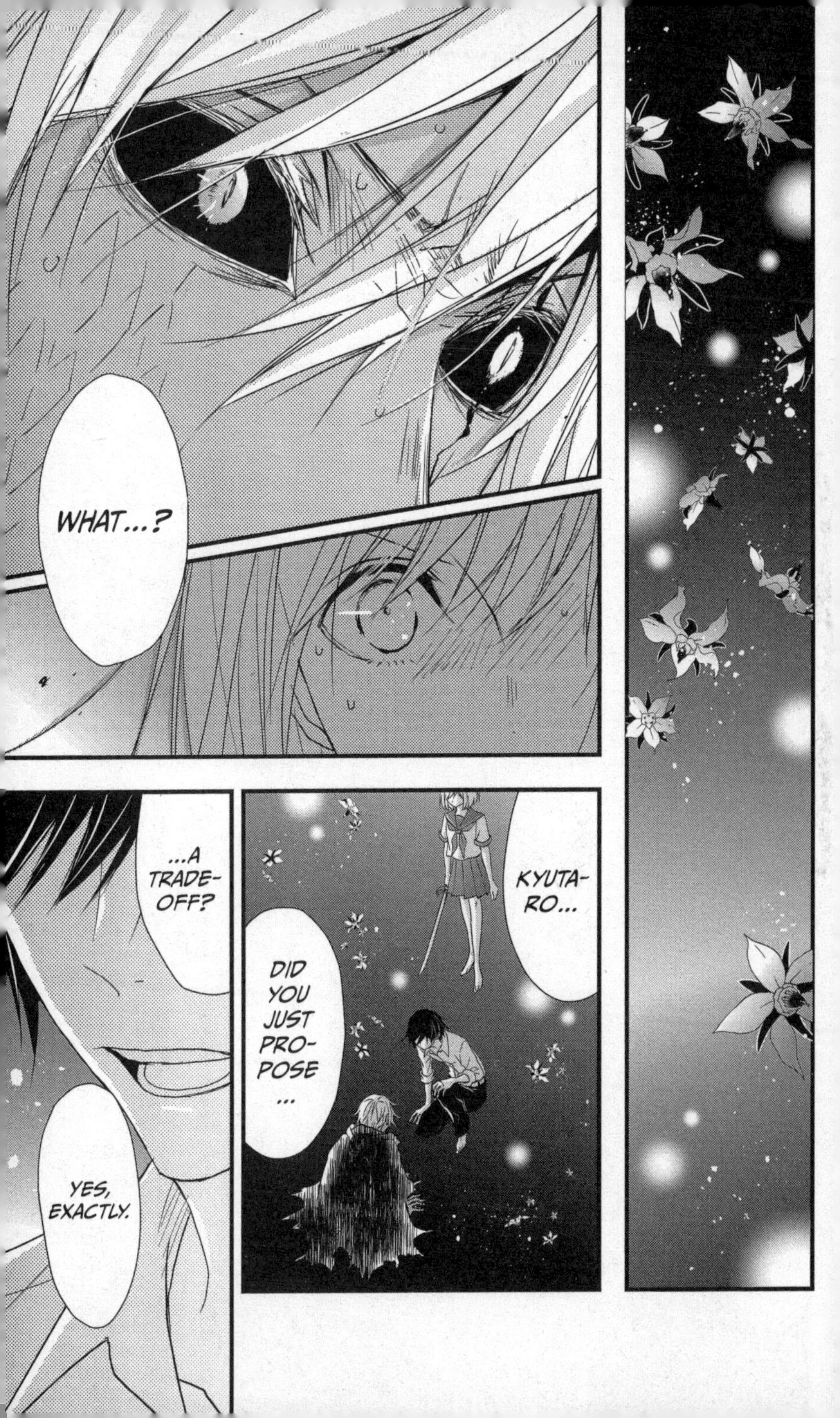
WHAT...?
KYUTA-RO...
DID YOU JUST PRO-POSE...
...A TRADE-OFF?
YES, EXACTLY.

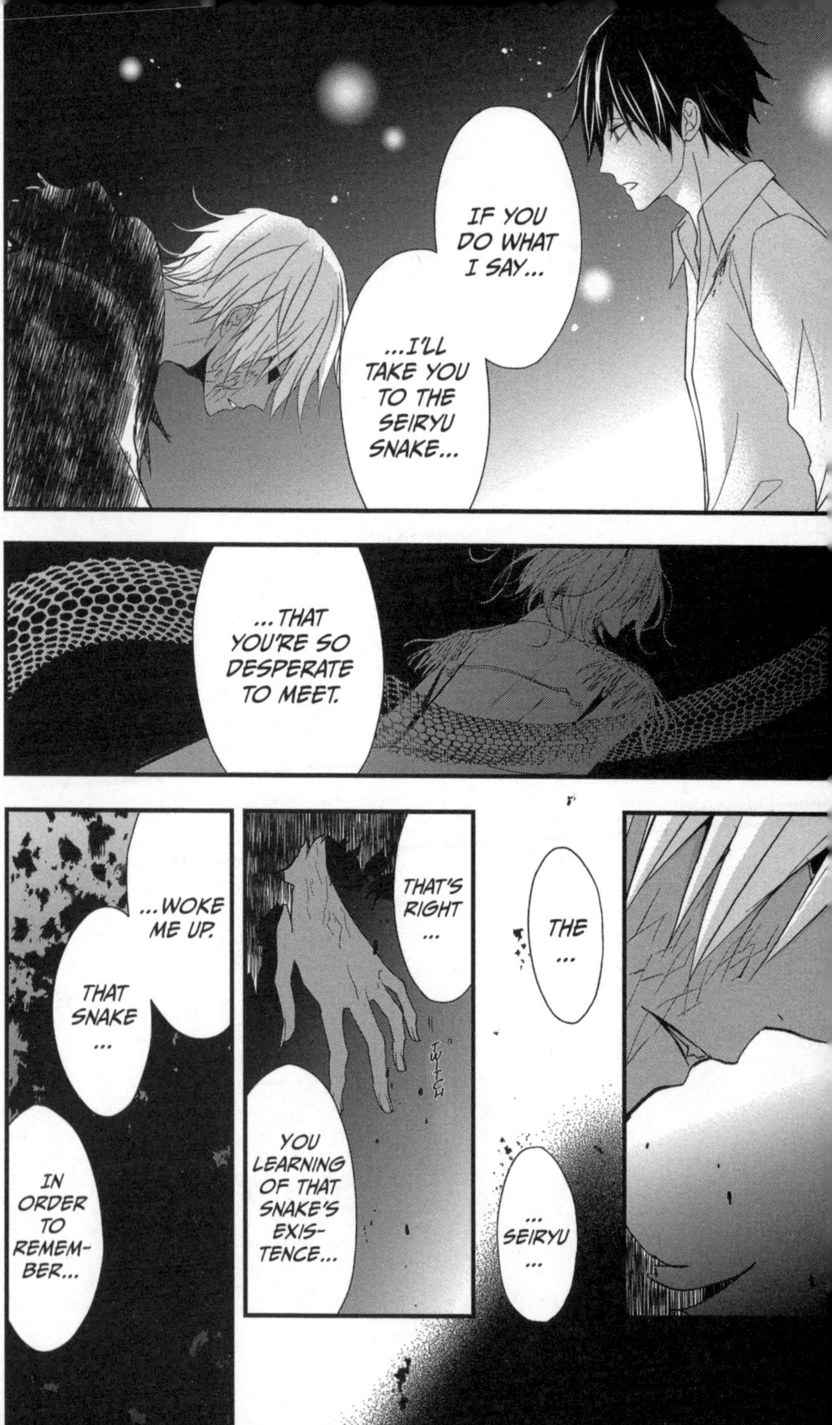
IF YOU DO WHAT I SAY...
...I'LL TAKE YOU TO THE SEIRYU SNAKE...
...THAT YOU'RE SO DESPERATE TO MEET.
THE ...
... SEIRYU ...
THAT'S RIGHT ...
TWITCH
YOU LEARNING OF THAT SNAKE'S EXIS-TENCE...
...WOKE ME UP.
THAT SNAKE ...
IN ORDER TO REMEM-BER...

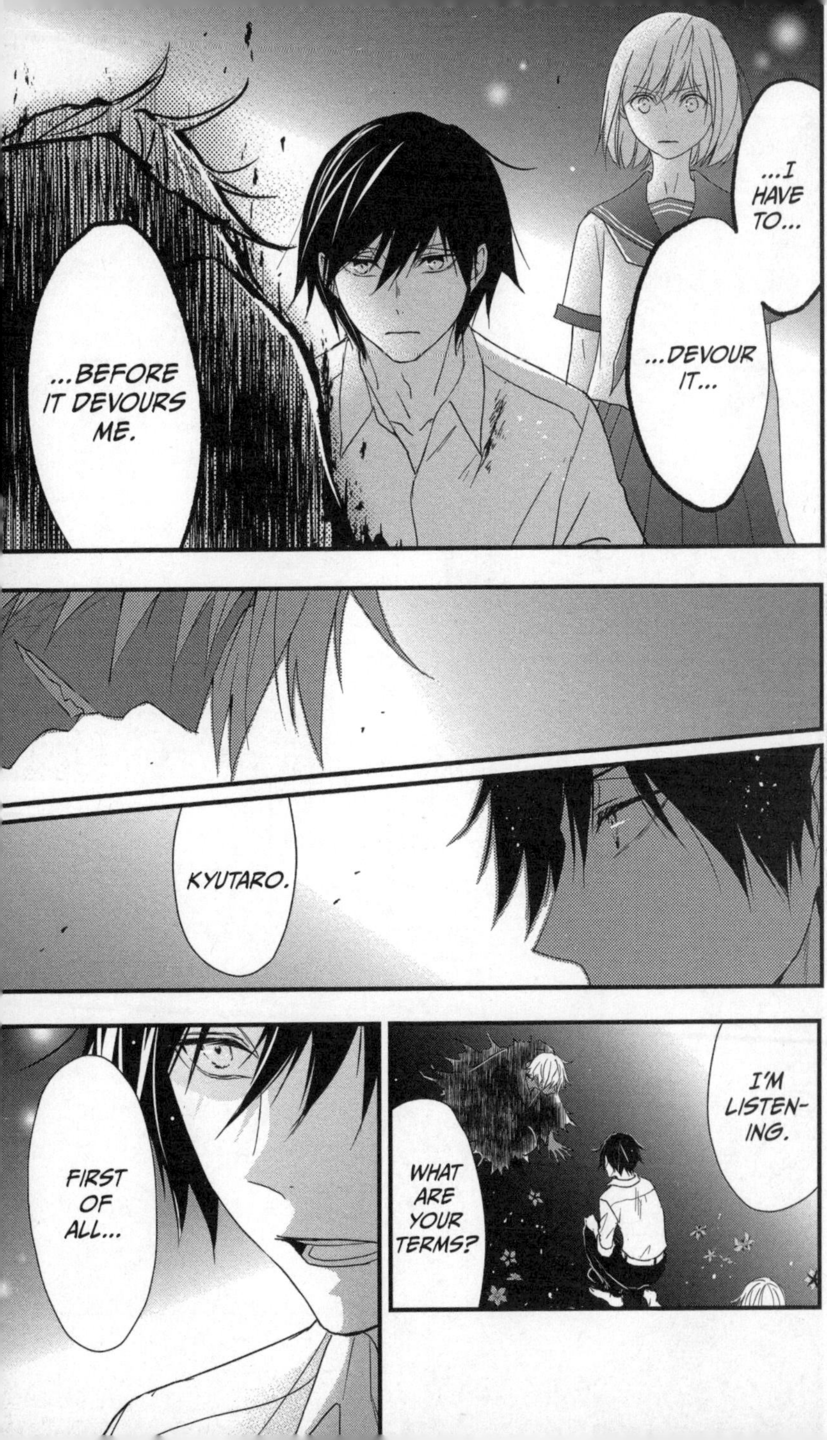
...I HAVE TO...
...DEVOUR IT...
...BEFORE IT DEVOURS ME.
KYUTARO.
I'M LISTEN-ING.
WHAT ARE YOUR TERMS?
FIRST OF ALL...

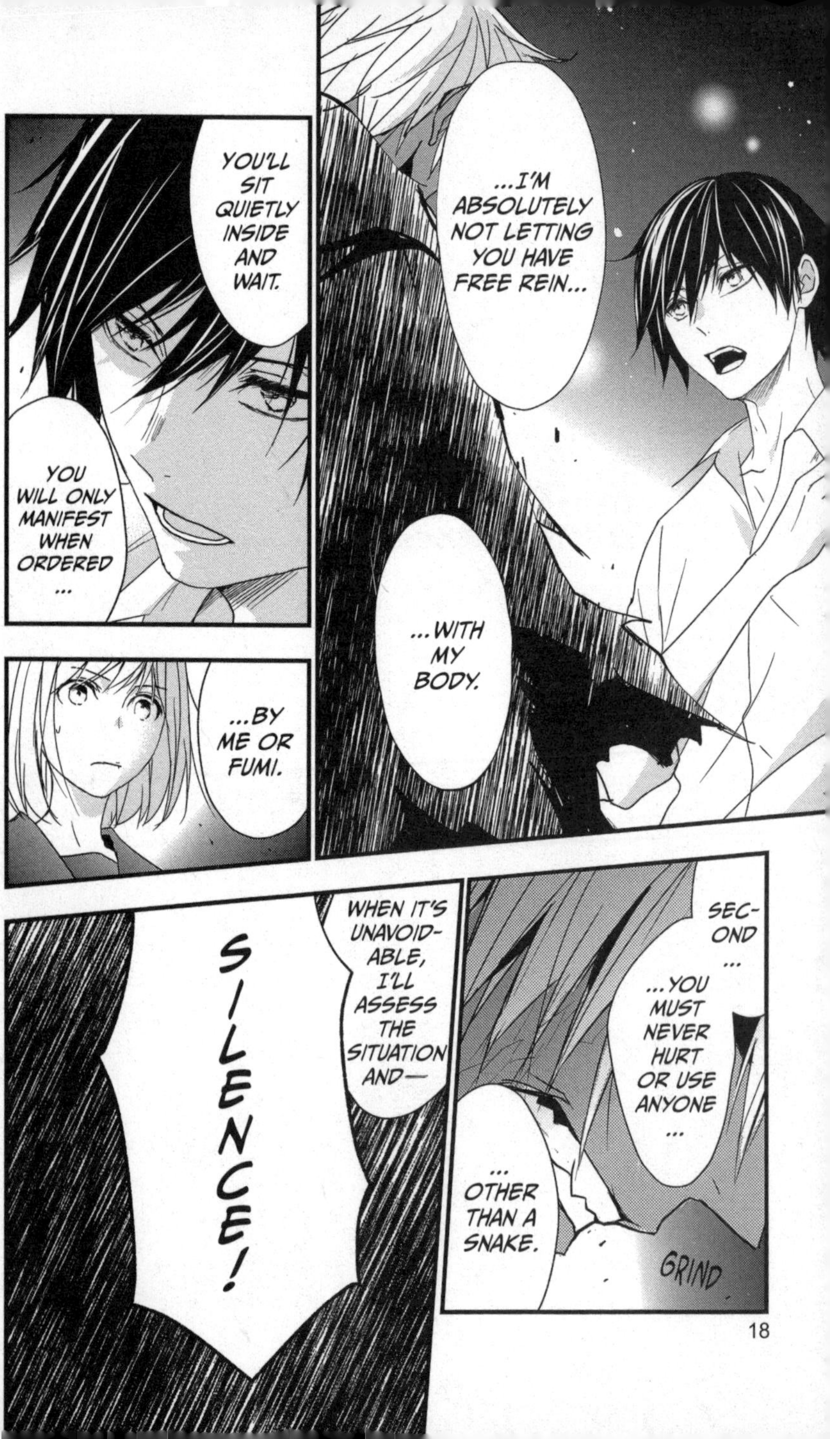
...I'M ABSOLUTELY NOT LETTING YOU HAVE FREE REIN...
...WITH MY BODY.
YOU'LL SIT QUIETLY INSIDE AND WAIT.
YOU WILL ONLY MANIFEST WHEN ORDERED ...
...BY ME OR FUMI.
SEC-OND ...
...YOU MUST NEVER HURT OR USE ANYONE ...
... OTHER THAN A SNAKE.
GRIND
WHEN IT'S UNAVOID-ABLE, I'LL ASSESS THE SITUATION AND—
SILENCE!

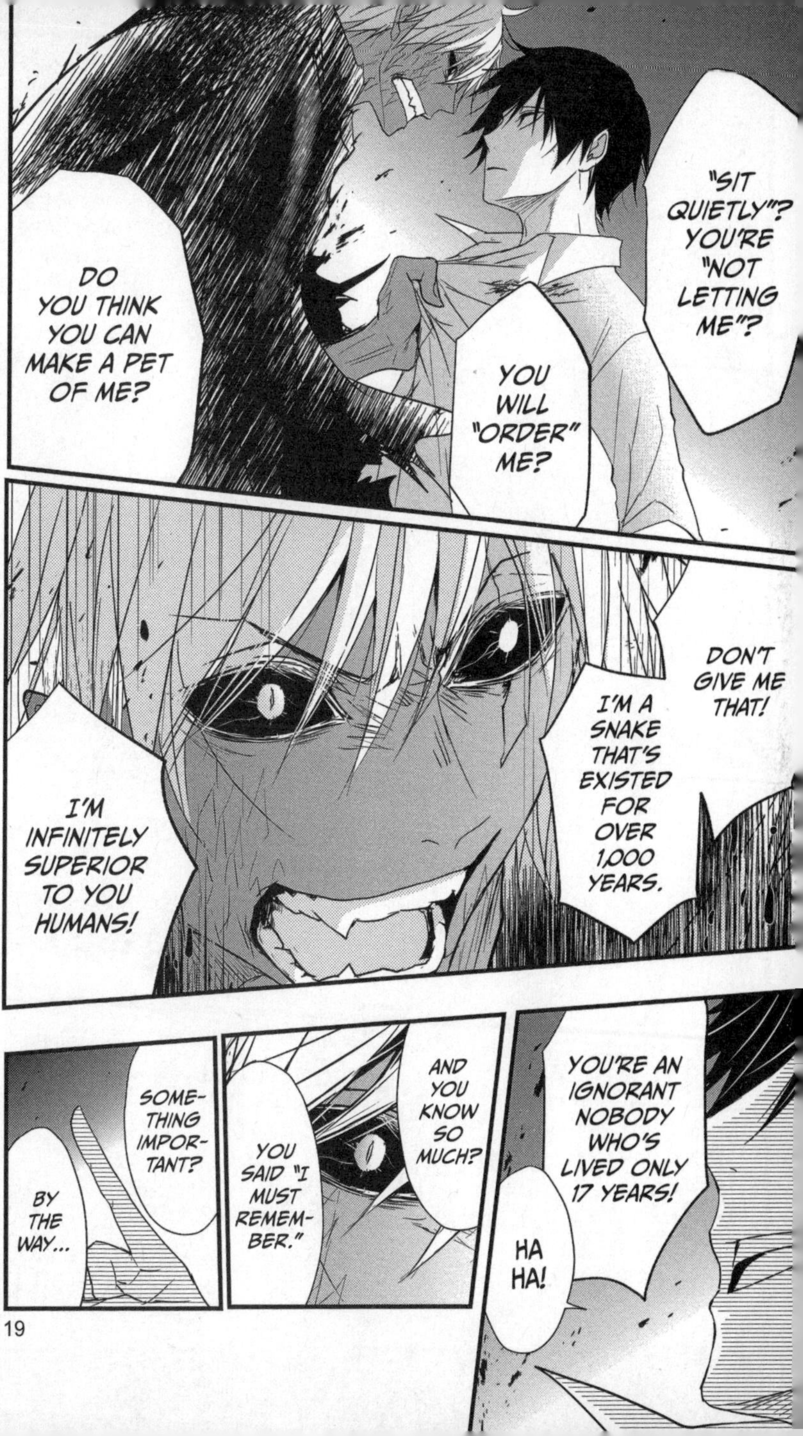
"SIT QUIETLY"? YOU'RE "NOT LETTING ME"?
YOU WILL "ORDER" ME?
DO YOU THINK YOU CAN MAKE A PET OF ME?
DON'T GIVE ME THAT!
I'M A SNAKE THAT'S EXISTED FOR OVER 1,000 YEARS.
I'M INFINITELY SUPERIOR TO YOU HUMANS!
YOU'RE AN IGNORANT NOBODY WHO'S LIVED ONLY 17 YEARS!
HA HA!
AND YOU KNOW SO MUCH?
YOU SAID "I MUST REMEMBER."
SOME-THING IMPOR-TANT?
BY THE WAY...

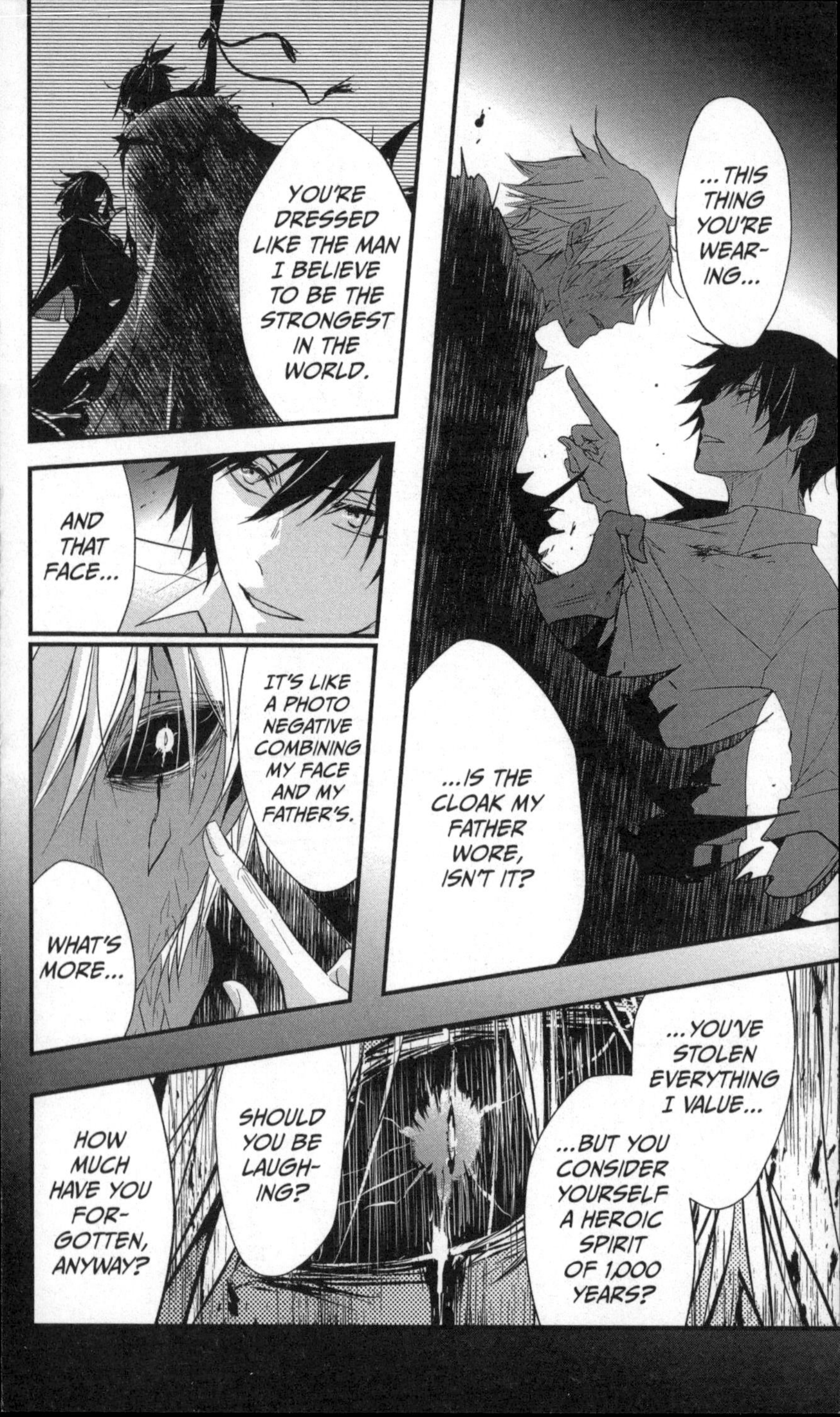
...THIS THING YOU'RE WEAR-ING...
...IS THE CLOAK MY FATHER WORE, ISN'T IT?
YOU'RE DRESSED LIKE THE MAN I BELIEVE TO BE THE STRONGEST IN THE WORLD.
AND THAT FACE...
IT'S LIKE A PHOTO NEGATIVE COMBINING MY FACE AND MY FATHER'S.
WHAT'S MORE...
...YOU'VE STOLEN EVERYTHING I VALUE...
...BUT YOU CONSIDER YOURSELF A HEROIC SPIRIT OF 1,000 YEARS?
SHOULD YOU BE LAUGH-ING?
HOW MUCH HAVE YOU FOR-GOTTEN, ANYWAY?

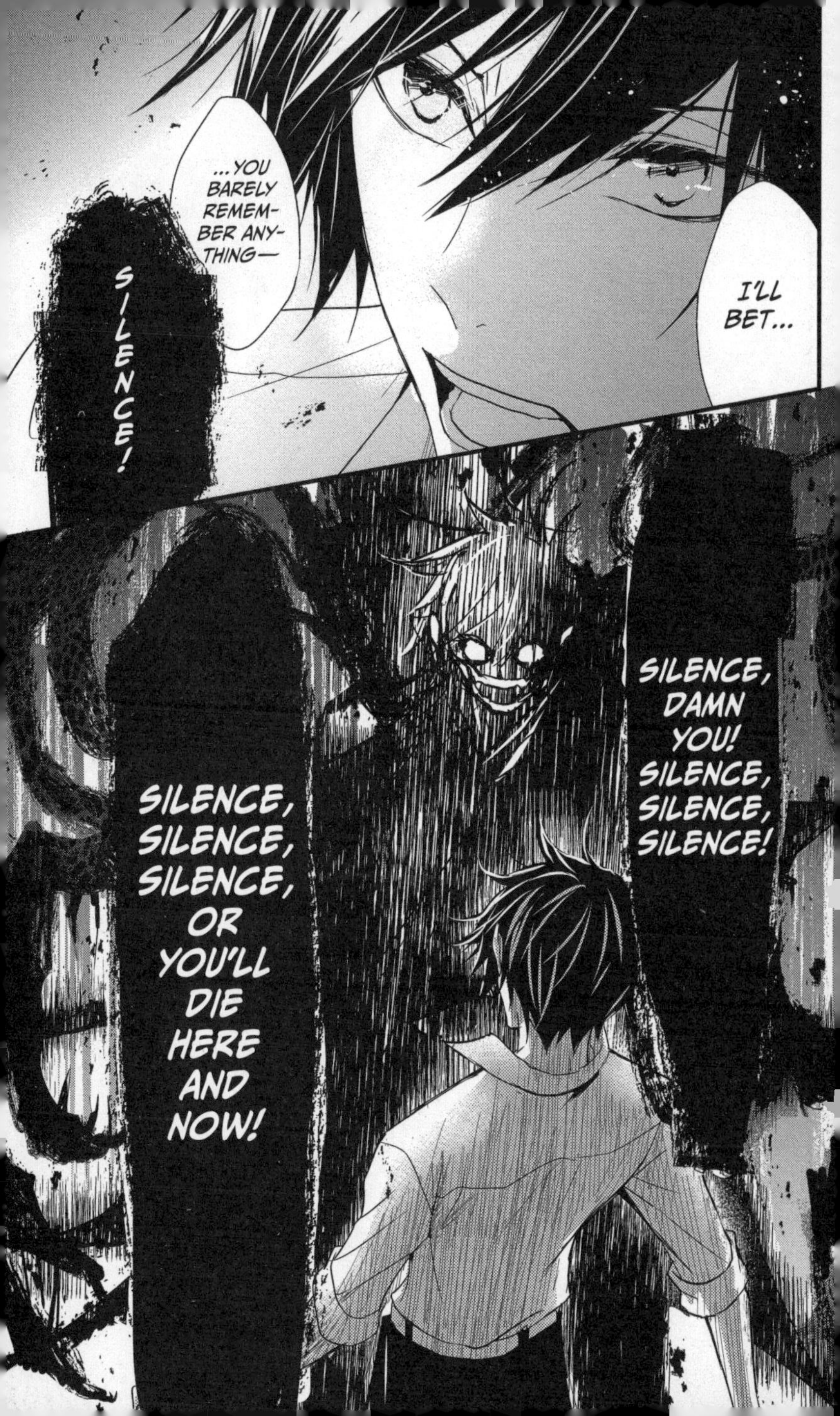
I'LL BET...
...YOU BARELY REMEMBER ANYTHING—
SILENCE!
SILENCE, DAMN YOU! SILENCE, SILENCE, SILENCE!
SILENCE, SILENCE, SILENCE, OR YOU'LL DIE HERE AND NOW!

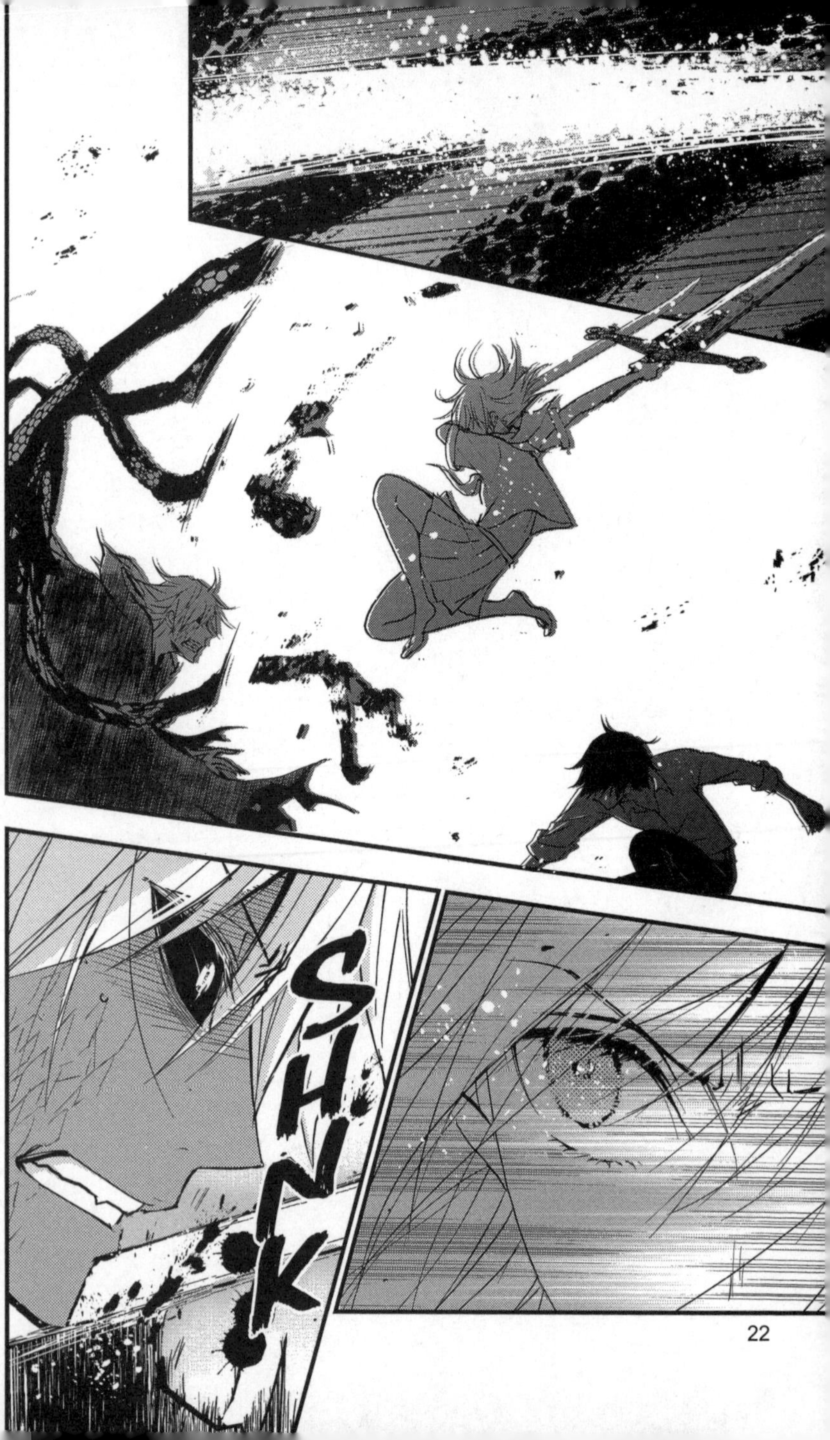
SHNK

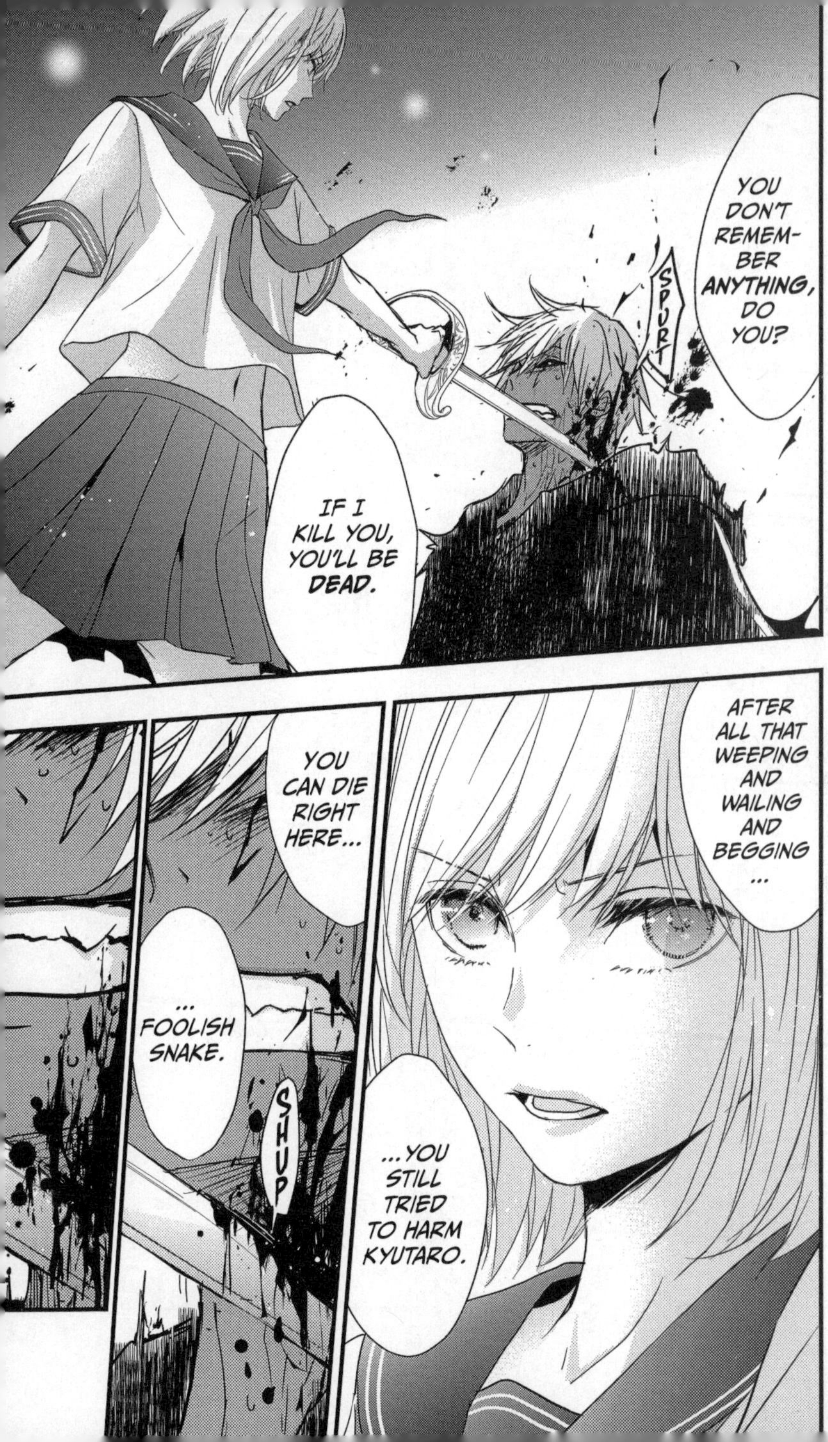
YOU DON'T REMEMBER ANYTHING, DO YOU?
SPURT
IF I KILL YOU, YOU'LL BE DEAD.
AFTER ALL THAT WEEPING AND WAILING AND BEGGING...
...YOU STILL TRIED TO HARM KYUTARO.
YOU CAN DIE RIGHT HERE...
...FOOLISH SNAKE.
SHUP

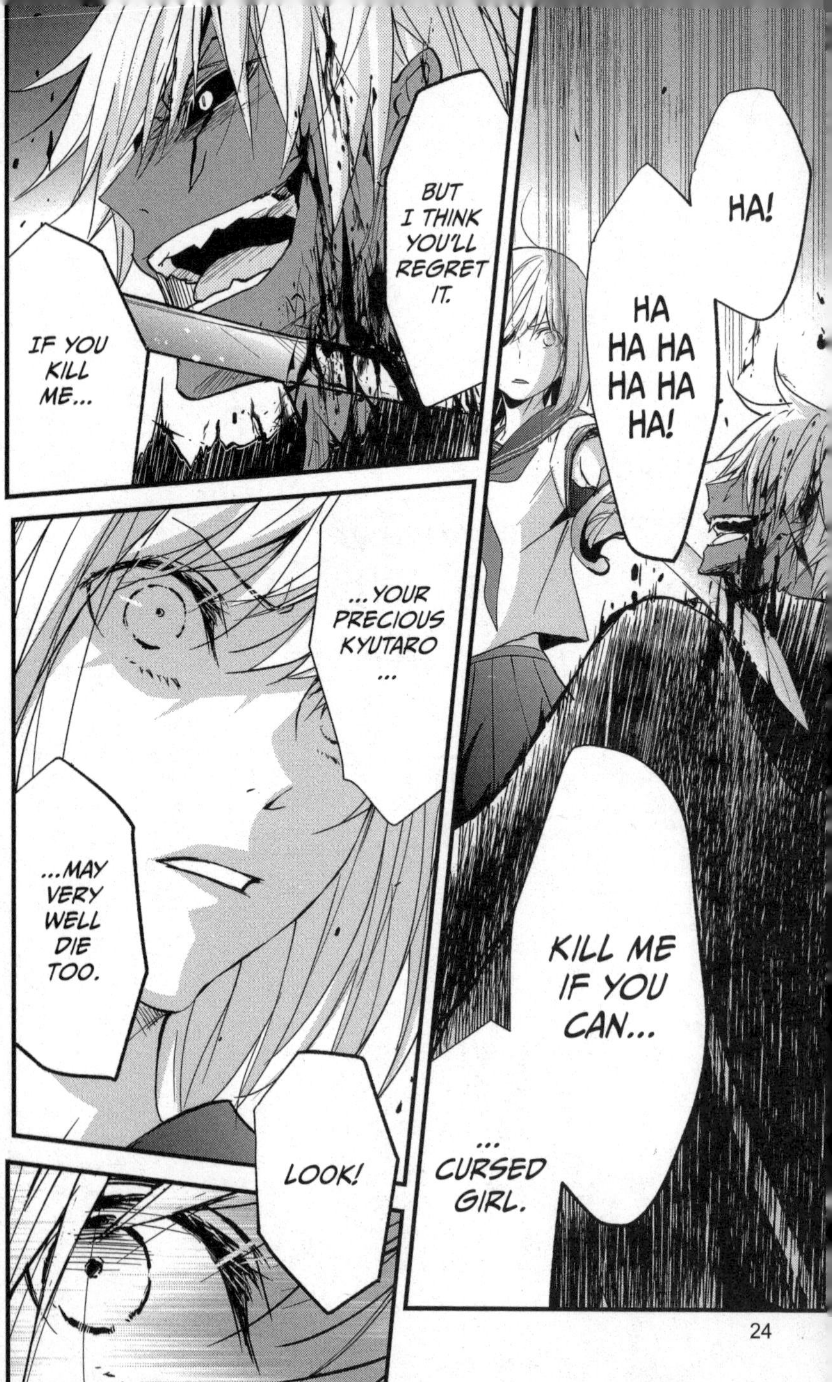
HA!
HA HA HA HA HA HA!
KILL ME IF YOU CAN...
...CURSED GIRL.
BUT I THINK YOU'LL REGRET IT.
IF YOU KILL ME...
...YOUR PRECIOUS KYUTARO...
...MAY VERY WELL DIE TOO.
LOOK!

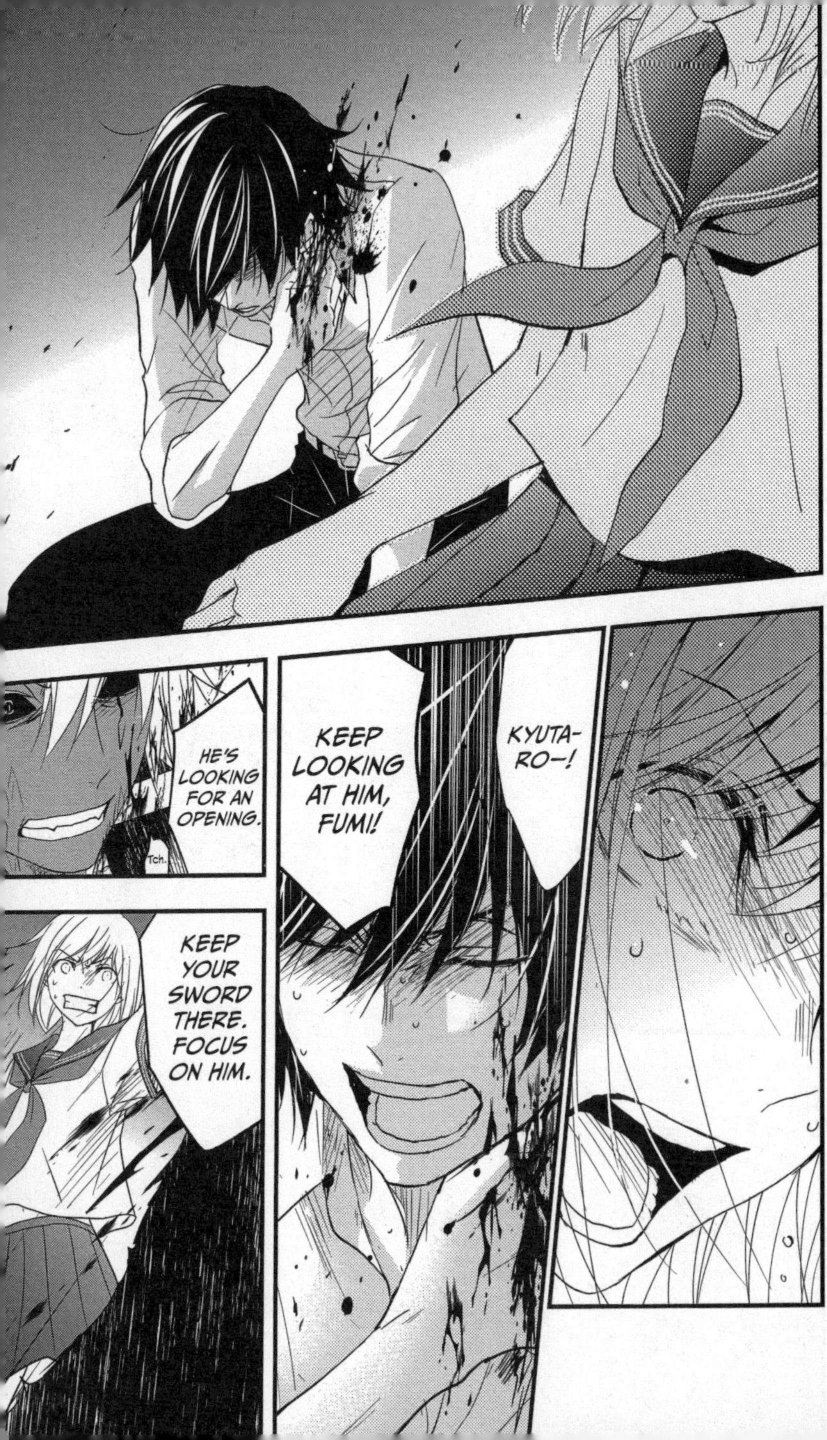
KYUTA-RO--!
KEEP LOOKING AT HIM, FUMI!
HE'S LOOKING FOR AN OPENING.
Tch.
KEEP YOUR SWORD THERE. FOCUS ON HIM.

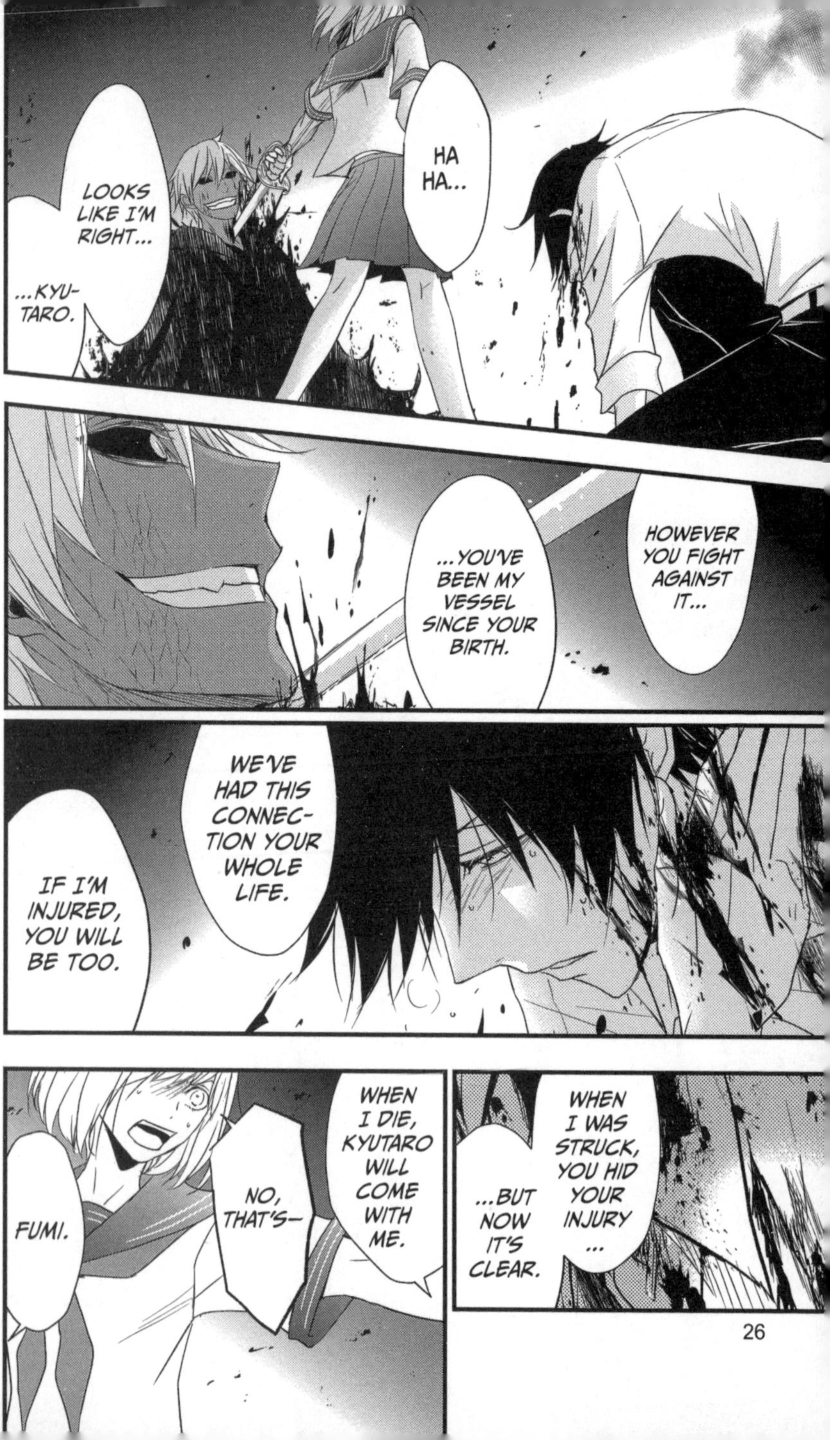
HA HA...
LOOKS LIKE I'M RIGHT...
...KYU-TARO.
HOWEVER YOU FIGHT AGAINST IT...
...YOU'VE BEEN MY VESSEL SINCE YOUR BIRTH.
WE'VE HAD THIS CONNEC-TION YOUR WHOLE LIFE.
IF I'M INJURED, YOU WILL BE TOO.
WHEN I WAS STRUCK, YOU HID YOUR INJURY ...
...BUT NOW IT'S CLEAR.
WHEN I DIE, KYUTARO WILL COME WITH ME.
NO, THAT'S—
FUMI.

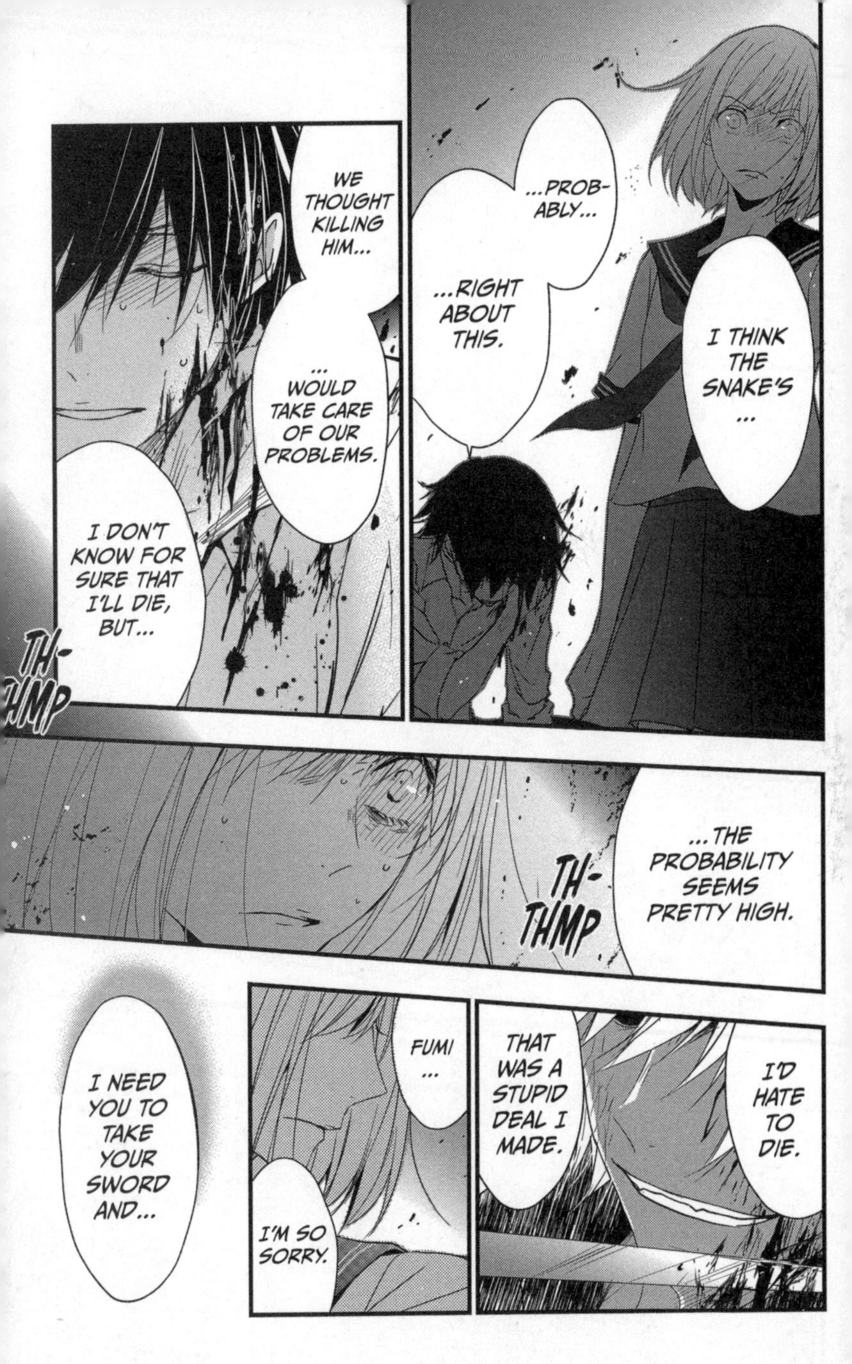
I THINK THE SNAKE'S ...
...PROB-ABLY...
...RIGHT ABOUT THIS.
WE THOUGHT KILLING HIM...
... WOULD TAKE CARE OF OUR PROBLEMS.
I DON'T KNOW FOR SURE THAT I'LL DIE, BUT...
TH-THMP
...THE PROBABILITY SEEMS PRETTY HIGH.
TH-THMP
I'D HATE TO DIE.
THAT WAS A STUPID DEAL I MADE.
FUMI ...
I'M SO SORRY.
I NEED YOU TO TAKE YOUR SWORD AND...

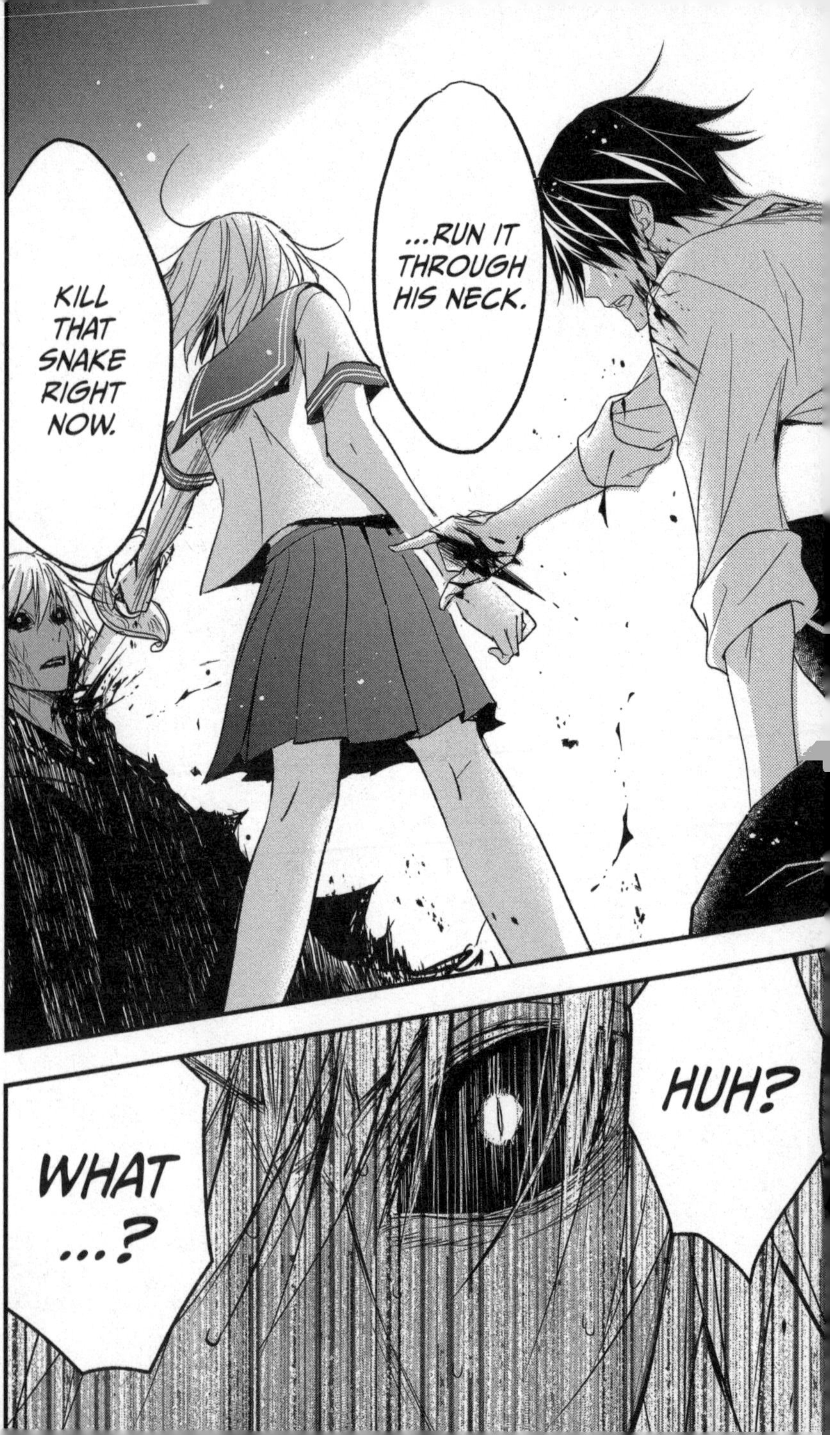
...RUN IT THROUGH HIS NECK.
KILL THAT SNAKE RIGHT NOW.
HUH?
WHAT ...?

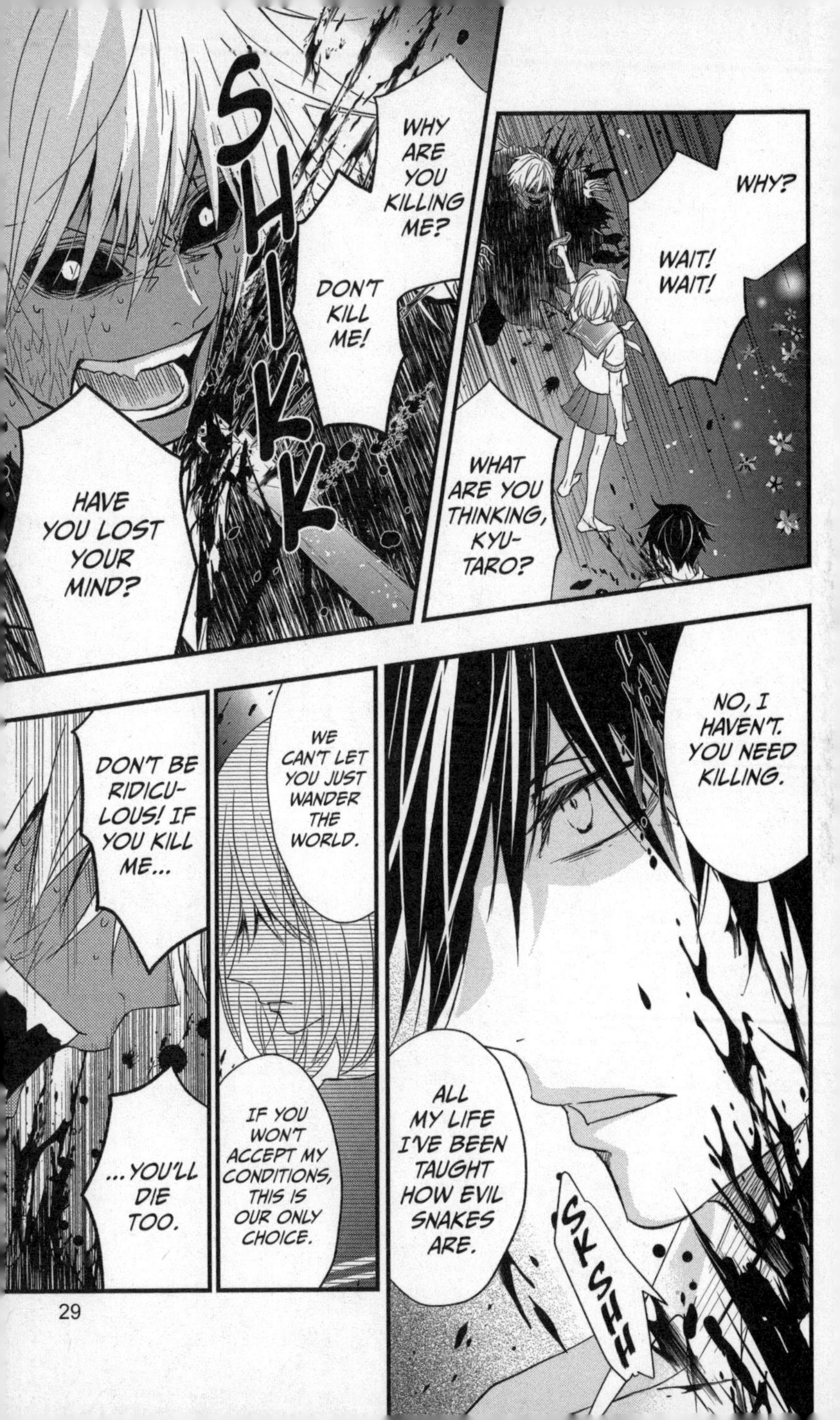
WHY?
WAIT! WAIT!
WHAT ARE YOU THINKING, KYU-TARO?
SHIKK
WHY ARE YOU KILLING ME?
DON'T KILL ME!
HAVE YOU LOST YOUR MIND?
NO, I HAVEN'T. YOU NEED KILLING.
ALL MY LIFE I'VE BEEN TAUGHT HOW EVIL SNAKES ARE.
SKSHH
WE CAN'T LET YOU JUST WANDER THE WORLD.
IF YOU WON'T ACCEPT MY CONDITIONS, THIS IS OUR ONLY CHOICE.
DON'T BE RIDICU-LOUS! IF YOU KILL ME...
...YOU'LL DIE TOO.

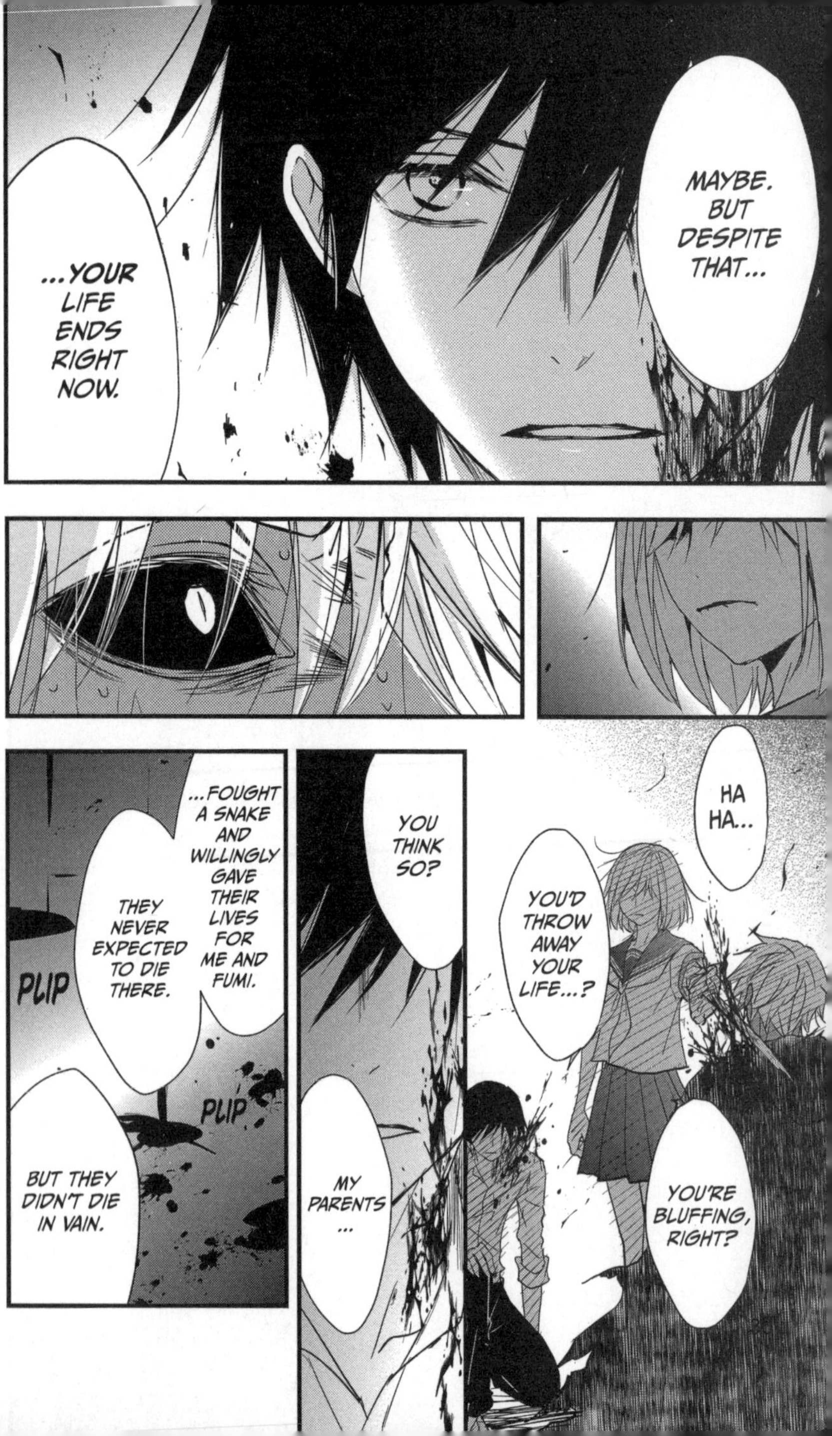
MAYBE. BUT DESPITE THAT...
...YOUR LIFE ENDS RIGHT NOW.
HA HA...
YOU'D THROW AWAY YOUR LIFE...?
YOU'RE BLUFFING, RIGHT?
YOU THINK SO?
MY PARENTS ...
...FOUGHT A SNAKE AND WILLINGLY GAVE THEIR LIVES FOR ME AND FUMI.
THEY NEVER EXPECTED TO DIE THERE.
PLIP
PLIP
BUT THEY DIDN'T DIE IN VAIN.

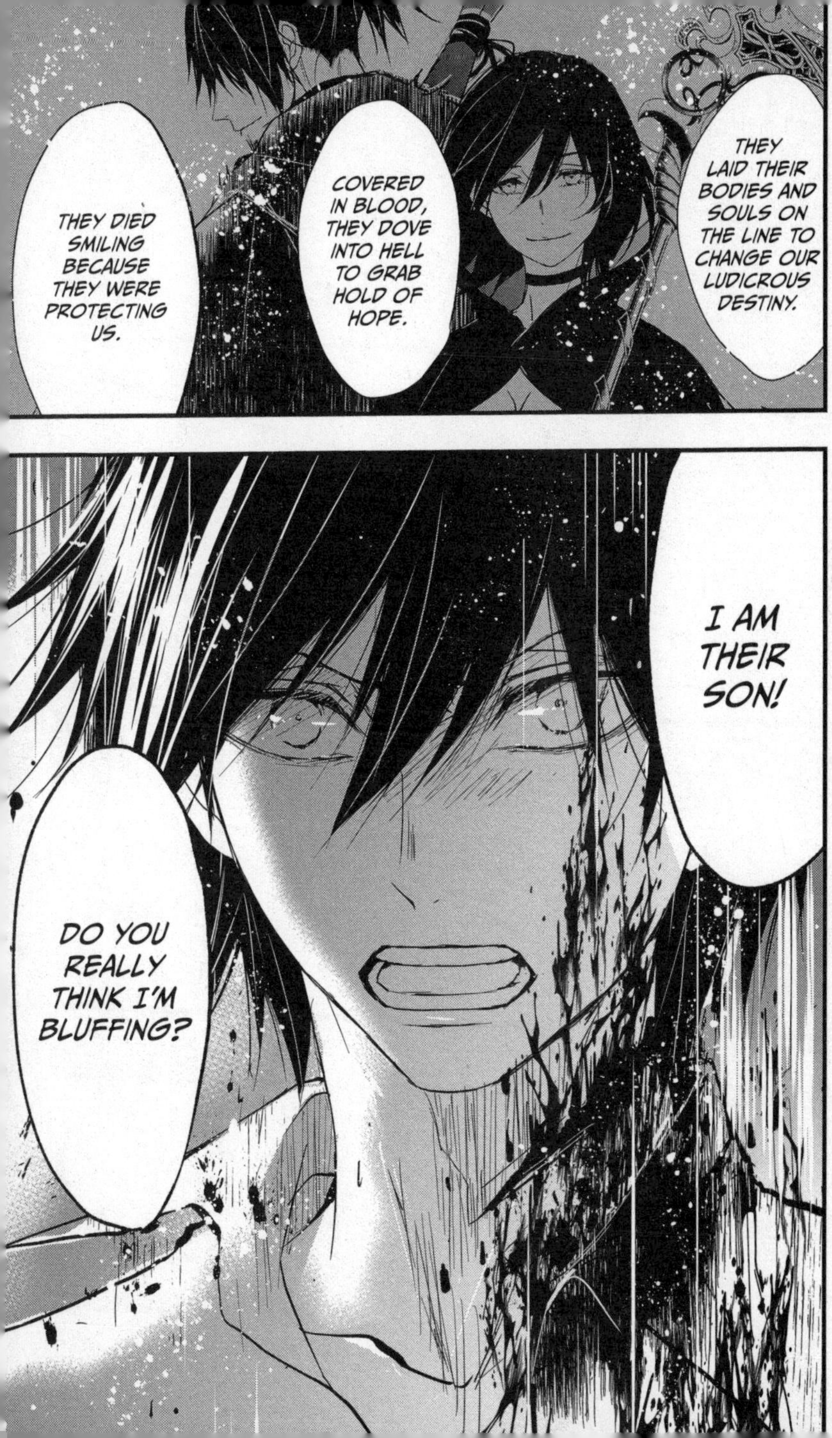
THEY LAID THEIR BODIES AND SOULS ON THE LINE TO CHANGE OUR LUDICROUS DESTINY.
COVERED IN BLOOD, THEY DOVE INTO HELL TO GRAB HOLD OF HOPE.
THEY DIED SMILING BECAUSE THEY WERE PROTECTING US.
I AM THEIR SON!
DO YOU REALLY THINK I'M BLUFFING?

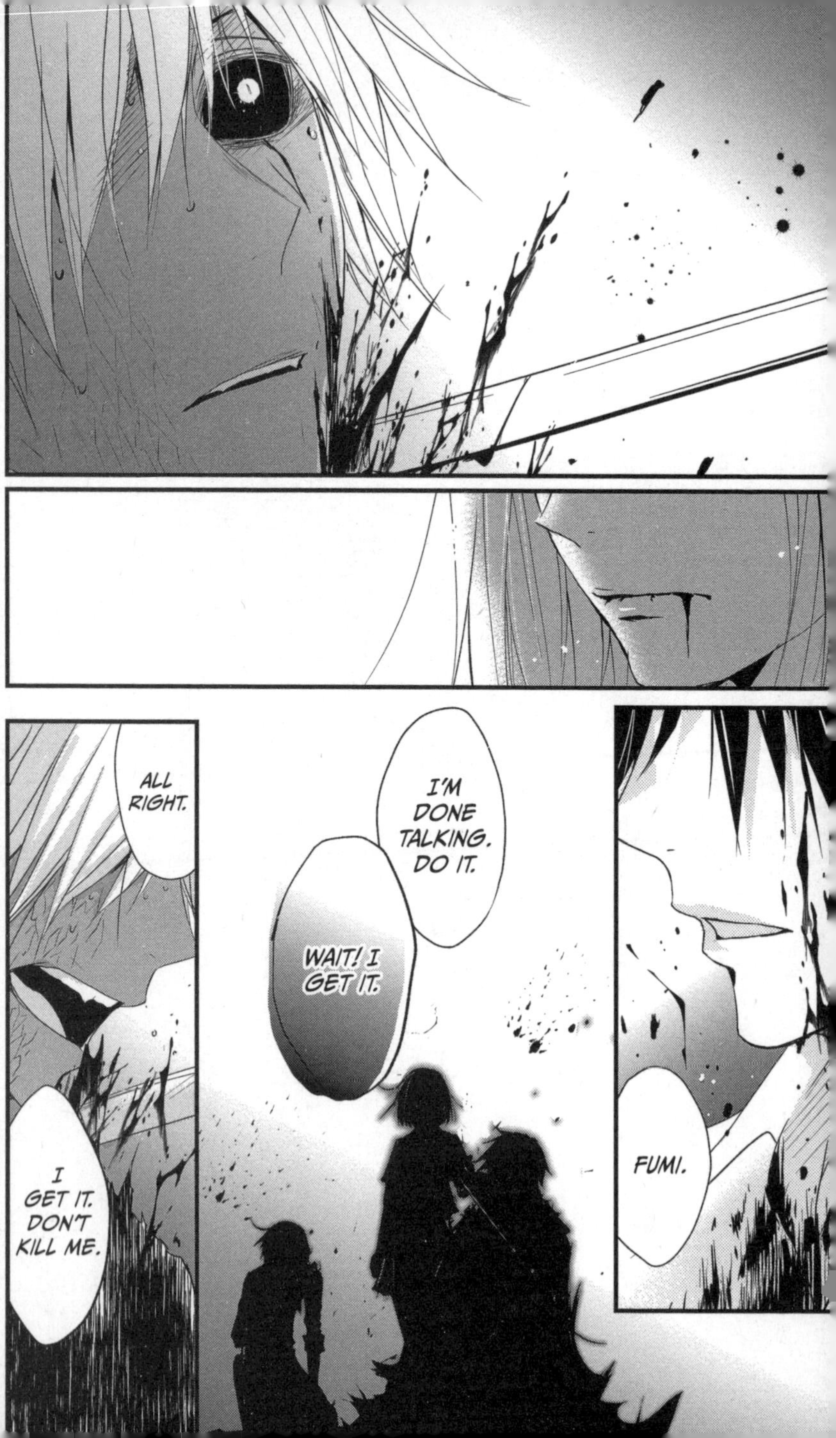
FUMI.
I'M DONE TALKING. DO IT.
WAIT! I GET IT.
ALL RIGHT.
I GET IT. DON'T KILL ME.

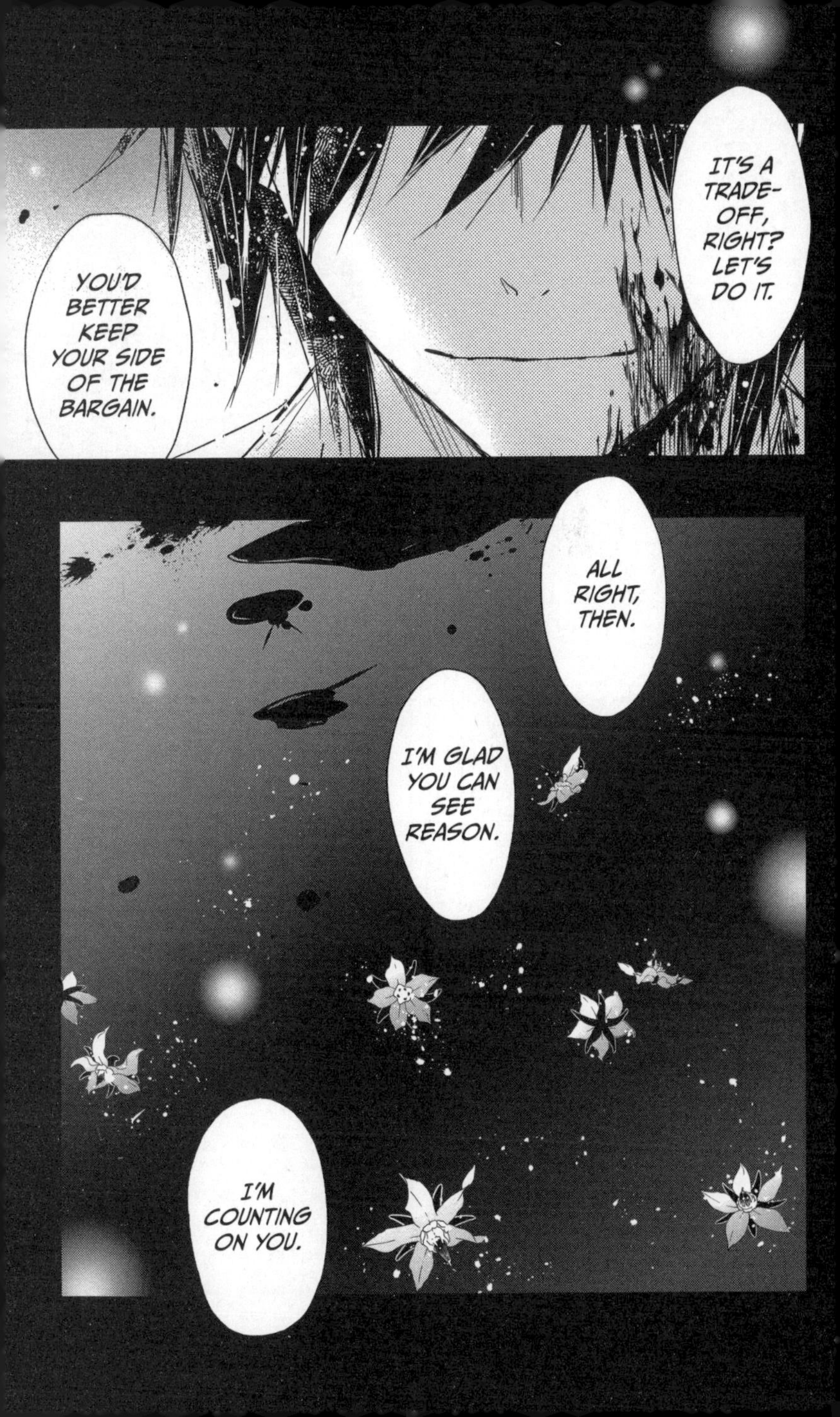
IT'S A TRADE-OFF, RIGHT? LET'S DO IT.
YOU'D BETTER KEEP YOUR SIDE OF THE BARGAIN.
ALL RIGHT, THEN.
I'M GLAD YOU CAN SEE REASON.
I'M COUNTING ON YOU.

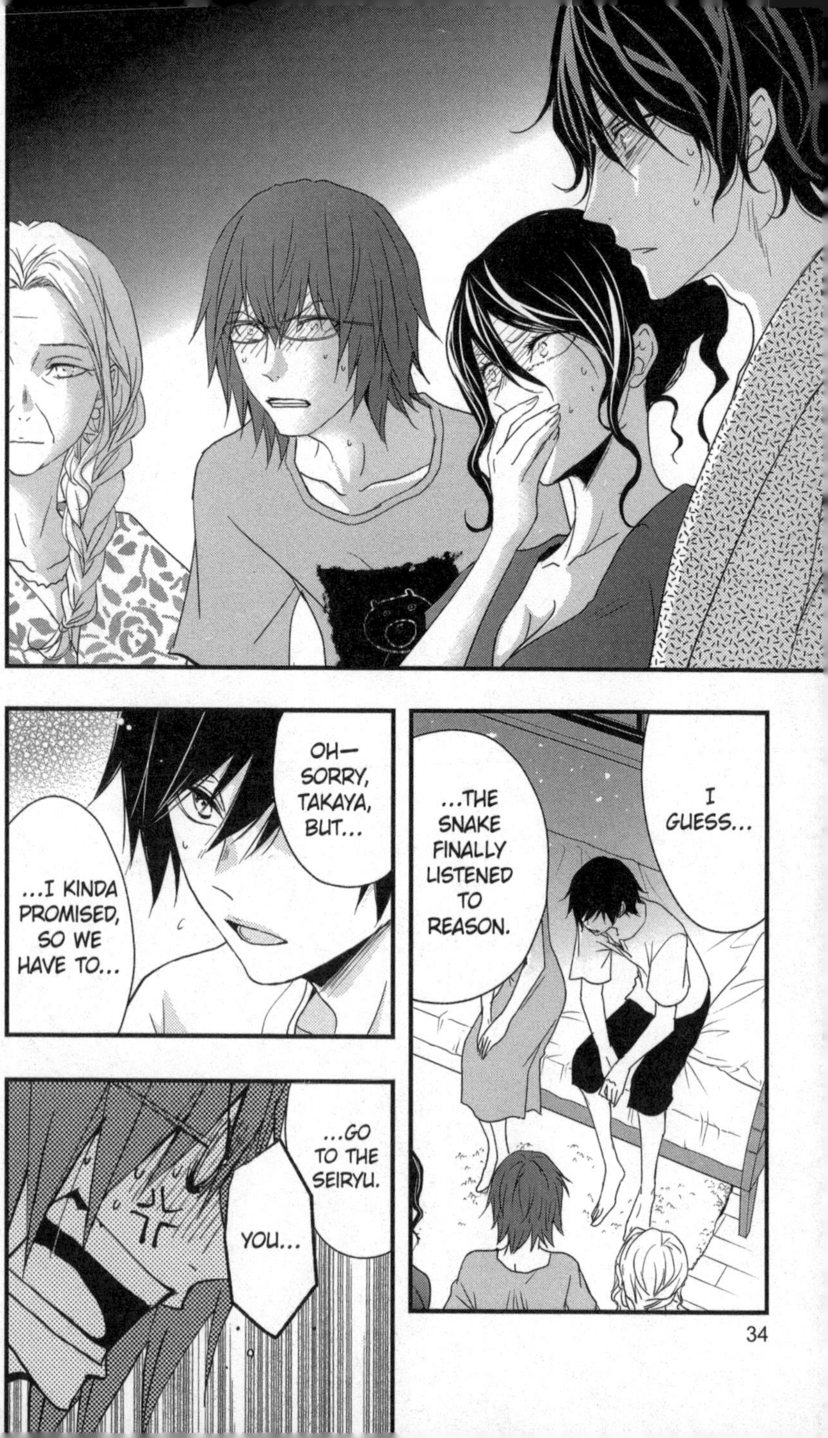
I GUESS...
...THE SNAKE FINALLY LISTENED TO REASON.
OH— SORRY, TAKAYA, BUT...
...I KINDA PROMISED, SO WE HAVE TO...
...GO TO THE SEIRYU.
YOU...

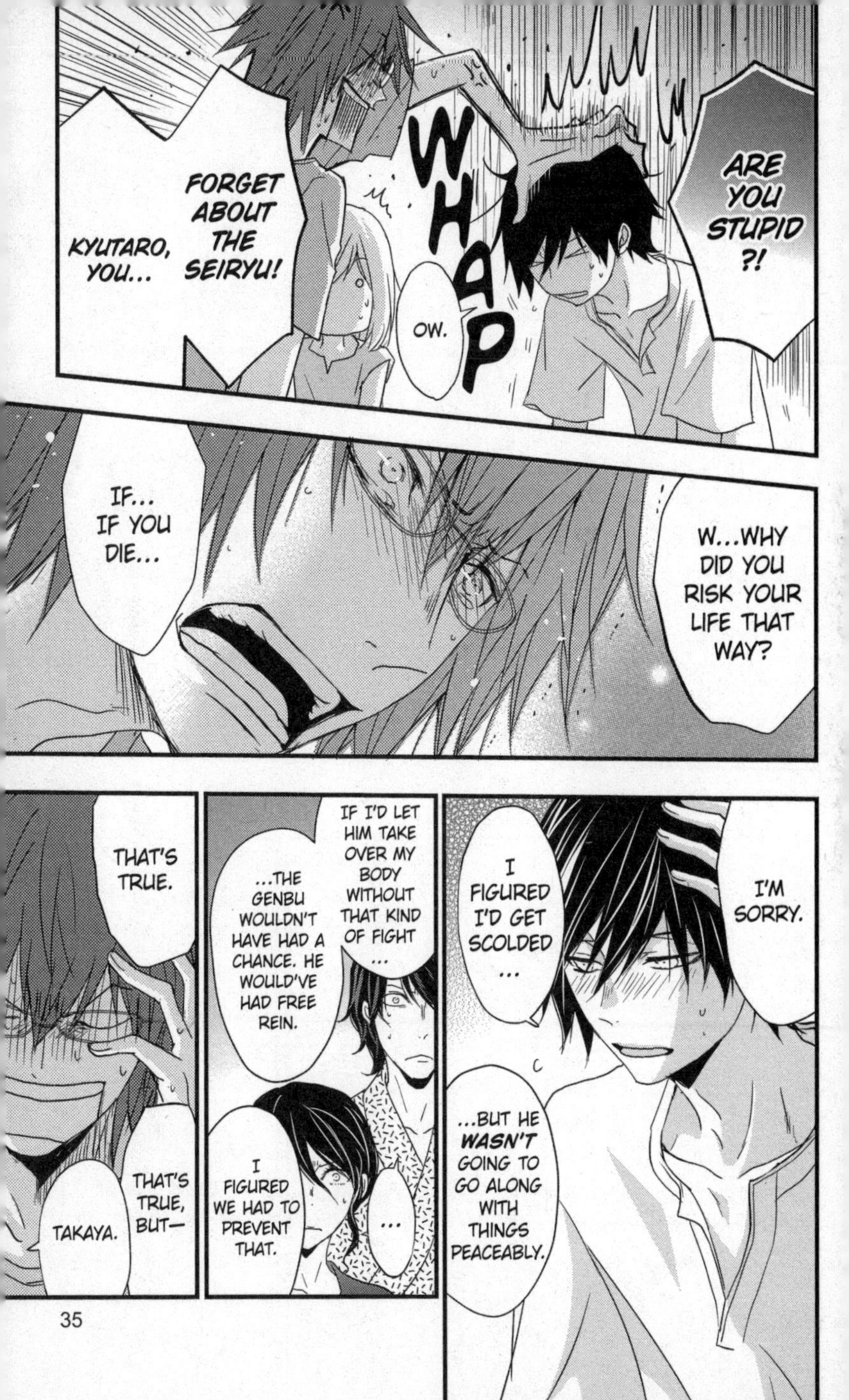
ARE YOU STUPID?!
WHAP
OW.
FORGET ABOUT THE SEIRYU!
KYUTARO, YOU...
W...WHY DID YOU RISK YOUR LIFE THAT WAY?
IF... IF YOU DIE...
I'M SORRY.
I FIGURED I'D GET SCOLDED...
...BUT HE *WASN'T* GOING TO GO ALONG WITH THINGS PEACEABLY.
IF I'D LET HIM TAKE OVER MY BODY WITHOUT THAT KIND OF FIGHT...
...THE GENBU WOULDN'T HAVE HAD A CHANCE. HE WOULD'VE HAD FREE REIN.
...
I FIGURED WE HAD TO PREVENT THAT.
THAT'S TRUE.
THAT'S TRUE, BUT—
TAKAYA.

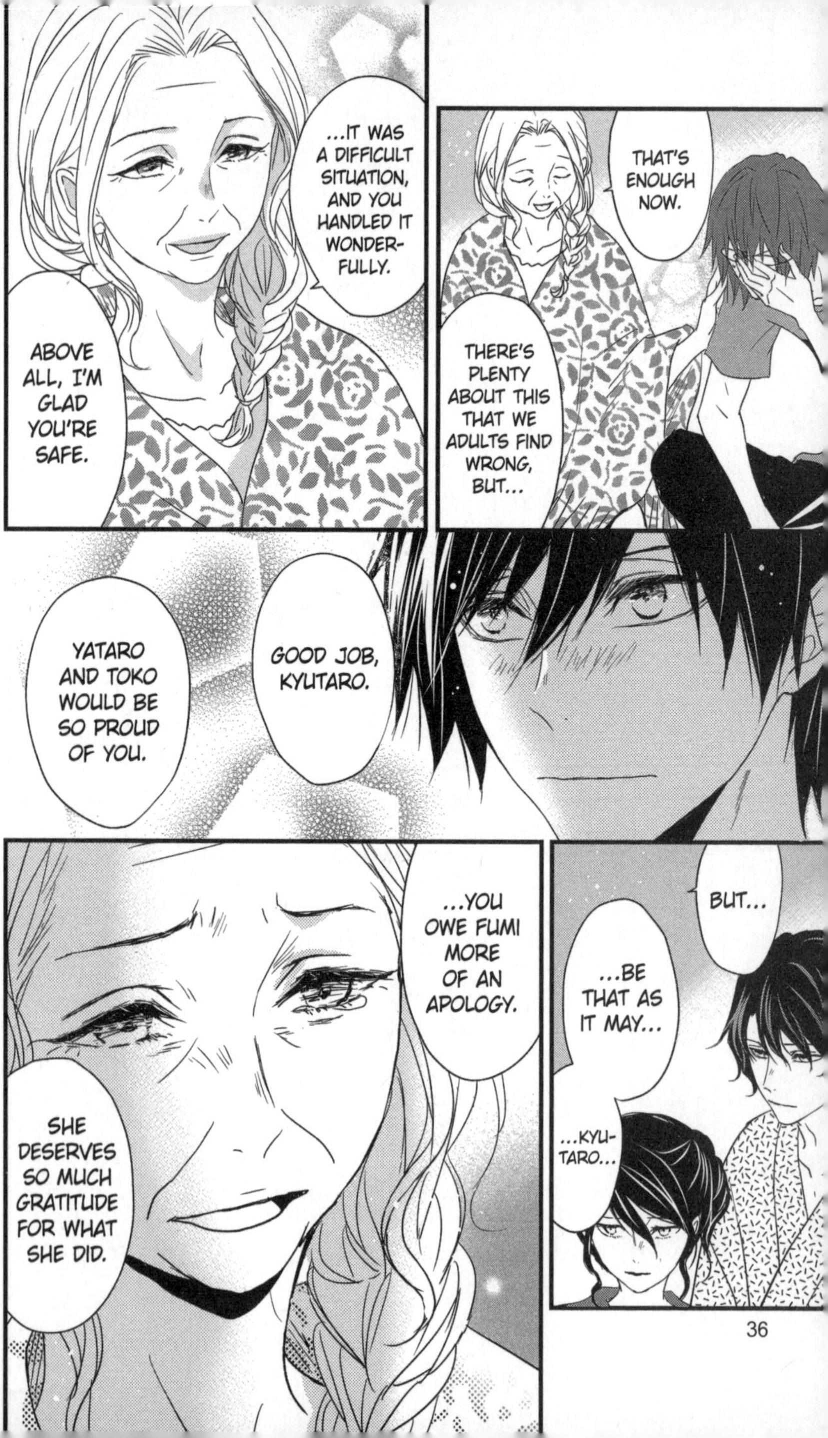
THAT'S ENOUGH NOW.
THERE'S PLENTY ABOUT THIS THAT WE ADULTS FIND WRONG, BUT...
...IT WAS A DIFFICULT SITUATION, AND YOU HANDLED IT WONDER-FULLY.
ABOVE ALL, I'M GLAD YOU'RE SAFE.
GOOD JOB, KYUTARO.
YATARO AND TOKO WOULD BE SO PROUD OF YOU.
BUT...
...BE THAT AS IT MAY...
...KYU-TARO...
...YOU OWE FUMI MORE OF AN APOLOGY.
SHE DESERVES SO MUCH GRATITUDE FOR WHAT SHE DID.

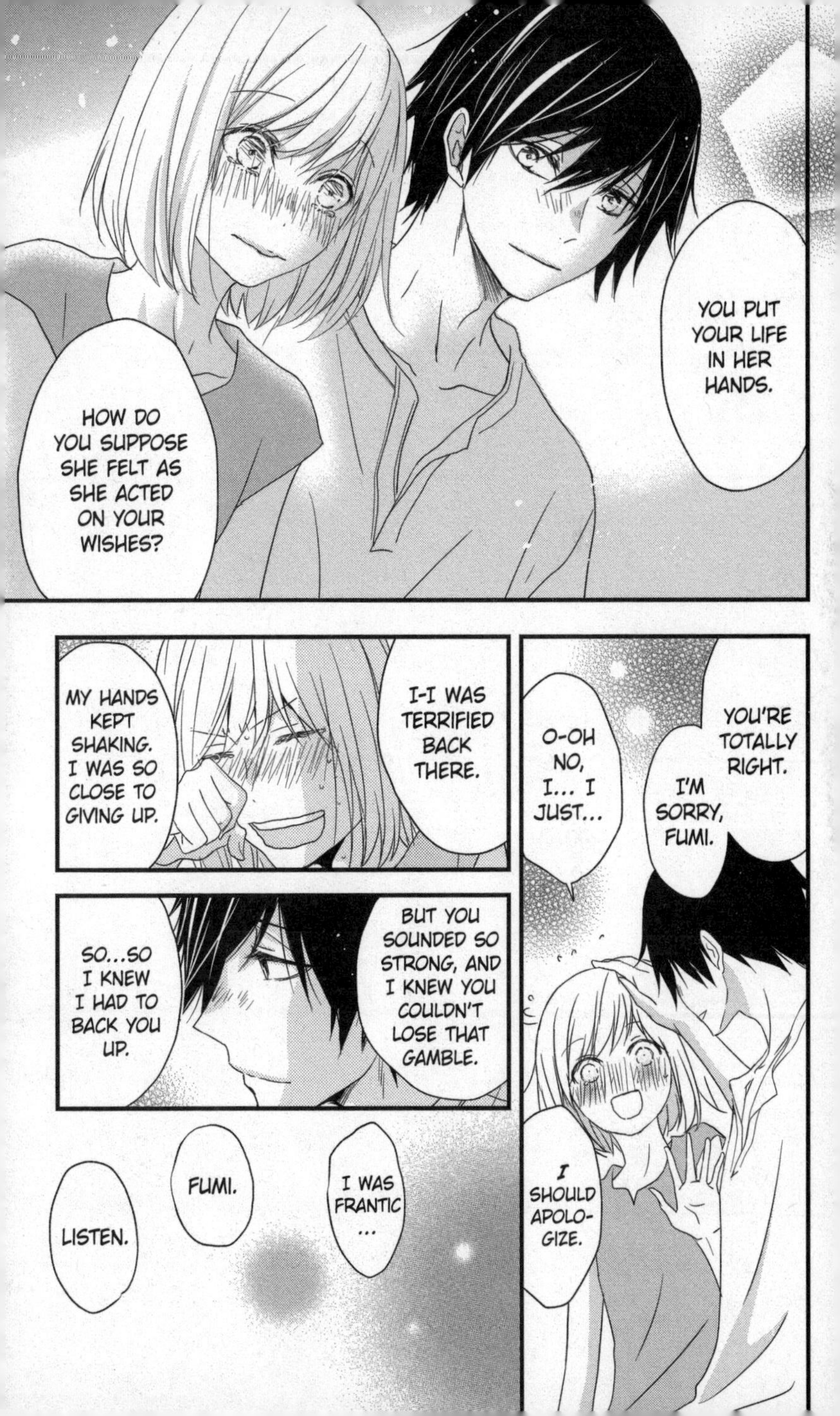
YOU PUT YOUR LIFE IN HER HANDS.
HOW DO YOU SUPPOSE SHE FELT AS SHE ACTED ON YOUR WISHES?
YOU'RE TOTALLY RIGHT.
I'M SORRY, FUMI.
O-OH NO, I... I JUST...
I SHOULD APOLOGIZE.
I-I WAS TERRIFIED BACK THERE.
MY HANDS KEPT SHAKING. I WAS SO CLOSE TO GIVING UP.
BUT YOU SOUNDED SO STRONG, AND I KNEW YOU COULDN'T LOSE THAT GAMBLE.
SO...SO I KNEW I HAD TO BACK YOU UP.
I WAS FRANTIC ...
FUMI.
LISTEN.

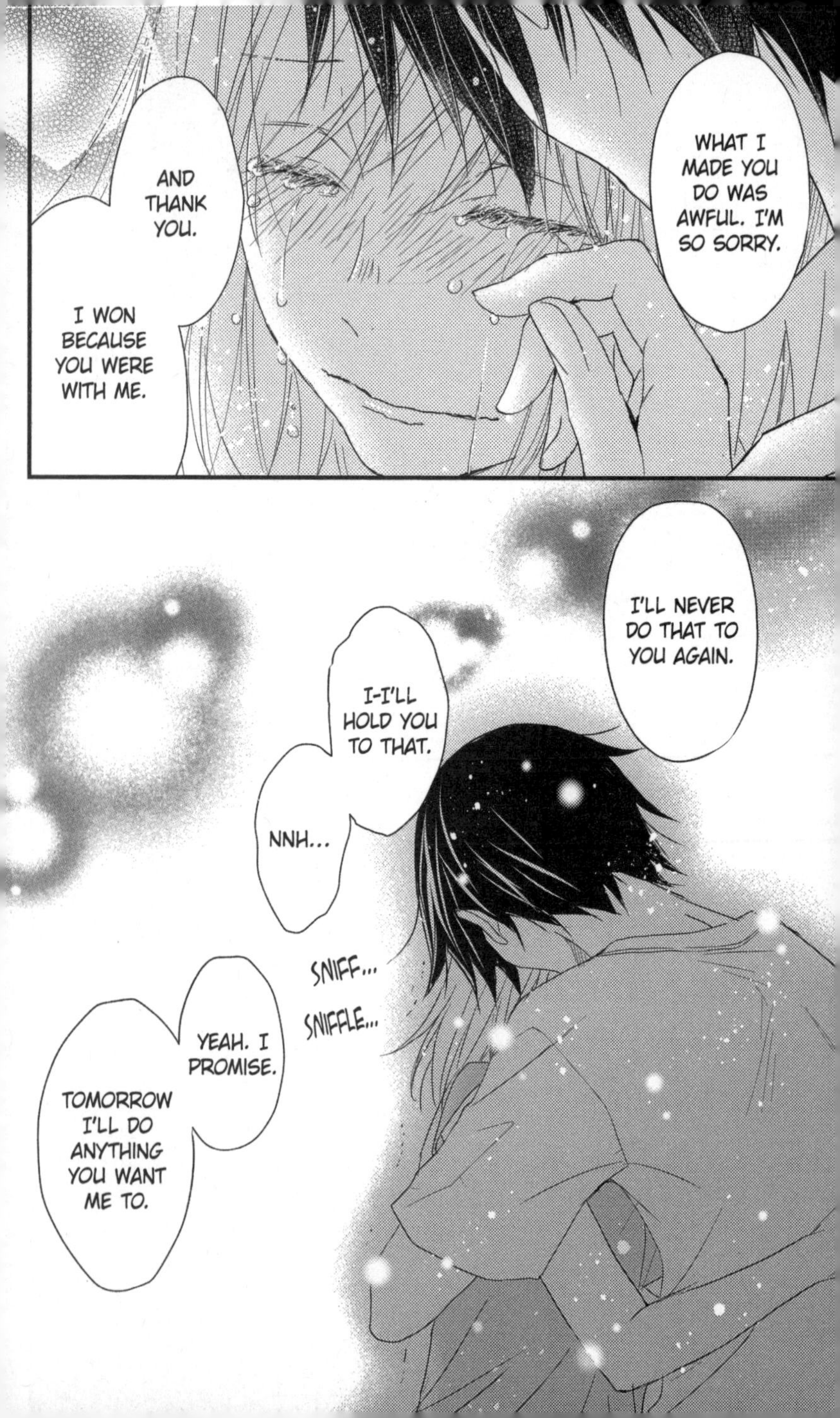
WHAT I MADE YOU DO WAS AWFUL. I'M SO SORRY.
AND THANK YOU.
I WON BECAUSE YOU WERE WITH ME.
I'LL NEVER DO THAT TO YOU AGAIN.
I-I'LL HOLD YOU TO THAT.
NNH...
SNIFF...
SNIFFLE...
YEAH. I PROMISE.
TOMORROW I'LL DO ANYTHING YOU WANT ME TO.

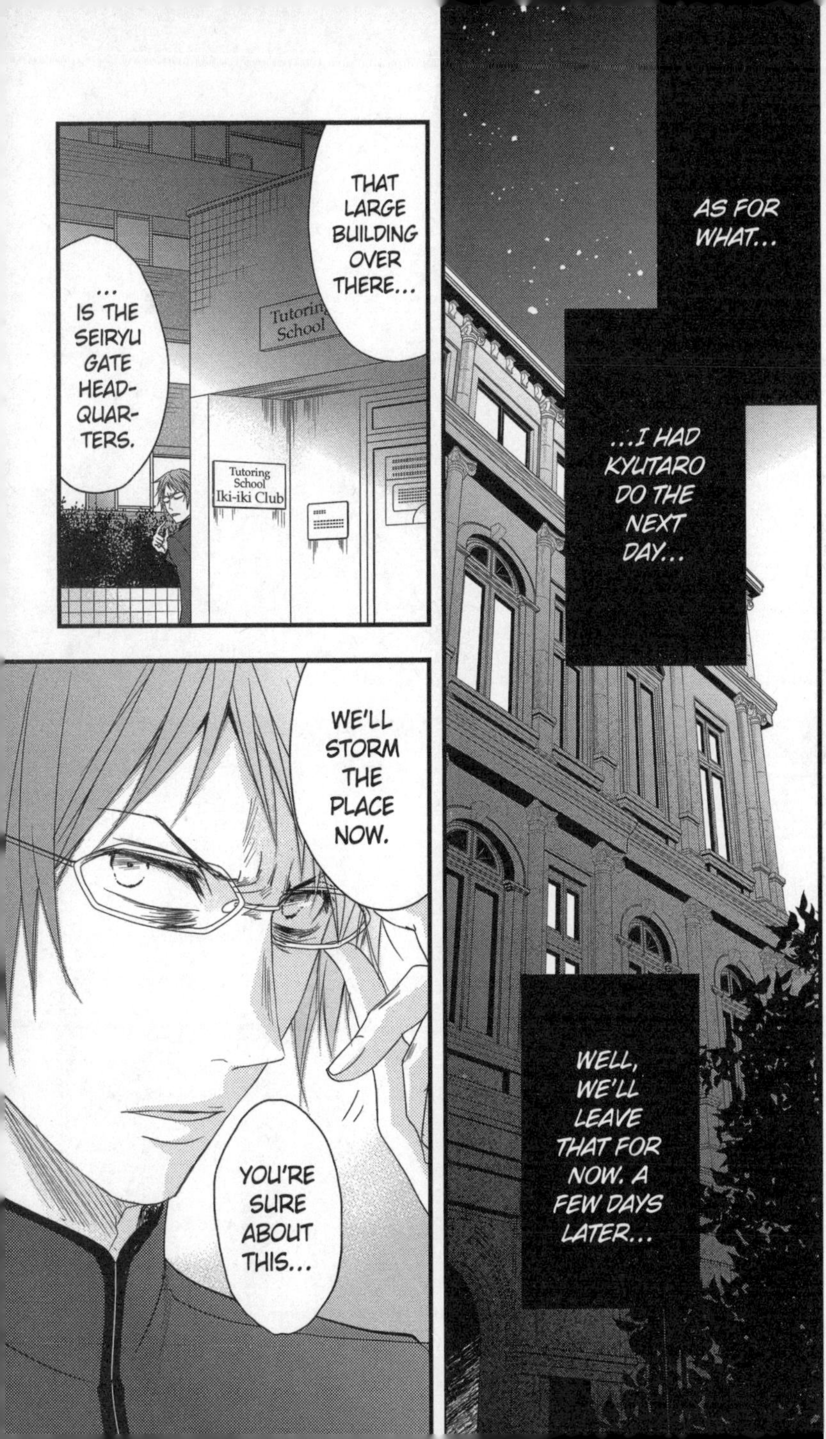
AS FOR WHAT...
...I HAD KYUTARO DO THE NEXT DAY...
WELL, WE'LL LEAVE THAT FOR NOW. A FEW DAYS LATER...
THAT LARGE BUILDING OVER THERE...
...IS THE SEIRYU GATE HEAD-QUARTERS.
Tutoring School
Tutoring School Iki-iki Club
WE'LL STORM THE PLACE NOW.
YOU'RE SURE ABOUT THIS...

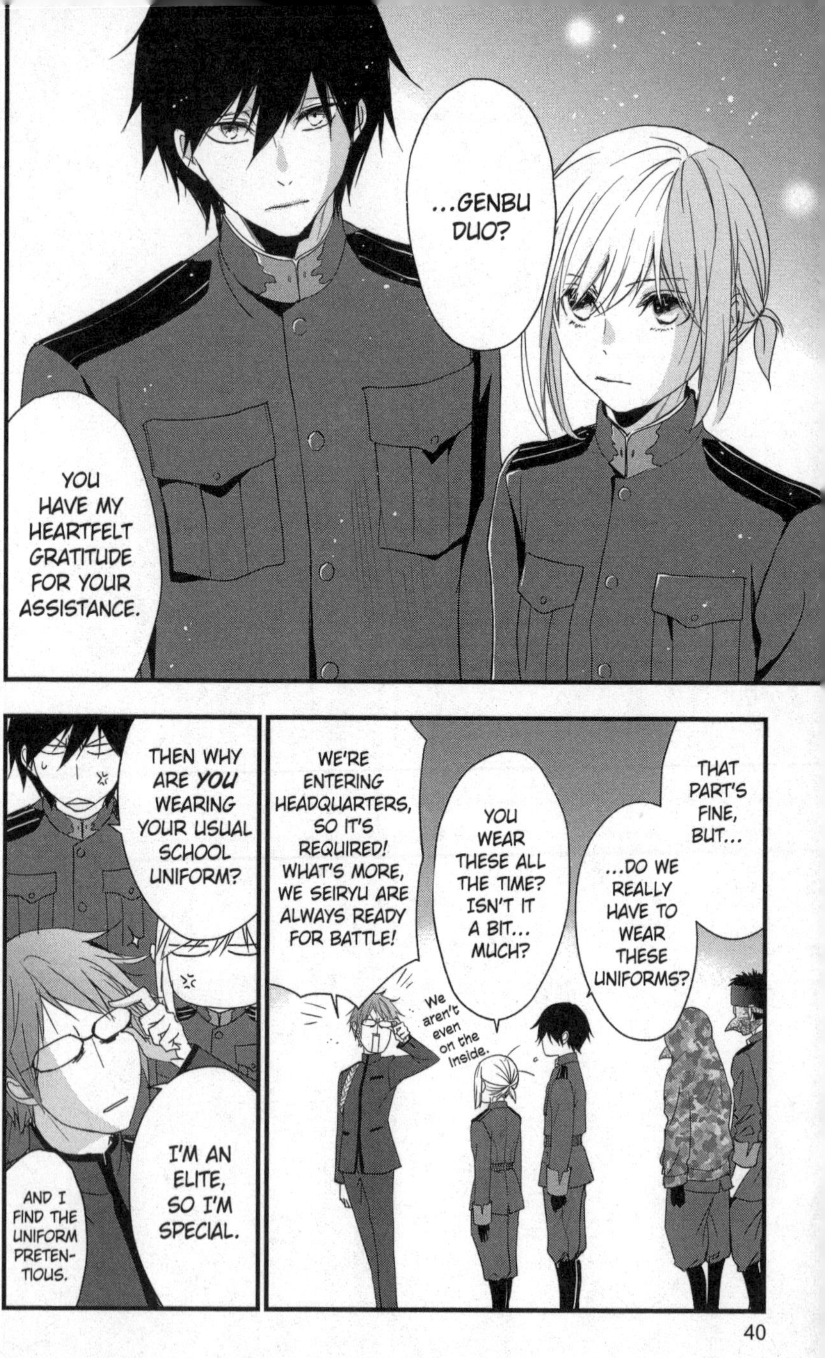
...GENBU DUO?
YOU HAVE MY HEARTFELT GRATITUDE FOR YOUR ASSISTANCE.
THAT PART'S FINE, BUT...
...DO WE REALLY HAVE TO WEAR THESE UNIFORMS?
YOU WEAR THESE ALL THE TIME? ISN'T IT A BIT... MUCH?
WE'RE ENTERING HEADQUARTERS, SO IT'S REQUIRED! WHAT'S MORE, WE SEIRYU ARE ALWAYS READY FOR BATTLE!
We aren't even on the inside.
THEN WHY ARE *YOU* WEARING YOUR USUAL SCHOOL UNIFORM?
I'M AN ELITE, SO I'M SPECIAL.
AND I FIND THE UNIFORM PRETEN-TIOUS.

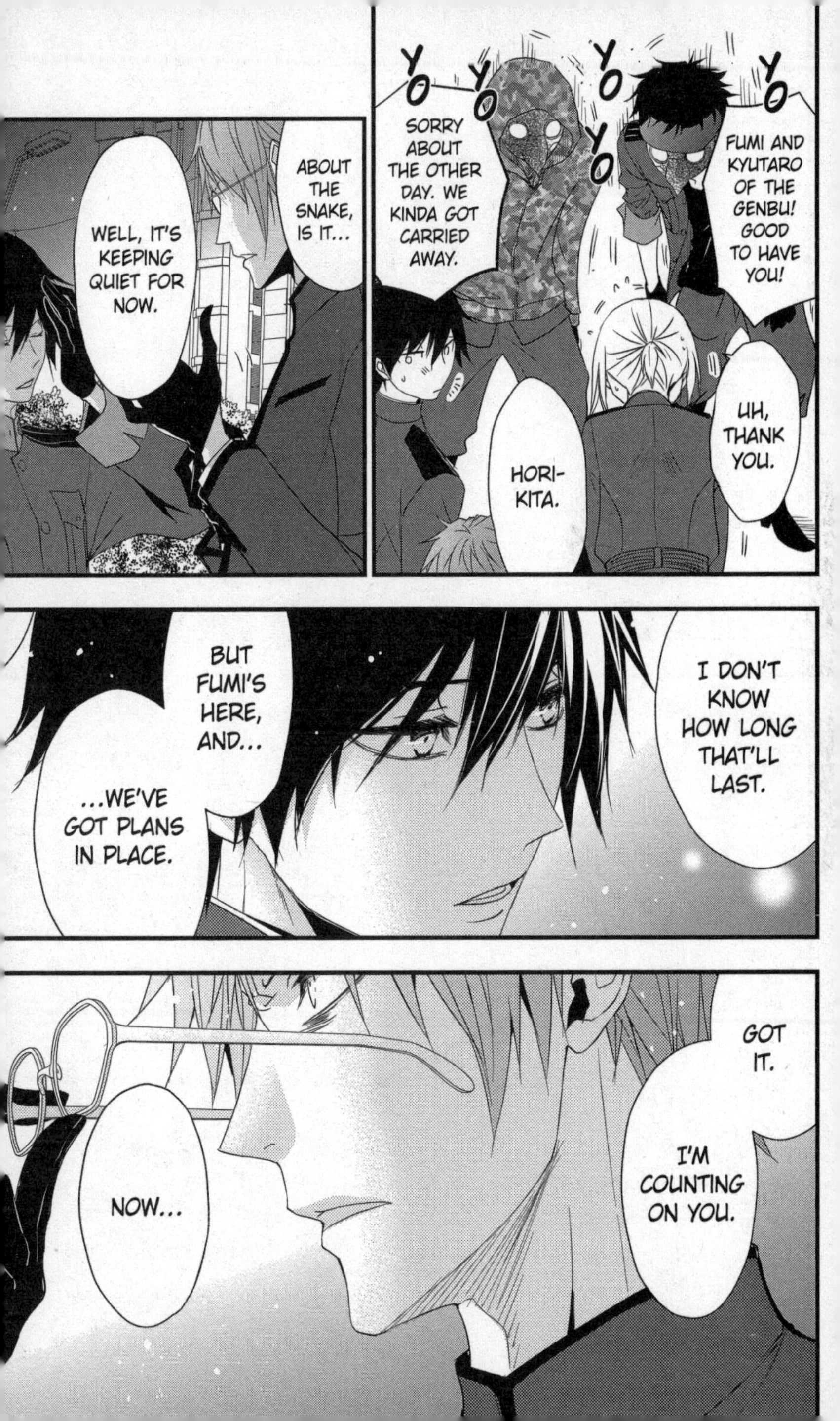
YO YO YO YO YO
FUMI AND KYUTARO OF THE GENBU! GOOD TO HAVE YOU!
SORRY ABOUT THE OTHER DAY. WE KINDA GOT CARRIED AWAY.
UH, THANK YOU.
HORI-KITA.
ABOUT THE SNAKE, IS IT...
WELL, IT'S KEEPING QUIET FOR NOW.
I DON'T KNOW HOW LONG THAT'LL LAST.
BUT FUMI'S HERE, AND...
...WE'VE GOT PLANS IN PLACE.
GOT IT.
I'M COUNTING ON YOU.
NOW...

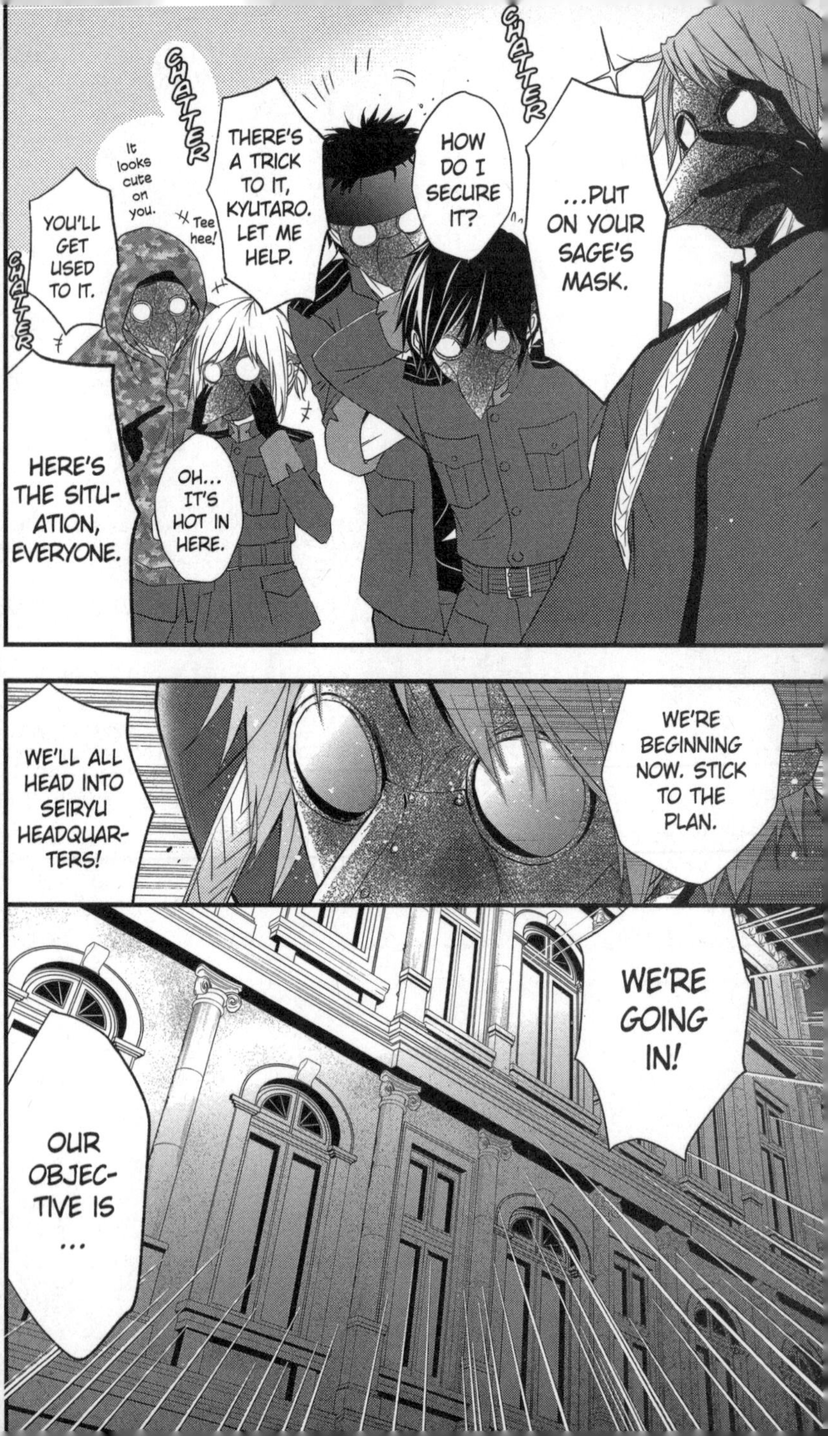
CHATTER
...PUT ON YOUR SAGE'S MASK.
HOW DO I SECURE IT?
THERE'S A TRICK TO IT, KYUTARO. LET ME HELP.
CHATTER
It looks cute on you.
Tee hee!
YOU'LL GET USED TO IT.
CHATTER
OH... IT'S HOT IN HERE.
HERE'S THE SITUATION, EVERYONE.
WE'RE BEGINNING NOW. STICK TO THE PLAN.
WE'LL ALL HEAD INTO SEIRYU HEADQUARTERS!
WE'RE GOING IN!
OUR OBJECTIVE IS ...

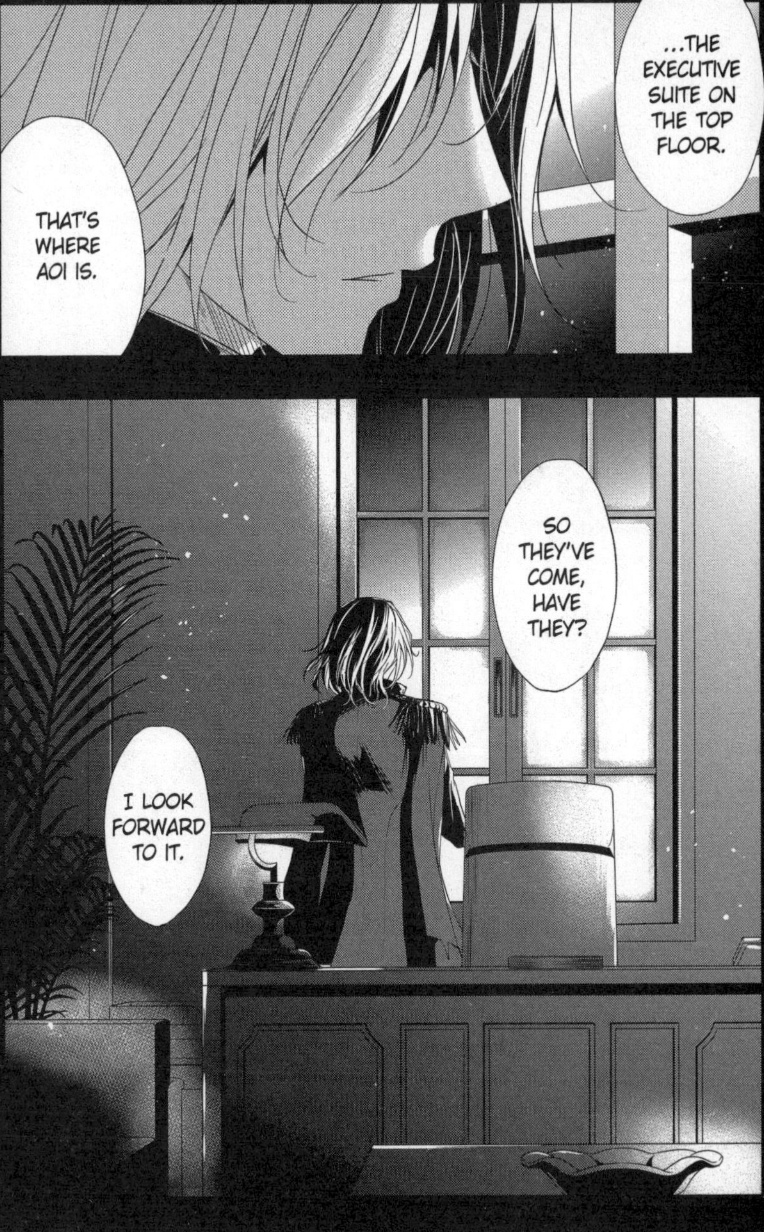
...THE EXECUTIVE SUITE ON THE TOP FLOOR.
THAT'S WHERE AOI IS.
SO THEY'VE COME, HAVE THEY?
I LOOK FORWARD TO IT.

KYOUSUKE MOTOMI
C/O QUEEN'S QUALITY EDITOR
P.O. BOX 77010
SAN FRANCISCO, CA 94107

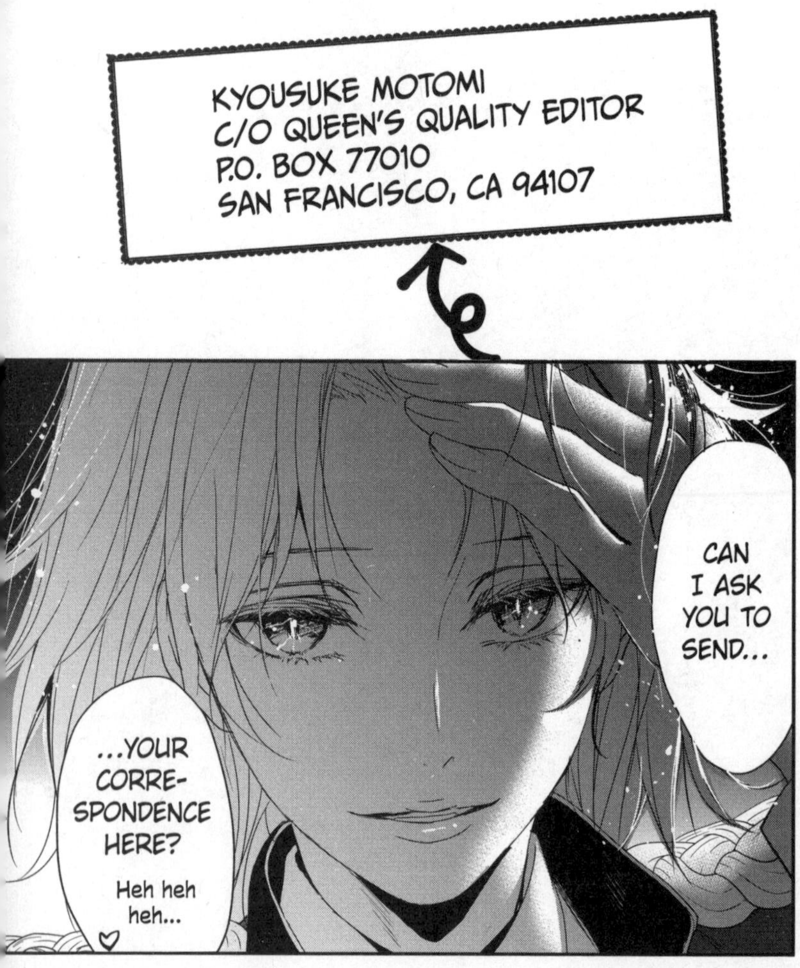
CAN I ASK YOU TO SEND...
...YOUR CORRE-SPONDENCE HERE?
Heh heh heh...

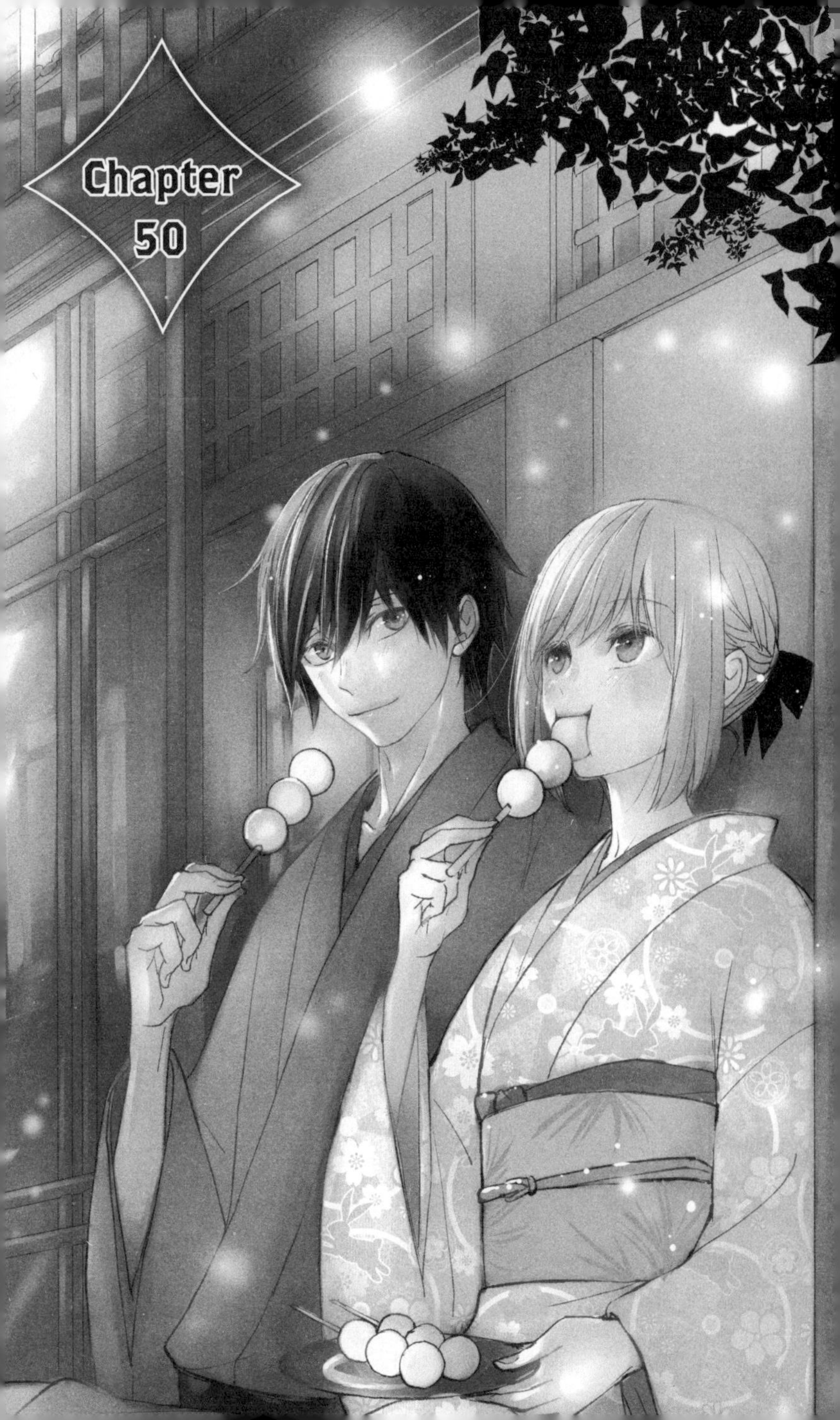
Chapter
50

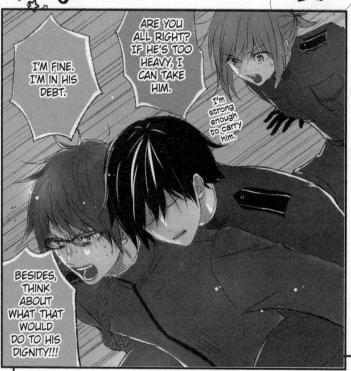

MONTHLY BETSUCOMI SALE DATE NOTICE ON TWITTER

CHAPTER 50

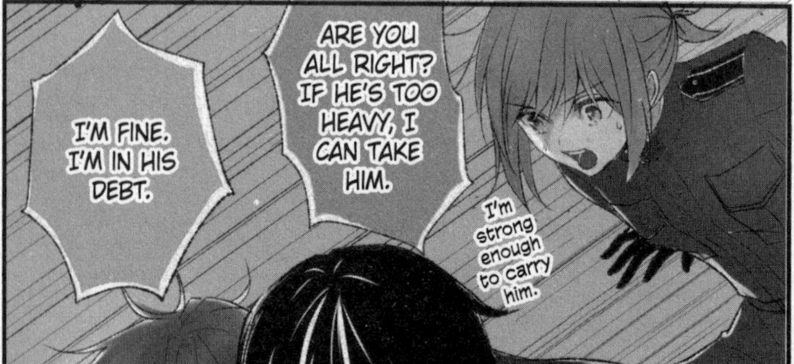
ARE YOU ALL RIGHT? IF HE'S TOO HEAVY, I CAN TAKE HIM.
I'm strong enough to carry him.
I'M FINE. I'M IN HIS DEBT.
BESIDES, THINK ABOUT WHAT THAT WOULD DO TO HIS DIGNITY!!!

LET'S SEE... WHAT'S UP IN *QUEEN'S QUALITY* THIS MONTH?
(1) THE THING IN TOSHIHIKO'S MOUTH IS A CHEESE-COD SNACK.
(2) HE'S READY TO MAKE OUT EVEN IN AN ENEMY'S ELEVATOR.
(3) LOOKS LIKE HE WAS READY TO RUN OFF WITH FUMI IN HIS ARMS.

IN THIS NEW VOLUME, THE SNAKE INSIDE KYUTARO SHOWS HIS TRUE STRENGTH (HIS SERIOUS FACE)!

AN UNCONSCIOUS PERSON IS VERY HEAVY, SO I DON'T THINK A GIRL WOULD BE ABLE TO CARRY HIM AND RUN. EXCEPT FUMI IS THE TRUE QUEEN NOW, SO SHE SHOULD BE ABLE TO ORDER HERSELF TO DO IT.

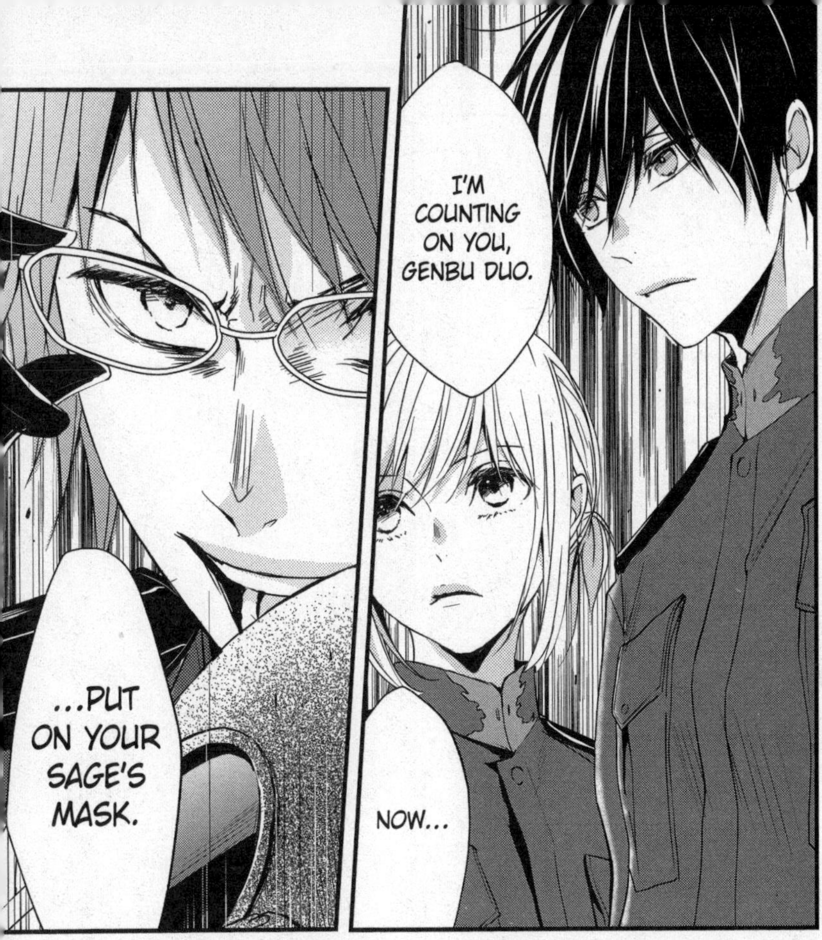
I'M COUNTING ON YOU, GENBU DUO.
NOW...
...PUT ON YOUR SAGE'S MASK.

Why is it that I get the urge to declutter when I'm super busy working on manga pages or a storyboard? I don't have to time to do a major job, so I just choose one or two items to throw away—books or clothes. It feels good! You should try it.

The art tools of my analog days... I just can't get rid of them even if I don't think I'll ever use them again. They hold too many memories.

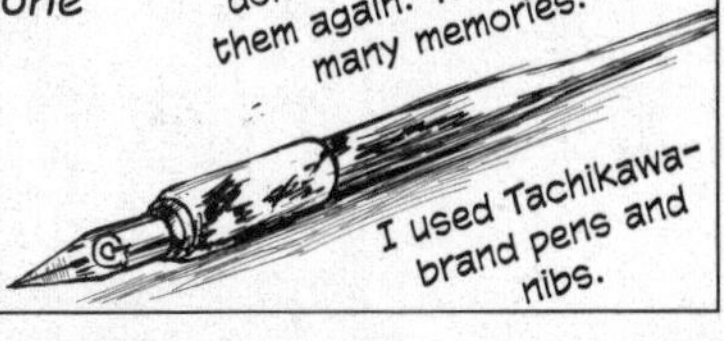
I used Tachikawa-brand pens and nibs.

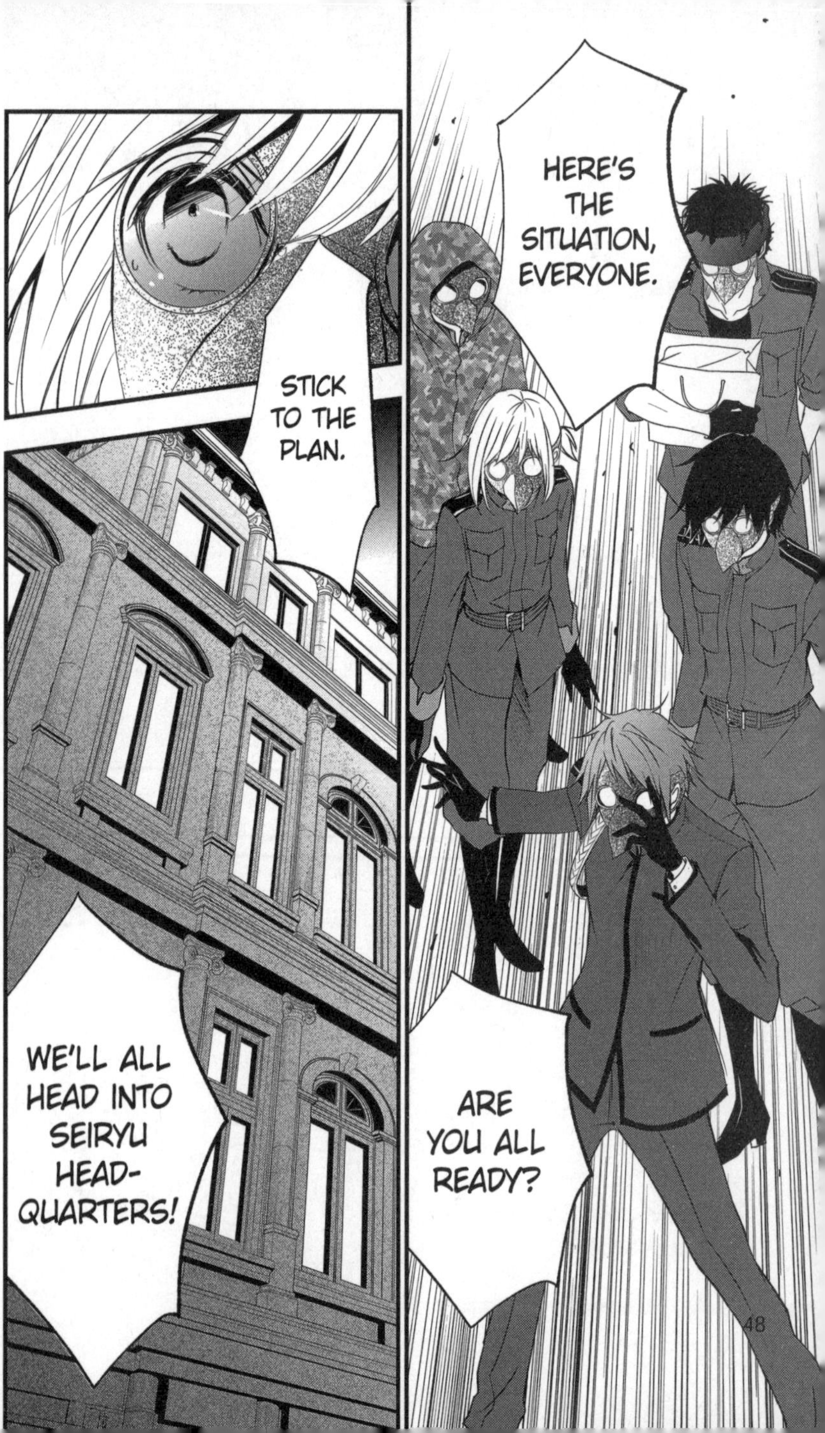
HERE'S THE SITUATION, EVERYONE.
ARE YOU ALL READY?
STICK TO THE PLAN.
WE'LL ALL HEAD INTO SEIRYU HEAD-QUARTERS!

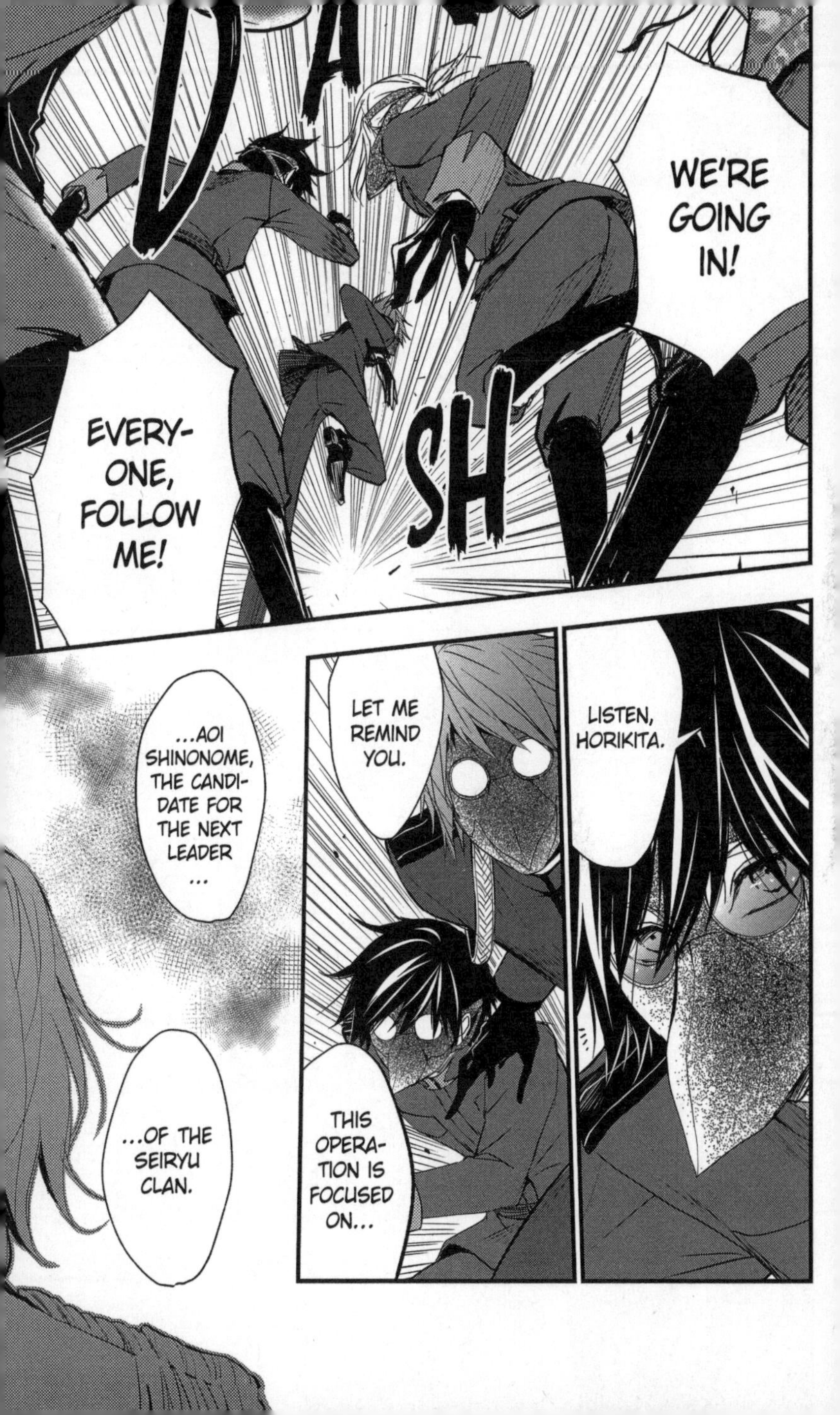
WE'RE GOING IN!
DA
SH
EVERY-ONE, FOLLOW ME!
LISTEN, HORIKITA.
LET ME REMIND YOU.
THIS OPERA-TION IS FOCUSED ON...
...AOI SHINONOME, THE CANDI-DATE FOR THE NEXT LEADER ...
...OF THE SEIRYU CLAN.

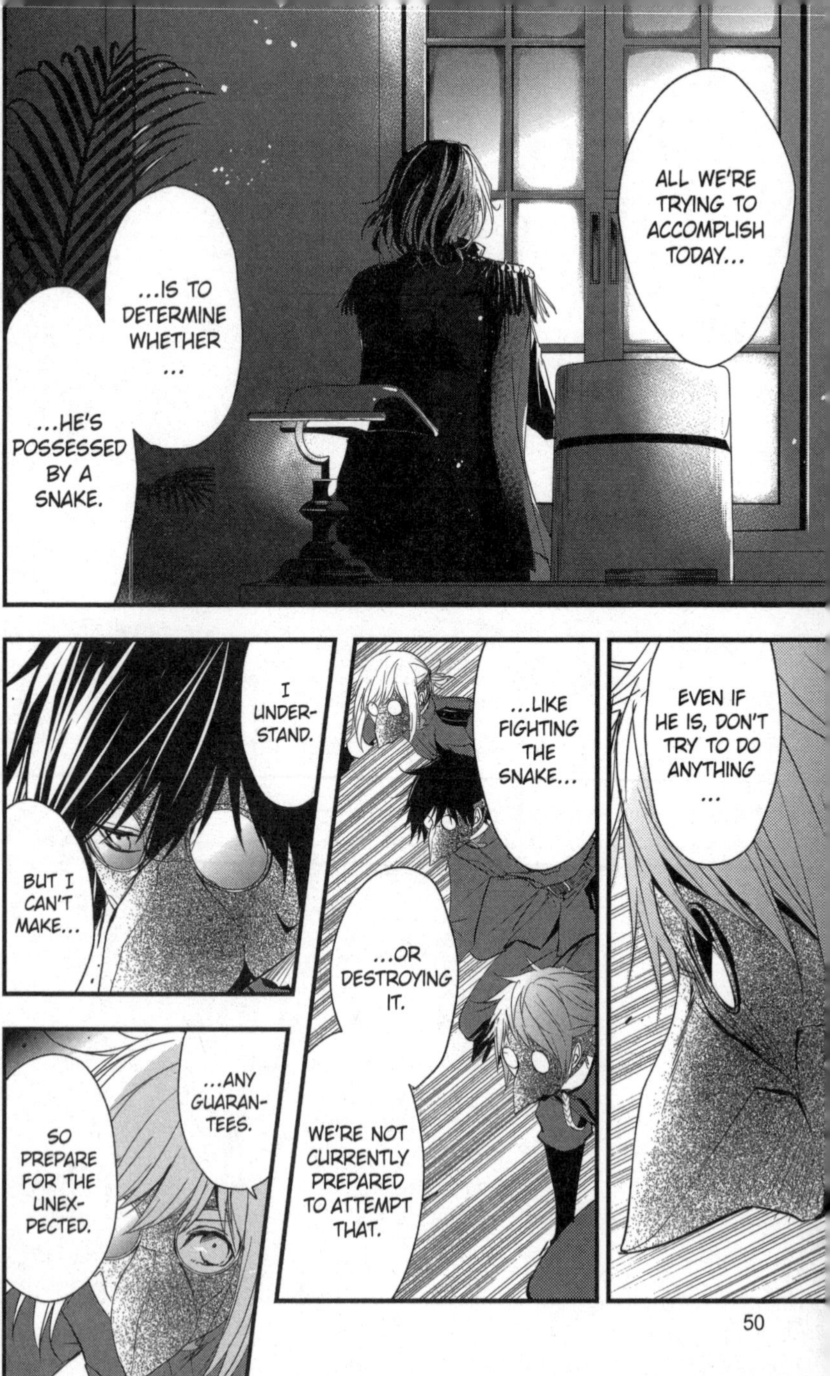
ALL WE'RE TRYING TO ACCOMPLISH TODAY...
...IS TO DETERMINE WHETHER...
...HE'S POSSESSED BY A SNAKE.
EVEN IF HE IS, DON'T TRY TO DO ANYTHING...
...LIKE FIGHTING THE SNAKE...
...OR DESTROYING IT.
WE'RE NOT CURRENTLY PREPARED TO ATTEMPT THAT.
I UNDER-STAND.
BUT I CAN'T MAKE...
...ANY GUARAN-TEES.
SO PREPARE FOR THE UNEX-PECTED.

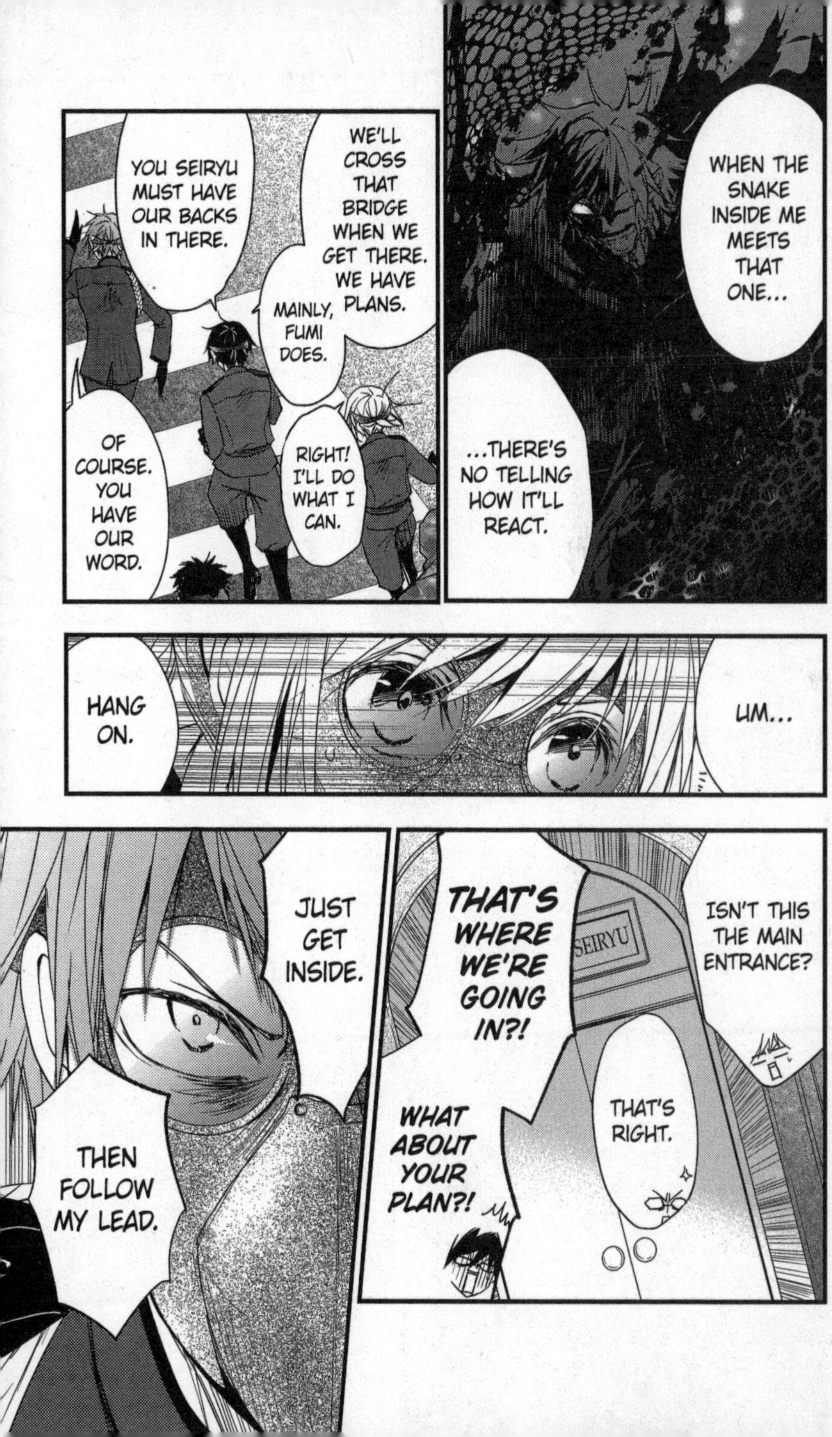
WHEN THE SNAKE INSIDE ME MEETS THAT ONE...
...THERE'S NO TELLING HOW IT'LL REACT.
WE'LL CROSS THAT BRIDGE WHEN WE GET THERE. WE HAVE PLANS.
MAINLY, FUMI DOES.
YOU SEIRYU MUST HAVE OUR BACKS IN THERE.
RIGHT! I'LL DO WHAT I CAN.
OF COURSE. YOU HAVE OUR WORD.
UM...
HANG ON.
ISN'T THIS THE MAIN ENTRANCE?
SEIRYU
THAT'S WHERE WE'RE GOING IN?!
THAT'S RIGHT.
WHAT ABOUT YOUR PLAN?!
JUST GET INSIDE.
THEN FOLLOW MY LEAD.

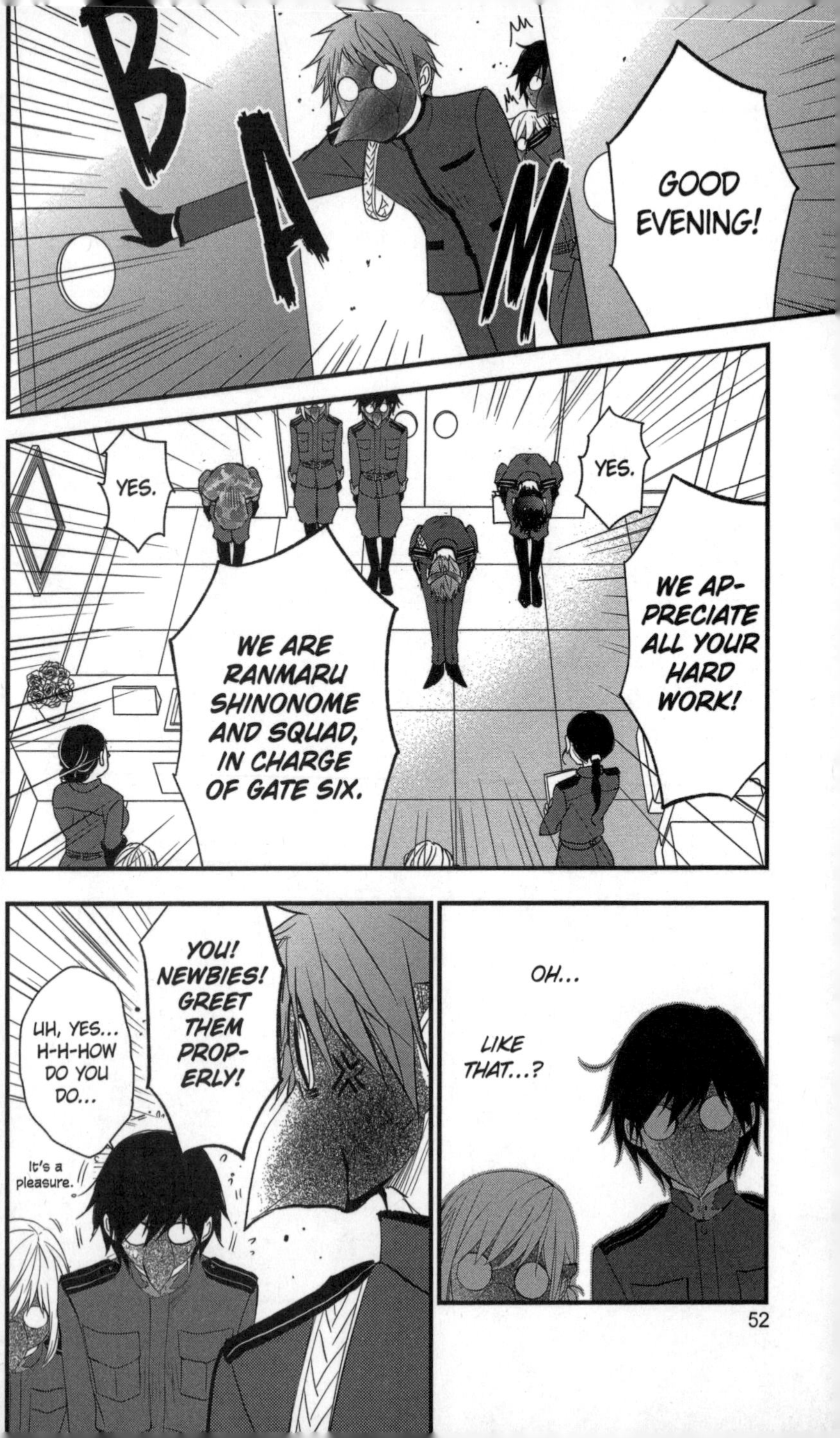
BAM
GOOD EVENING!
YES.
YES.
WE APPRECIATE ALL YOUR HARD WORK!
WE ARE RANMARU SHINONOME AND SQUAD, IN CHARGE OF GATE SIX.
OH...
LIKE THAT...?
YOU! NEWBIES! GREET THEM PROPERLY!
UH, YES... H-H-HOW DO YOU DO...
It's a pleasure.

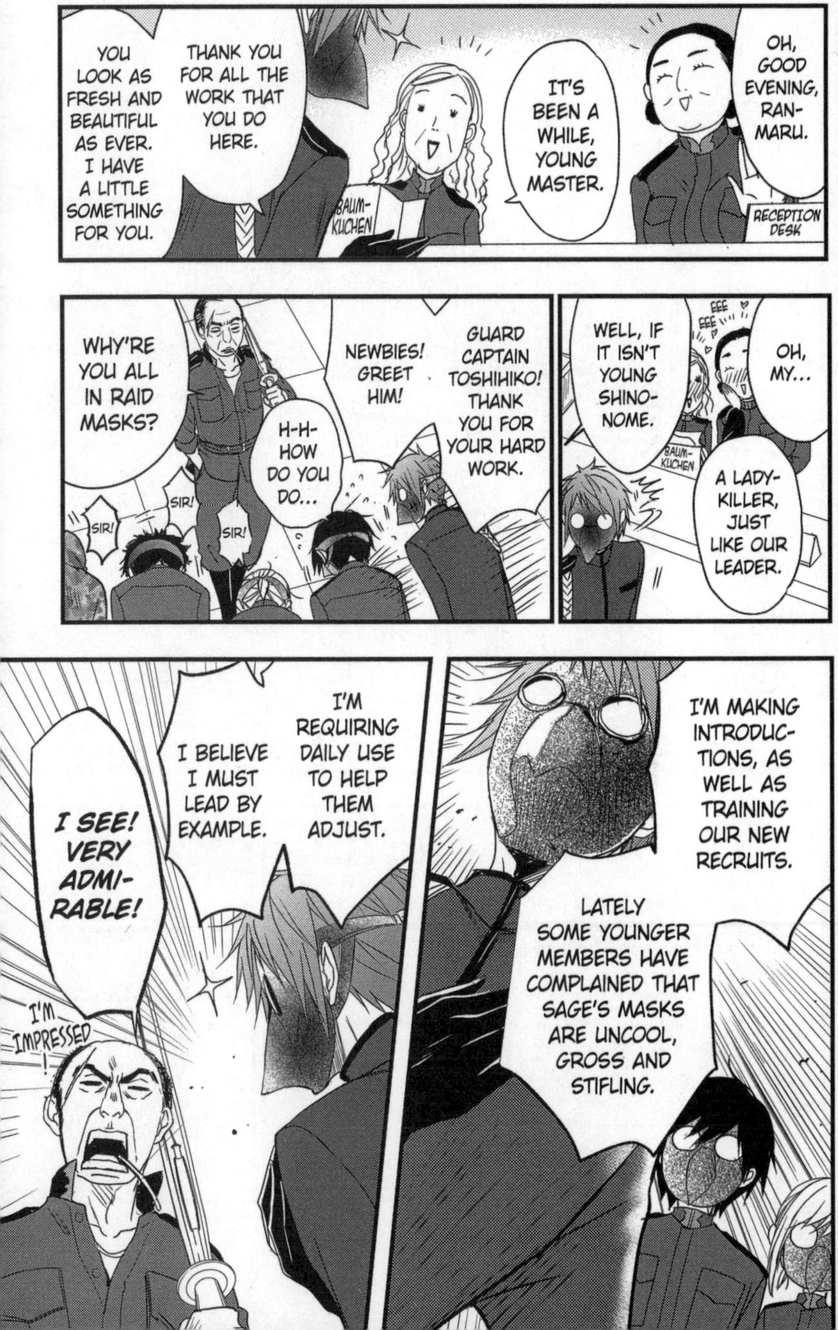
OH, GOOD EVENING, RAN-MARU.
RECEPTION DESK
IT'S BEEN A WHILE, YOUNG MASTER.
BAUM-KUCHEN
THANK YOU FOR ALL THE WORK THAT YOU DO HERE.
YOU LOOK AS FRESH AND BEAUTIFUL AS EVER. I HAVE A LITTLE SOMETHING FOR YOU.
EEE EEE
OH, MY...
WELL, IF IT ISN'T YOUNG SHINO-NOME.
BAUM-KUCHEN
A LADY-KILLER, JUST LIKE OUR LEADER.
GUARD CAPTAIN TOSHIHIKO! THANK YOU FOR YOUR HARD WORK.
NEWBIES! GREET HIM!
H-H-HOW DO YOU DO...
WHY'RE YOU ALL IN RAID MASKS?
SIR!
SIR!
SIR!
I'M MAKING INTRODUC-TIONS, AS WELL AS TRAINING OUR NEW RECRUITS.
LATELY SOME YOUNGER MEMBERS HAVE COMPLAINED THAT SAGE'S MASKS ARE UNCOOL, GROSS AND STIFLING.
I'M REQUIRING DAILY USE TO HELP THEM ADJUST.
I BELIEVE I MUST LEAD BY EXAMPLE.
I SEE! VERY ADMI-RABLE!
I'M IMPRESSED!

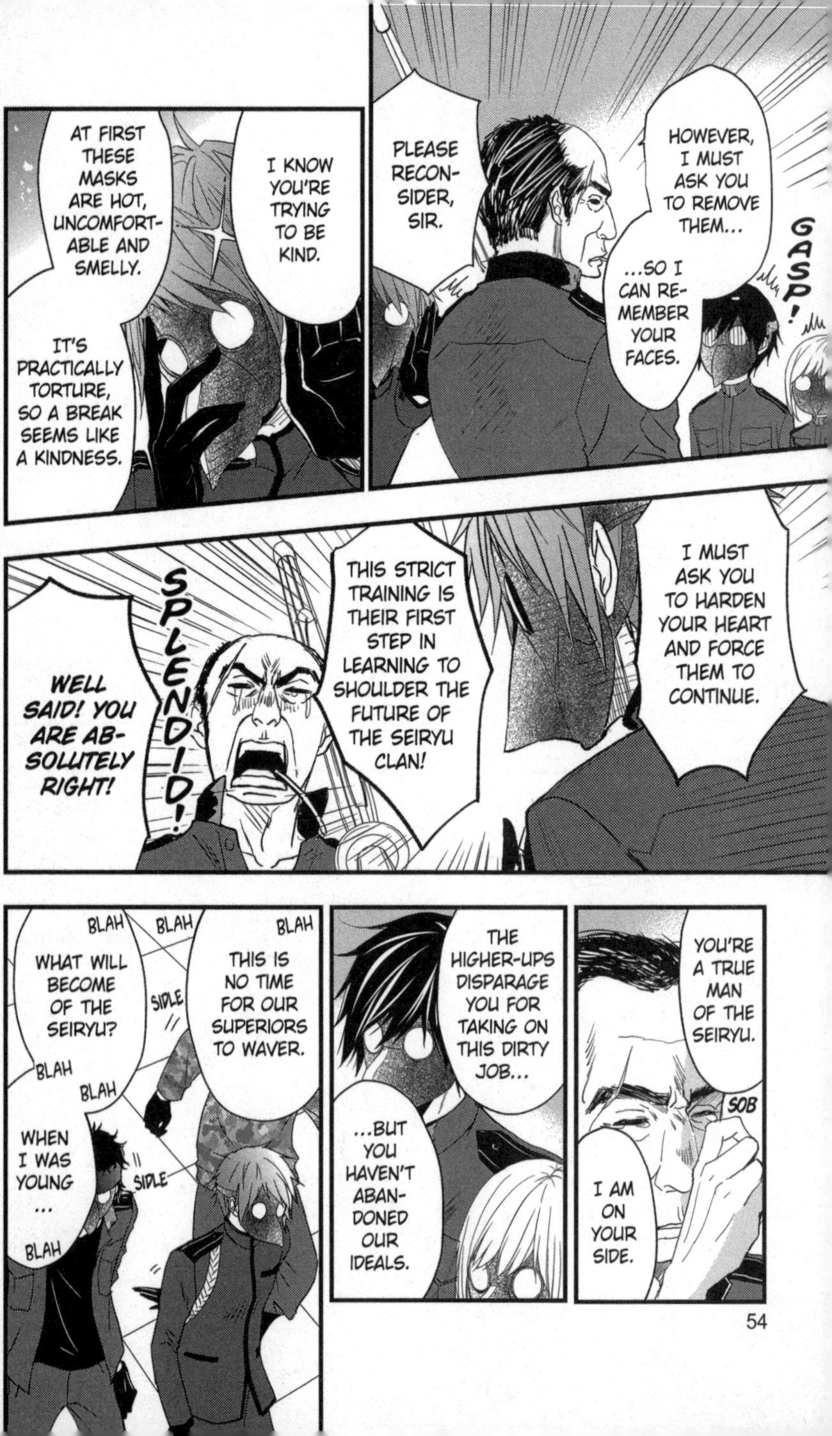
HOWEVER, I MUST ASK YOU TO REMOVE THEM...
GASP!
...SO I CAN REMEMBER YOUR FACES.
PLEASE RECONSIDER, SIR.
I KNOW YOU'RE TRYING TO BE KIND.
AT FIRST THESE MASKS ARE HOT, UNCOMFORTABLE AND SMELLY.
IT'S PRACTICALLY TORTURE, SO A BREAK SEEMS LIKE A KINDNESS.
I MUST ASK YOU TO HARDEN YOUR HEART AND FORCE THEM TO CONTINUE.
THIS STRICT TRAINING IS THEIR FIRST STEP IN LEARNING TO SHOULDER THE FUTURE OF THE SEIRYU CLAN!
SPLENDID!
WELL SAID! YOU ARE ABSOLUTELY RIGHT!
YOU'RE A TRUE MAN OF THE SEIRYU.
SOB
I AM ON YOUR SIDE.
THE HIGHER-UPS DISPARAGE YOU FOR TAKING ON THIS DIRTY JOB...
...BUT YOU HAVEN'T ABANDONED OUR IDEALS.
BLAH
THIS IS NO TIME FOR OUR SUPERIORS TO WAVER.
BLAH
BLAH
WHAT WILL BECOME OF THE SEIRYU?
SIDLE
BLAH
BLAH
SIDLE
WHEN I WAS YOUNG...
BLAH

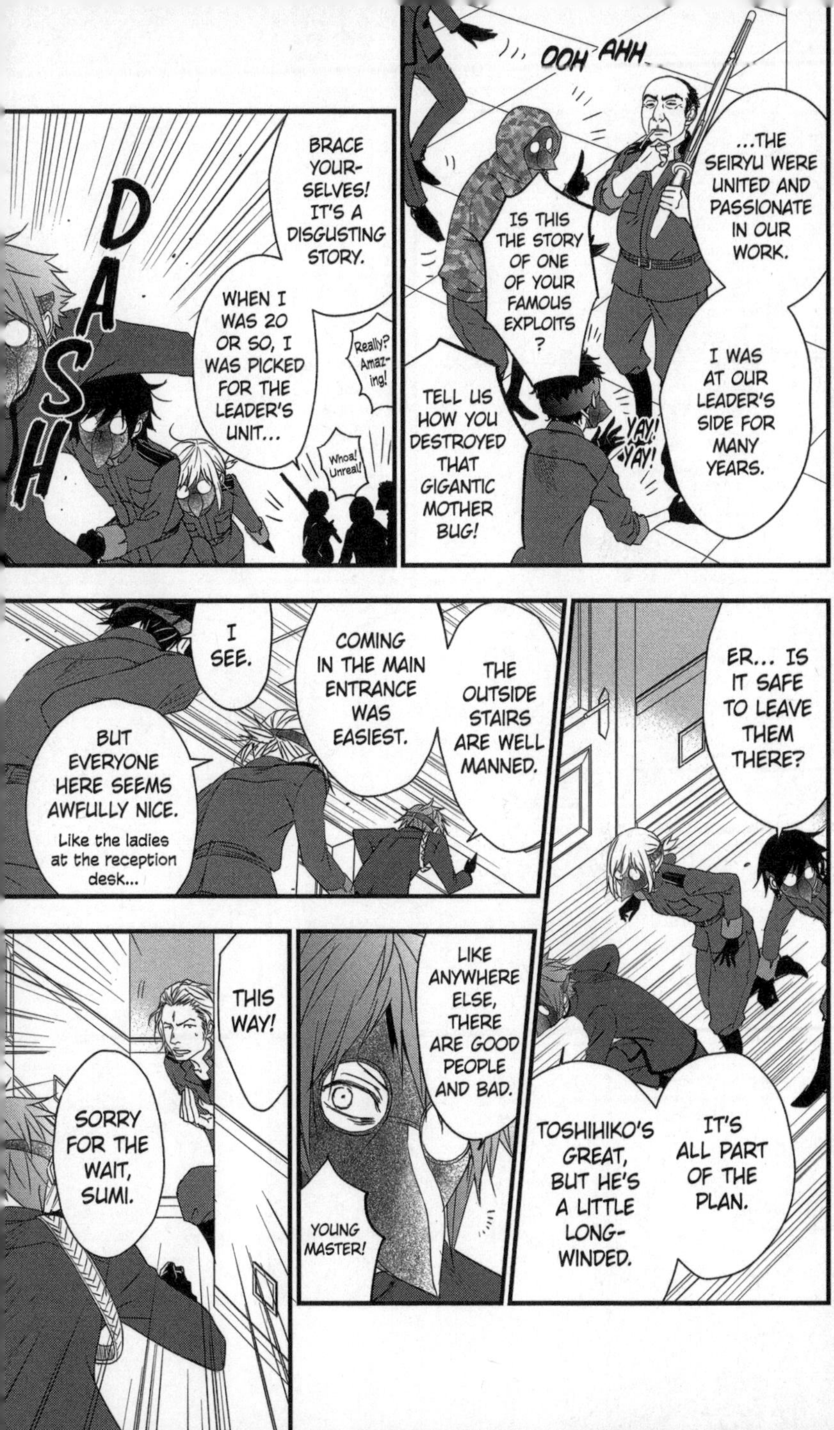
OOH AHH
...THE SEIRYU WERE UNITED AND PASSIONATE IN OUR WORK.
IS THIS THE STORY OF ONE OF YOUR FAMOUS EXPLOITS?
I WAS AT OUR LEADER'S SIDE FOR MANY YEARS.
TELL US HOW YOU DESTROYED THAT GIGANTIC MOTHER BUG!
YAY! YAY!
BRACE YOURSELVES! IT'S A DISGUSTING STORY.
WHEN I WAS 20 OR SO, I WAS PICKED FOR THE LEADER'S UNIT...
Really? Amazing!
Whoa! Unreal!
DASH
ER... IS IT SAFE TO LEAVE THEM THERE?
IT'S ALL PART OF THE PLAN.
TOSHIHIKO'S GREAT, BUT HE'S A LITTLE LONG-WINDED.
THE OUTSIDE STAIRS ARE WELL MANNED.
COMING IN THE MAIN ENTRANCE WAS EASIEST.
I SEE.
BUT EVERYONE HERE SEEMS AWFULLY NICE.
Like the ladies at the reception desk...
LIKE ANYWHERE ELSE, THERE ARE GOOD PEOPLE AND BAD.
YOUNG MASTER!
THIS WAY!
SORRY FOR THE WAIT, SUMI.

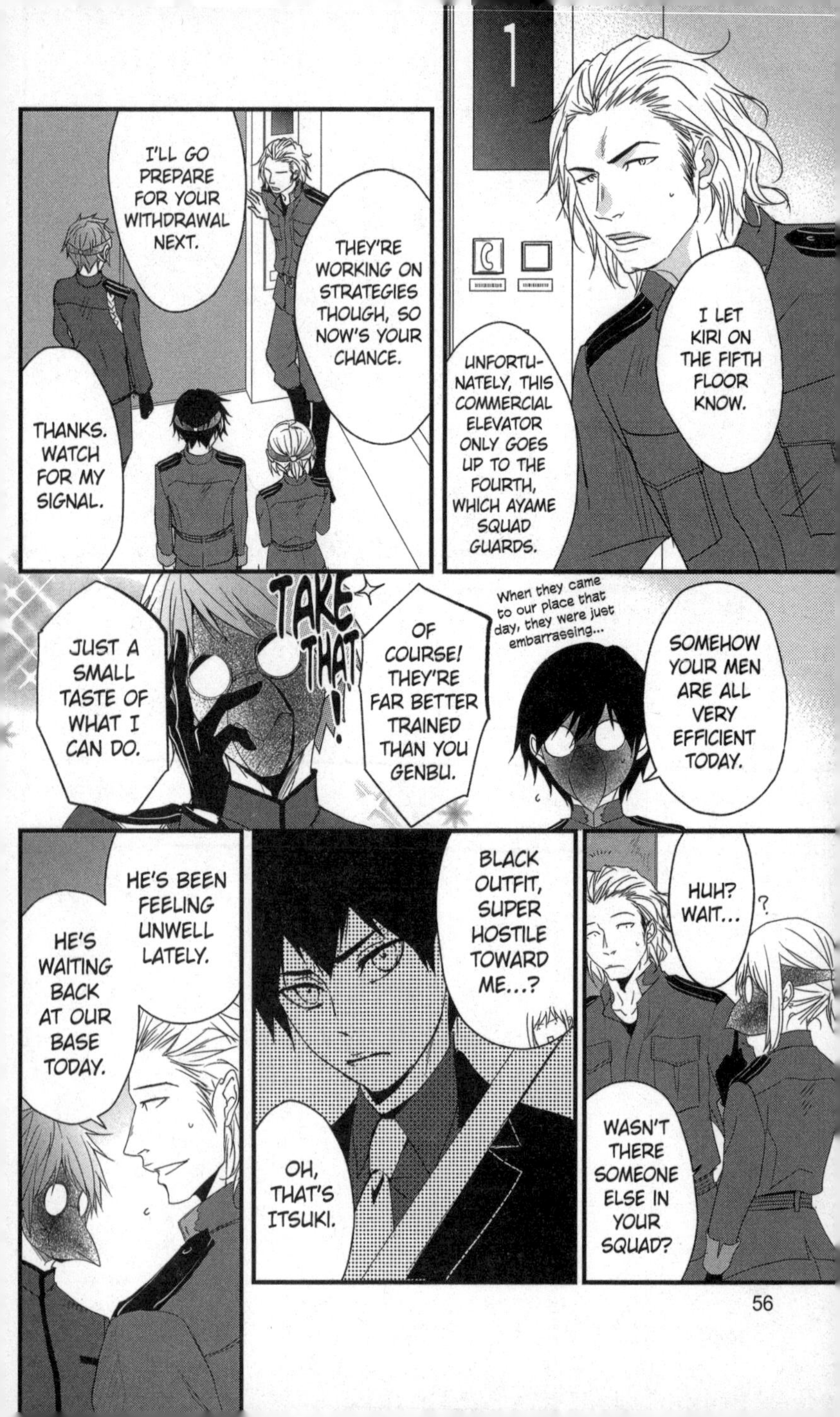
I LET KIRI ON THE FIFTH FLOOR KNOW.
UNFORTUNATELY, THIS COMMERCIAL ELEVATOR ONLY GOES UP TO THE FOURTH, WHICH AYAME SQUAD GUARDS.
THEY'RE WORKING ON STRATEGIES THOUGH, SO NOW'S YOUR CHANCE.
I'LL GO PREPARE FOR YOUR WITHDRAWAL NEXT.
THANKS. WATCH FOR MY SIGNAL.
SOMEHOW YOUR MEN ARE ALL VERY EFFICIENT TODAY.
When they came to our place that day, they were just embarrassing...
OF COURSE! THEY'RE FAR BETTER TRAINED THAN YOU GENBU.
TAKE THAT!
JUST A SMALL TASTE OF WHAT I CAN DO.
HUH? WAIT...
?
WASN'T THERE SOMEONE ELSE IN YOUR SQUAD?
BLACK OUTFIT, SUPER HOSTILE TOWARD ME...?
OH, THAT'S ITSUKI.
HE'S BEEN FEELING UNWELL LATELY.
HE'S WAITING BACK AT OUR BASE TODAY.

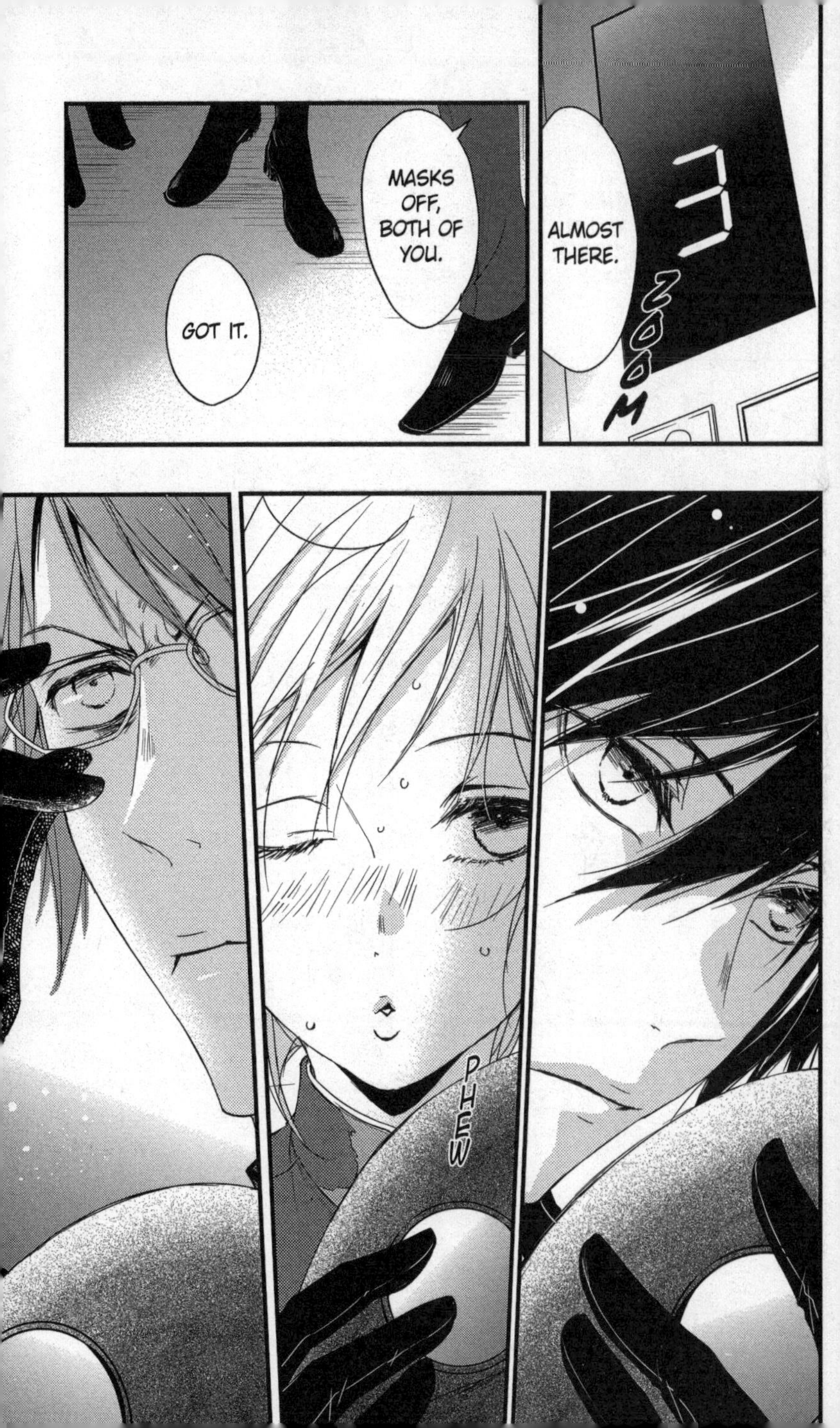
ALMOST THERE.
ZOOM
MASKS OFF, BOTH OF YOU.
GOT IT.
PHEW

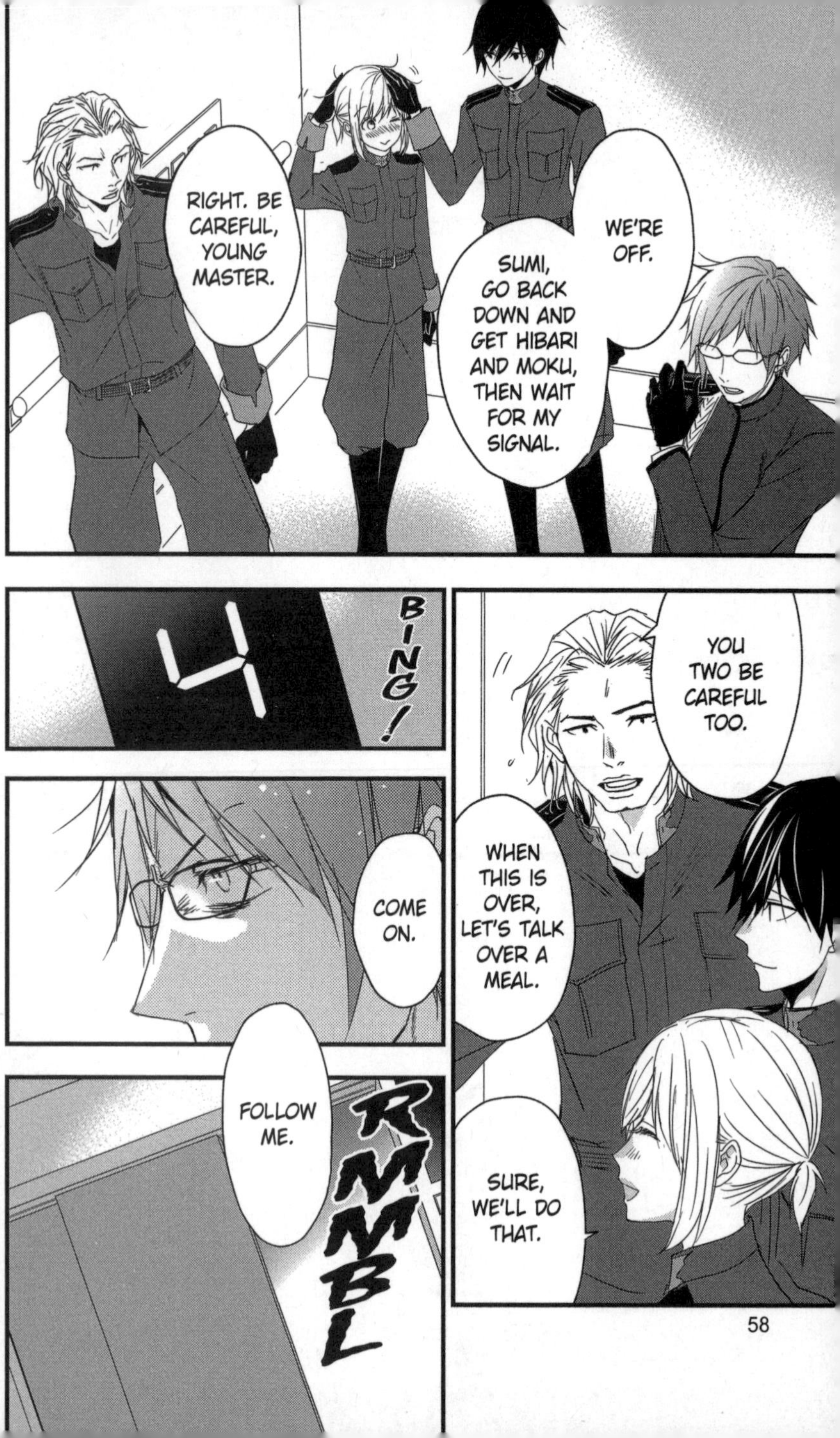
WE'RE OFF.
SUMI, GO BACK DOWN AND GET HIBARI AND MOKU, THEN WAIT FOR MY SIGNAL.
RIGHT. BE CAREFUL, YOUNG MASTER.
YOU TWO BE CAREFUL TOO.
WHEN THIS IS OVER, LET'S TALK OVER A MEAL.
SURE, WE'LL DO THAT.
4
BING!
COME ON.
FOLLOW ME.
RMMBL

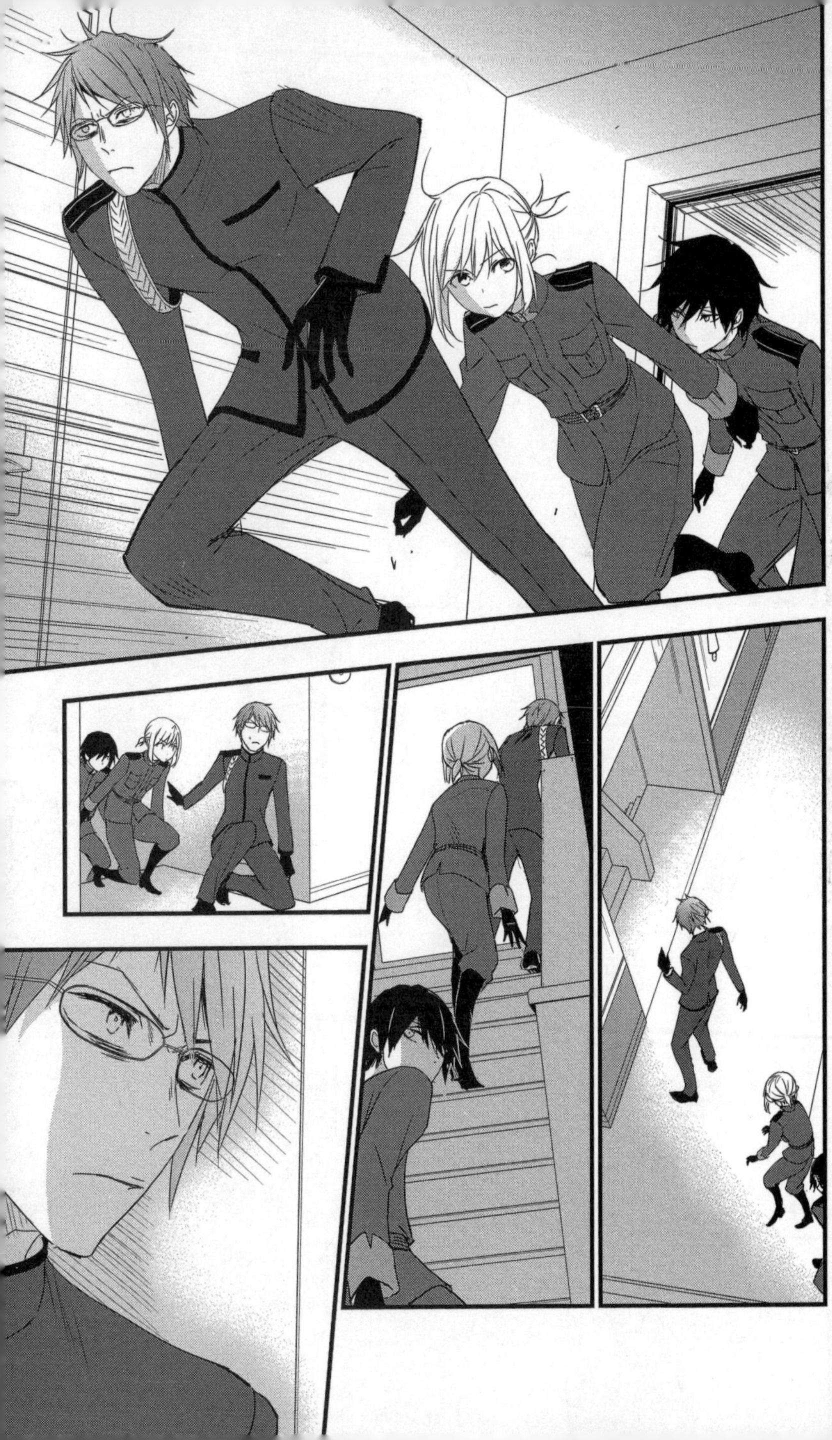

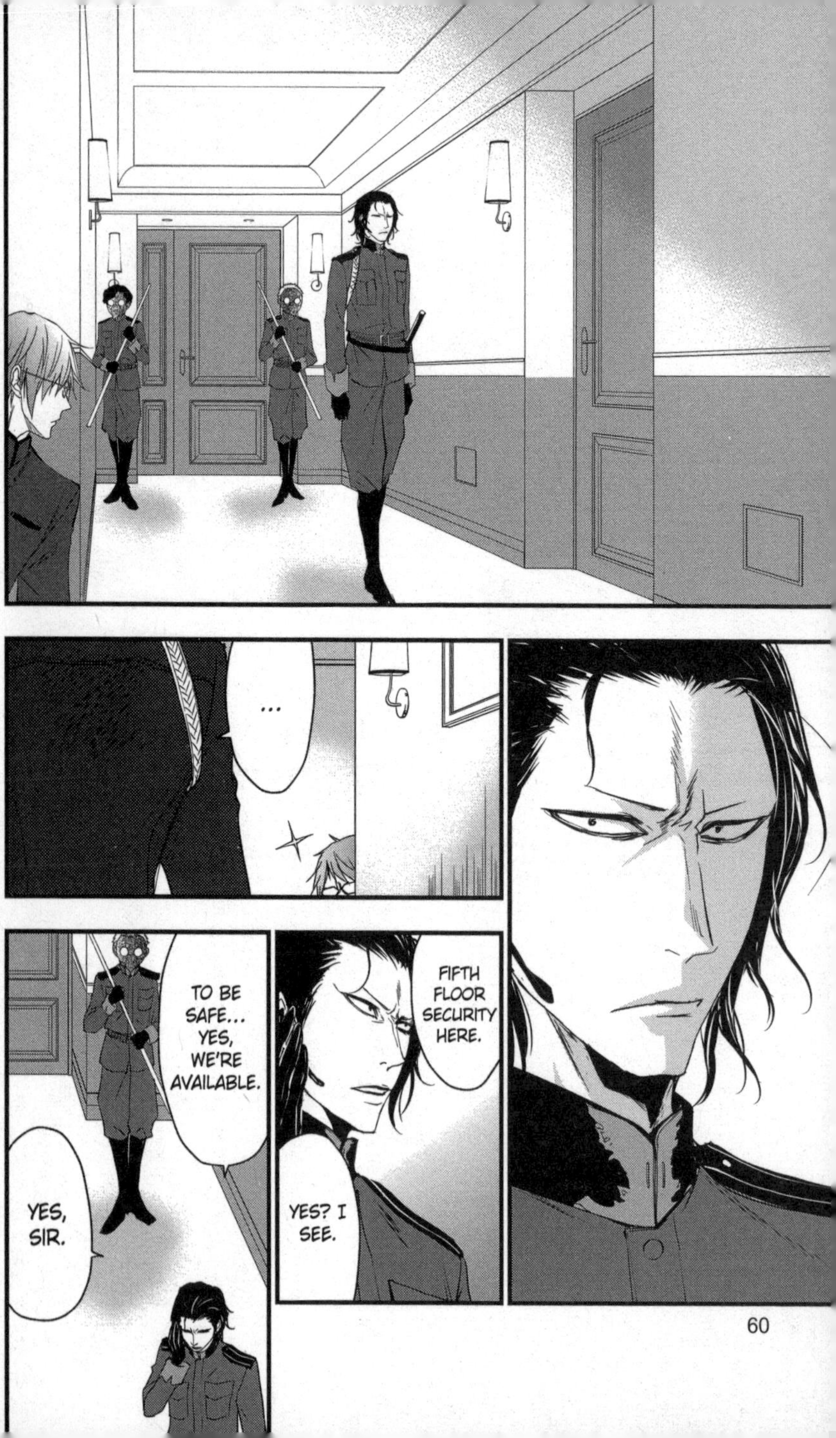
...
FIFTH FLOOR SECURITY HERE.
YES? I SEE.
TO BE SAFE... YES, WE'RE AVAILABLE.
YES, SIR.

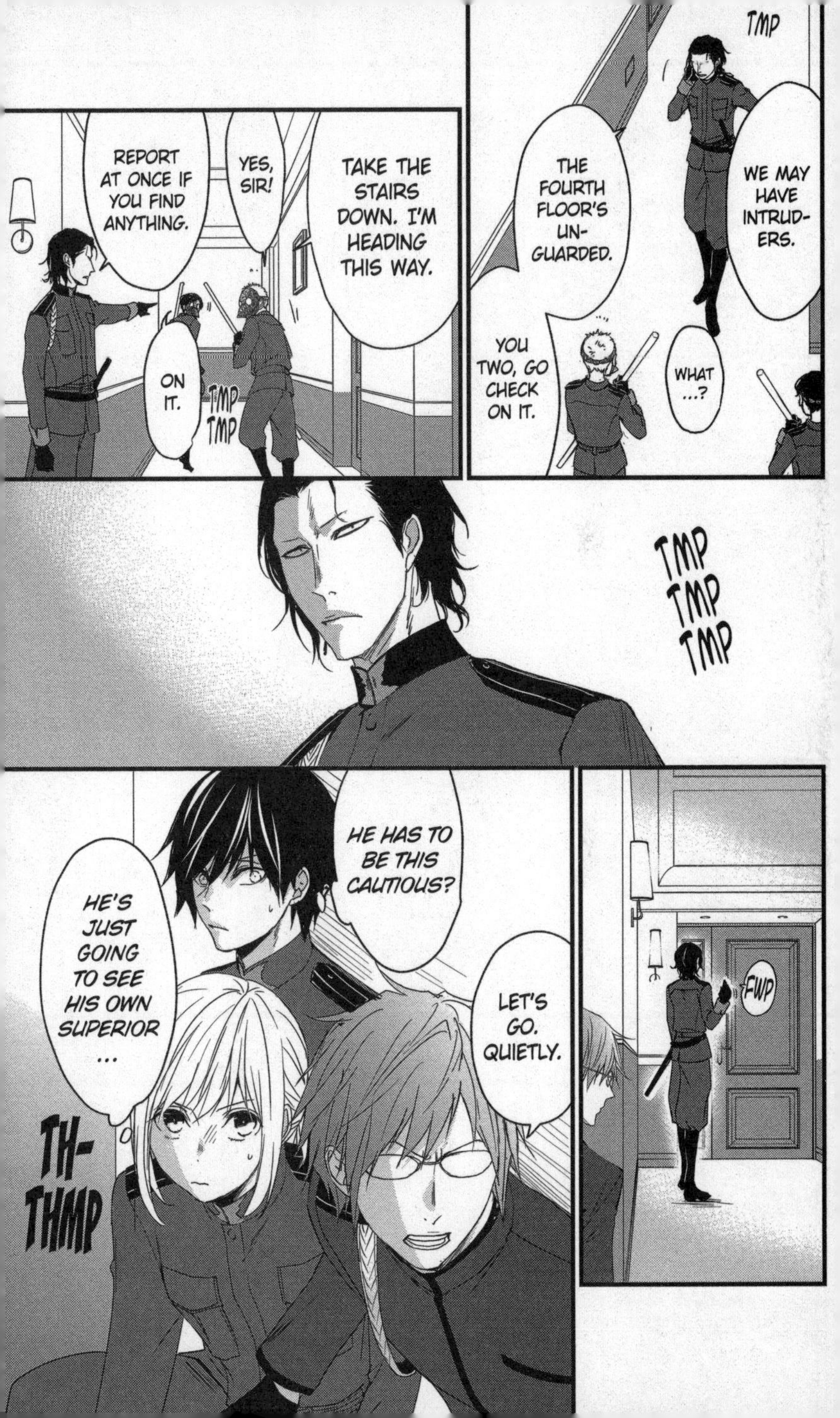
TMP
WE MAY HAVE INTRUDERS.
THE FOURTH FLOOR'S UNGUARDED.
WHAT ...?
YOU TWO, GO CHECK ON IT.
TAKE THE STAIRS DOWN. I'M HEADING THIS WAY.
YES, SIR!
REPORT AT ONCE IF YOU FIND ANYTHING.
ON IT.
TMP TMP
TMP TMP TMP
FWP
HE HAS TO BE THIS CAUTIOUS?
HE'S JUST GOING TO SEE HIS OWN SUPERIOR ...
LET'S GO. QUIETLY.
TH-THMP

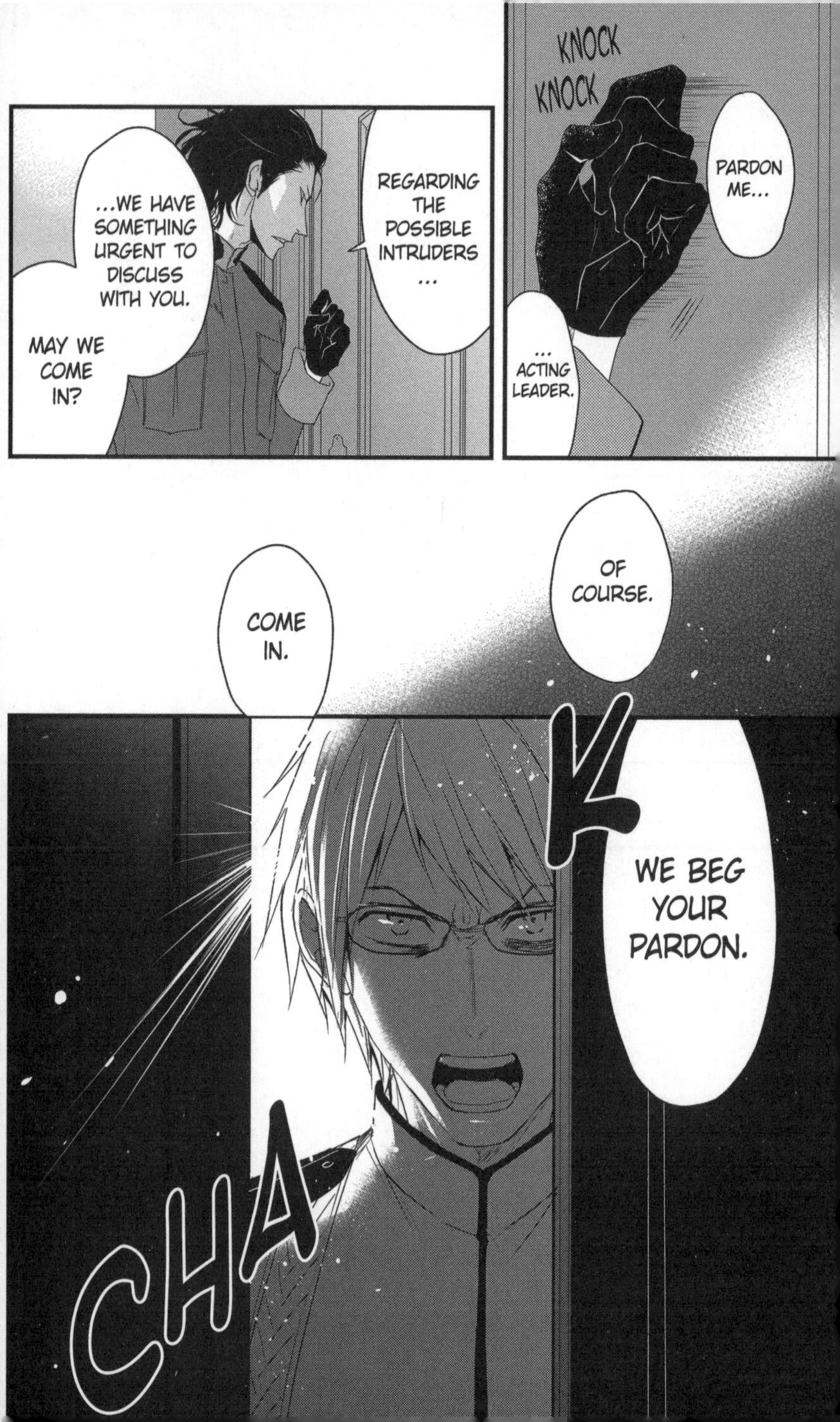
KNOCK KNOCK
PARDON ME...
...ACTING LEADER.
REGARDING THE POSSIBLE INTRUDERS...
...WE HAVE SOMETHING URGENT TO DISCUSS WITH YOU.
MAY WE COME IN?
OF COURSE.
COME IN.
K
WE BEG YOUR PARDON.
CHA

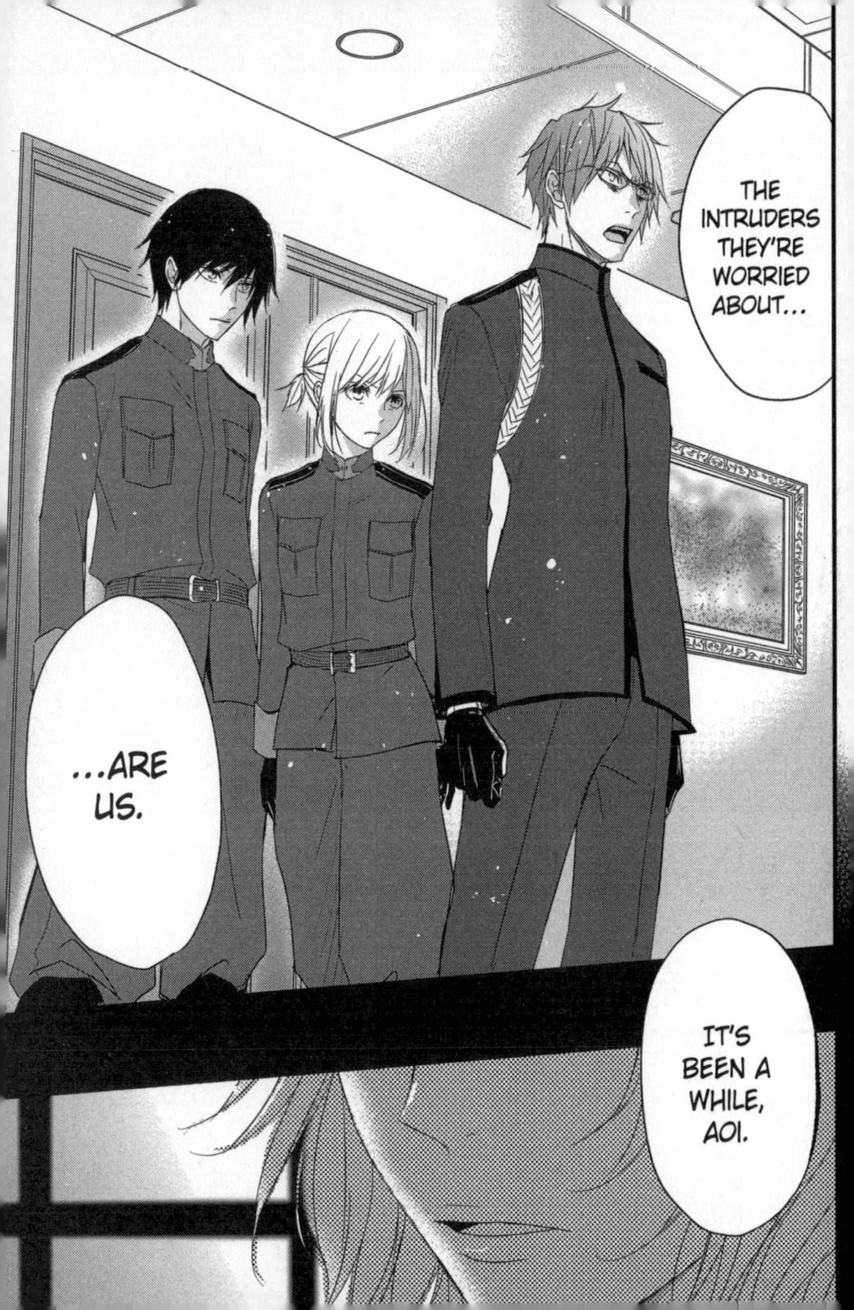
THE INTRUDERS THEY'RE WORRIED ABOUT...
...ARE US.
IT'S BEEN A WHILE, AOI.

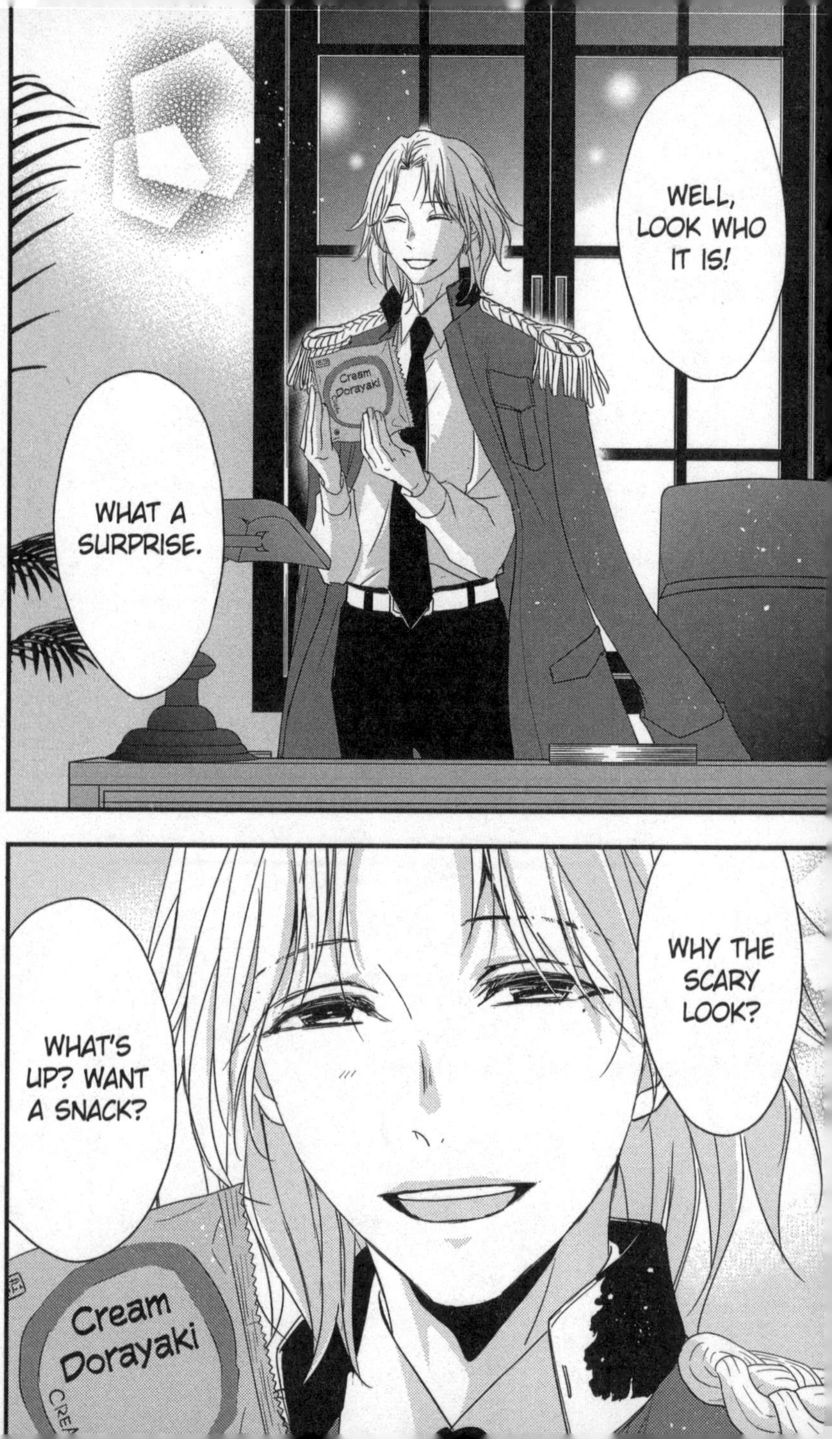
WELL, LOOK WHO IT IS!
Cream Dorayaki
WHAT A SURPRISE.
WHY THE SCARY LOOK?
WHAT'S UP? WANT A SNACK?
Cream Dorayaki

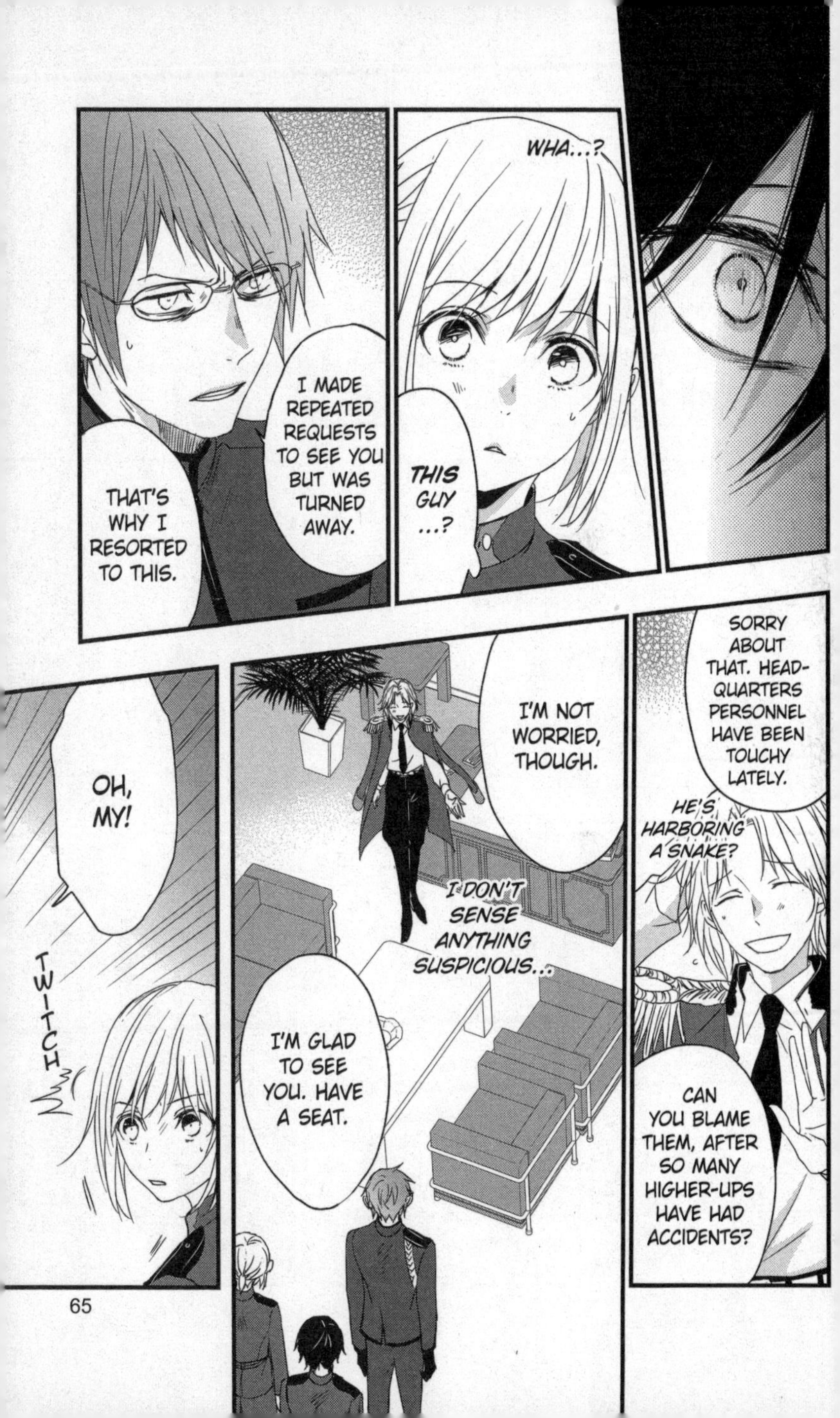
WHA...?
THIS GUY ...?
I MADE REPEATED REQUESTS TO SEE YOU BUT WAS TURNED AWAY.
THAT'S WHY I RESORTED TO THIS.
SORRY ABOUT THAT. HEAD-QUARTERS PERSONNEL HAVE BEEN TOUCHY LATELY.
HE'S HARBORING A SNAKE?
CAN YOU BLAME THEM, AFTER SO MANY HIGHER-UPS HAVE HAD ACCIDENTS?
I'M NOT WORRIED, THOUGH.
I DON'T SENSE ANYTHING SUSPICIOUS...
I'M GLAD TO SEE YOU. HAVE A SEAT.
OH, MY!
TWITCH

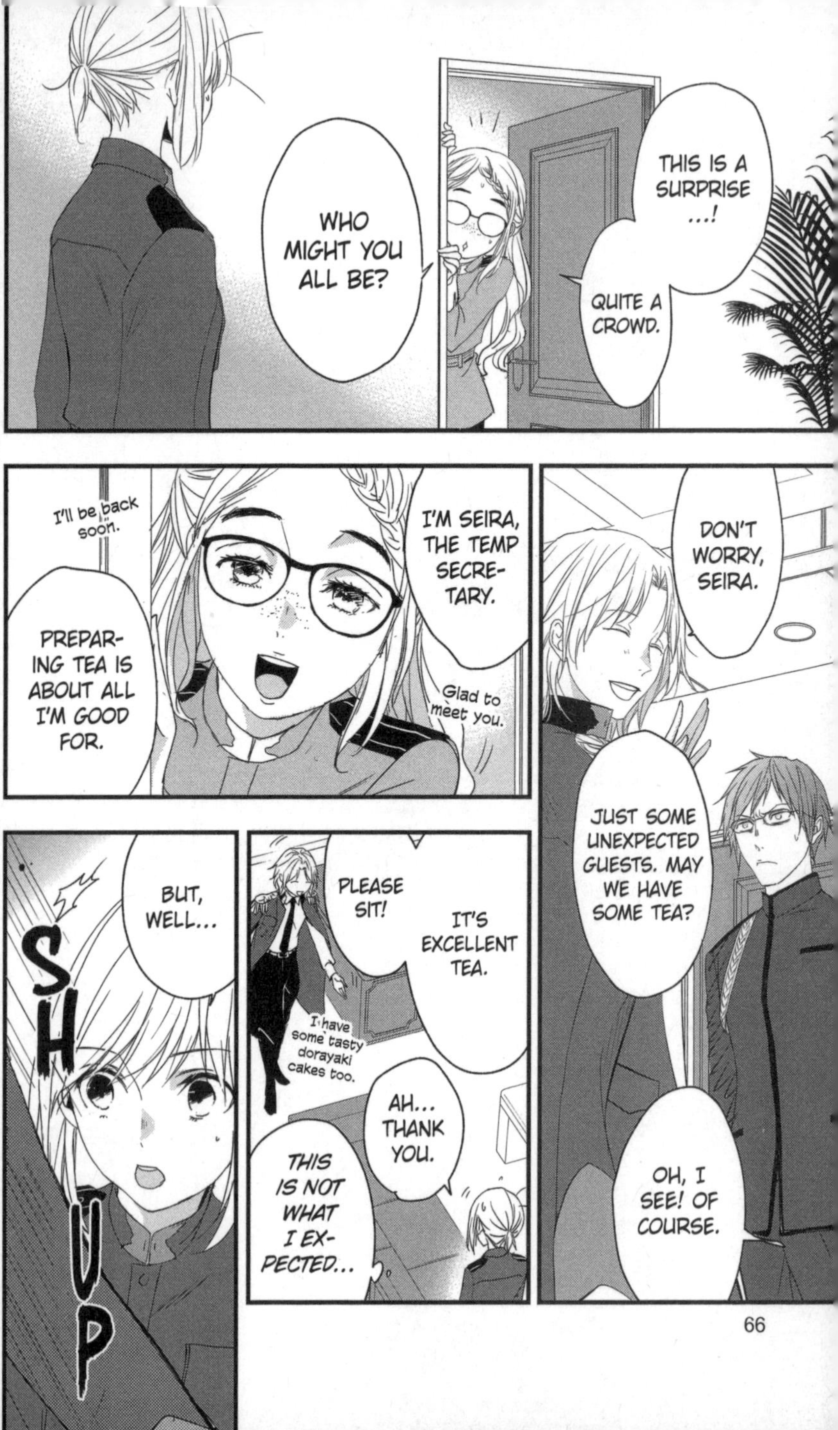
THIS IS A SURPRISE ...!
QUITE A CROWD.
WHO MIGHT YOU ALL BE?
DON'T WORRY, SEIRA.
JUST SOME UNEXPECTED GUESTS. MAY WE HAVE SOME TEA?
OH, I SEE! OF COURSE.
I'M SEIRA, THE TEMP SECRE-TARY.
Glad to meet you.
I'll be back soon.
PREPAR-ING TEA IS ABOUT ALL I'M GOOD FOR.
PLEASE SIT!
IT'S EXCELLENT TEA.
I have some tasty dorayaki cakes too.
AH... THANK YOU.
THIS IS NOT WHAT I EX-PECTED...
BUT, WELL...
SHUP

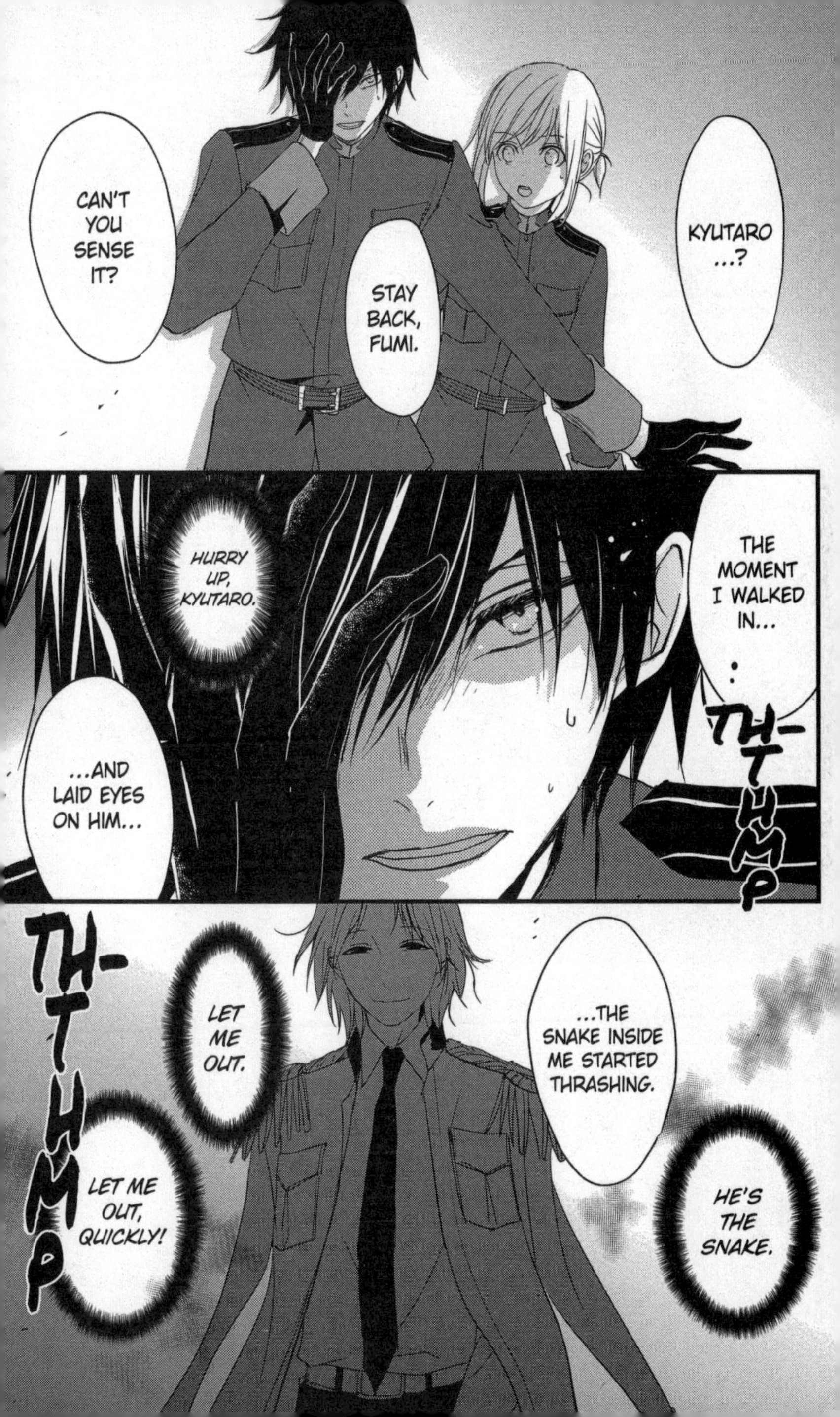
KYUTARO ...?
STAY BACK, FUMI.
CAN'T YOU SENSE IT?
THE MOMENT I WALKED IN...
TH-THUMP
HURRY UP, KYUTARO.
...AND LAID EYES ON HIM...
...THE SNAKE INSIDE ME STARTED THRASHING.
HE'S THE SNAKE.
LET ME OUT.
LET ME OUT, QUICKLY!
TH-THUMP

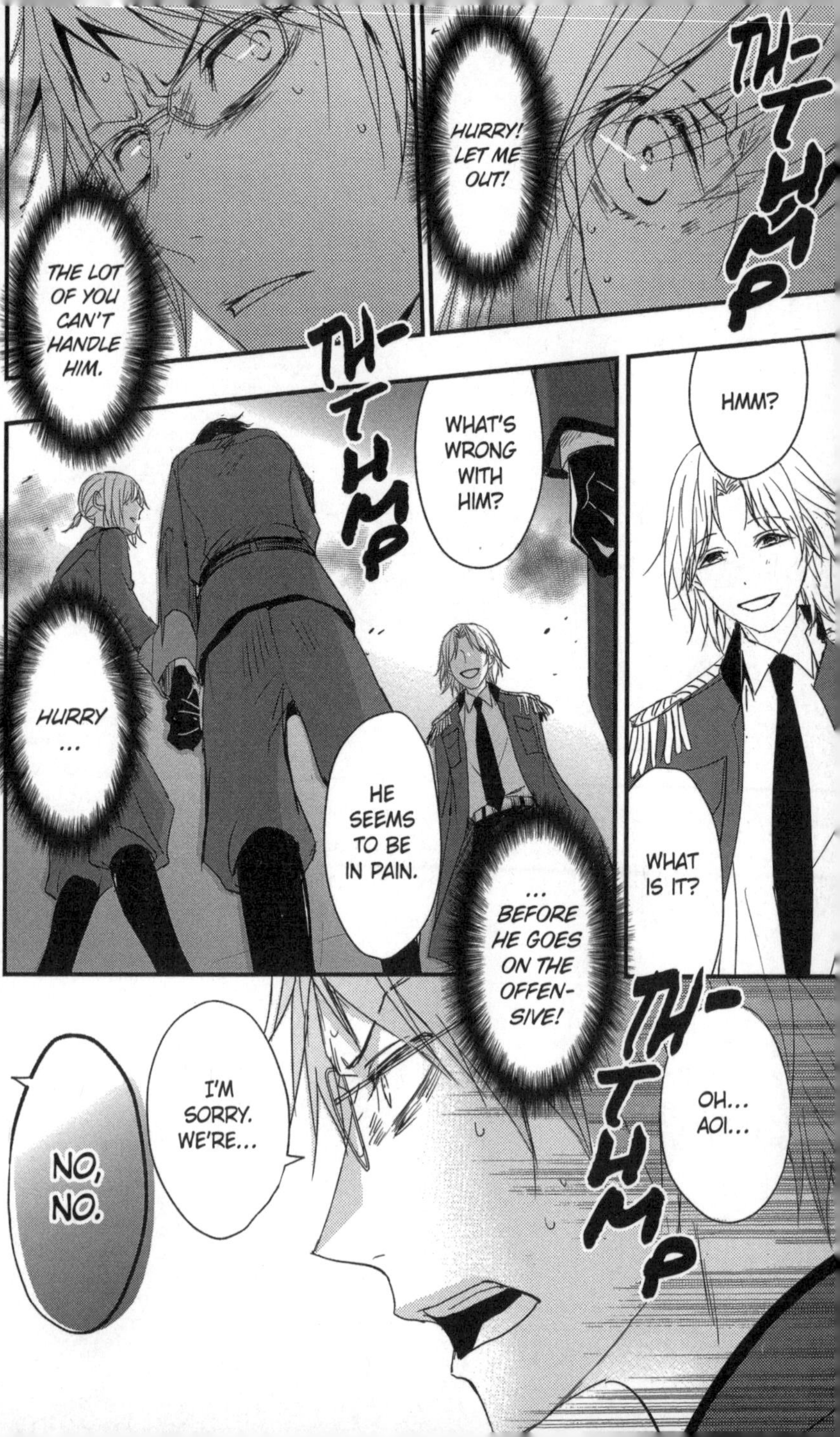
TH-THUMP
HURRY! LET ME OUT!
THE LOT OF YOU CAN'T HANDLE HIM.
HMM?
WHAT IS IT?
TH-THUMP
WHAT'S WRONG WITH HIM?
HE SEEMS TO BE IN PAIN.
HURRY …
… BEFORE HE GOES ON THE OFFEN-SIVE!
TH-THUMP
OH… AOI…
I'M SORRY. WE'RE…
NO, NO.

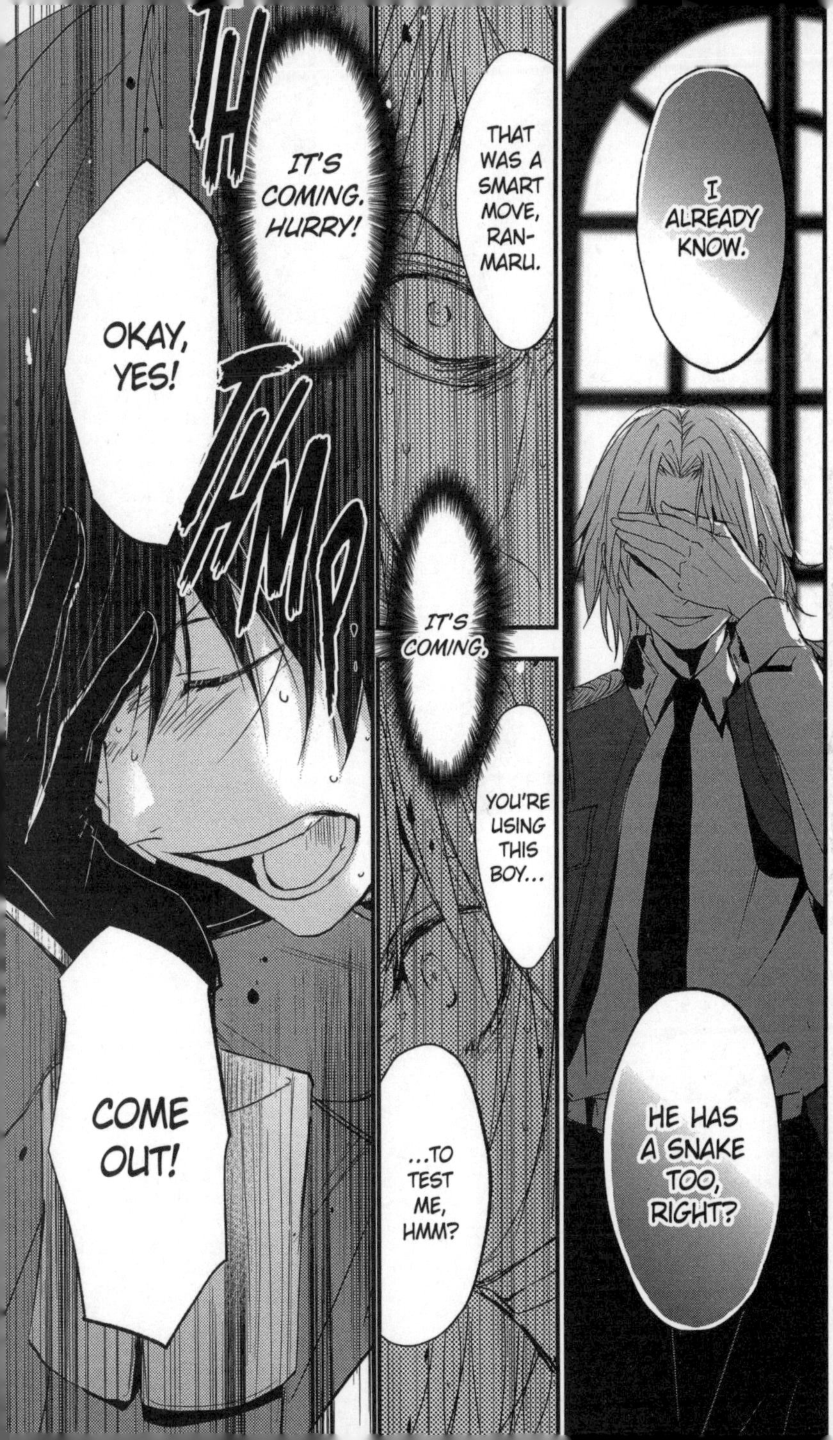
I ALREADY KNOW.
HE HAS A SNAKE TOO, RIGHT?
THAT WAS A SMART MOVE, RAN-MARU.
IT'S COMING.
YOU'RE USING THIS BOY...
...TO TEST ME, HMM?
TH
IT'S COMING. HURRY!
OKAY, YES!
THMP
COME OUT!

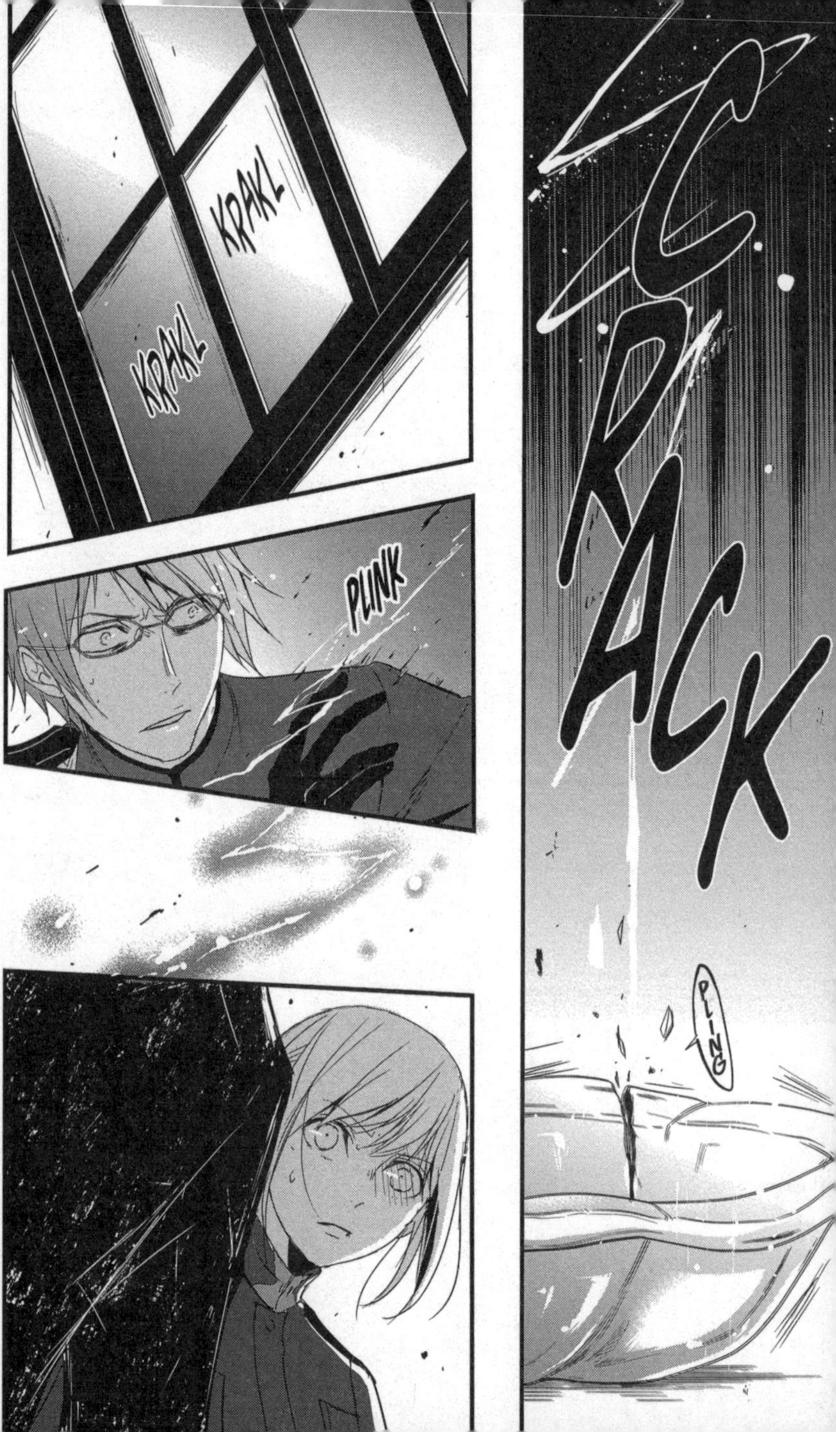
CRACK
PLING
KRAKL
KRAKL
PLINK

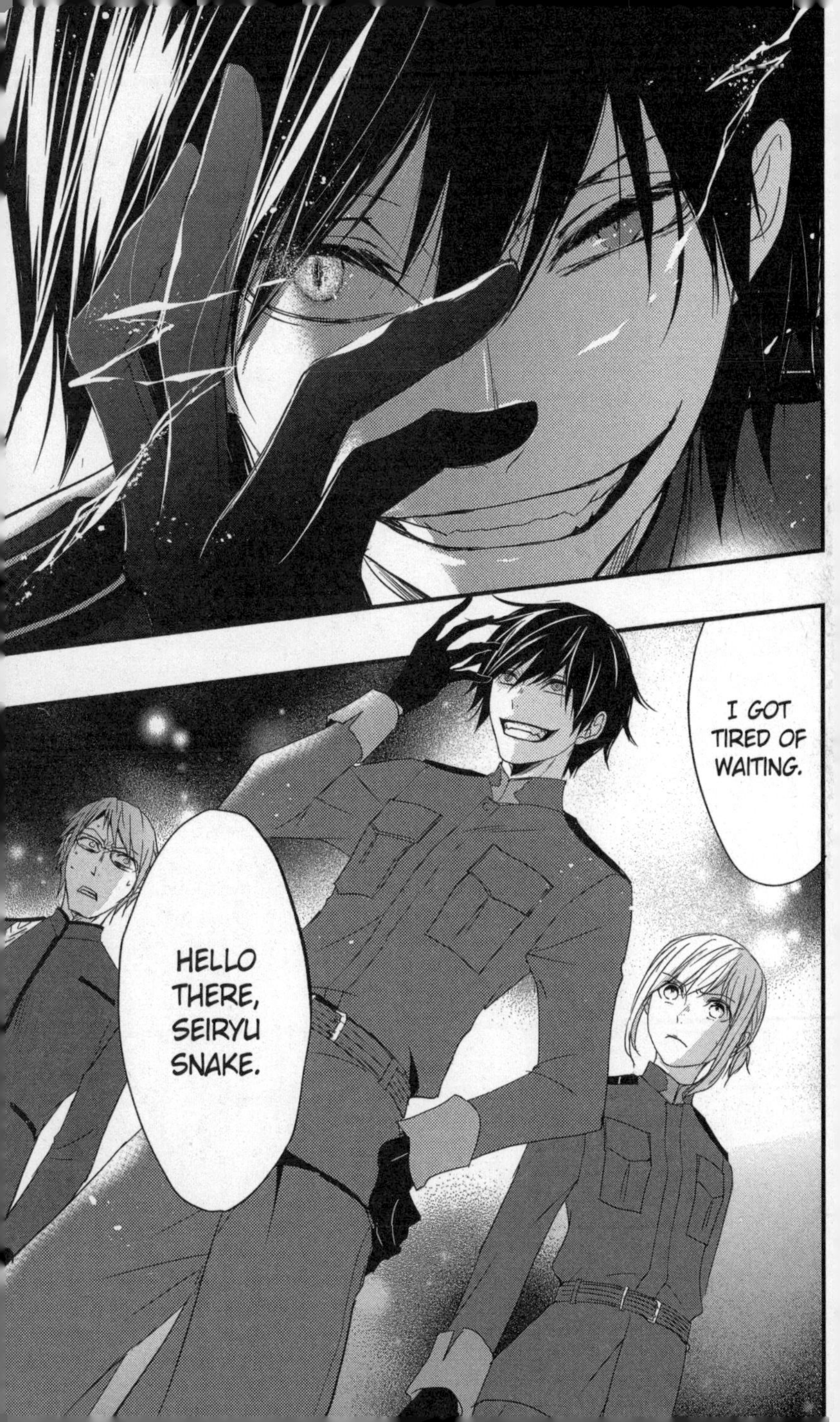
I GOT TIRED OF WAITING.
HELLO THERE, SEIRYU SNAKE.

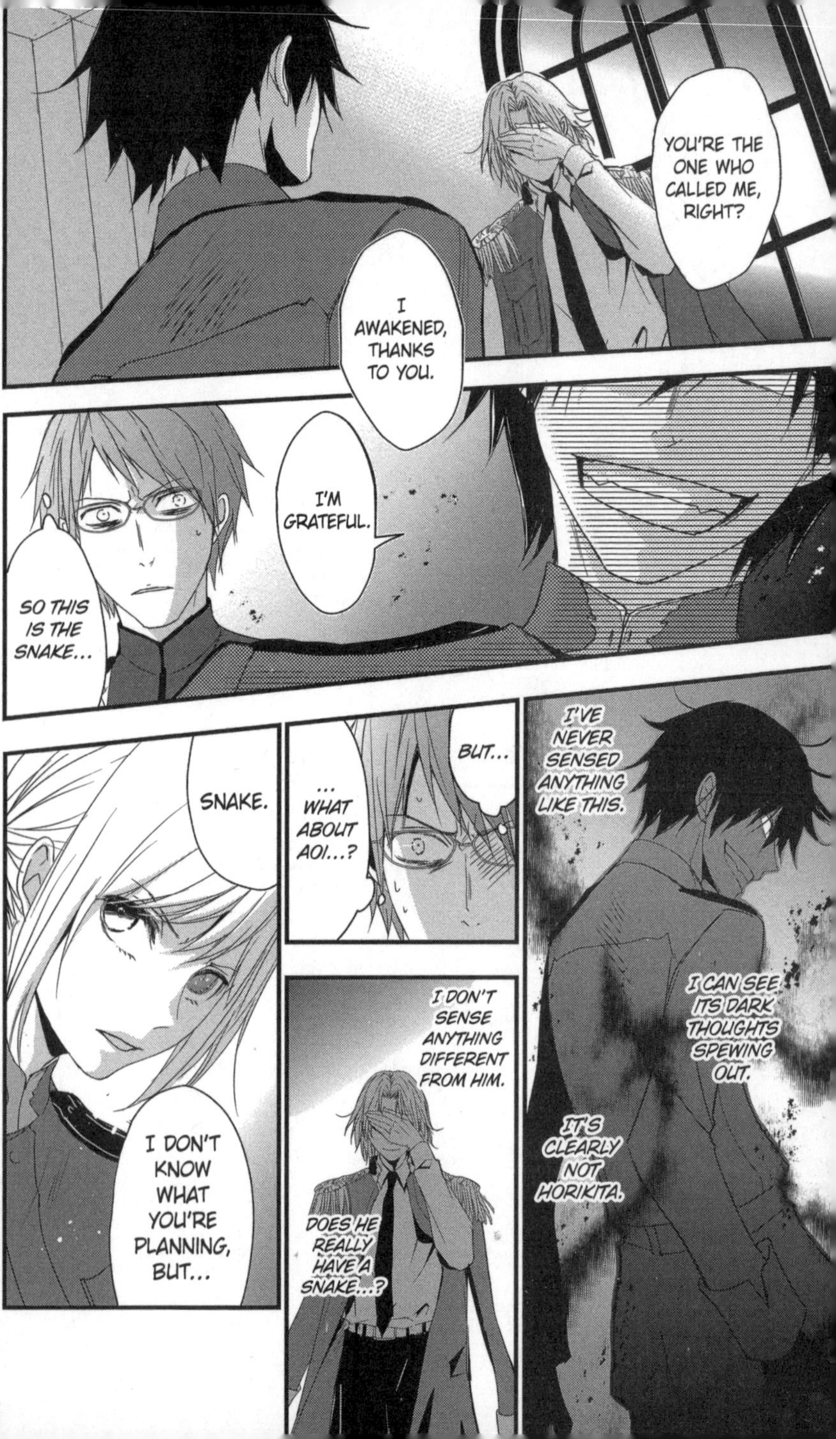

YOU'RE THE ONE WHO CALLED ME, RIGHT?
I AWAKENED, THANKS TO YOU.
I'M GRATEFUL.
SO THIS IS THE SNAKE...
I'VE NEVER SENSED ANYTHING LIKE THIS.
I CAN SEE ITS DARK THOUGHTS SPEWING OUT.
IT'S CLEARLY NOT HORIKITA.
BUT...
...WHAT ABOUT AOI...?
I DON'T SENSE ANYTHING DIFFERENT FROM HIM.
DOES HE REALLY HAVE A SNAKE...?
SNAKE.
I DON'T KNOW WHAT YOU'RE PLANNING, BUT...

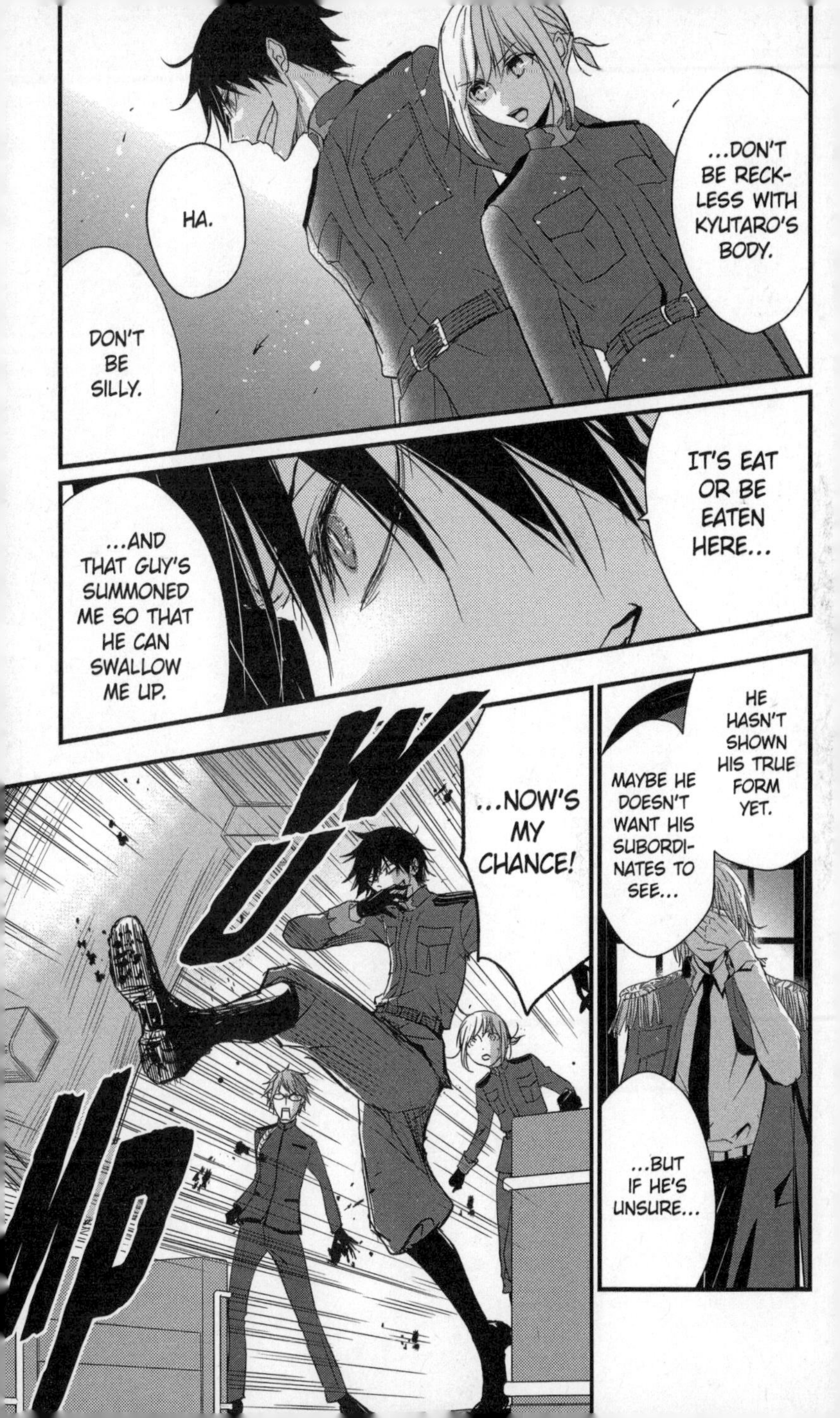
...DON'T BE RECK-LESS WITH KYUTARO'S BODY.
HA.
DON'T BE SILLY.
IT'S EAT OR BE EATEN HERE...
...AND THAT GUY'S SUMMONED ME SO THAT HE CAN SWALLOW ME UP.
HE HASN'T SHOWN HIS TRUE FORM YET.
MAYBE HE DOESN'T WANT HIS SUBORDI-NATES TO SEE...
...BUT IF HE'S UNSURE...
...NOW'S MY CHANCE!

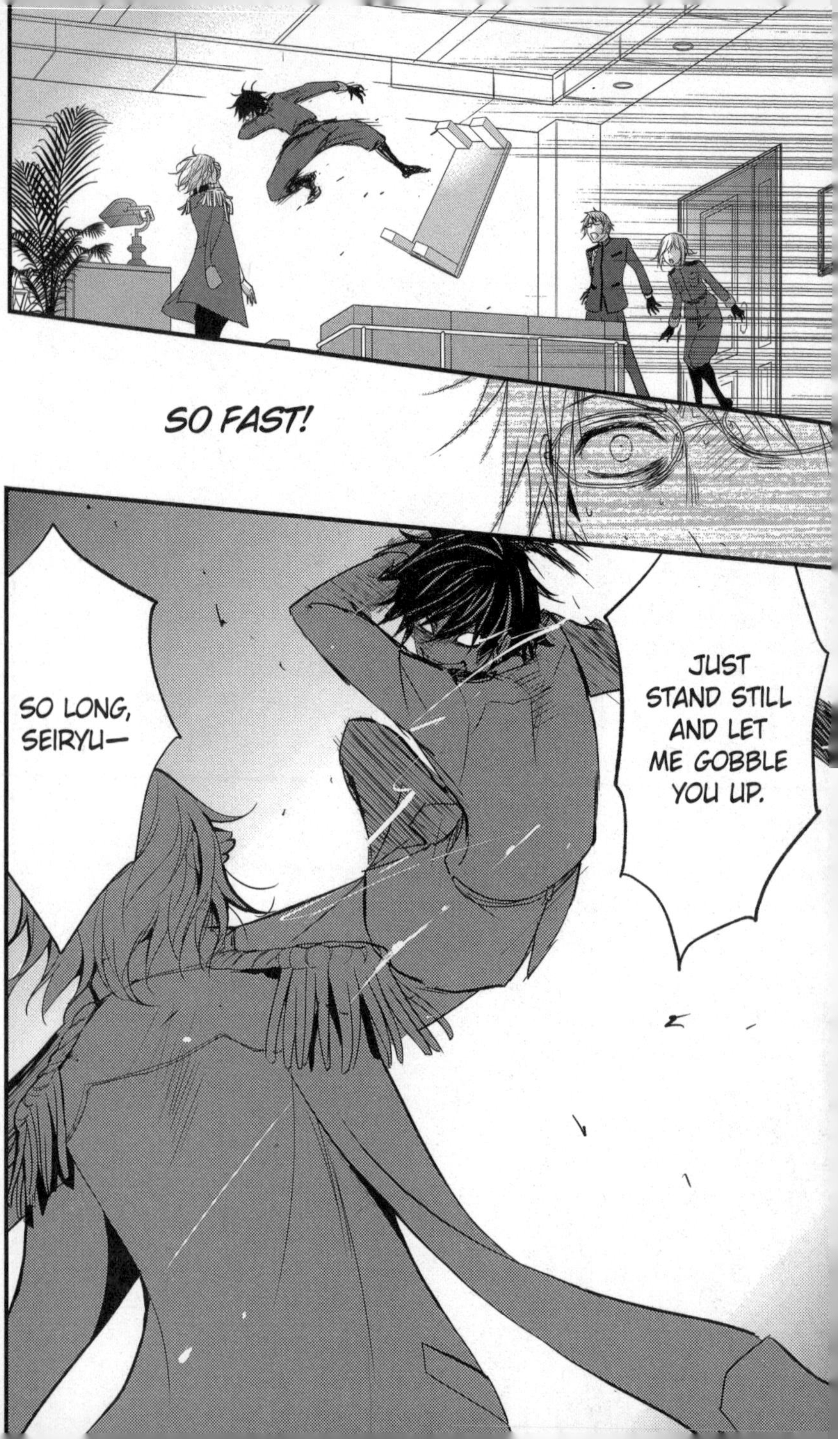
SO FAST!
JUST STAND STILL AND LET ME GOBBLE YOU UP.
SO LONG, SEIRYU—

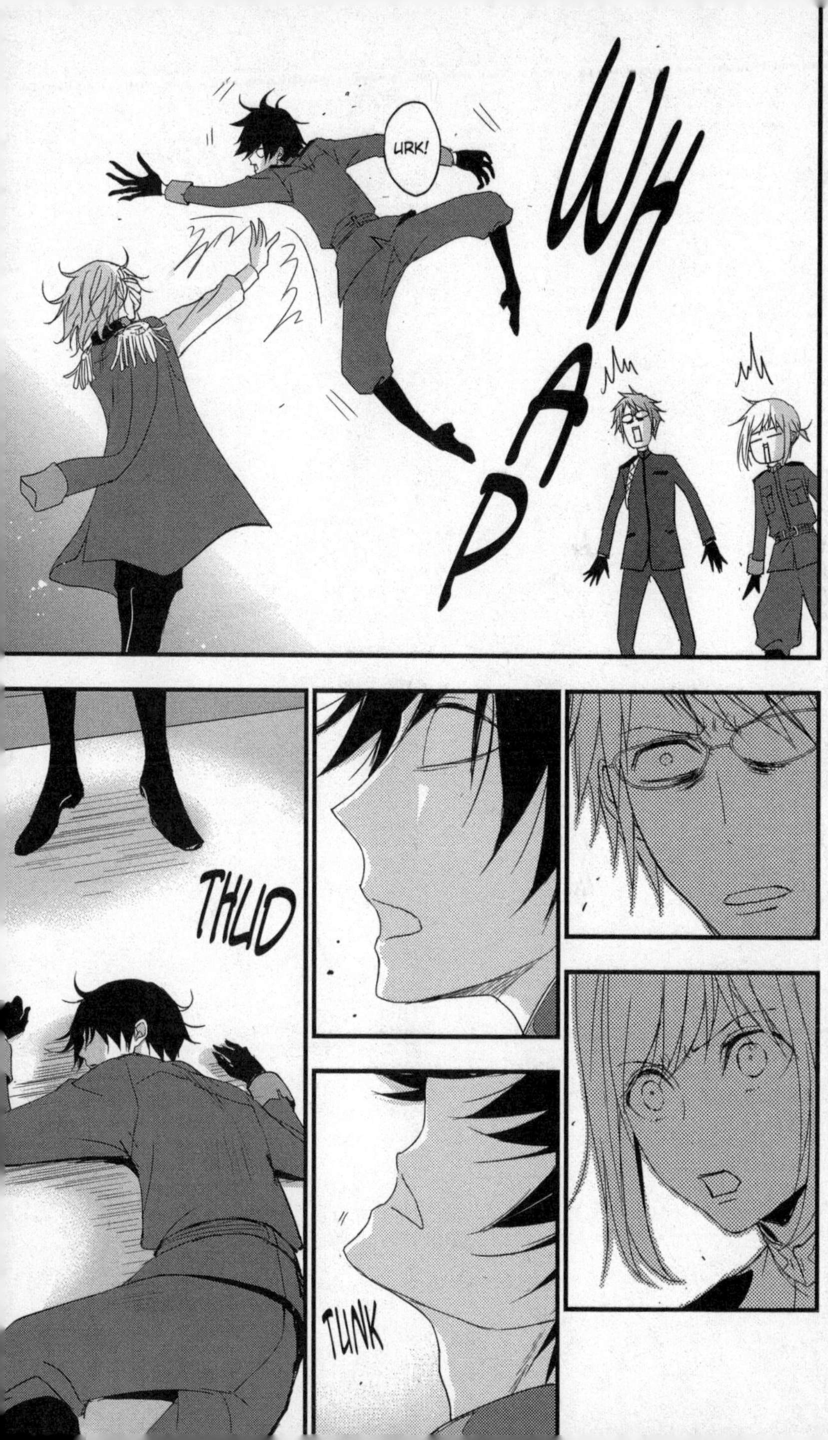
WHAP
URK!
THUD
TUNK

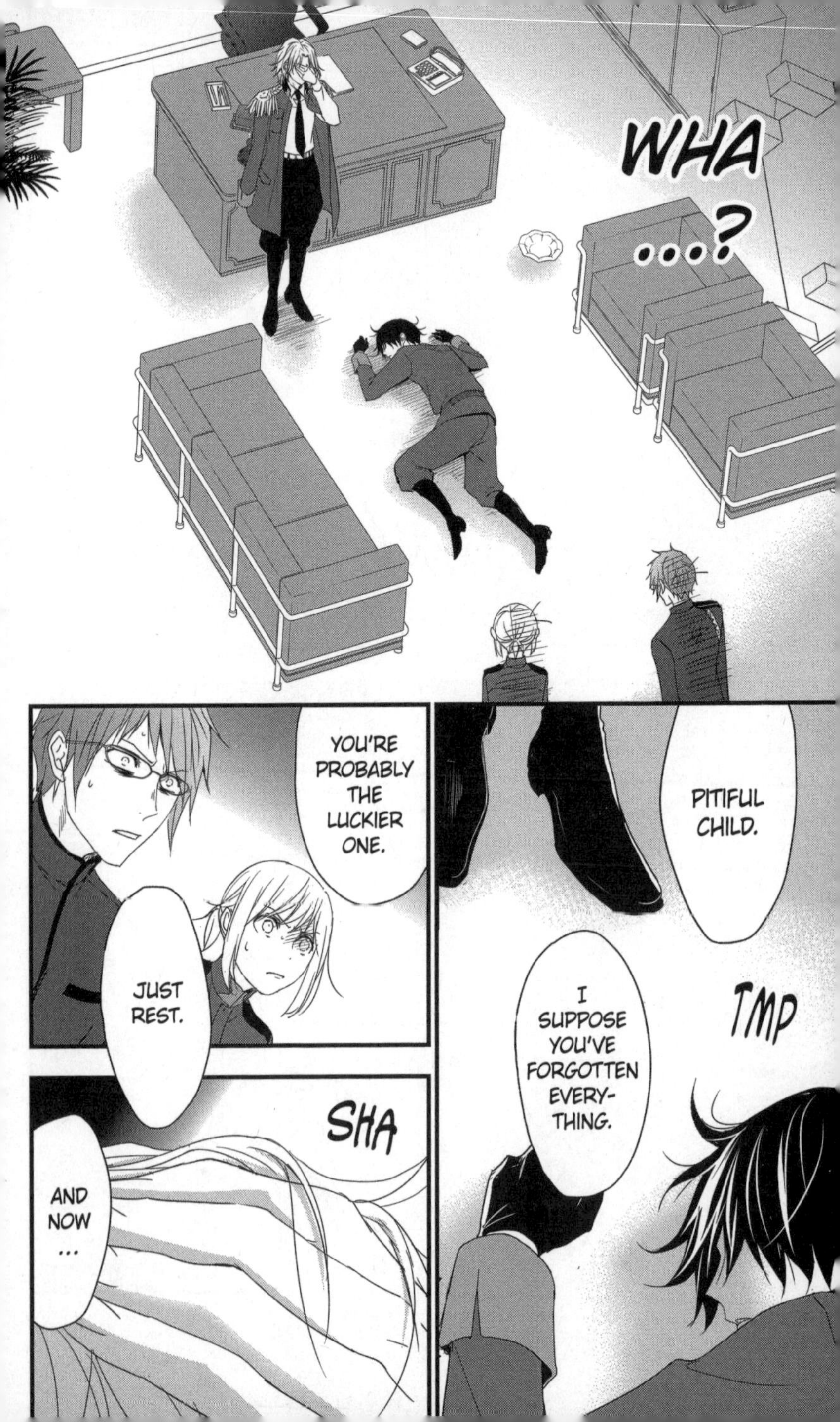
WHA ...?
PITIFUL CHILD.
I SUPPOSE YOU'VE FORGOTTEN EVERY-THING.
TMP
YOU'RE PROBABLY THE LUCKIER ONE.
JUST REST.
SHA
AND NOW ...

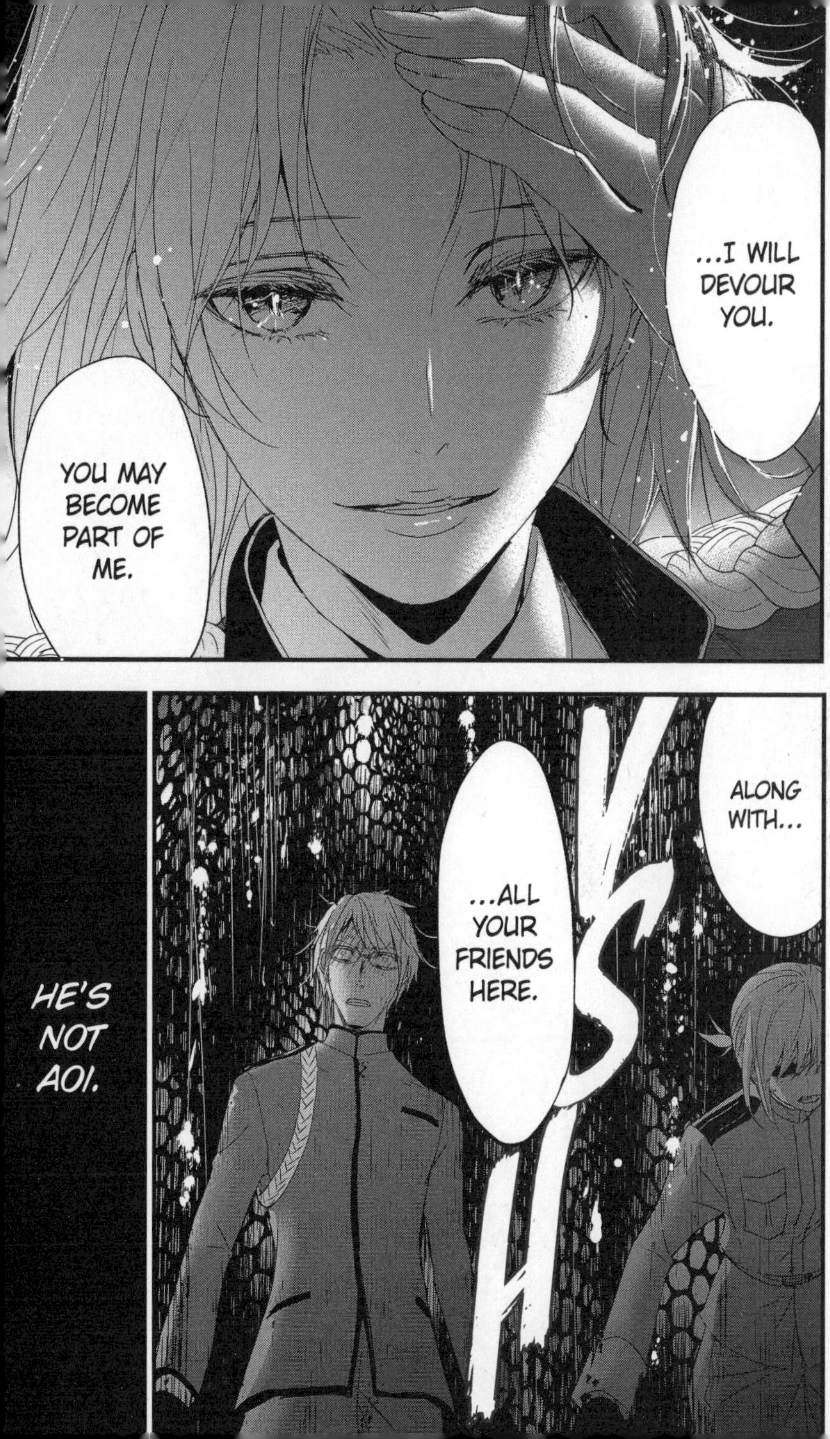
...I WILL DEVOUR YOU.
YOU MAY BECOME PART OF ME.
ALONG WITH...
...ALL YOUR FRIENDS HERE.
HE'S NOT AOI.

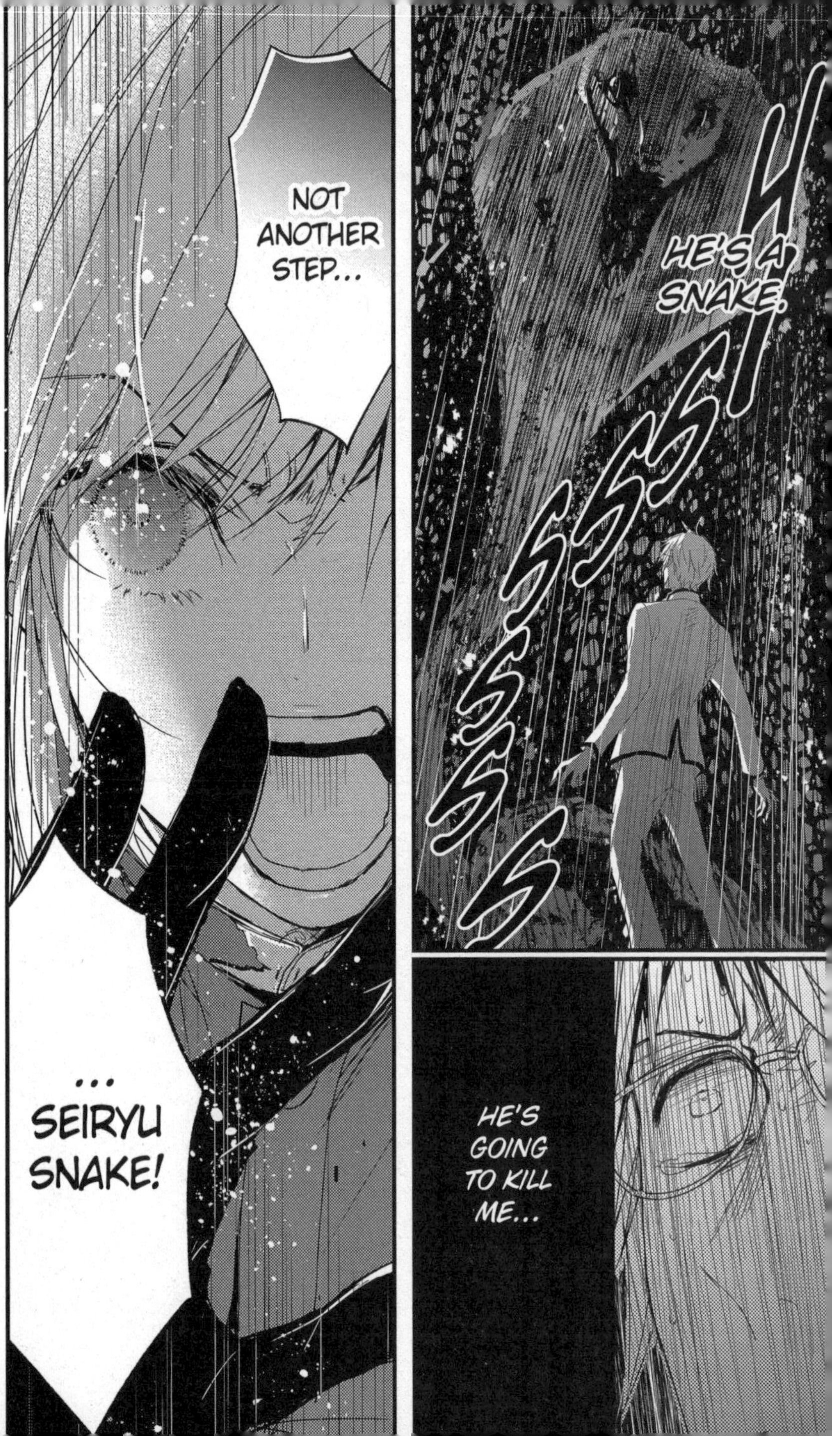
HE'S A SNAKE.
SSSSSSSH
HE'S GOING TO KILL ME...
NOT ANOTHER STEP...
...SEIRYU SNAKE!

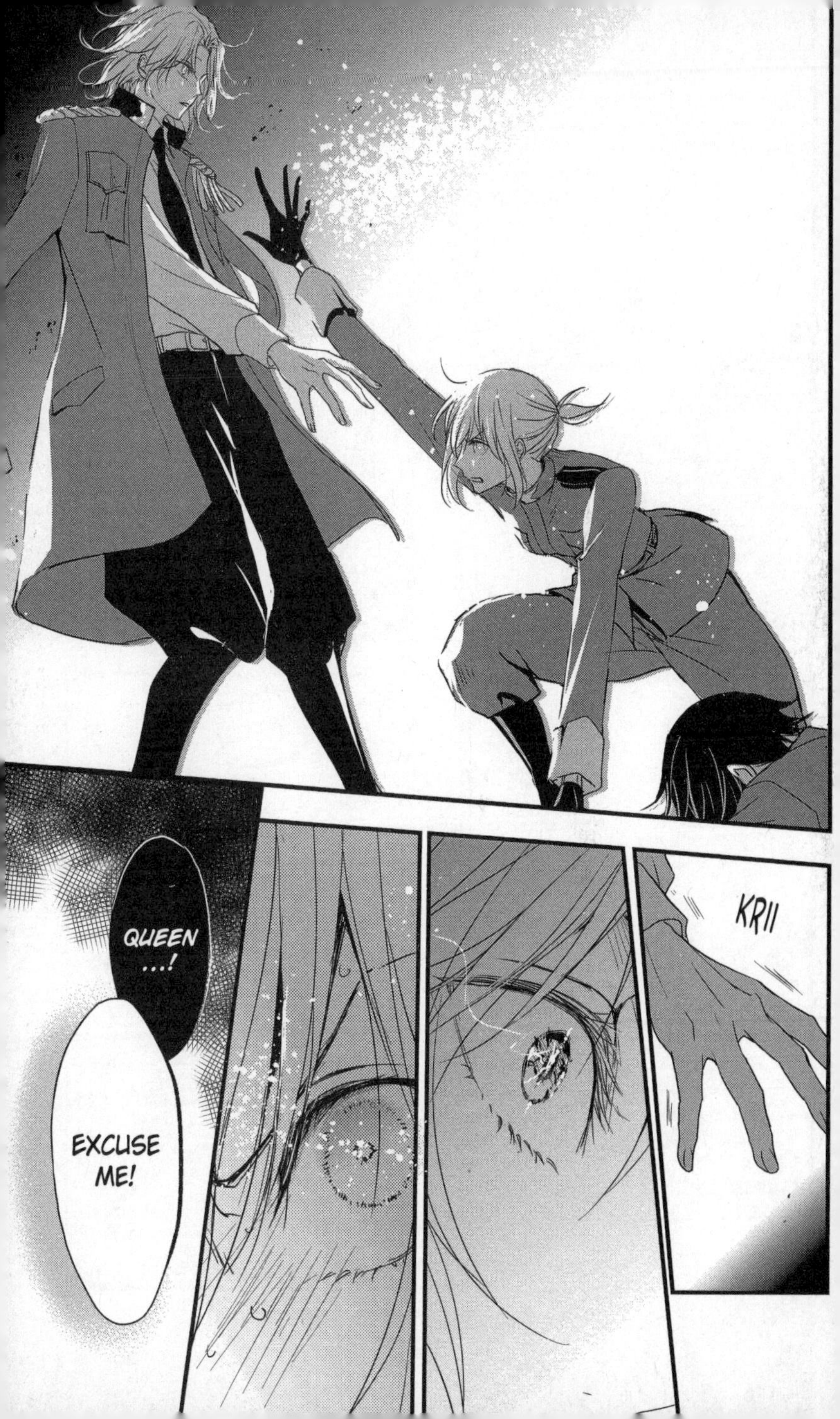
KRII
QUEEN ...!
EXCUSE ME!

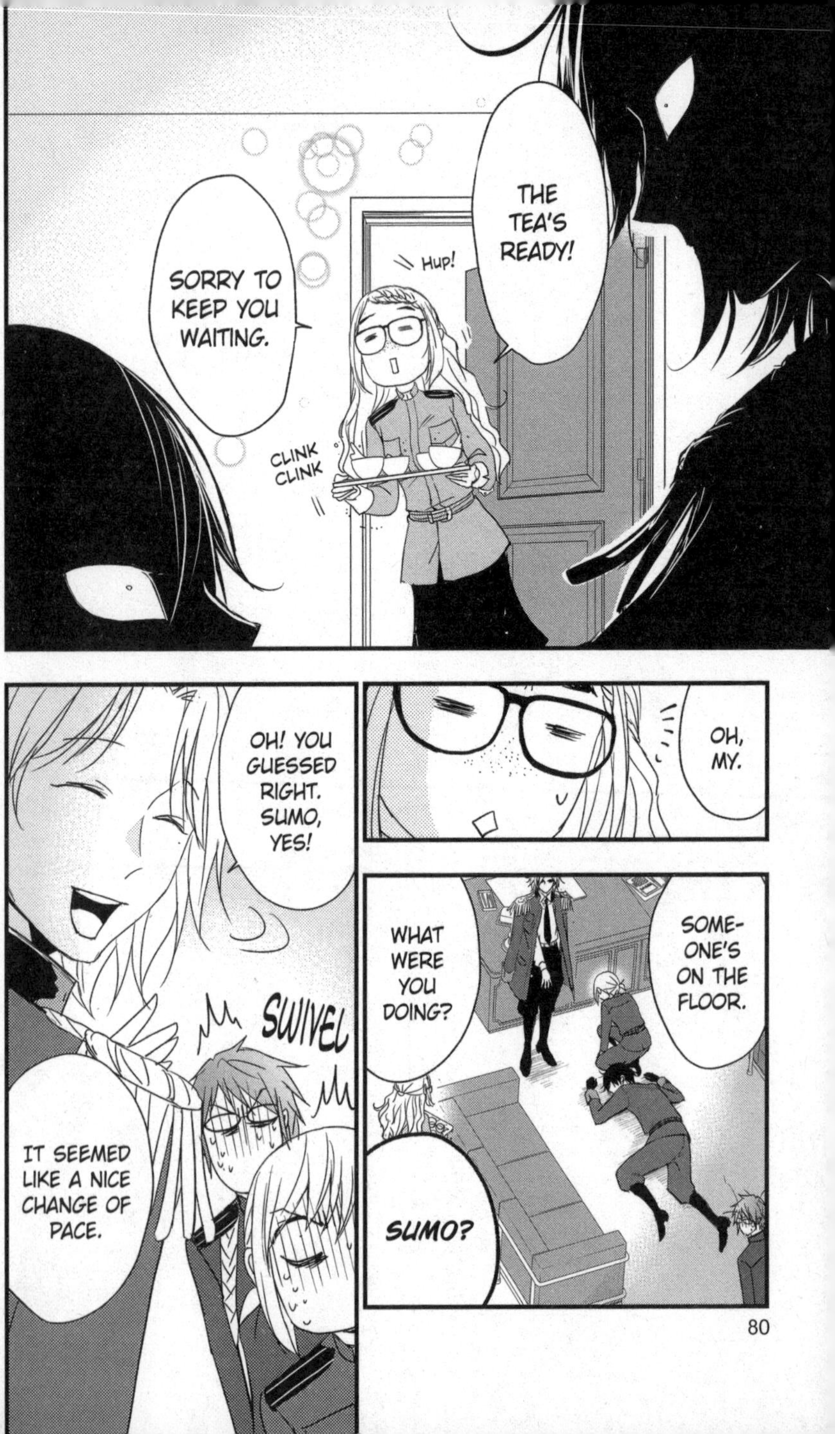
THE TEA'S READY!
Hup!
SORRY TO KEEP YOU WAITING.
CLINK CLINK
OH, MY.
SOME-ONE'S ON THE FLOOR.
WHAT WERE YOU DOING?
SUMO?
OH! YOU GUESSED RIGHT. SUMO, YES!
SWIVEL
IT SEEMED LIKE A NICE CHANGE OF PACE.

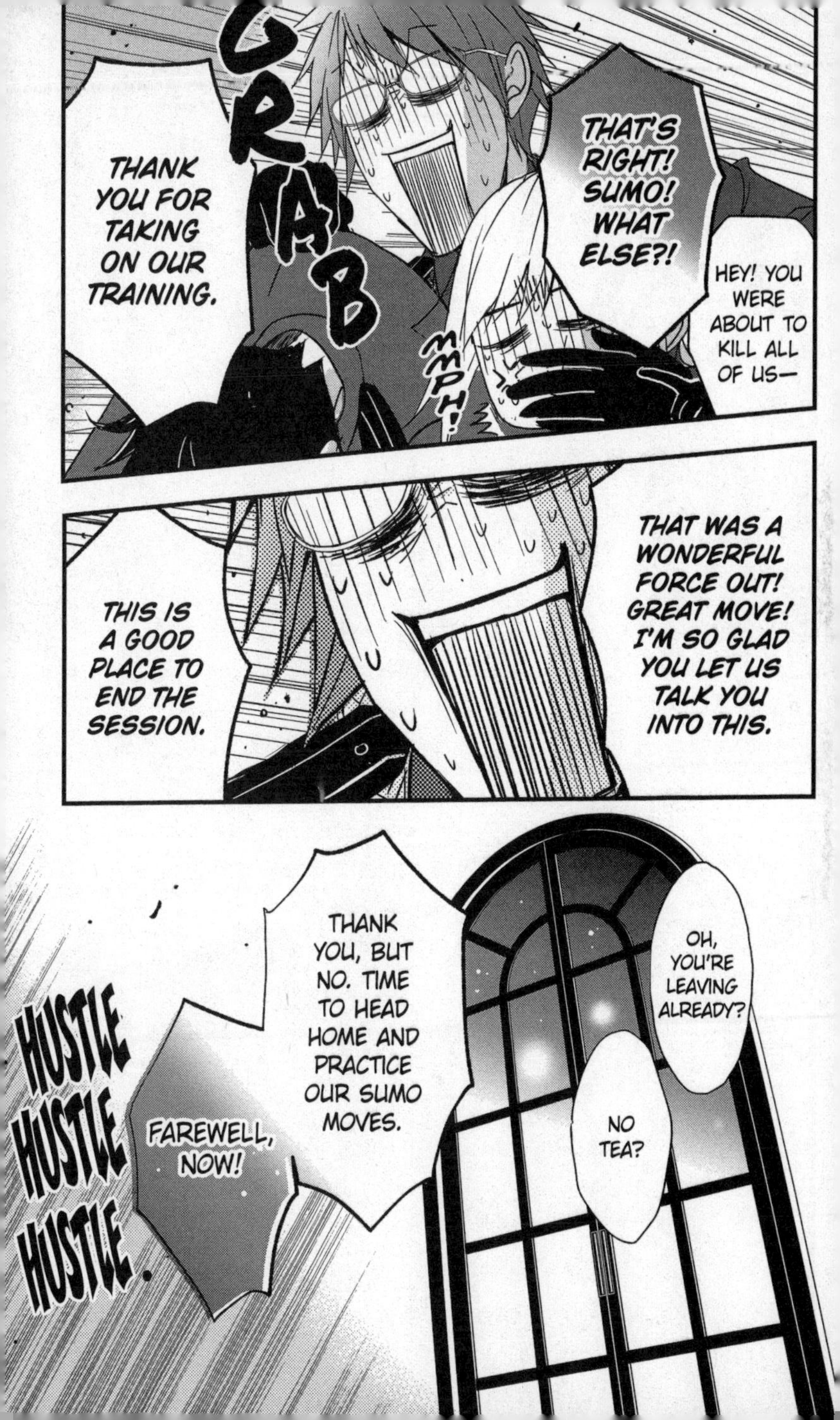
THAT'S RIGHT! SUMO! WHAT ELSE?!
HEY! YOU WERE ABOUT TO KILL ALL OF US—
GRAB
MMPH!
THANK YOU FOR TAKING ON OUR TRAINING.
THAT WAS A WONDERFUL FORCE OUT! GREAT MOVE! I'M SO GLAD YOU LET US TALK YOU INTO THIS.
THIS IS A GOOD PLACE TO END THE SESSION.
OH, YOU'RE LEAVING ALREADY?
NO TEA?
THANK YOU, BUT NO. TIME TO HEAD HOME AND PRACTICE OUR SUMO MOVES.
FAREWELL, NOW!
HUSTLE HUSTLE HUSTLE

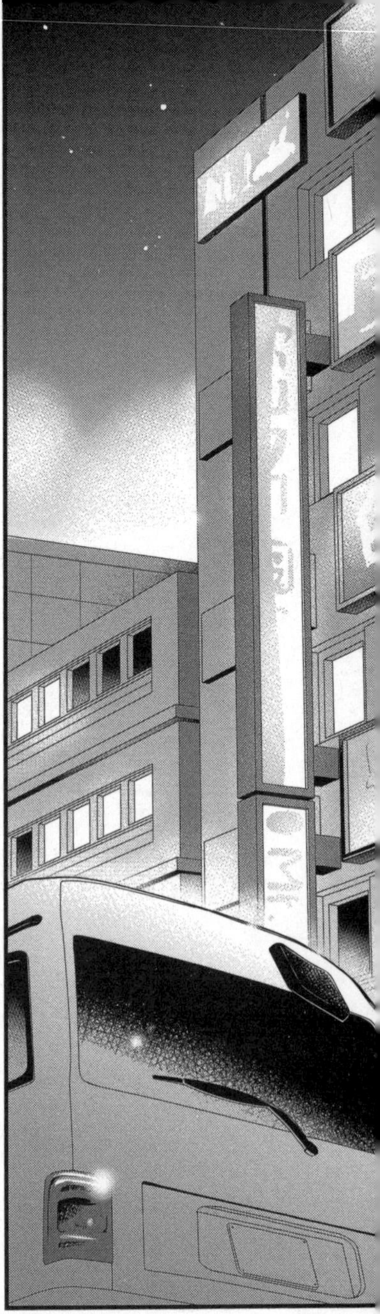

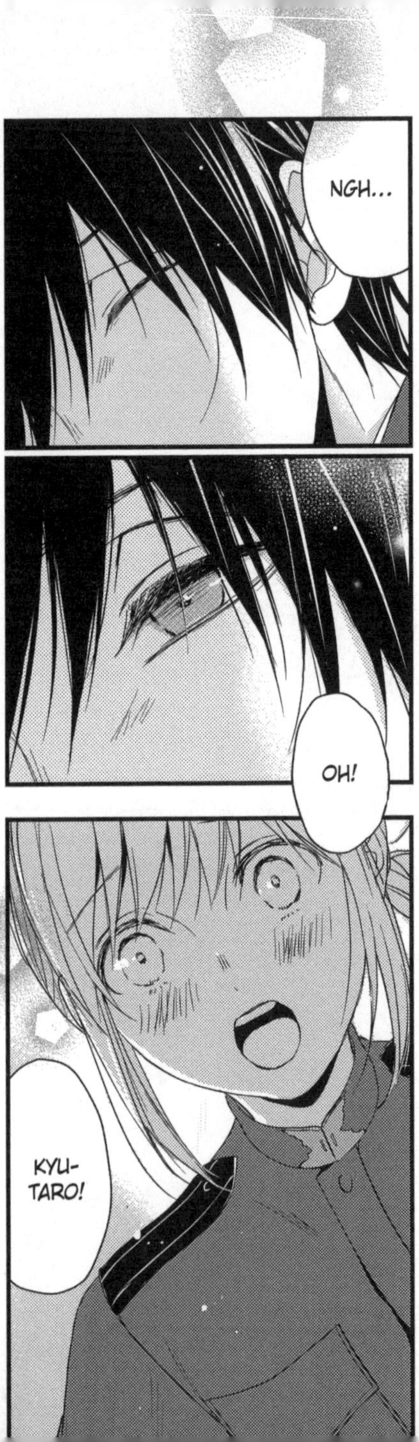
NGH...
OH!
KYU-TARO!

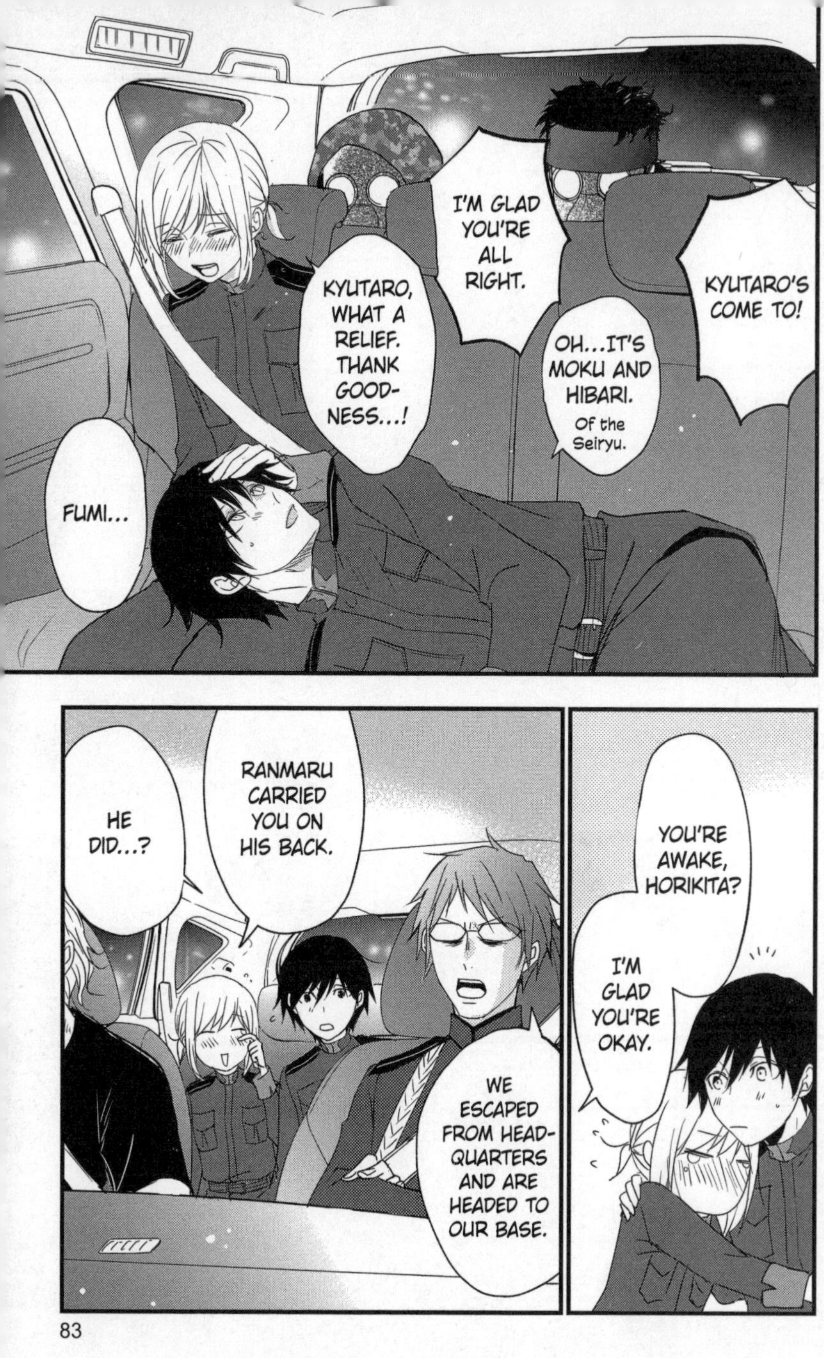
KYUTARO'S COME TO!
I'M GLAD YOU'RE ALL RIGHT.
OH...IT'S MOKU AND HIBARI.
Of the Seiryu.
KYUTARO, WHAT A RELIEF. THANK GOOD-NESS...!
FUMI...
YOU'RE AWAKE, HORIKITA?
I'M GLAD YOU'RE OKAY.
WE ESCAPED FROM HEAD-QUARTERS AND ARE HEADED TO OUR BASE.
RANMARU CARRIED YOU ON HIS BACK.
HE DID...?

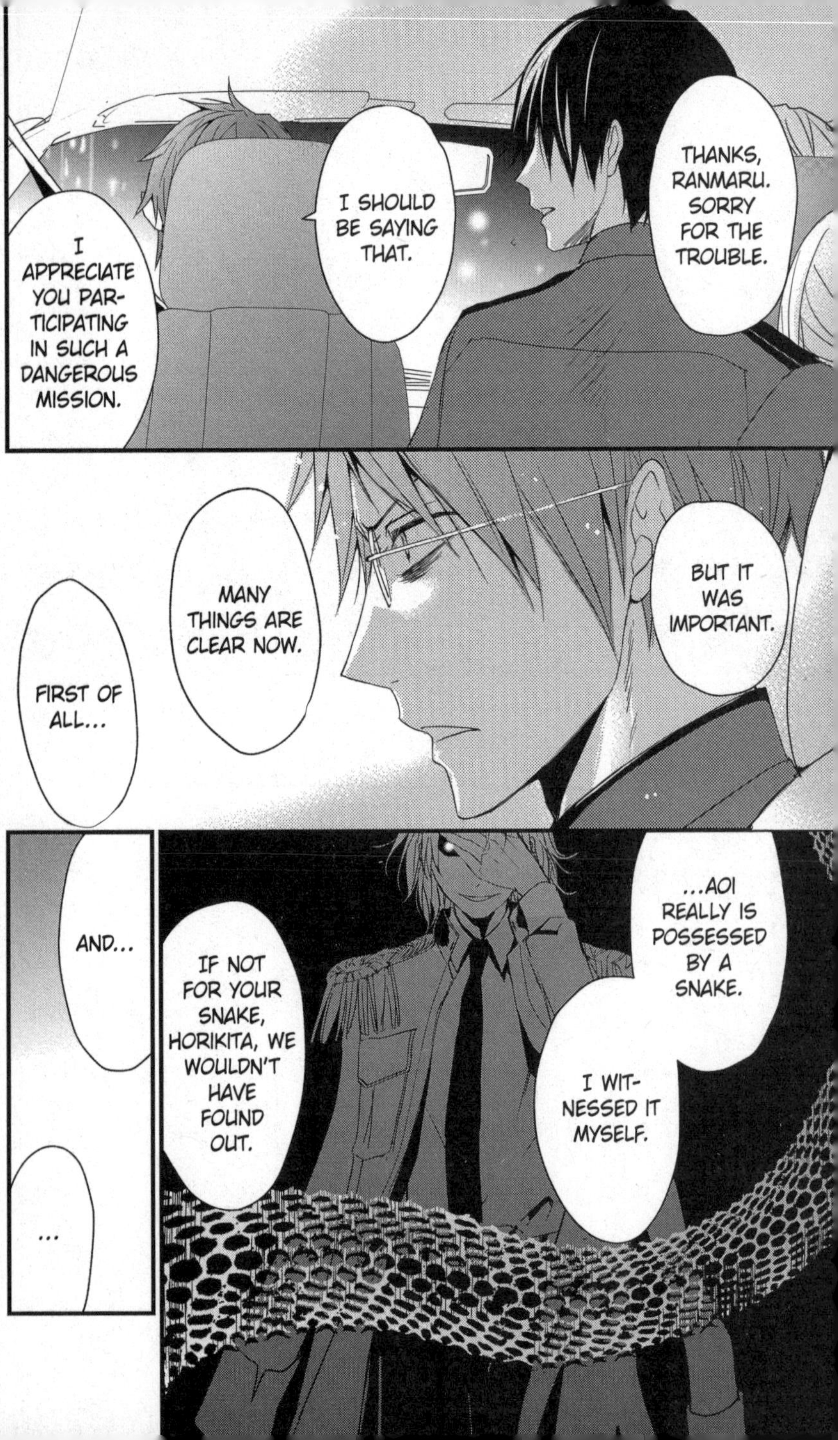
THANKS, RANMARU. SORRY FOR THE TROUBLE.
I SHOULD BE SAYING THAT.
I APPRECIATE YOU PAR-TICIPATING IN SUCH A DANGEROUS MISSION.
BUT IT WAS IMPORTANT.
MANY THINGS ARE CLEAR NOW.
FIRST OF ALL...
...AOI REALLY IS POSSESSED BY A SNAKE.
I WIT-NESSED IT MYSELF.
IF NOT FOR YOUR SNAKE, HORIKITA, WE WOULDN'T HAVE FOUND OUT.
AND...
...

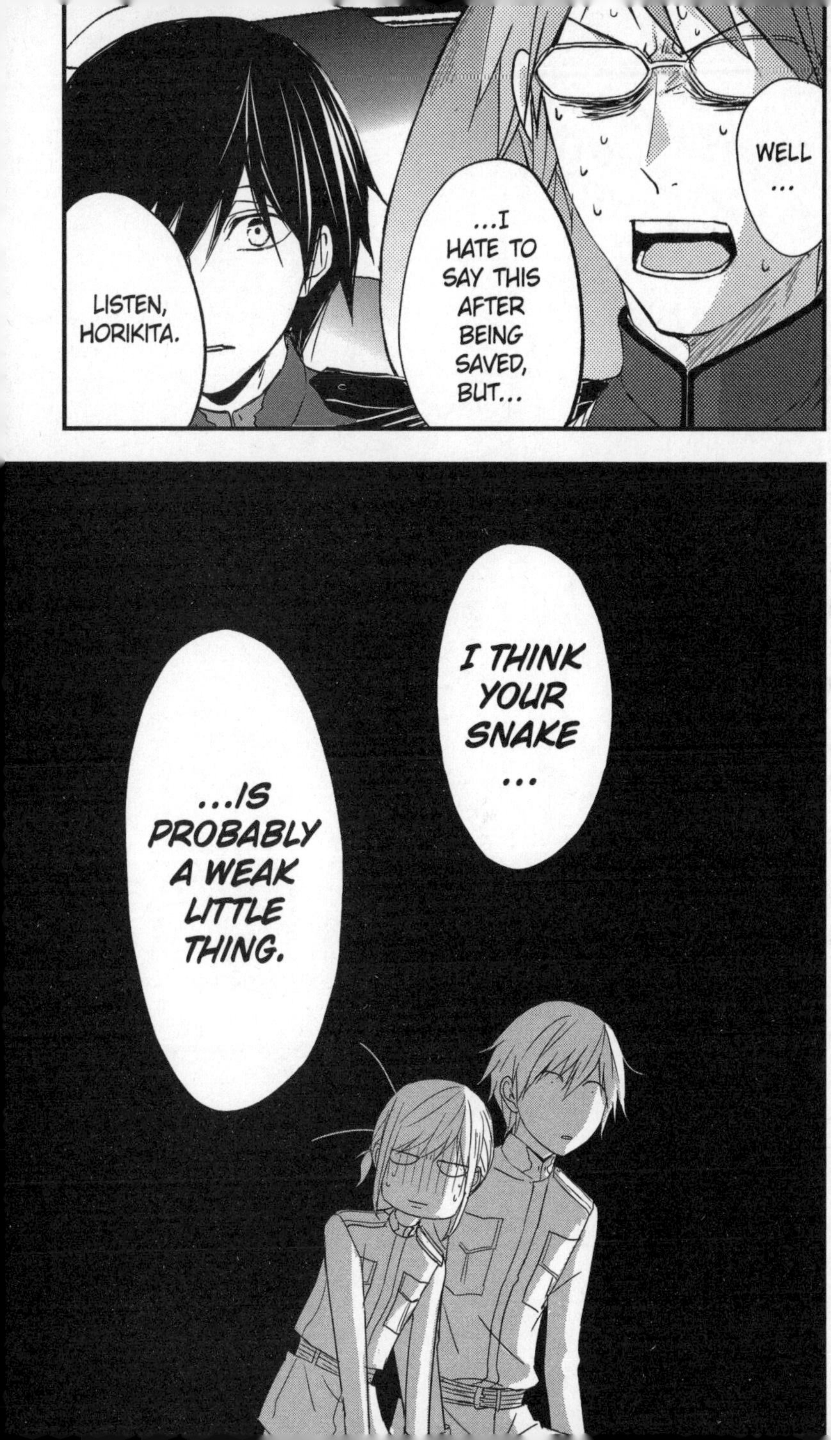
WELL ...
...I HATE TO SAY THIS AFTER BEING SAVED, BUT...
LISTEN, HORIKITA.
I THINK YOUR SNAKE ...
...IS PROBABLY A WEAK LITTLE THING.

CHAPTER 51

MONTHLY BETSUCOMI SALE DATE NOTICE ON TWITTER

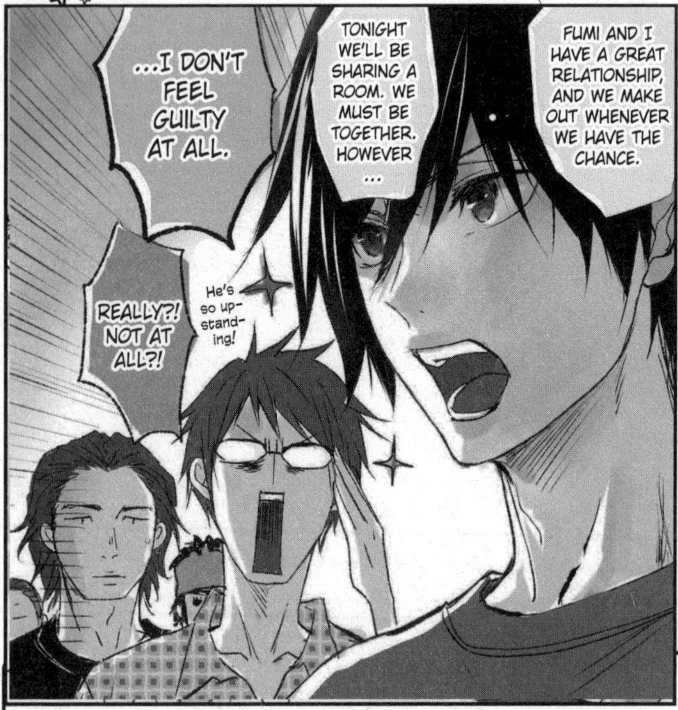
FUMI AND I HAVE A GREAT RELATIONSHIP, AND WE MAKE OUT WHENEVER WE HAVE THE CHANCE.
TONIGHT WE'LL BE SHARING A ROOM. WE MUST BE TOGETHER. HOWEVER ...
...I DON'T FEEL GUILTY AT ALL.
He's so up-standing!
REALLY?! NOT AT ALL?!

LET'S SEE... WHAT'S UP IN *QUEEN'S QUALITY* THIS MONTH?

(1) AN APRON THAT'S NO LAUGHING MATTER.
(2) RANMARU IS PROBABLY THE ONLY ONE WHO BELIEVES KYUTARO'S PROFESSED INTENTION.
(3) MY EDITOR PRAISED THAT BUTT.
IN THIS VOLUME, SOMETHING THAT MY READERS MAY HAVE BEEN AWARE OF FROM AROUND VOLUME 3 BECOMES OBVIOUS IN CHAPTER 51!

RANMARU IS GOOD AT COOKING, IS SERIOUS-MINDED AND A VIRGIN. I THINK HE AND KYUTARO COULD BECOME GOOD FRIENDS. BOTH VIRGINS.

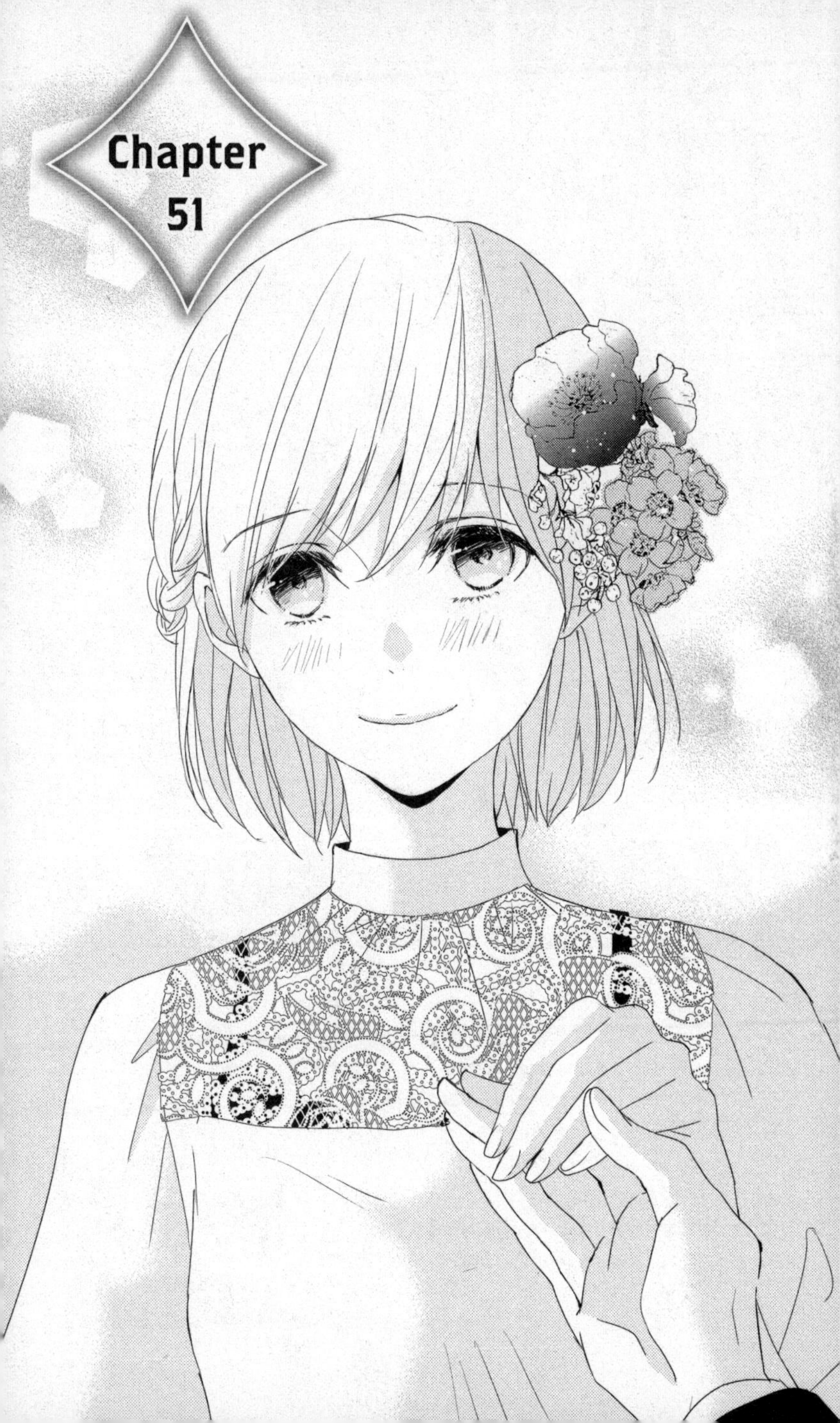
Chapter
51

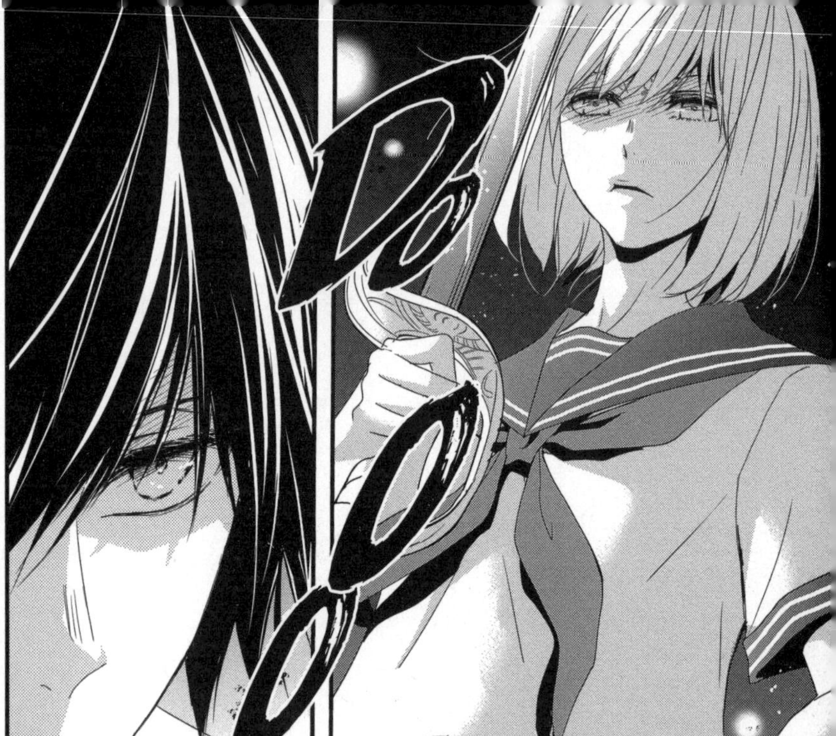

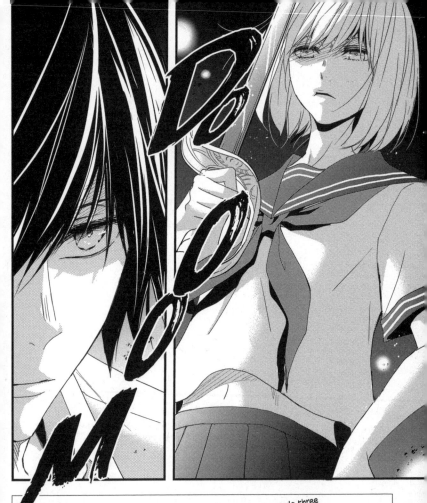

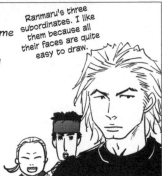

Oh, whoops… Back in chapter 46 (volume 10), Sumi had a goatee. I guess he just happened to shave it between now and then. Yeah, that's what happened.

Just so you know, Sumi's full name is Sumire, Moku is Mokuren and Hibari is Hibari. Those are all words that evoke spring in Japanese poetry.

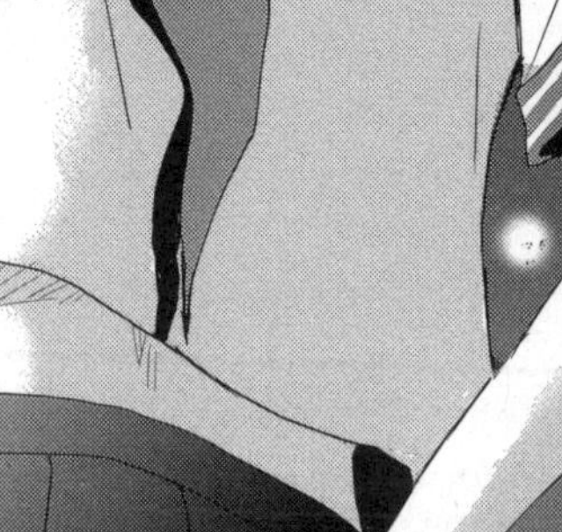
Ranmaru's three subordinates. I like them because all their faces are quite easy to draw.

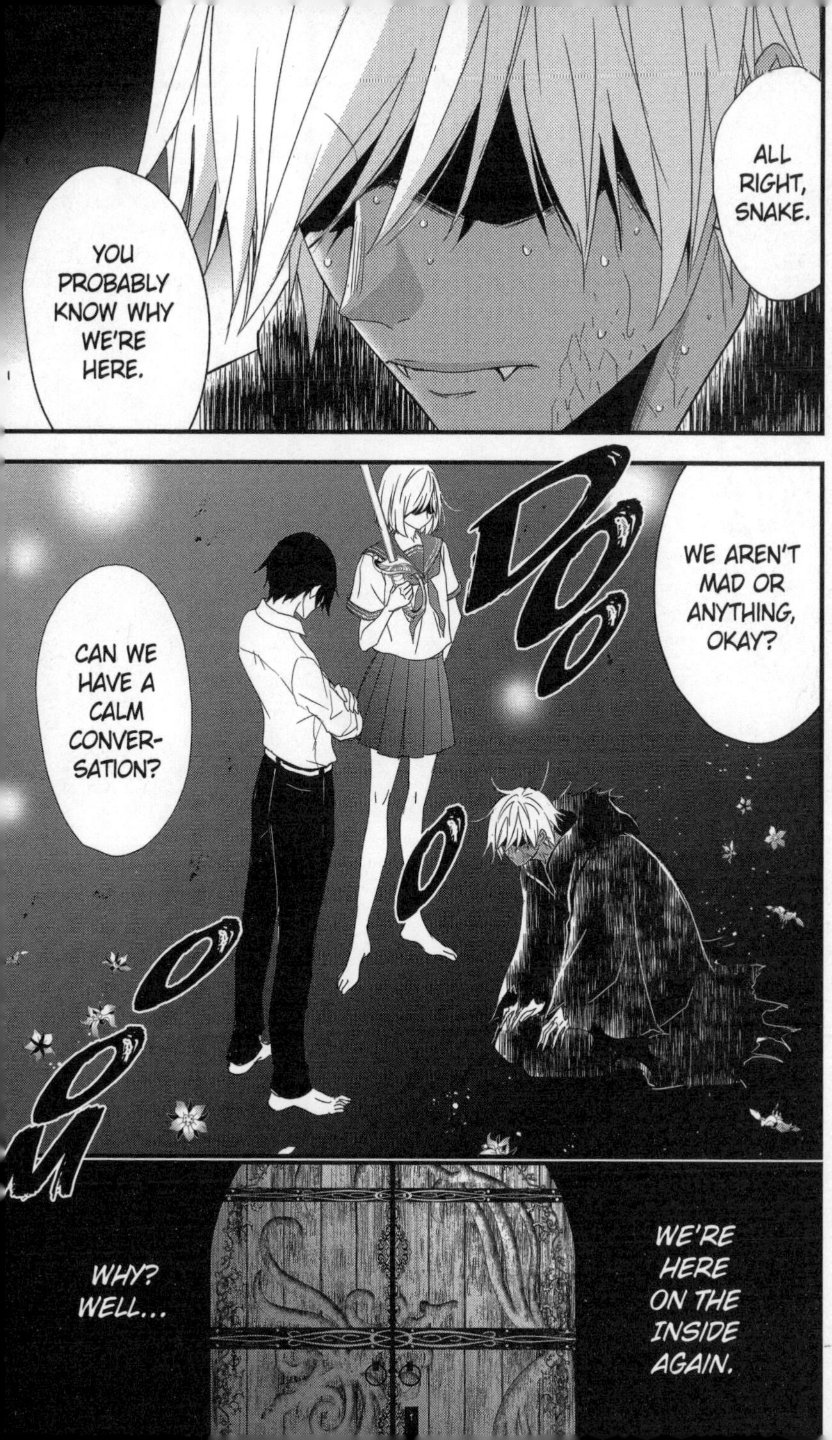
ALL RIGHT, SNAKE.
YOU PROBABLY KNOW WHY WE'RE HERE.
WE AREN'T MAD OR ANYTHING, OKAY?
CAN WE HAVE A CALM CONVERSATION?
WE'RE HERE ON THE INSIDE AGAIN.
WHY? WELL...

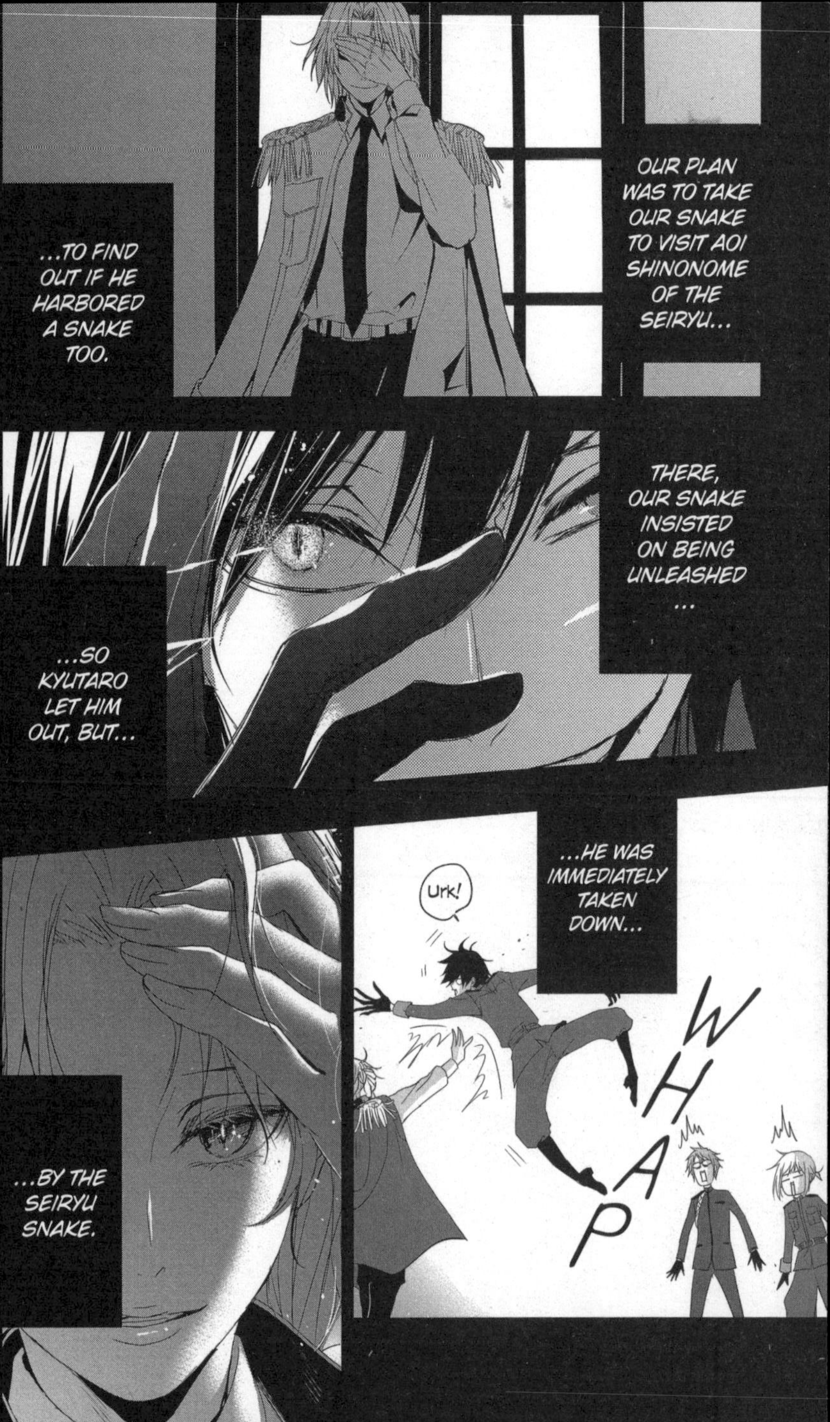

OUR PLAN WAS TO TAKE OUR SNAKE TO VISIT AOI SHINONOME OF THE SEIRYU...
...TO FIND OUT IF HE HARBORED A SNAKE TOO.
THERE, OUR SNAKE INSISTED ON BEING UNLEASHED...
...SO KYUTARO LET HIM OUT, BUT...
...HE WAS IMMEDIATELY TAKEN DOWN...
Urk!
WHAP
...BY THE SEIRYU SNAKE.

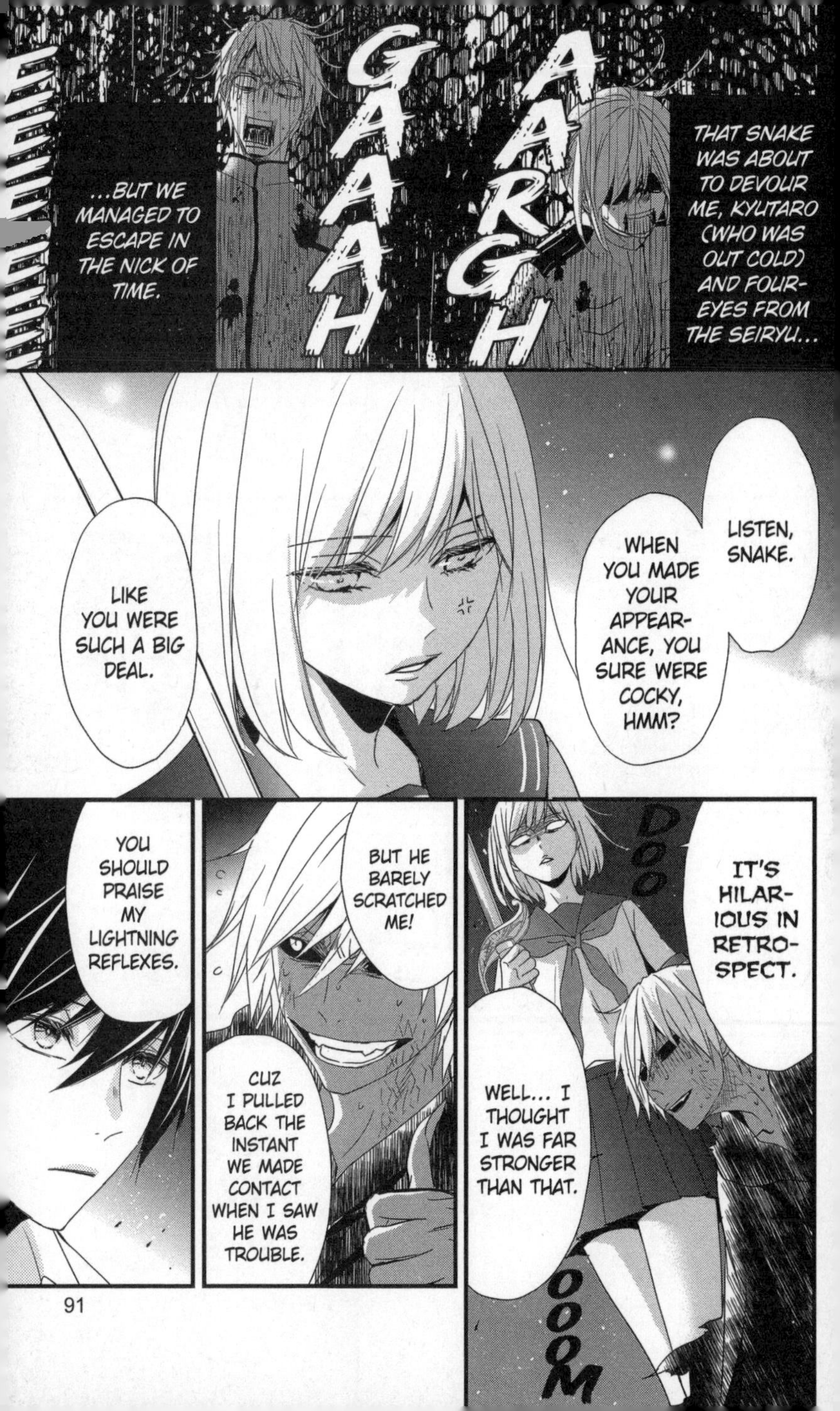
THAT SNAKE WAS ABOUT TO DEVOUR ME, KYUTARO (WHO WAS OUT COLD) AND FOUR-EYES FROM THE SEIRYU...
AARGH
GAAAH
...BUT WE MANAGED TO ESCAPE IN THE NICK OF TIME.
LISTEN, SNAKE.
WHEN YOU MADE YOUR APPEAR-ANCE, YOU SURE WERE COCKY, HMM?
LIKE YOU WERE SUCH A BIG DEAL.
IT'S HILAR-IOUS IN RETRO-SPECT.
DOOOOOOOM
WELL... I THOUGHT I WAS FAR STRONGER THAN THAT.
BUT HE BARELY SCRATCHED ME!
CUZ I PULLED BACK THE INSTANT WE MADE CONTACT WHEN I SAW HE WAS TROUBLE.
YOU SHOULD PRAISE MY LIGHTNING REFLEXES.

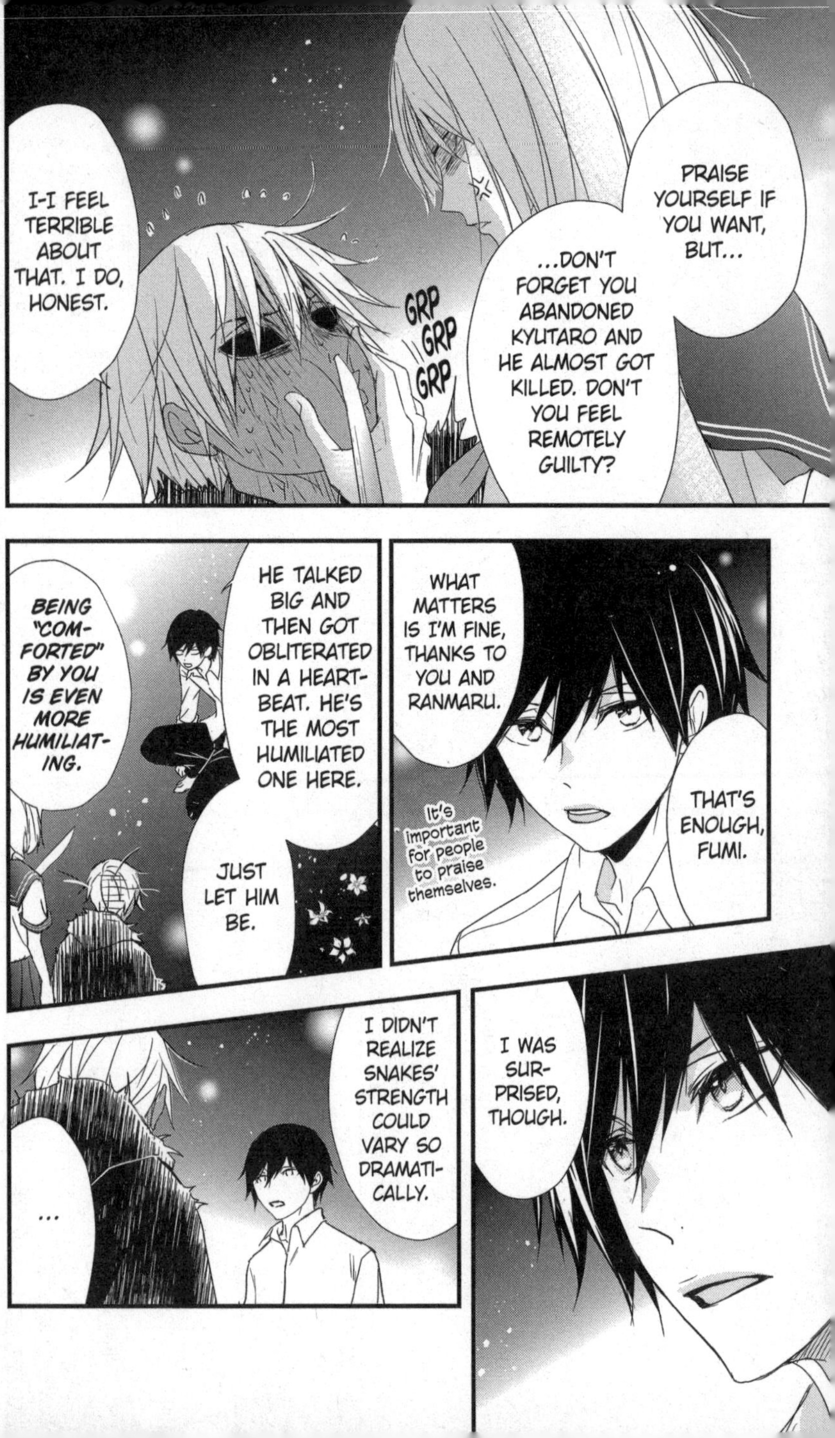
PRAISE YOURSELF IF YOU WANT, BUT...
...DON'T FORGET YOU ABANDONED KYUTARO AND HE ALMOST GOT KILLED. DON'T YOU FEEL REMOTELY GUILTY?
GRP GRP GRP
I-I FEEL TERRIBLE ABOUT THAT. I DO, HONEST.
THAT'S ENOUGH, FUMI.
WHAT MATTERS IS I'M FINE, THANKS TO YOU AND RANMARU.
It's important for people to praise themselves.
JUST LET HIM BE.
HE TALKED BIG AND THEN GOT OBLITERATED IN A HEART-BEAT. HE'S THE MOST HUMILIATED ONE HERE.
BEING "COM-FORTED" BY YOU IS EVEN MORE HUMILIAT-ING.
I WAS SUR-PRISED, THOUGH.
I DIDN'T REALIZE SNAKES' STRENGTH COULD VARY SO DRAMATI-CALLY.
...

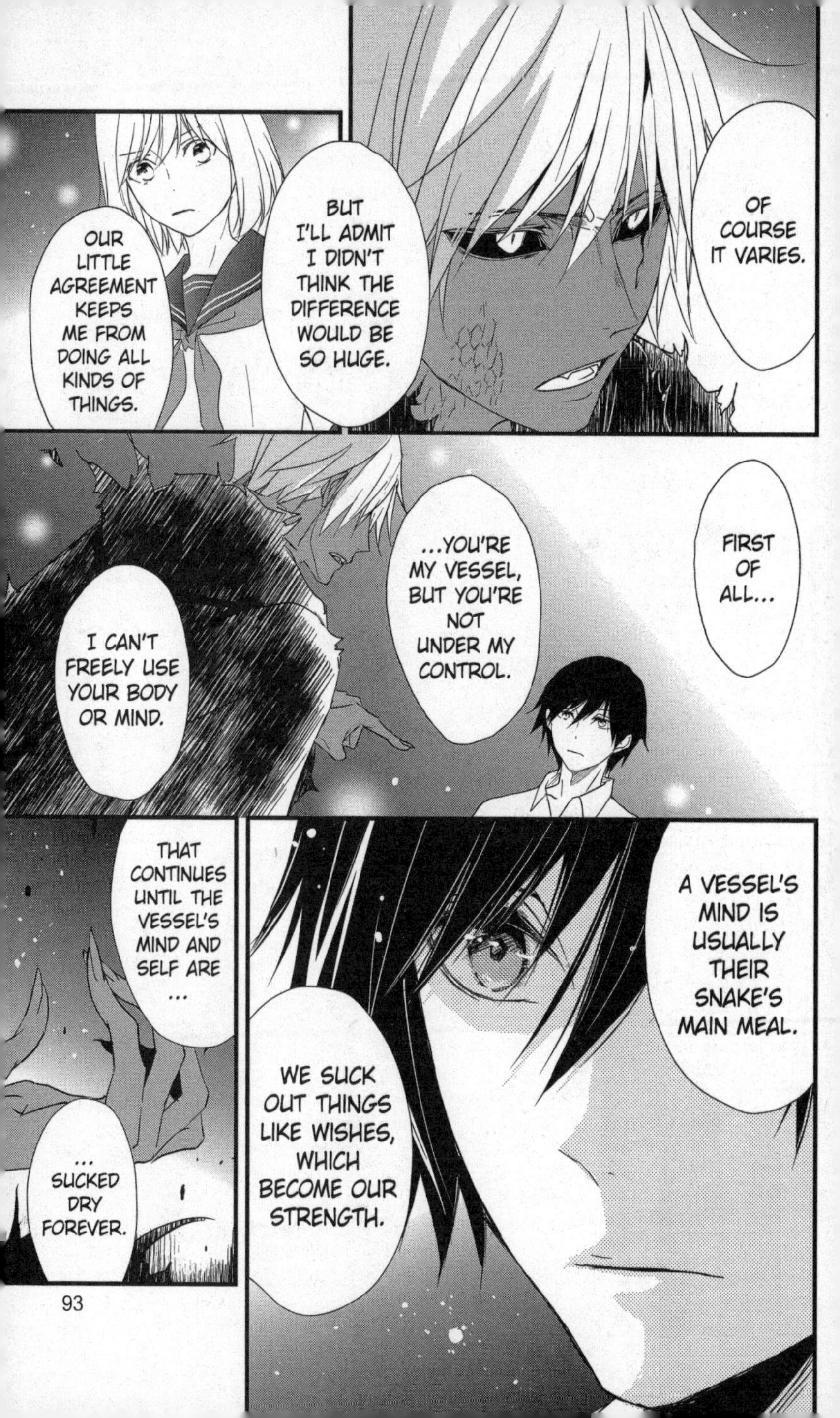
OF COURSE IT VARIES.
BUT I'LL ADMIT I DIDN'T THINK THE DIFFERENCE WOULD BE SO HUGE.
OUR LITTLE AGREEMENT KEEPS ME FROM DOING ALL KINDS OF THINGS.
FIRST OF ALL...
...YOU'RE MY VESSEL, BUT YOU'RE NOT UNDER MY CONTROL.
I CAN'T FREELY USE YOUR BODY OR MIND.
A VESSEL'S MIND IS USUALLY THEIR SNAKE'S MAIN MEAL.
WE SUCK OUT THINGS LIKE WISHES, WHICH BECOME OUR STRENGTH.
THAT CONTINUES UNTIL THE VESSEL'S MIND AND SELF ARE ...
...SUCKED DRY FOREVER.

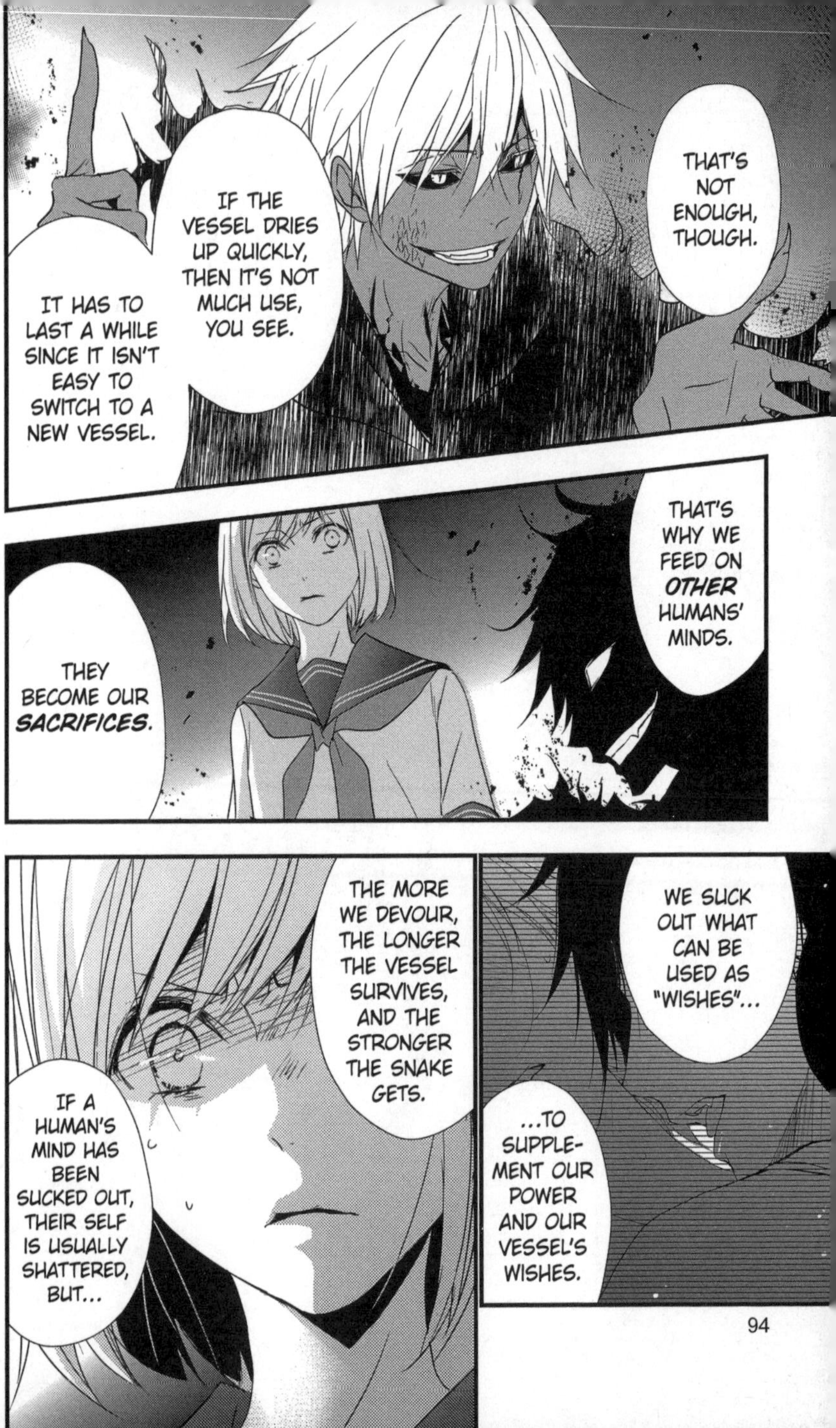
THAT'S NOT ENOUGH, THOUGH.
IF THE VESSEL DRIES UP QUICKLY, THEN IT'S NOT MUCH USE, YOU SEE.
IT HAS TO LAST A WHILE SINCE IT ISN'T EASY TO SWITCH TO A NEW VESSEL.
THAT'S WHY WE FEED ON *OTHER* HUMANS' MINDS.
THEY BECOME OUR *SACRIFICES*.
WE SUCK OUT WHAT CAN BE USED AS "WISHES"...
...TO SUPPLE-MENT OUR POWER AND OUR VESSEL'S WISHES.
THE MORE WE DEVOUR, THE LONGER THE VESSEL SURVIVES, AND THE STRONGER THE SNAKE GETS.
IF A HUMAN'S MIND HAS BEEN SUCKED OUT, THEIR SELF IS USUALLY SHATTERED, BUT...

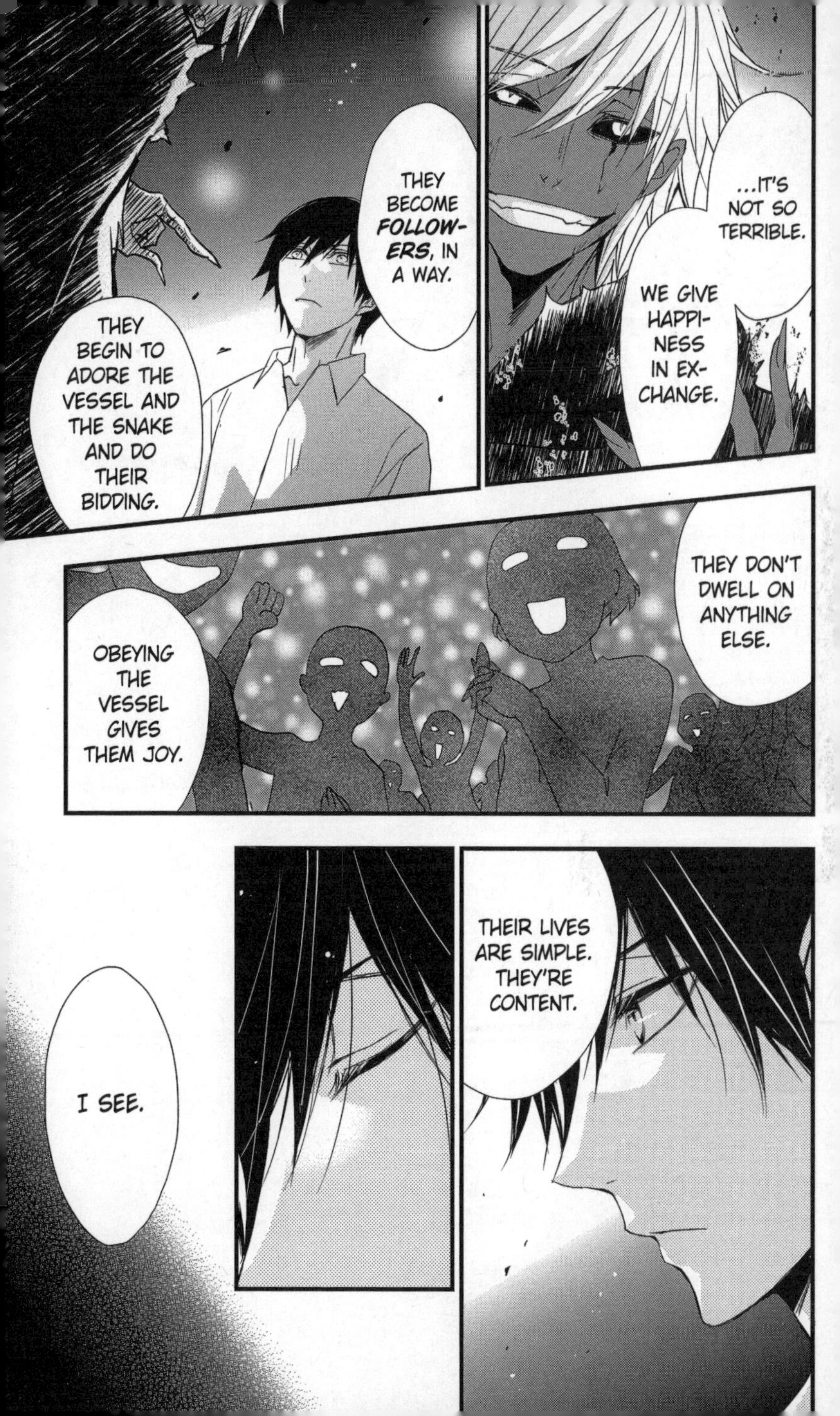
...IT'S NOT SO TERRIBLE.
WE GIVE HAPPINESS IN EXCHANGE.
THEY BECOME *FOLLOWERS*, IN A WAY.
THEY BEGIN TO ADORE THE VESSEL AND THE SNAKE AND DO THEIR BIDDING.
THEY DON'T DWELL ON ANYTHING ELSE.
OBEYING THE VESSEL GIVES THEM JOY.
THEIR LIVES ARE SIMPLE. THEY'RE CONTENT.
I SEE.

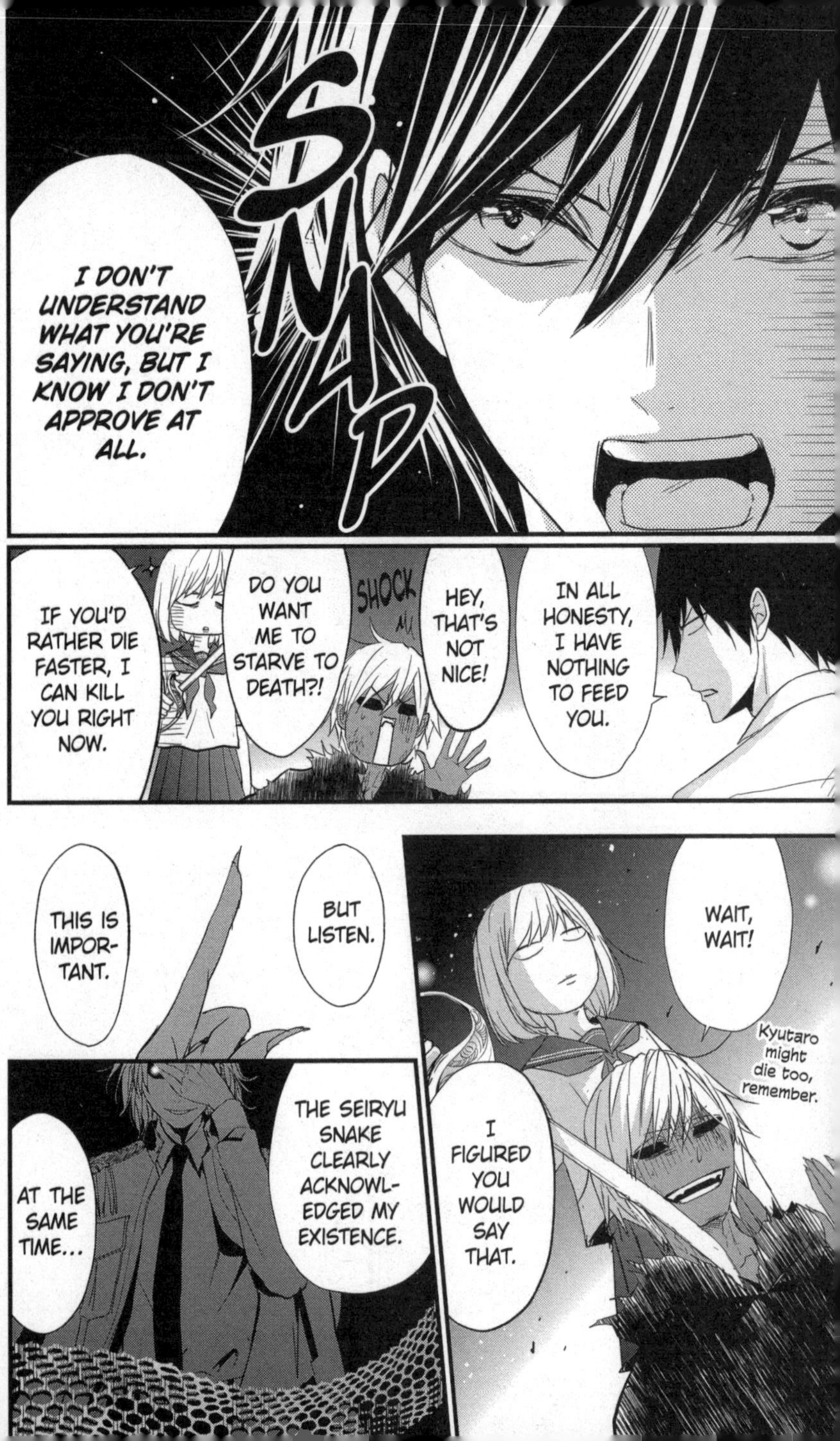
SNAP
I DON'T UNDERSTAND WHAT YOU'RE SAYING, BUT I KNOW I DON'T APPROVE AT ALL.
IN ALL HONESTY, I HAVE NOTHING TO FEED YOU.
HEY, THAT'S NOT NICE!
SHOCK
DO YOU WANT ME TO STARVE TO DEATH?!
IF YOU'D RATHER DIE FASTER, I CAN KILL YOU RIGHT NOW.
WAIT, WAIT!
Kyutaro might die too, remember.
I FIGURED YOU WOULD SAY THAT.
BUT LISTEN.
THIS IS IMPOR-TANT.
THE SEIRYU SNAKE CLEARLY ACKNOWL-EDGED MY EXISTENCE.
AT THE SAME TIME...

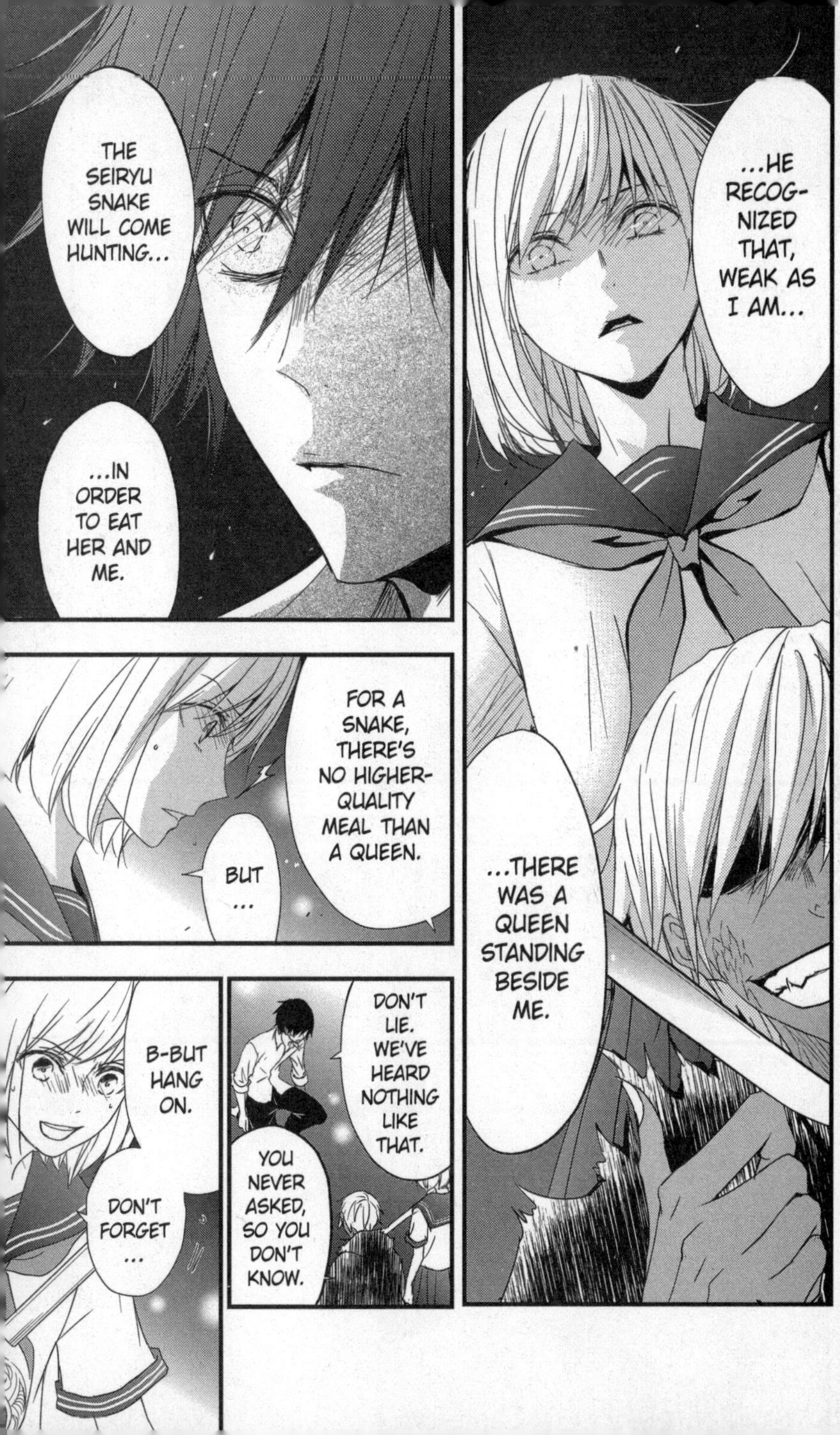
...HE RECOGNIZED THAT, WEAK AS I AM...
...THERE WAS A QUEEN STANDING BESIDE ME.
THE SEIRYU SNAKE WILL COME HUNTING...
...IN ORDER TO EAT HER AND ME.
FOR A SNAKE, THERE'S NO HIGHER-QUALITY MEAL THAN A QUEEN.
BUT ...
DON'T LIE. WE'VE HEARD NOTHING LIKE THAT.
YOU NEVER ASKED, SO YOU DON'T KNOW.
B-BUT HANG ON.
DON'T FORGET ...

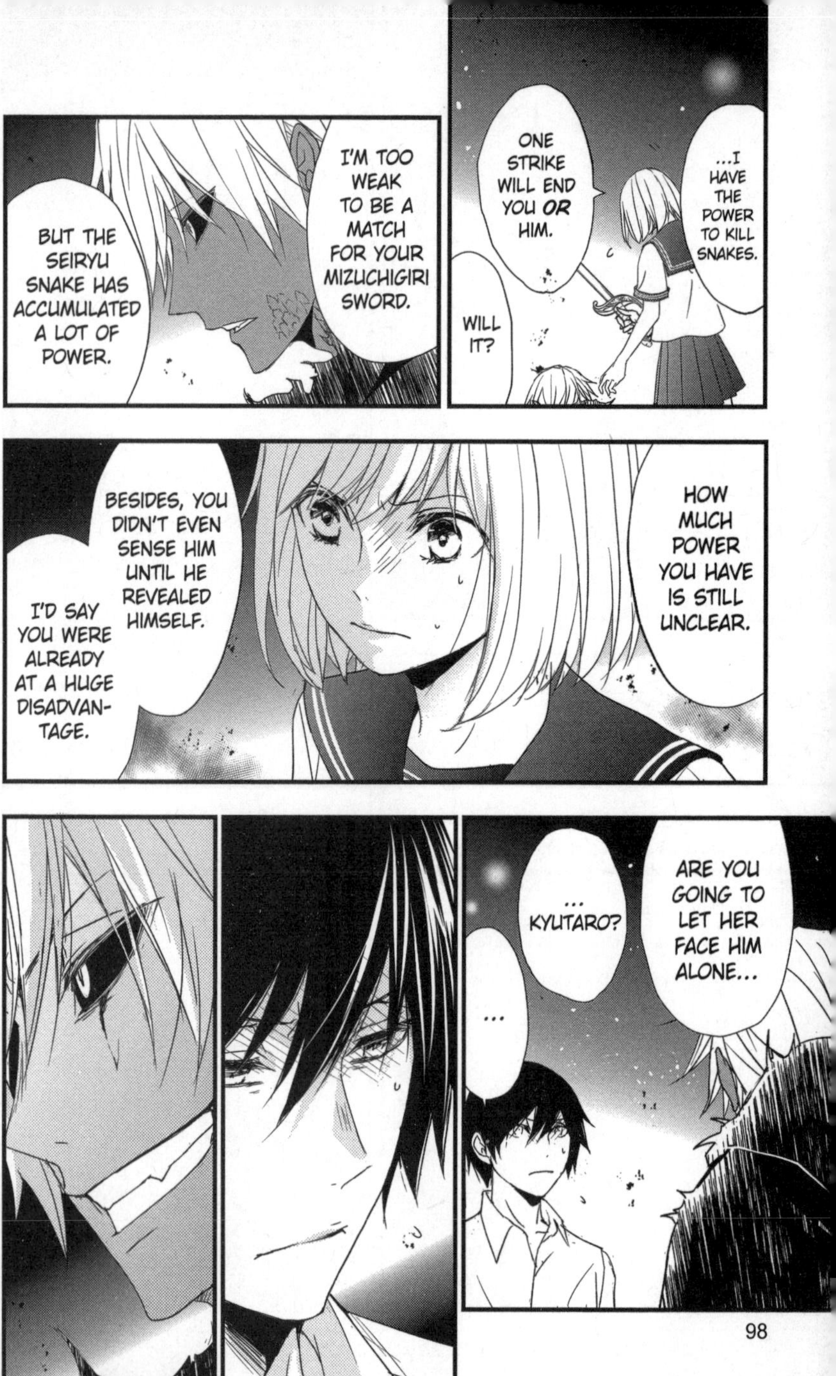
...I HAVE THE POWER TO KILL SNAKES.
ONE STRIKE WILL END YOU *OR* HIM.
WILL IT?
I'M TOO WEAK TO BE A MATCH FOR YOUR MIZUCHIGIRI SWORD.
BUT THE SEIRYU SNAKE HAS ACCUMULATED A LOT OF POWER.
HOW MUCH POWER YOU HAVE IS STILL UNCLEAR.
BESIDES, YOU DIDN'T EVEN SENSE HIM UNTIL HE REVEALED HIMSELF.
I'D SAY YOU WERE ALREADY AT A HUGE DISADVANTAGE.
ARE YOU GOING TO LET HER FACE HIM ALONE...
...KYUTARO?
...

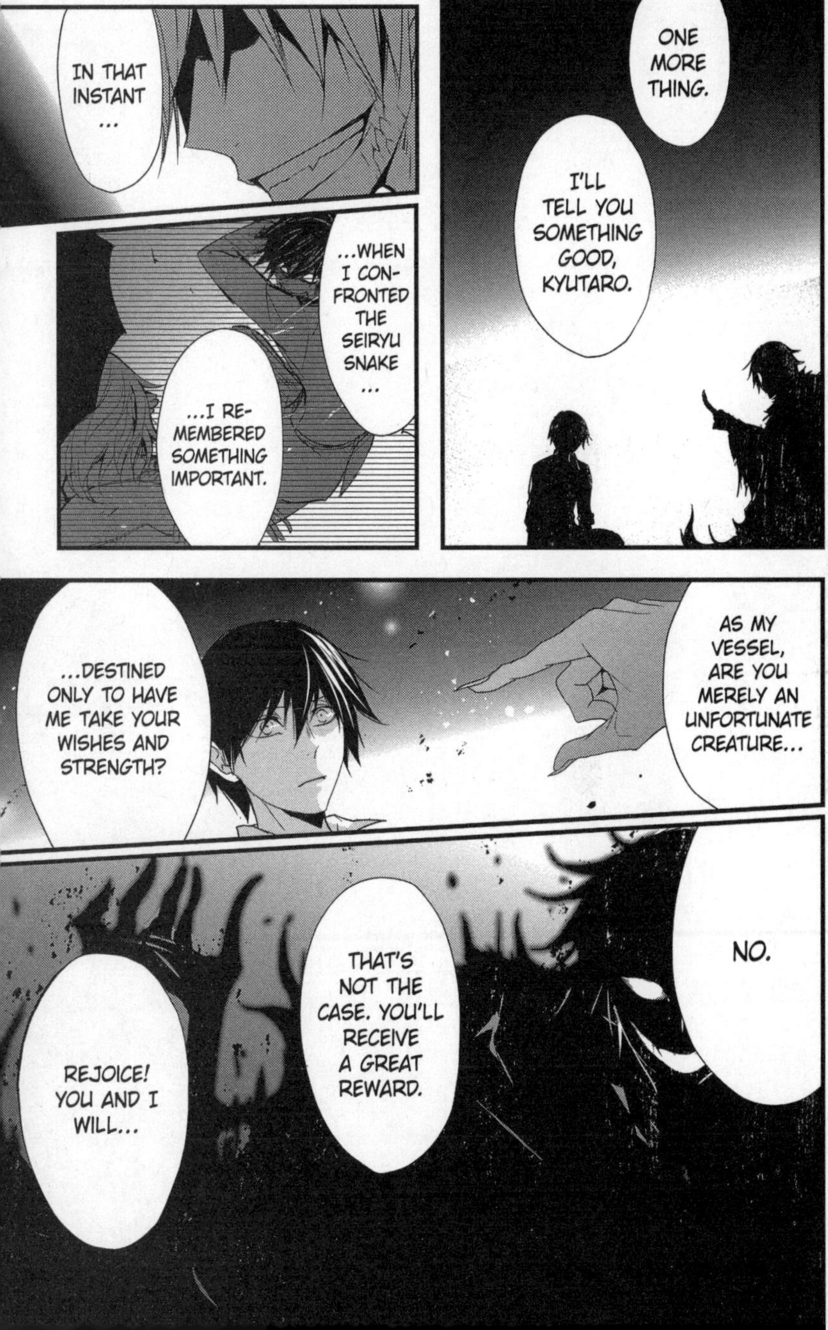
ONE MORE THING.
I'LL TELL YOU SOMETHING GOOD, KYUTARO.
IN THAT INSTANT...
...WHEN I CONFRONTED THE SEIRYU SNAKE...
...I REMEMBERED SOMETHING IMPORTANT.
AS MY VESSEL, ARE YOU MERELY AN UNFORTUNATE CREATURE...
...DESTINED ONLY TO HAVE ME TAKE YOUR WISHES AND STRENGTH?
NO.
THAT'S NOT THE CASE. YOU'LL RECEIVE A GREAT REWARD.
REJOICE! YOU AND I WILL...

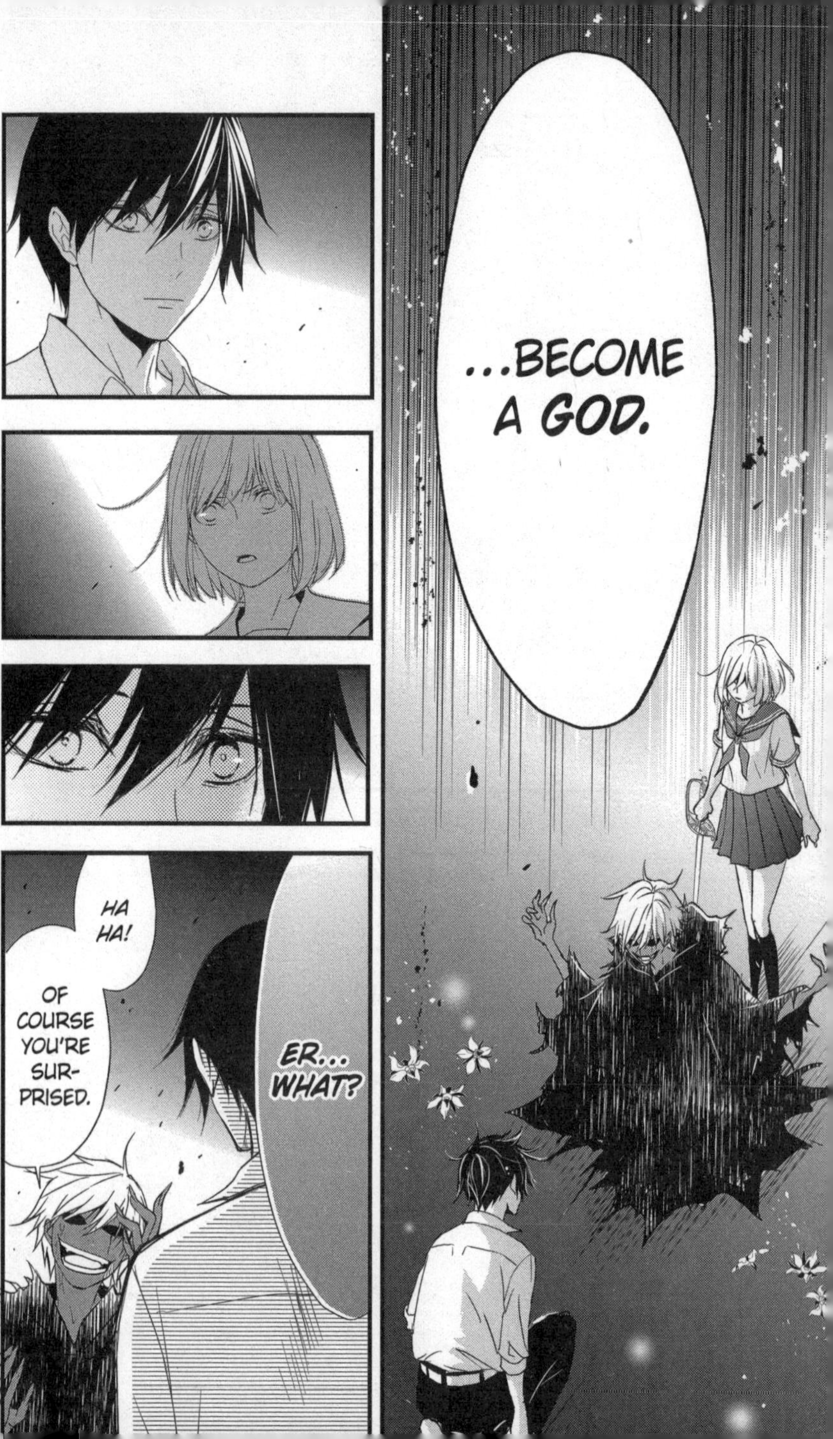
...BECOME A GOD.
ER... WHAT?
HA HA!
OF COURSE YOU'RE SUR-PRISED.

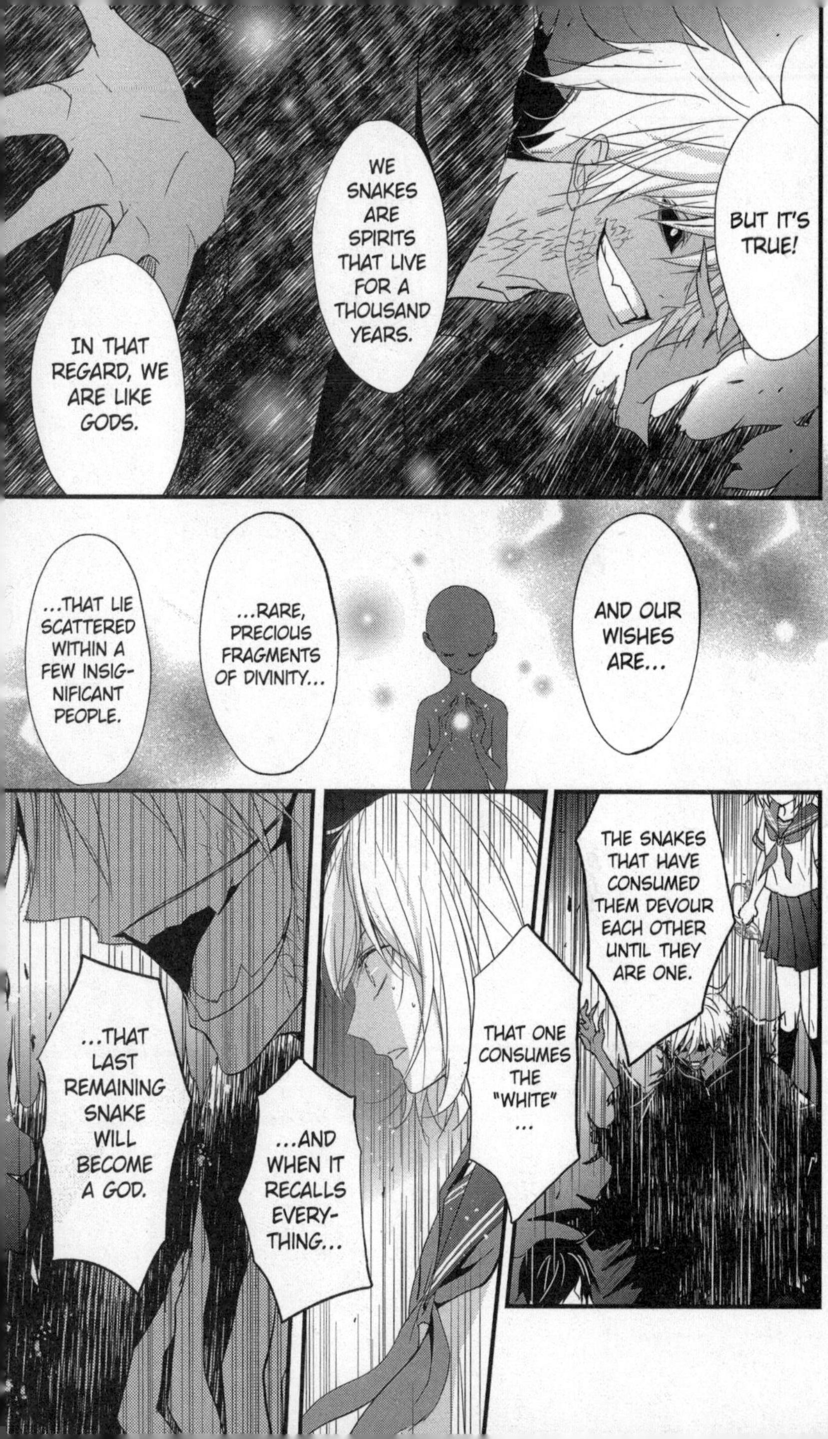
BUT IT'S TRUE!
WE SNAKES ARE SPIRITS THAT LIVE FOR A THOUSAND YEARS.
IN THAT REGARD, WE ARE LIKE GODS.
AND OUR WISHES ARE...
...RARE, PRECIOUS FRAGMENTS OF DIVINITY...
...THAT LIE SCATTERED WITHIN A FEW INSIGNIFICANT PEOPLE.
THE SNAKES THAT HAVE CONSUMED THEM DEVOUR EACH OTHER UNTIL THEY ARE ONE.
THAT ONE CONSUMES THE "WHITE"...
...AND WHEN IT RECALLS EVERYTHING...
...THAT LAST REMAINING SNAKE WILL BECOME A GOD.

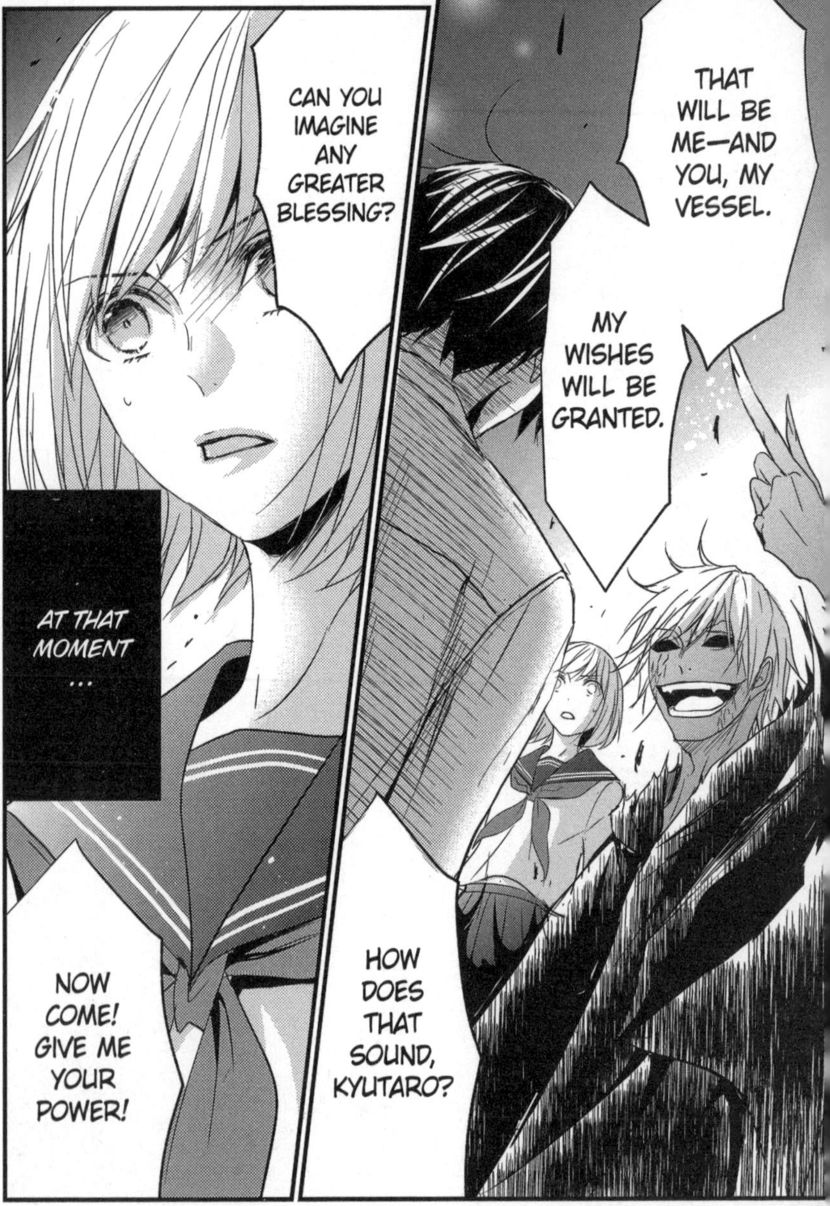
THAT WILL BE ME—AND YOU, MY VESSEL.
MY WISHES WILL BE GRANTED.
HOW DOES THAT SOUND, KYUTARO?
CAN YOU IMAGINE ANY GREATER BLESSING?
AT THAT MOMENT...
NOW COME! GIVE ME YOUR POWER!

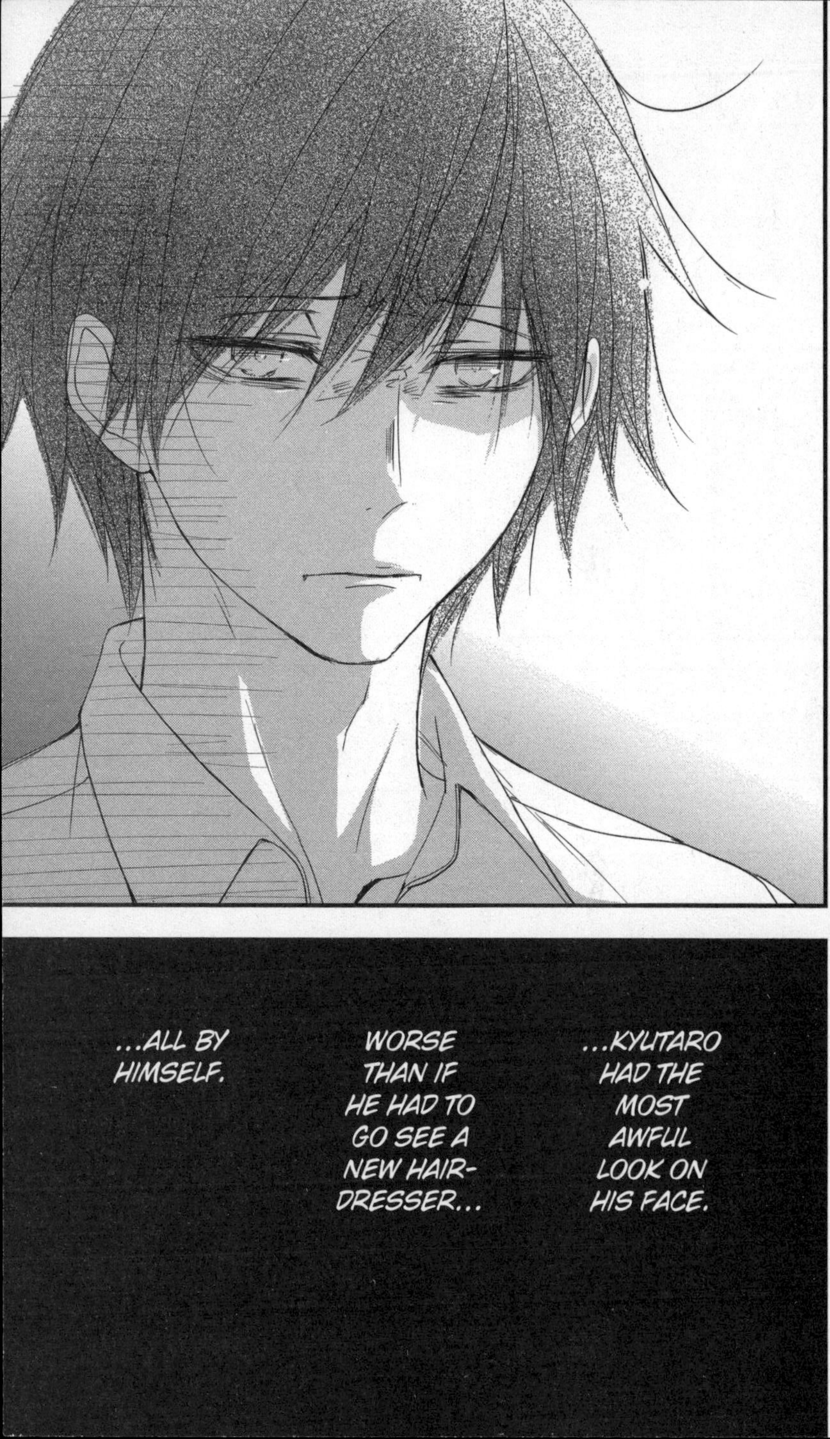
...KYUTARO HAD THE MOST AWFUL LOOK ON HIS FACE.
WORSE THAN IF HE HAD TO GO SEE A NEW HAIR-DRESSER...
...ALL BY HIMSELF.

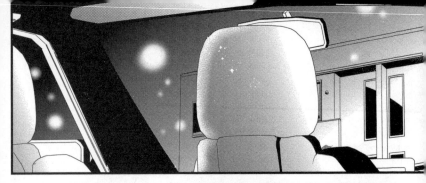

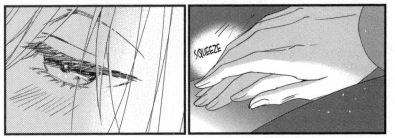

SQUEEZE

ARE YOU AWAKE, FUMI?

AH...

YAWN... KYUTARO?

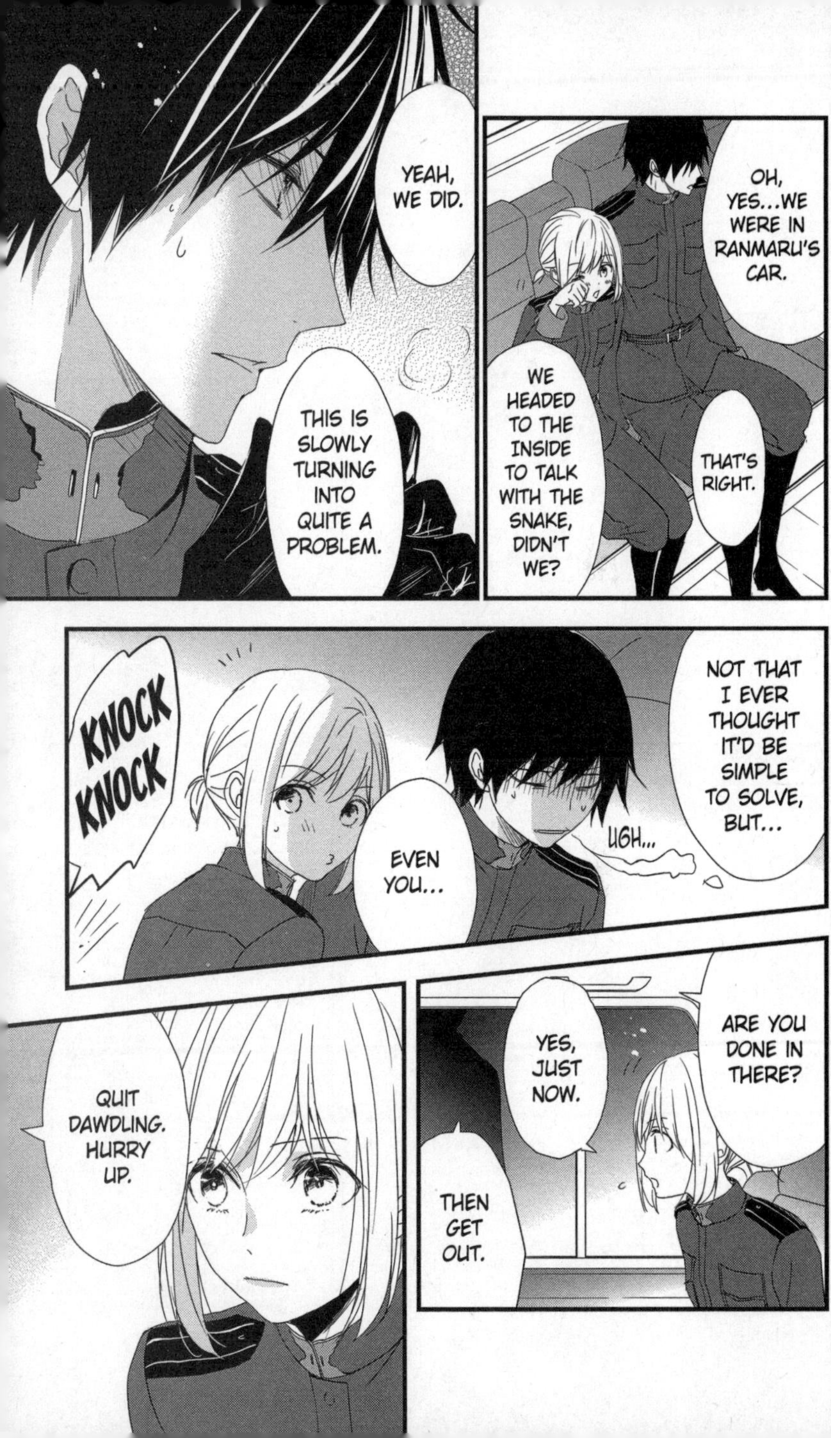
OH, YES...WE WERE IN RANMARU'S CAR.
WE HEADED TO THE INSIDE TO TALK WITH THE SNAKE, DIDN'T WE?
THAT'S RIGHT.
YEAH, WE DID.
THIS IS SLOWLY TURNING INTO QUITE A PROBLEM.
NOT THAT I EVER THOUGHT IT'D BE SIMPLE TO SOLVE, BUT...
UGH...
EVEN YOU...
KNOCK KNOCK
ARE YOU DONE IN THERE?
YES, JUST NOW.
THEN GET OUT.
QUIT DAWDLING. HURRY UP.

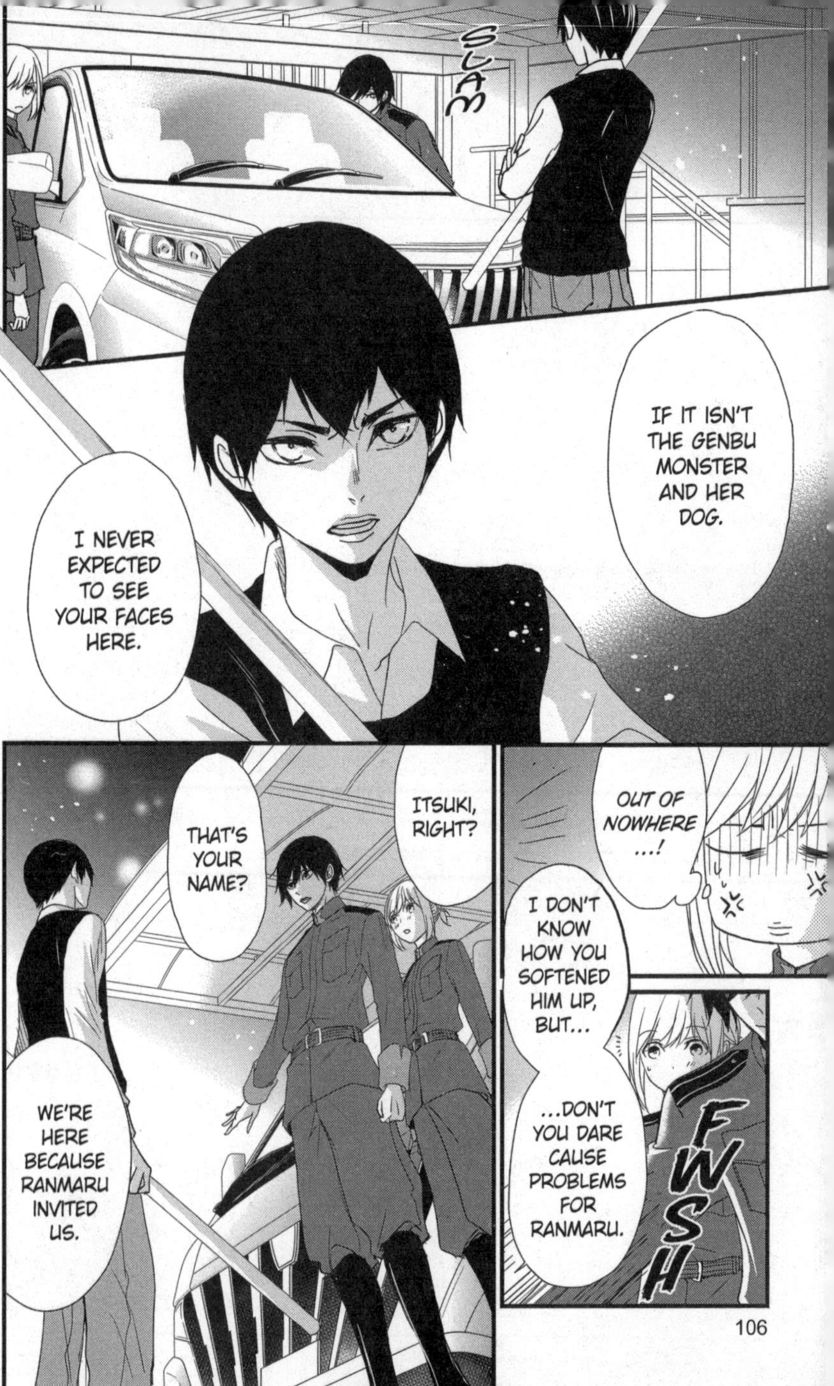
SLAM
IF IT ISN'T THE GENBU MONSTER AND HER DOG.
I NEVER EXPECTED TO SEE YOUR FACES HERE.
OUT OF NOWHERE...!
I DON'T KNOW HOW YOU SOFTENED HIM UP, BUT...
...DON'T YOU DARE CAUSE PROBLEMS FOR RANMARU.
FWSH
ITSUKI, RIGHT?
THAT'S YOUR NAME?
WE'RE HERE BECAUSE RANMARU INVITED US.

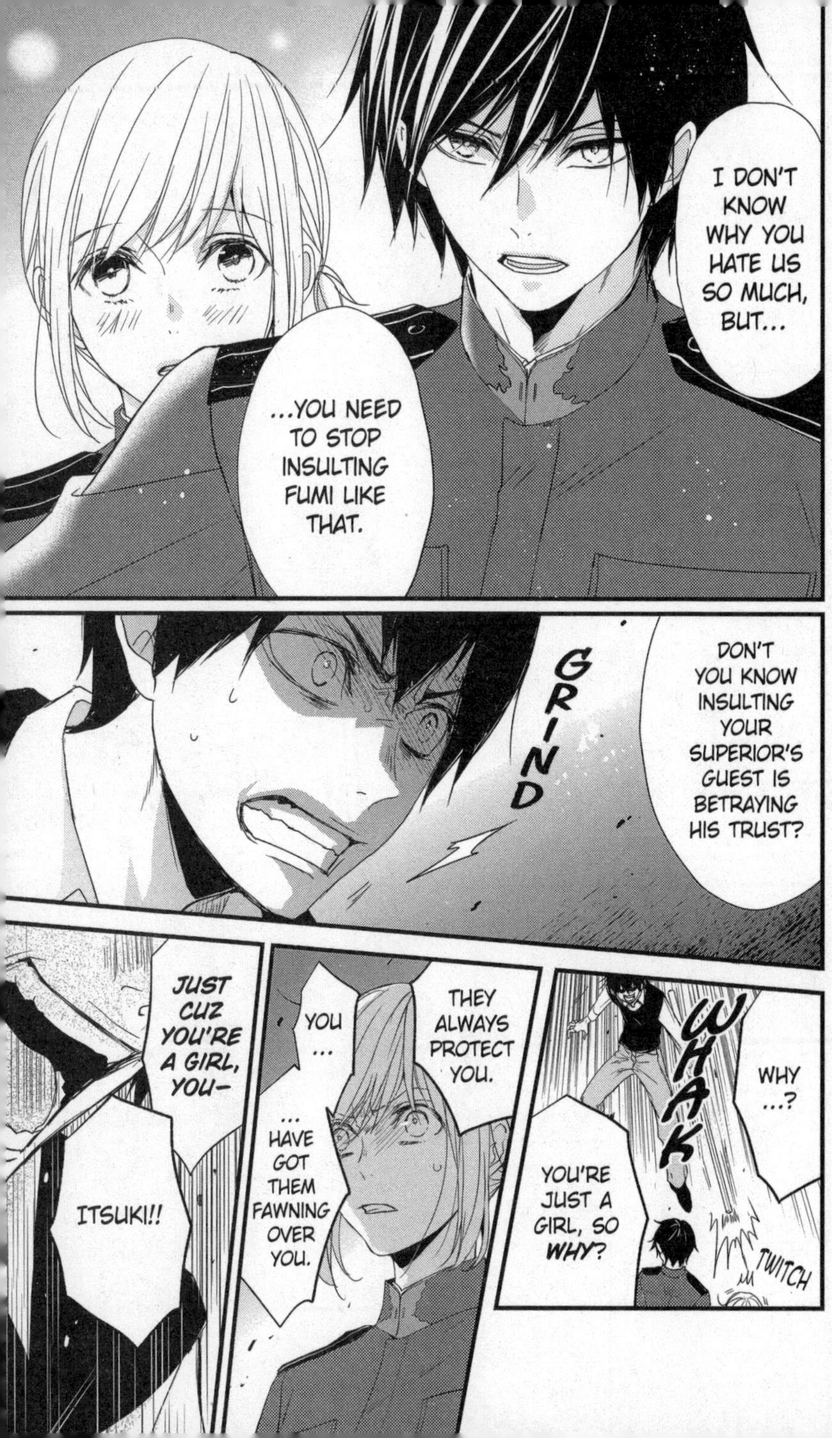
I DON'T KNOW WHY YOU HATE US SO MUCH, BUT...
...YOU NEED TO STOP INSULTING FUMI LIKE THAT.
DON'T YOU KNOW INSULTING YOUR SUPERIOR'S GUEST IS BETRAYING HIS TRUST?
GRIND
WHY ...?
WHAK
YOU'RE JUST A GIRL, SO *WHY*?
TWITCH
THEY ALWAYS PROTECT YOU.
YOU ...
... HAVE GOT THEM FAWNING OVER YOU.
JUST CUZ YOU'RE A GIRL, YOU—
ITSUKI!!

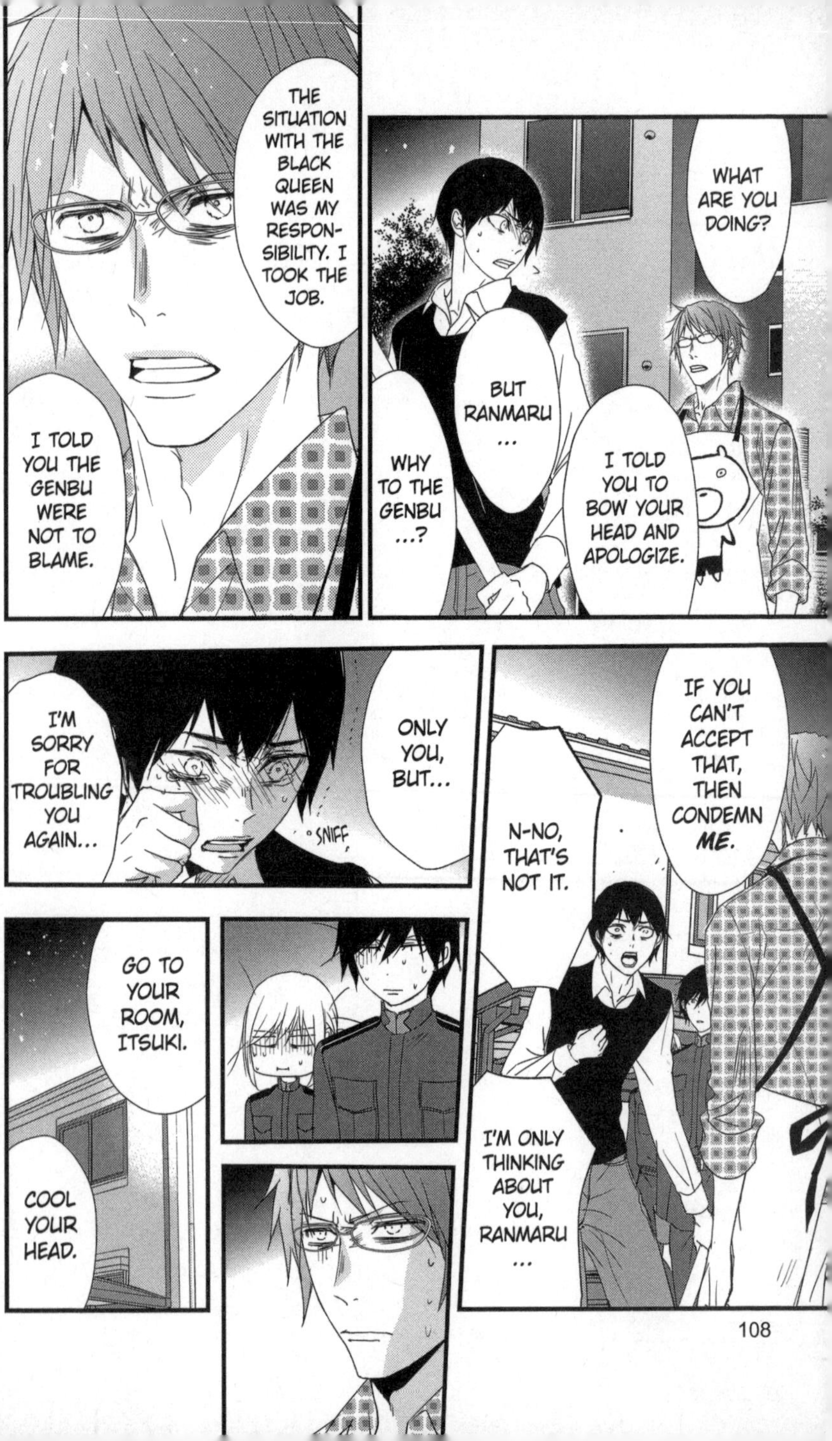

WHAT ARE YOU DOING?
I TOLD YOU TO BOW YOUR HEAD AND APOLOGIZE.
BUT RANMARU ...
WHY TO THE GENBU ...?
THE SITUATION WITH THE BLACK QUEEN WAS MY RESPON-SIBILITY. I TOOK THE JOB.
I TOLD YOU THE GENBU WERE NOT TO BLAME.
IF YOU CAN'T ACCEPT THAT, THEN CONDEMN *ME*.
N-NO, THAT'S NOT IT.
I'M ONLY THINKING ABOUT YOU, RANMARU ...
ONLY YOU, BUT...
I'M SORRY FOR TROUBLING YOU AGAIN...
SNIFF
GO TO YOUR ROOM, ITSUKI.
COOL YOUR HEAD.

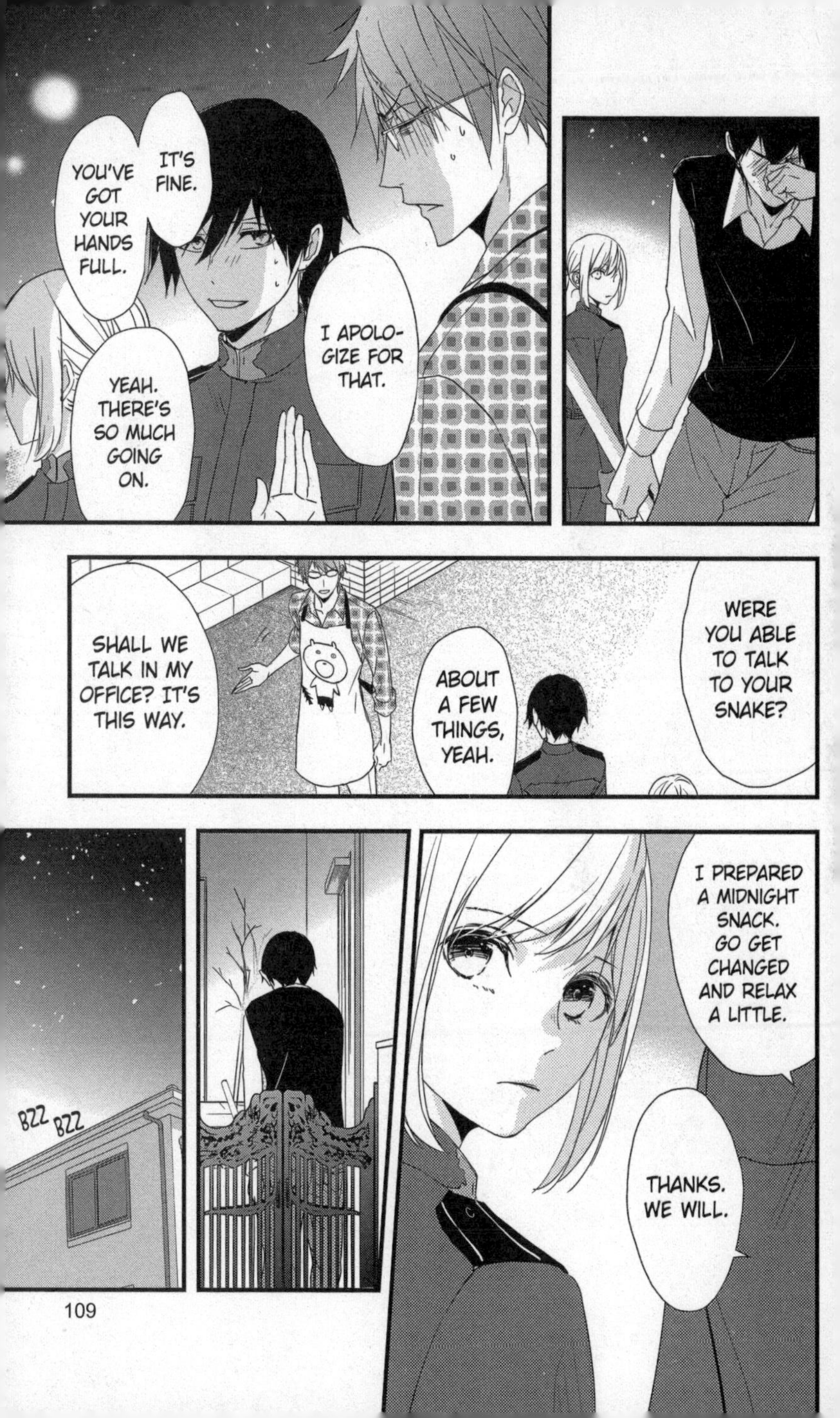
I APOLOGIZE FOR THAT.
IT'S FINE.
YOU'VE GOT YOUR HANDS FULL.
YEAH. THERE'S SO MUCH GOING ON.
WERE YOU ABLE TO TALK TO YOUR SNAKE?
ABOUT A FEW THINGS, YEAH.
SHALL WE TALK IN MY OFFICE? IT'S THIS WAY.
I PREPARED A MIDNIGHT SNACK. GO GET CHANGED AND RELAX A LITTLE.
THANKS. WE WILL.
BZZ BZZ

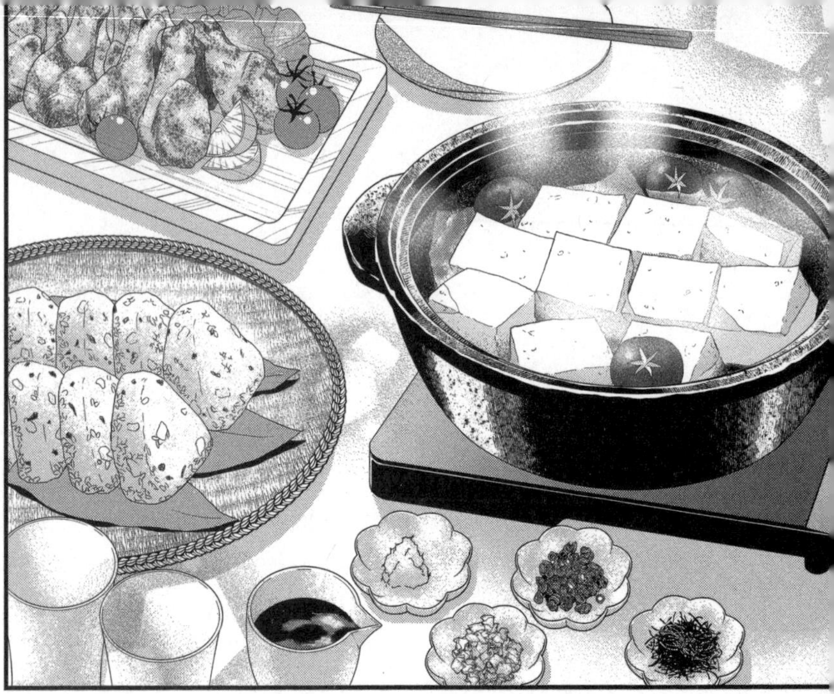

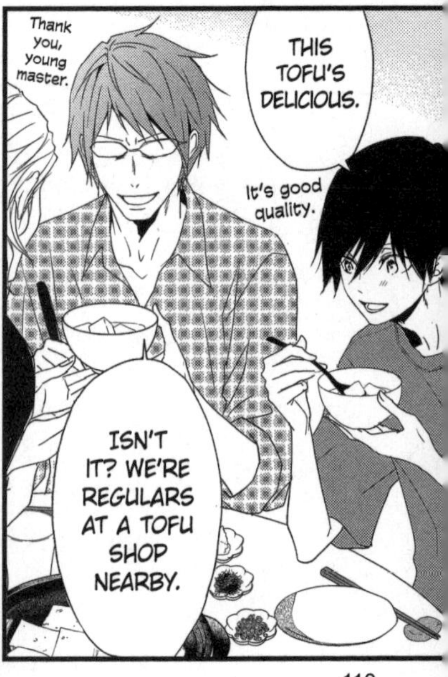
THIS TOFU'S DELICIOUS.
Thank you, young master.
It's good quality.
ISN'T IT? WE'RE REGULARS AT A TOFU SHOP NEARBY.

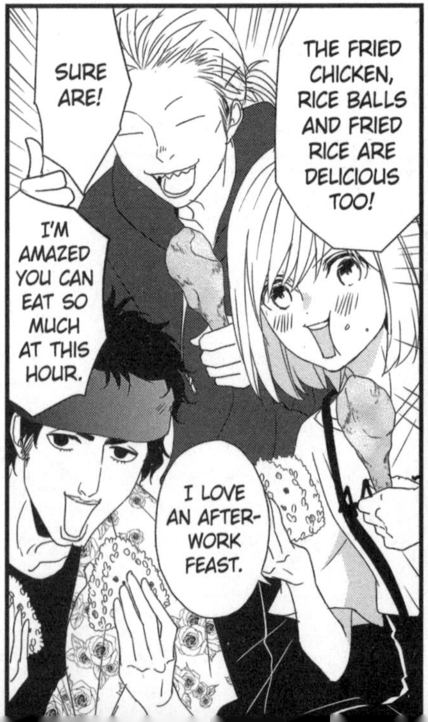
THE FRIED CHICKEN, RICE BALLS AND FRIED RICE ARE DELICIOUS TOO!
SURE ARE!
I'M AMAZED YOU CAN EAT SO MUCH AT THIS HOUR.
I LOVE AN AFTER-WORK FEAST.

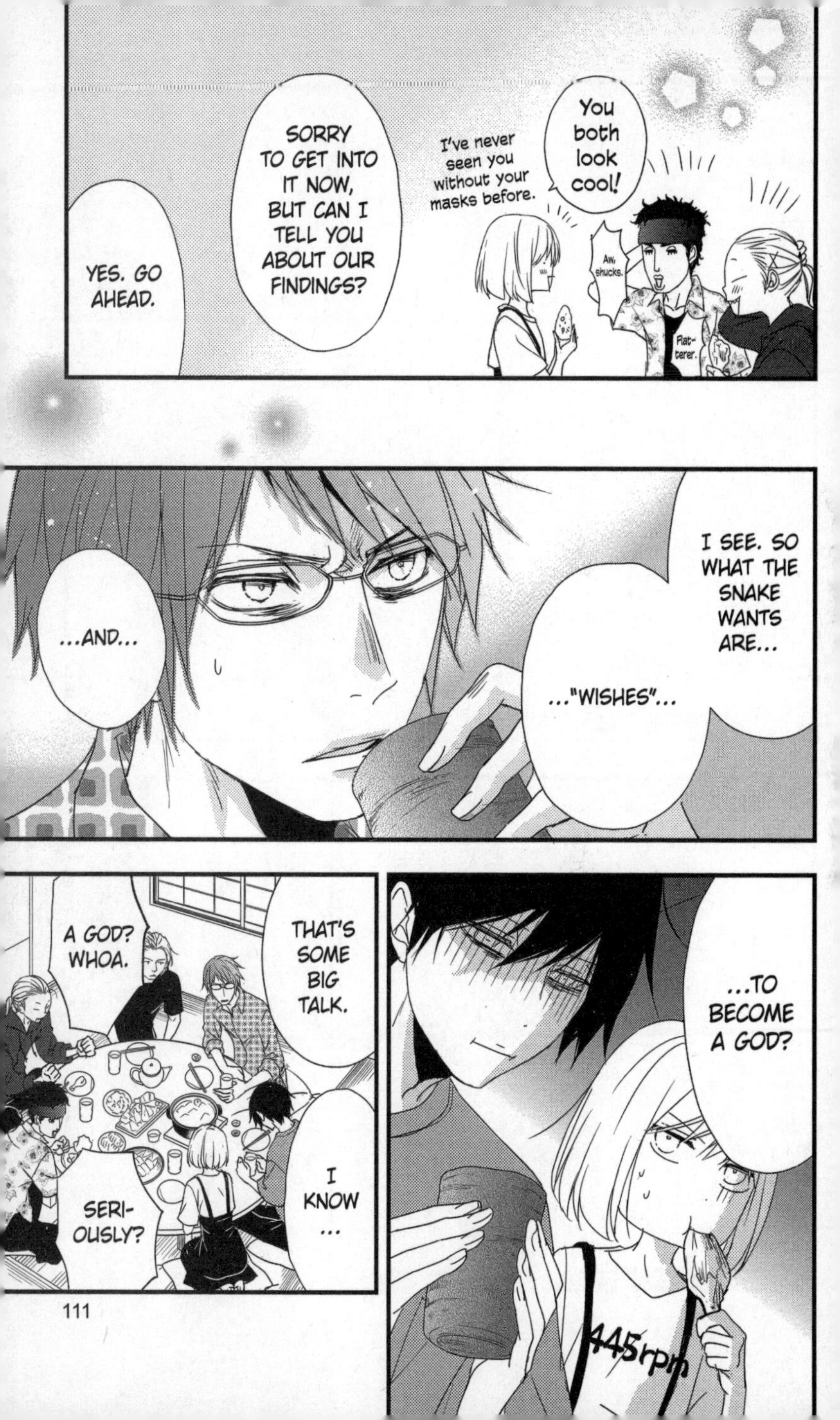

You both look cool!
I've never seen you without your masks before.
Aw, shucks.
Flat-terer.
SORRY TO GET INTO IT NOW, BUT CAN I TELL YOU ABOUT OUR FINDINGS?
YES. GO AHEAD.
I SEE. SO WHAT THE SNAKE WANTS ARE...
..."WISHES"...
...AND...
...TO BECOME A GOD?
445rpm
THAT'S SOME BIG TALK.
A GOD? WHOA.
I KNOW ...
SERI-OUSLY?

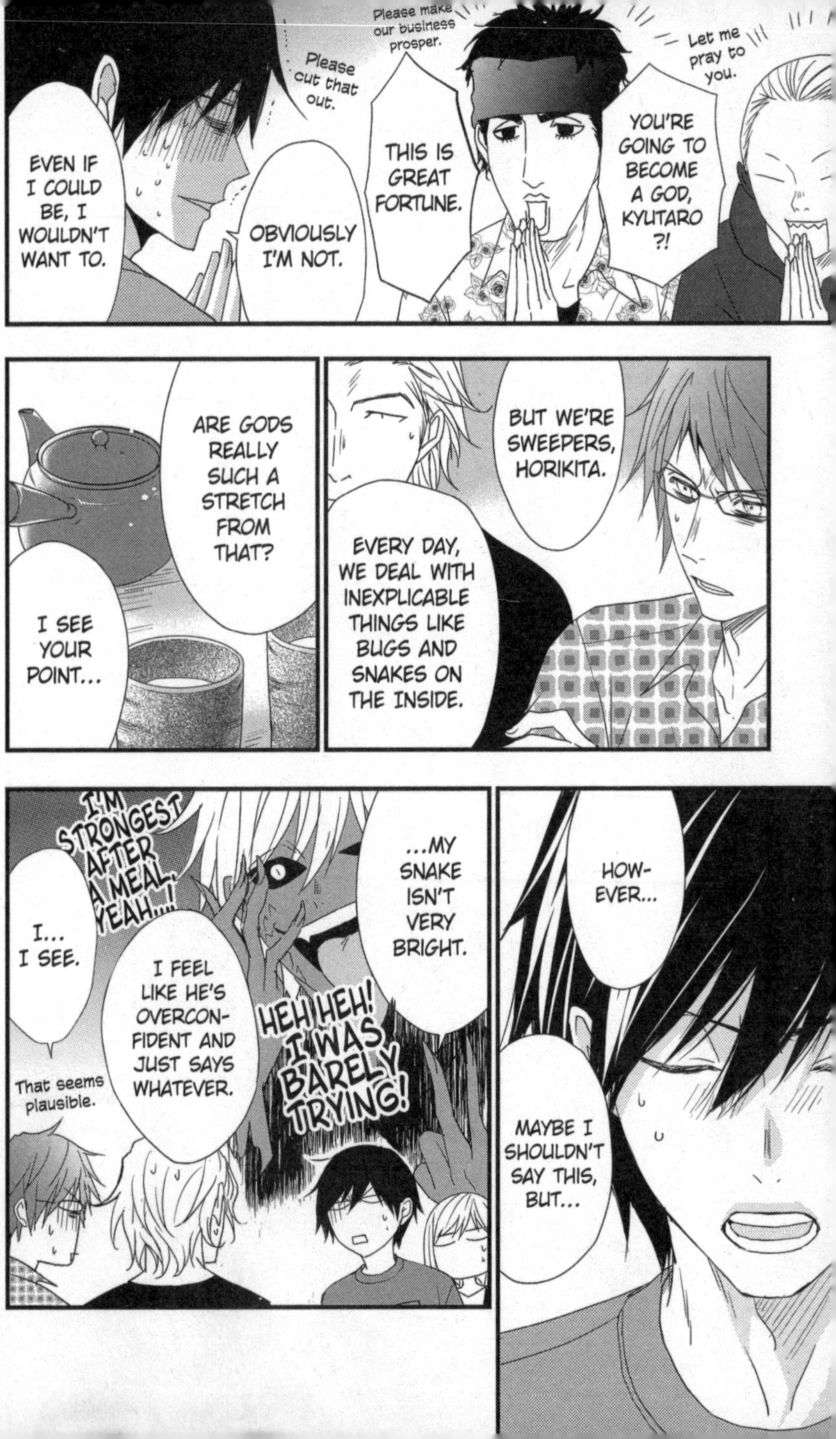
Let me pray to you.
YOU'RE GOING TO BECOME A GOD, KYUTARO?!
Please make our business prosper.
THIS IS GREAT FORTUNE.
Please cut that out.
OBVIOUSLY I'M NOT.
EVEN IF I COULD BE, I WOULDN'T WANT TO.
BUT WE'RE SWEEPERS, HORIKITA.
EVERY DAY, WE DEAL WITH INEXPLICABLE THINGS LIKE BUGS AND SNAKES ON THE INSIDE.
ARE GODS REALLY SUCH A STRETCH FROM THAT?
I SEE YOUR POINT...
HOW-EVER...
MAYBE I SHOULDN'T SAY THIS, BUT...
...MY SNAKE ISN'T VERY BRIGHT.
I'M STRONGEST AFTER A MEAL, YEAH...!
I... I SEE.
HEH HEH! I WAS BARELY TRYING!
I FEEL LIKE HE'S OVERCON-FIDENT AND JUST SAYS WHATEVER.
That seems plausible.

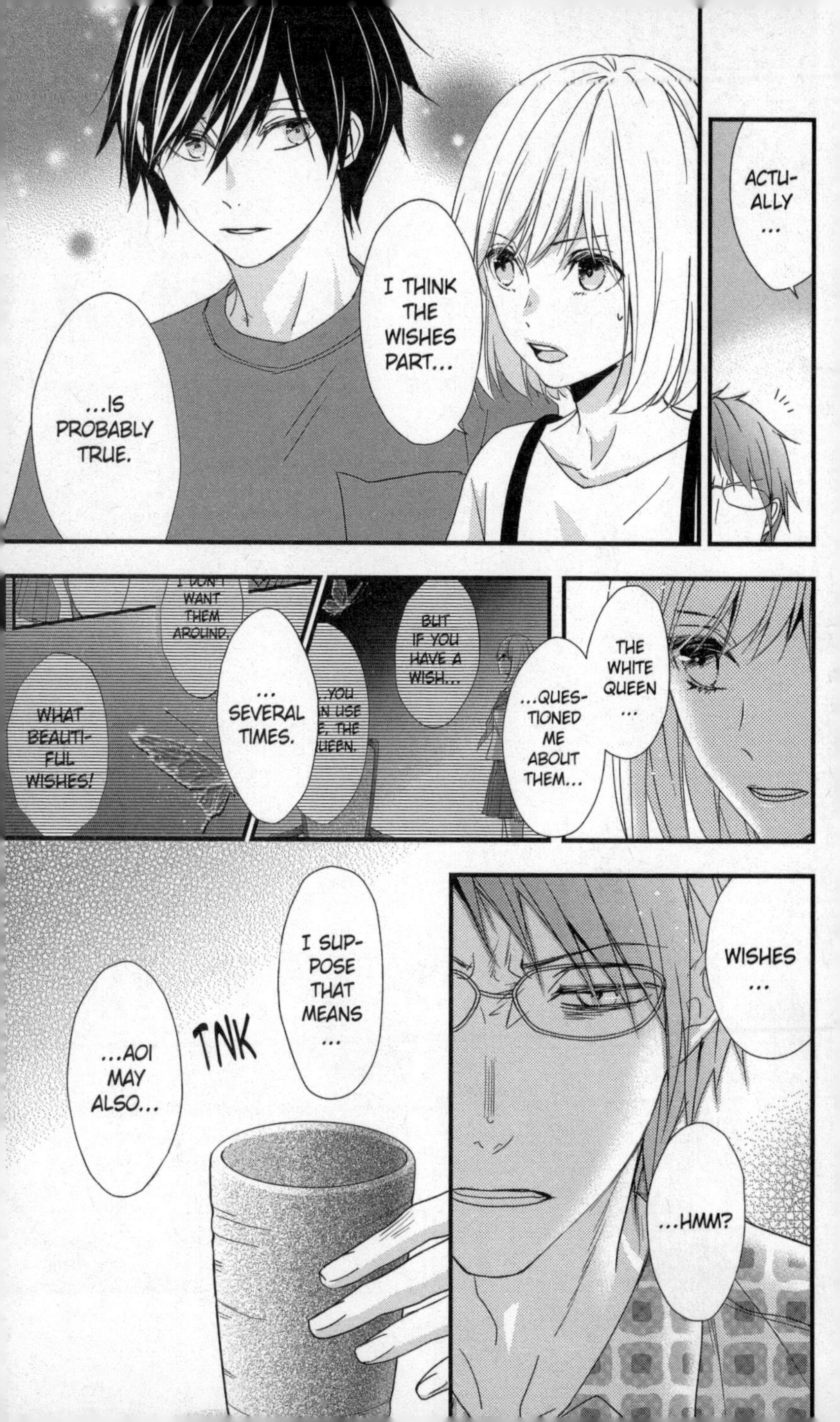
ACTU-ALLY...
I THINK THE WISHES PART...
...IS PROBABLY TRUE.
THE WHITE QUEEN...
...QUESTIONED ME ABOUT THEM...
BUT IF YOU HAVE A WISH...
...YOU
WANT THEM AROUND.
...SEVERAL TIMES.
WHAT BEAUTIFUL WISHES!
WISHES...
...HMM?
I SUPPOSE THAT MEANS...
TNK
...AOI MAY ALSO...

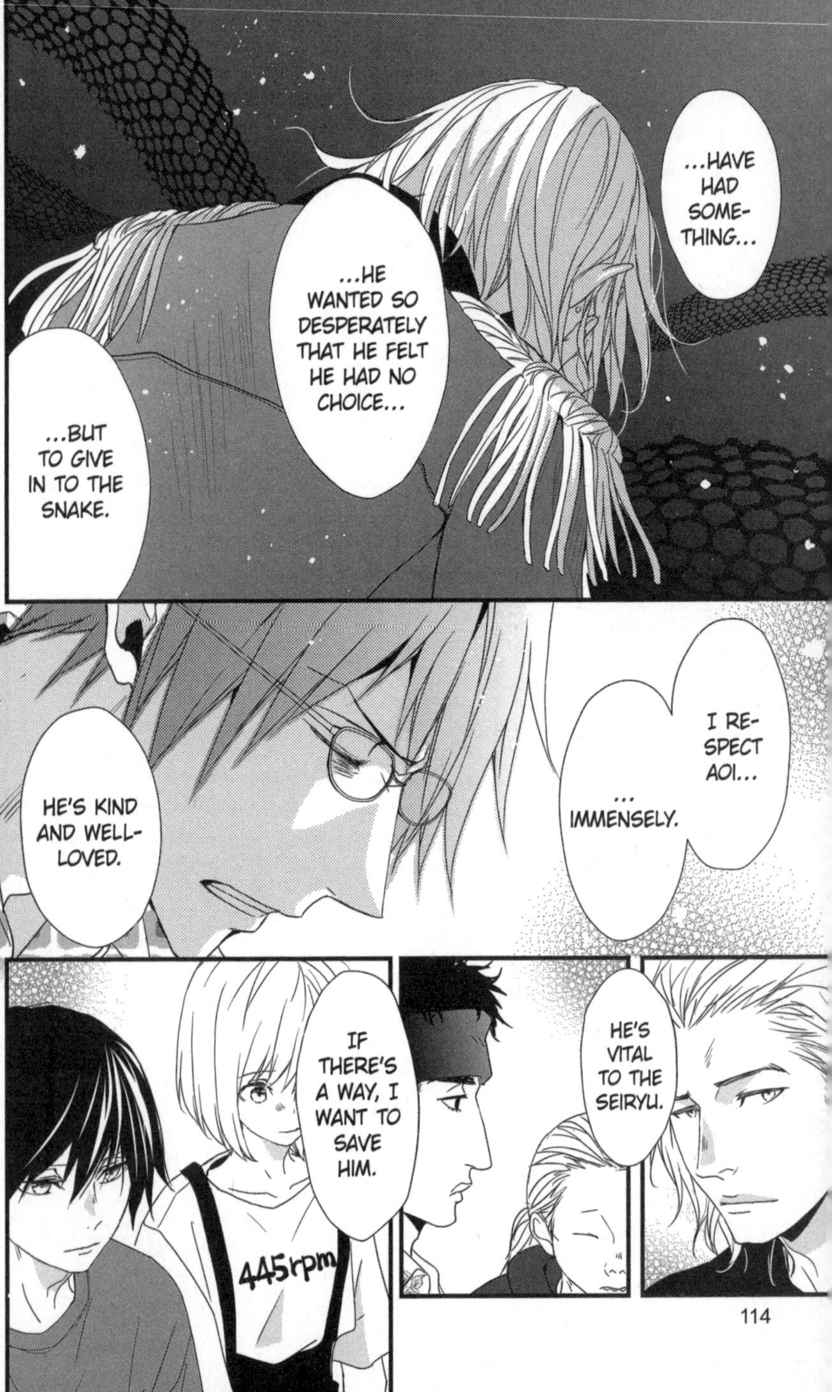
...HAVE HAD SOMETHING...
...HE WANTED SO DESPERATELY THAT HE FELT HE HAD NO CHOICE...
...BUT TO GIVE IN TO THE SNAKE.
I RESPECT AOI...
...IMMENSELY.
HE'S KIND AND WELL-LOVED.
HE'S VITAL TO THE SEIRYU.
IF THERE'S A WAY, I WANT TO SAVE HIM.
445rpm

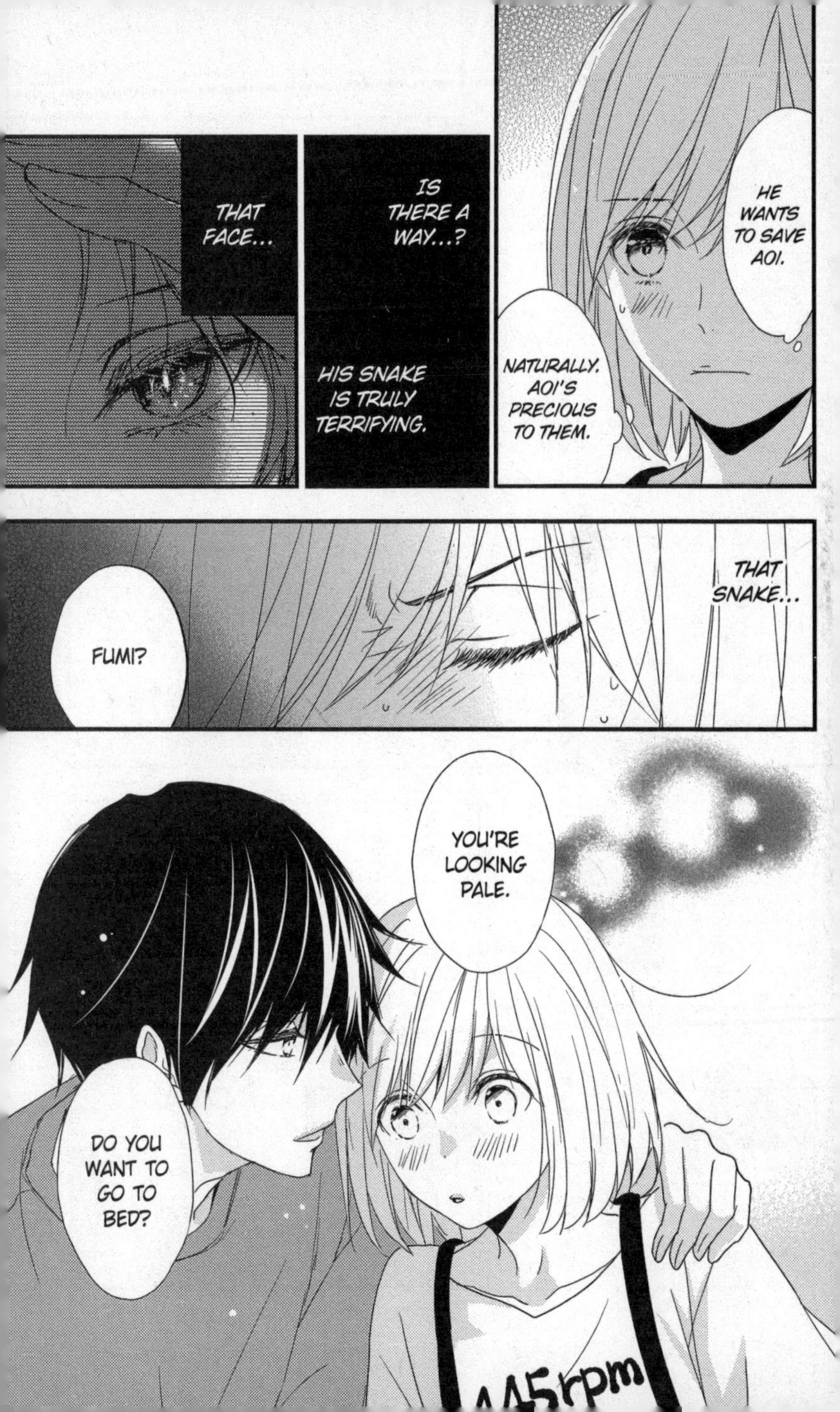
HE WANTS TO SAVE AOI.
NATURALLY. AOI'S PRECIOUS TO THEM.
IS THERE A WAY...?
HIS SNAKE IS TRULY TERRIFYING.
THAT FACE...
THAT SNAKE...
FUMI?
YOU'RE LOOKING PALE.
DO YOU WANT TO GO TO BED?

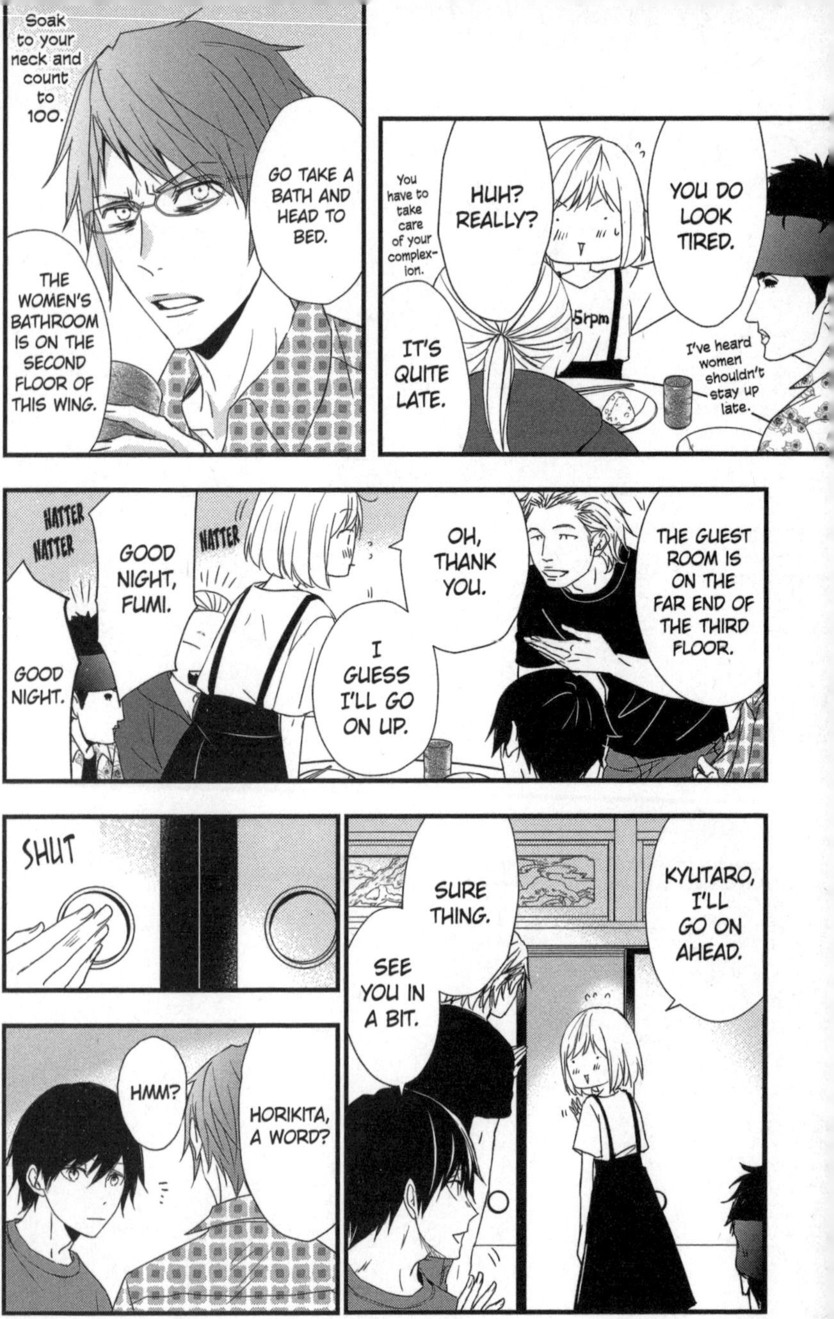
YOU DO LOOK TIRED.
I've heard women shouldn't stay up late.
HUH? REALLY?
You have to take care of your complexion.
IT'S QUITE LATE.
GO TAKE A BATH AND HEAD TO BED.
Soak to your neck and count to 100.
THE WOMEN'S BATHROOM IS ON THE SECOND FLOOR OF THIS WING.
THE GUEST ROOM IS ON THE FAR END OF THE THIRD FLOOR.
OH, THANK YOU.
I GUESS I'LL GO ON UP.
NATTER
GOOD NIGHT, FUMI.
NATTER NATTER
GOOD NIGHT.
KYUTARO, I'LL GO ON AHEAD.
SURE THING.
SEE YOU IN A BIT.
SHUT
HORIKITA, A WORD?
HMM?

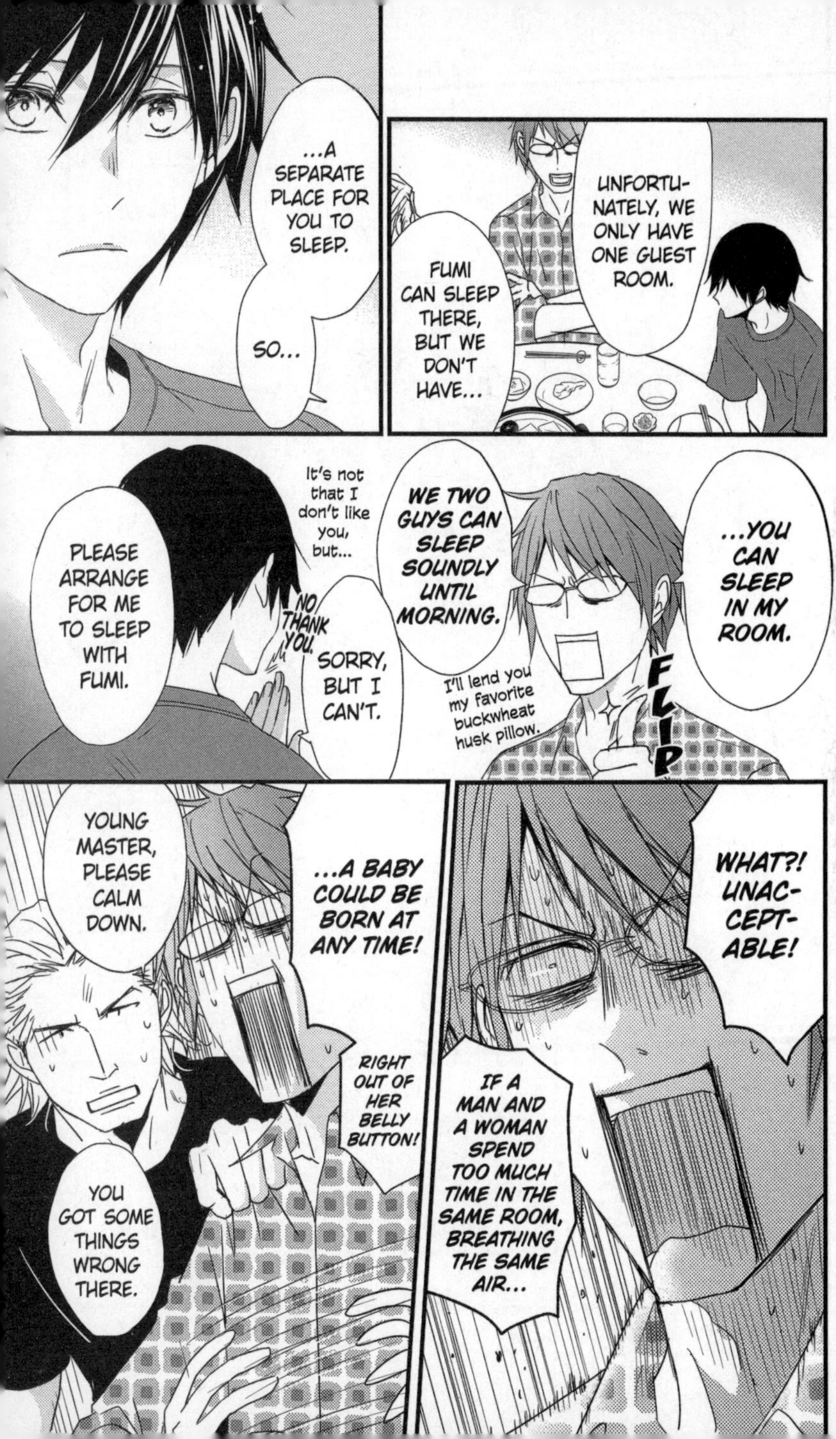
UNFORTUNATELY, WE ONLY HAVE ONE GUEST ROOM.
FUMI CAN SLEEP THERE, BUT WE DON'T HAVE...
...A SEPARATE PLACE FOR YOU TO SLEEP.
SO...
...YOU CAN SLEEP IN MY ROOM.
FLIP
I'll lend you my favorite buckwheat husk pillow.
WE TWO GUYS CAN SLEEP SOUNDLY UNTIL MORNING.
It's not that I don't like you, but...
SORRY, BUT I CAN'T.
NO THANK YOU.
PLEASE ARRANGE FOR ME TO SLEEP WITH FUMI.
WHAT?! UNACCEPTABLE!
IF A MAN AND A WOMAN SPEND TOO MUCH TIME IN THE SAME ROOM, BREATHING THE SAME AIR...
...A BABY COULD BE BORN AT ANY TIME!
RIGHT OUT OF HER BELLY BUTTON!
YOUNG MASTER, PLEASE CALM DOWN.
YOU GOT SOME THINGS WRONG THERE.

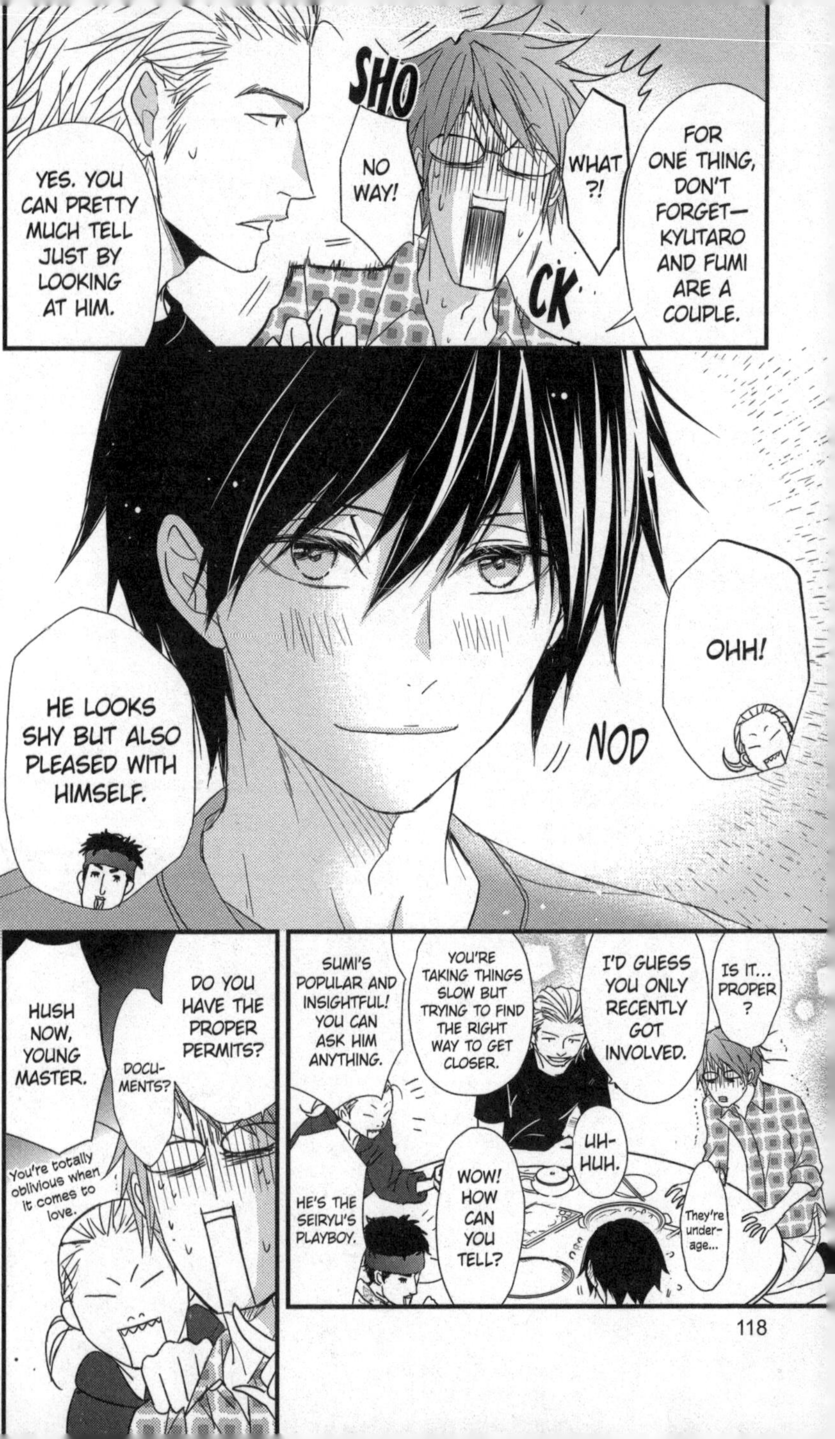
FOR ONE THING, DON'T FORGET—KYUTARO AND FUMI ARE A COUPLE.
WHAT?!
SHO
CK
NO WAY!
YES. YOU CAN PRETTY MUCH TELL JUST BY LOOKING AT HIM.
OHH!
NOD
HE LOOKS SHY BUT ALSO PLEASED WITH HIMSELF.
IS IT... PROPER?
I'D GUESS YOU ONLY RECENTLY GOT INVOLVED.
YOU'RE TAKING THINGS SLOW BUT TRYING TO FIND THE RIGHT WAY TO GET CLOSER.
SUMI'S POPULAR AND INSIGHTFUL! YOU CAN ASK HIM ANYTHING.
UH-HUH.
They're under-age...
WOW! HOW CAN YOU TELL?
HE'S THE SEIRYU'S PLAYBOY.
DO YOU HAVE THE PROPER PERMITS?
DOCU-MENTS?
HUSH NOW, YOUNG MASTER.
You're totally oblivious when it comes to love.

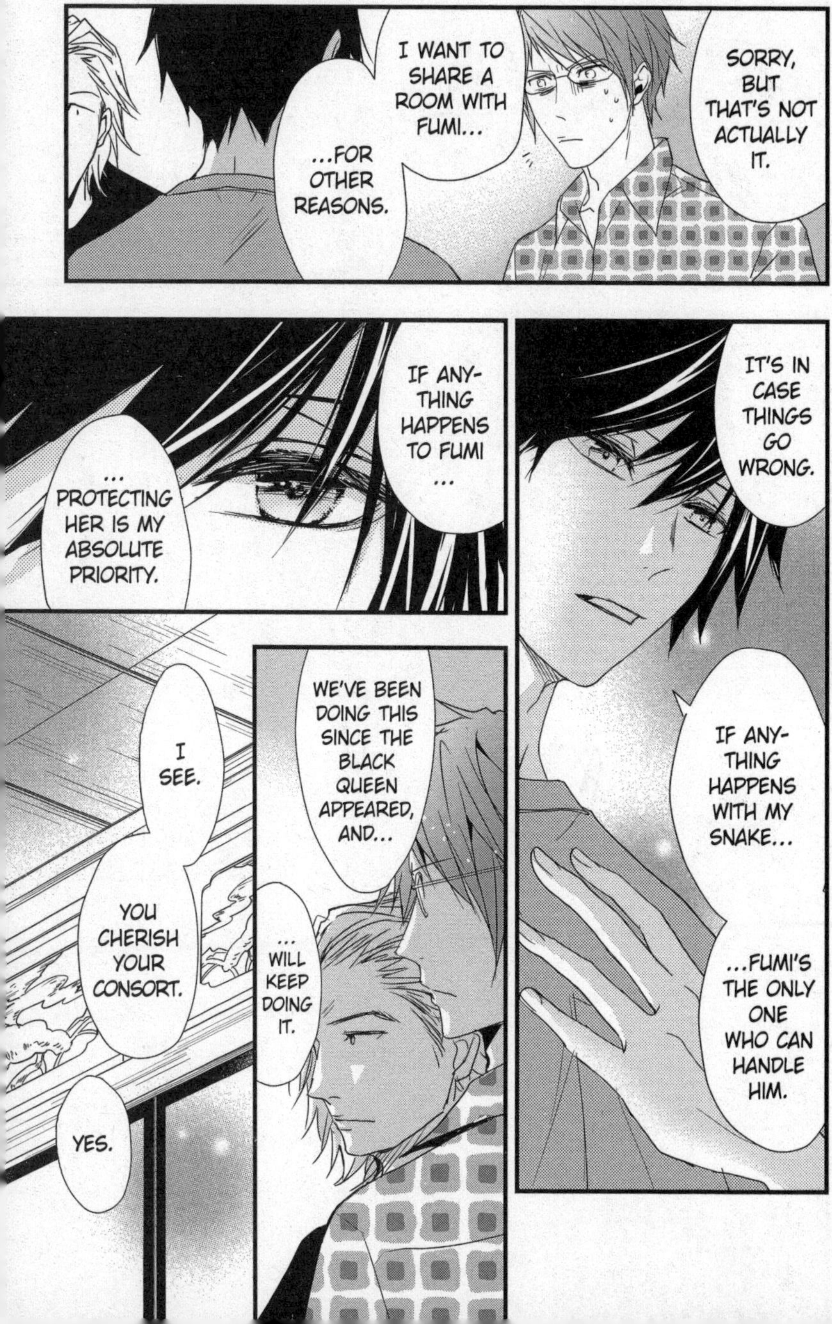
SORRY, BUT THAT'S NOT ACTUALLY IT.
I WANT TO SHARE A ROOM WITH FUMI...
...FOR OTHER REASONS.
IT'S IN CASE THINGS GO WRONG.
IF ANY-THING HAPPENS WITH MY SNAKE...
...FUMI'S THE ONLY ONE WHO CAN HANDLE HIM.
IF ANY-THING HAPPENS TO FUMI ...
... PROTECTING HER IS MY ABSOLUTE PRIORITY.
WE'VE BEEN DOING THIS SINCE THE BLACK QUEEN APPEARED, AND...
... WILL KEEP DOING IT.
I SEE.
YOU CHERISH YOUR CONSORT.
YES.

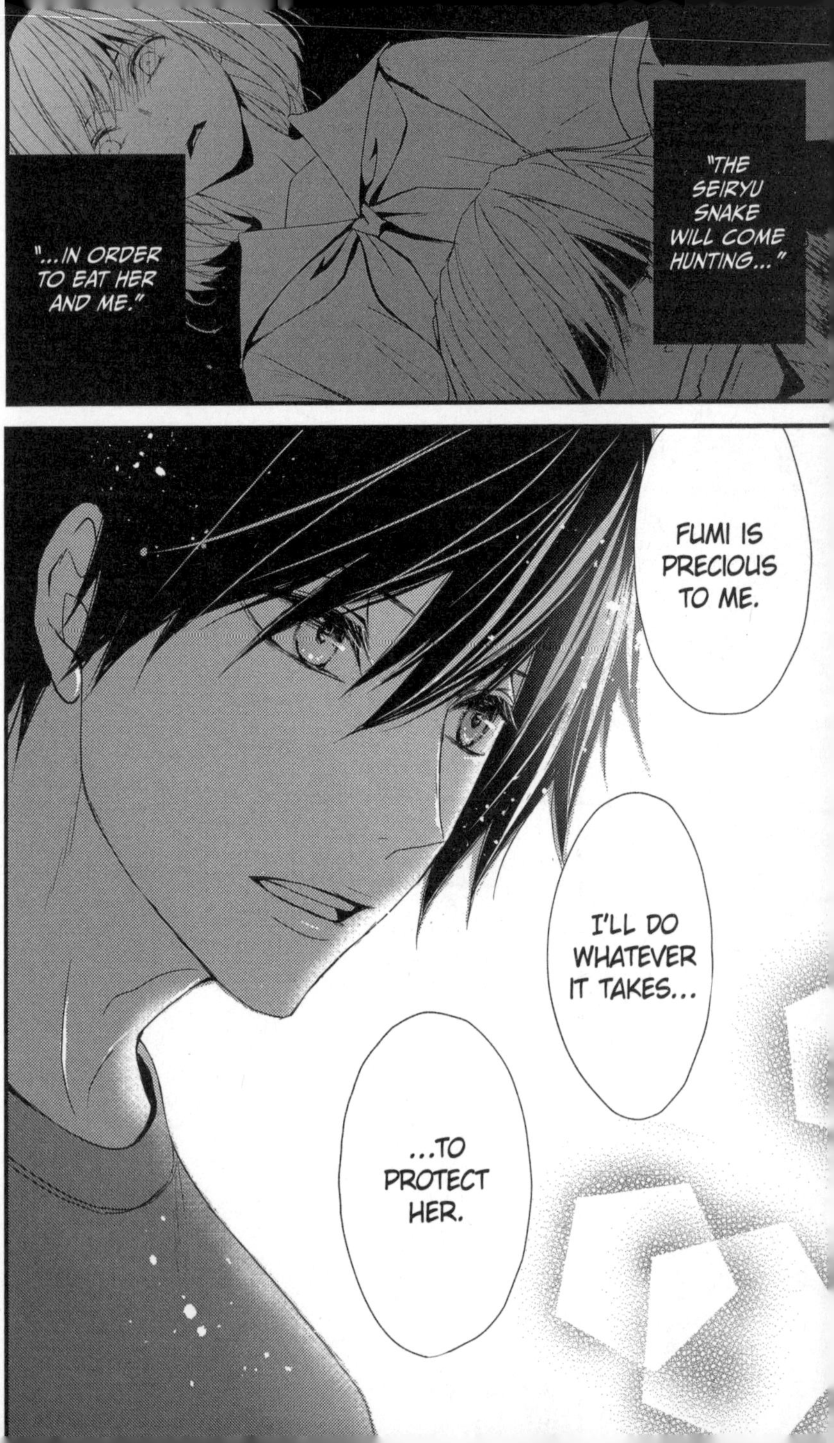
"THE SEIRYU SNAKE WILL COME HUNTING..."
"...IN ORDER TO EAT HER AND ME."
FUMI IS PRECIOUS TO ME.
I'LL DO WHATEVER IT TAKES...
...TO PROTECT HER.

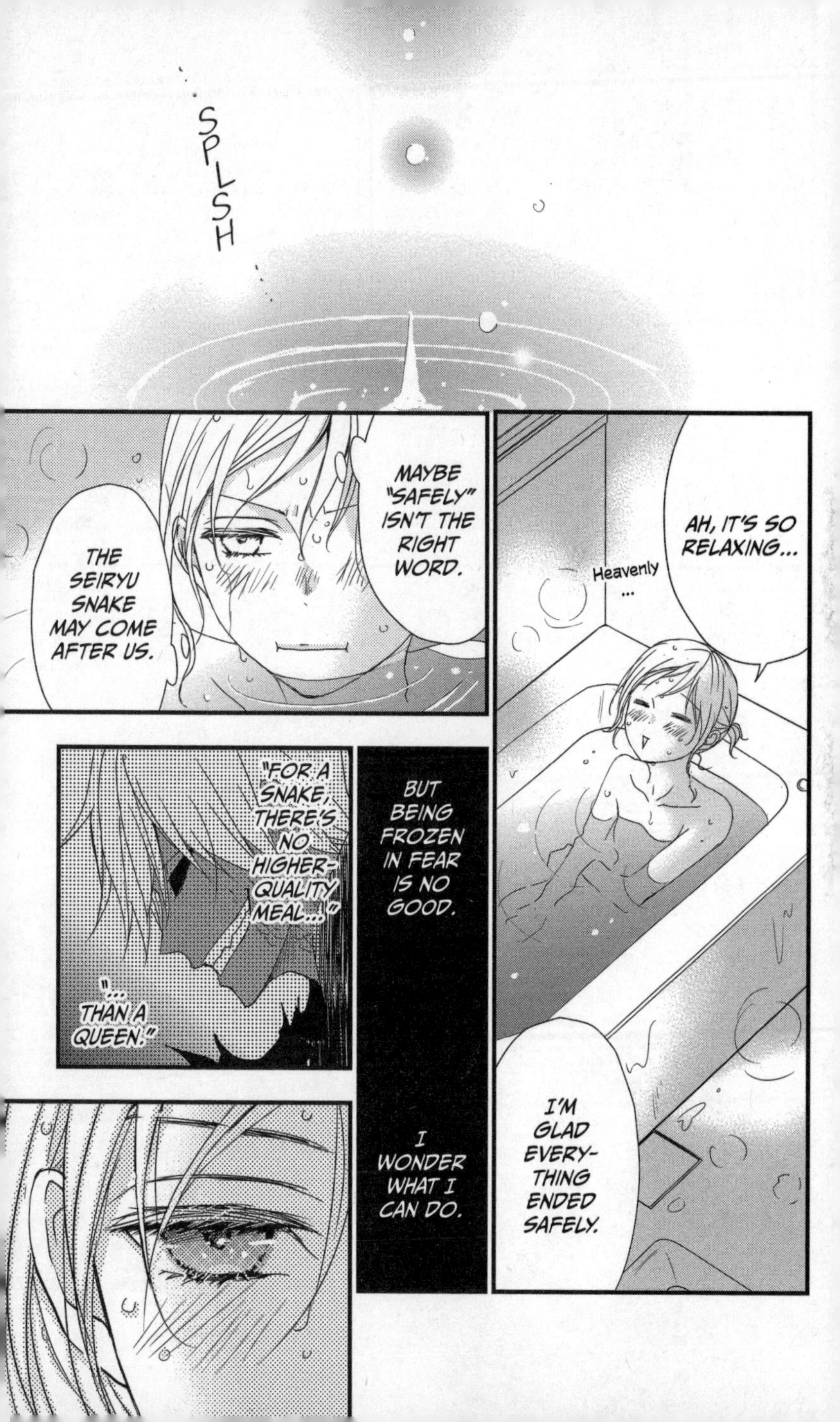
SPLSH
AH, IT'S SO RELAXING...
Heavenly ...
I'M GLAD EVERY-THING ENDED SAFELY.
MAYBE "SAFELY" ISN'T THE RIGHT WORD.
THE SEIRYU SNAKE MAY COME AFTER US.
BUT BEING FROZEN IN FEAR IS NO GOOD.
I WONDER WHAT I CAN DO.
"FOR A SNAKE, THERE'S NO HIGHER-QUALITY MEAL..."
"...THAN A QUEEN."

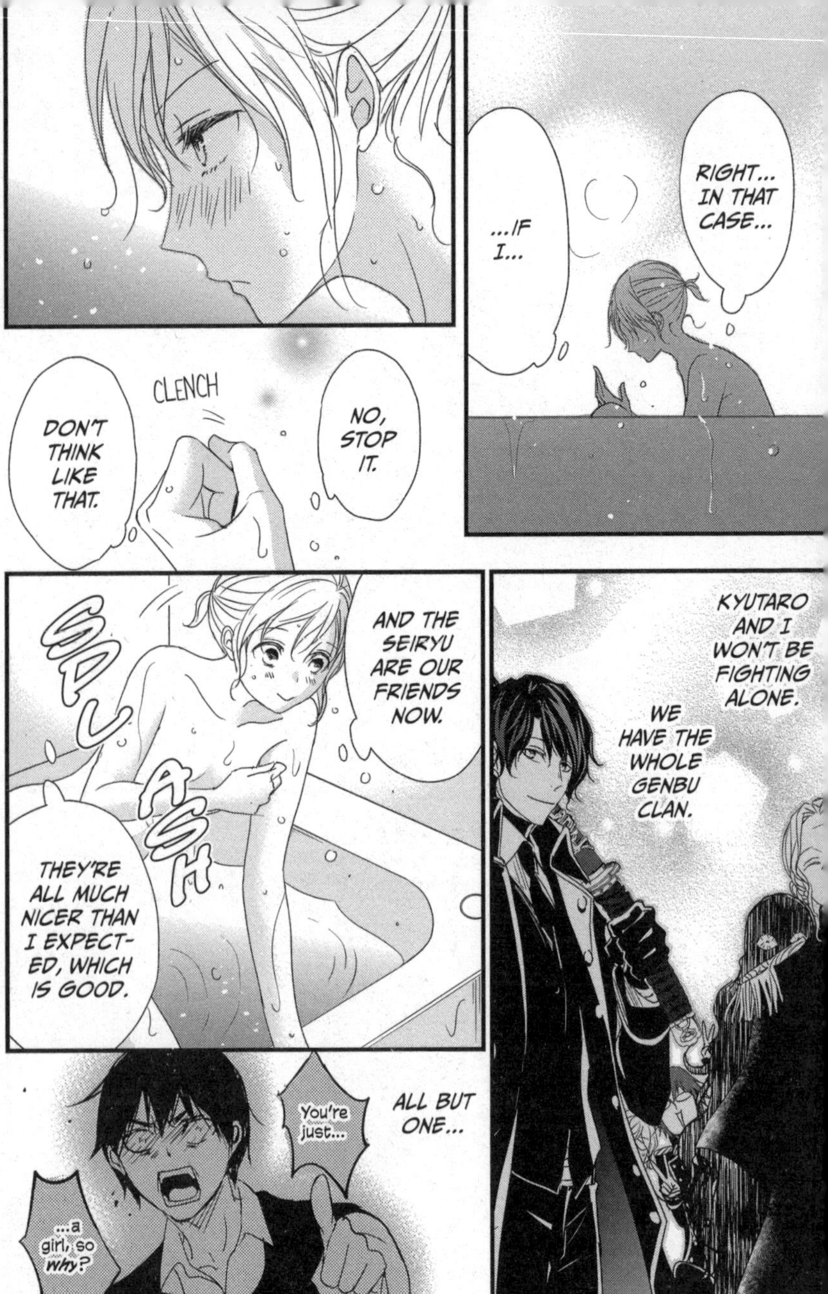
RIGHT... IN THAT CASE...
...IF I...
NO, STOP IT.
CLENCH
DON'T THINK LIKE THAT.
KYUTARO AND I WON'T BE FIGHTING ALONE.
WE HAVE THE WHOLE GENBU CLAN.
AND THE SEIRYU ARE OUR FRIENDS NOW.
SPLASH
THEY'RE ALL MUCH NICER THAN I EXPECT-ED, WHICH IS GOOD.
ALL BUT ONE...
You're just...
...a girl, so *why*?

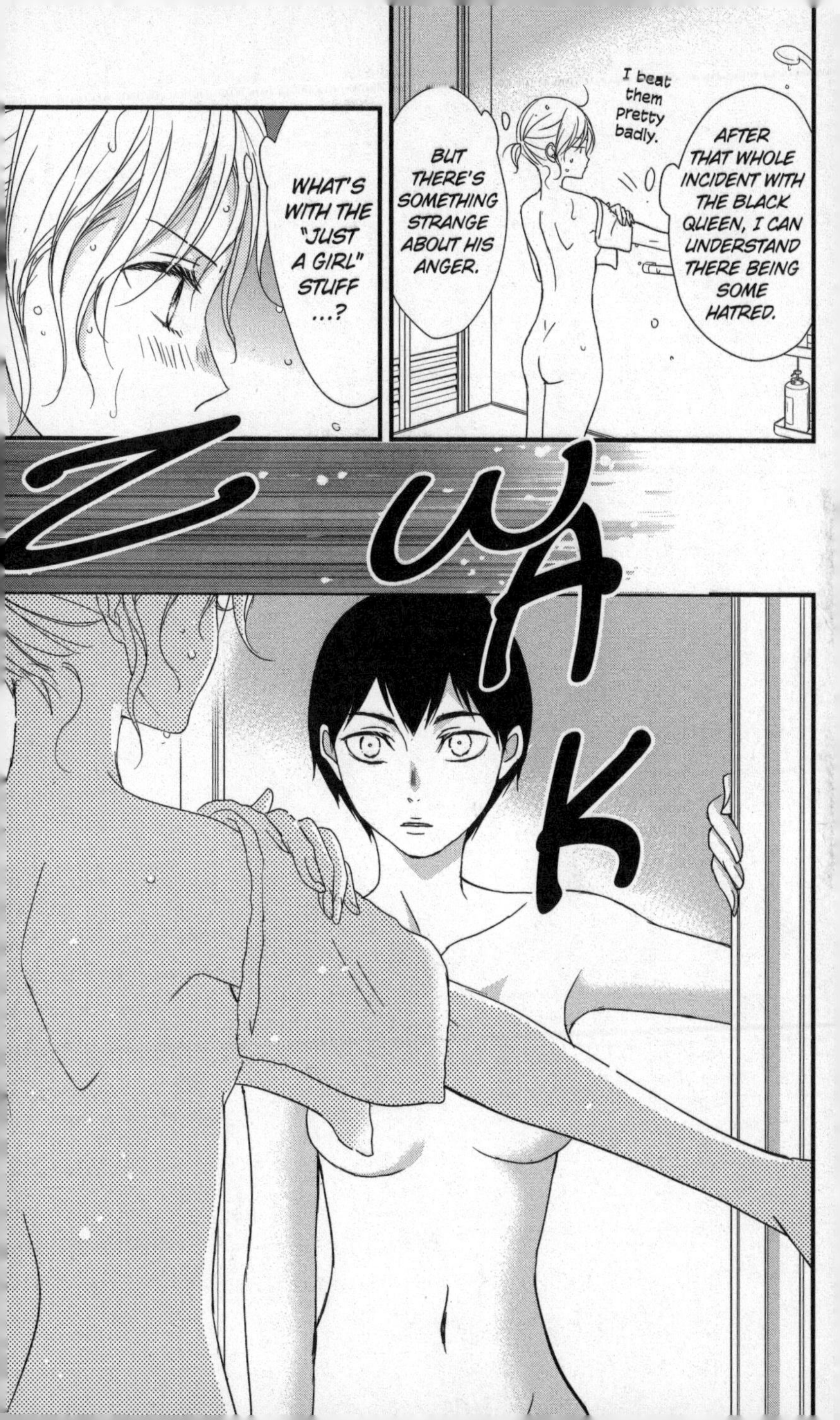
AFTER THAT WHOLE INCIDENT WITH THE BLACK QUEEN, I CAN UNDERSTAND THERE BEING SOME HATRED.
I beat them pretty badly.
BUT THERE'S SOMETHING STRANGE ABOUT HIS ANGER.
WHAT'S WITH THE "JUST A GIRL" STUFF ...?
ZWAK

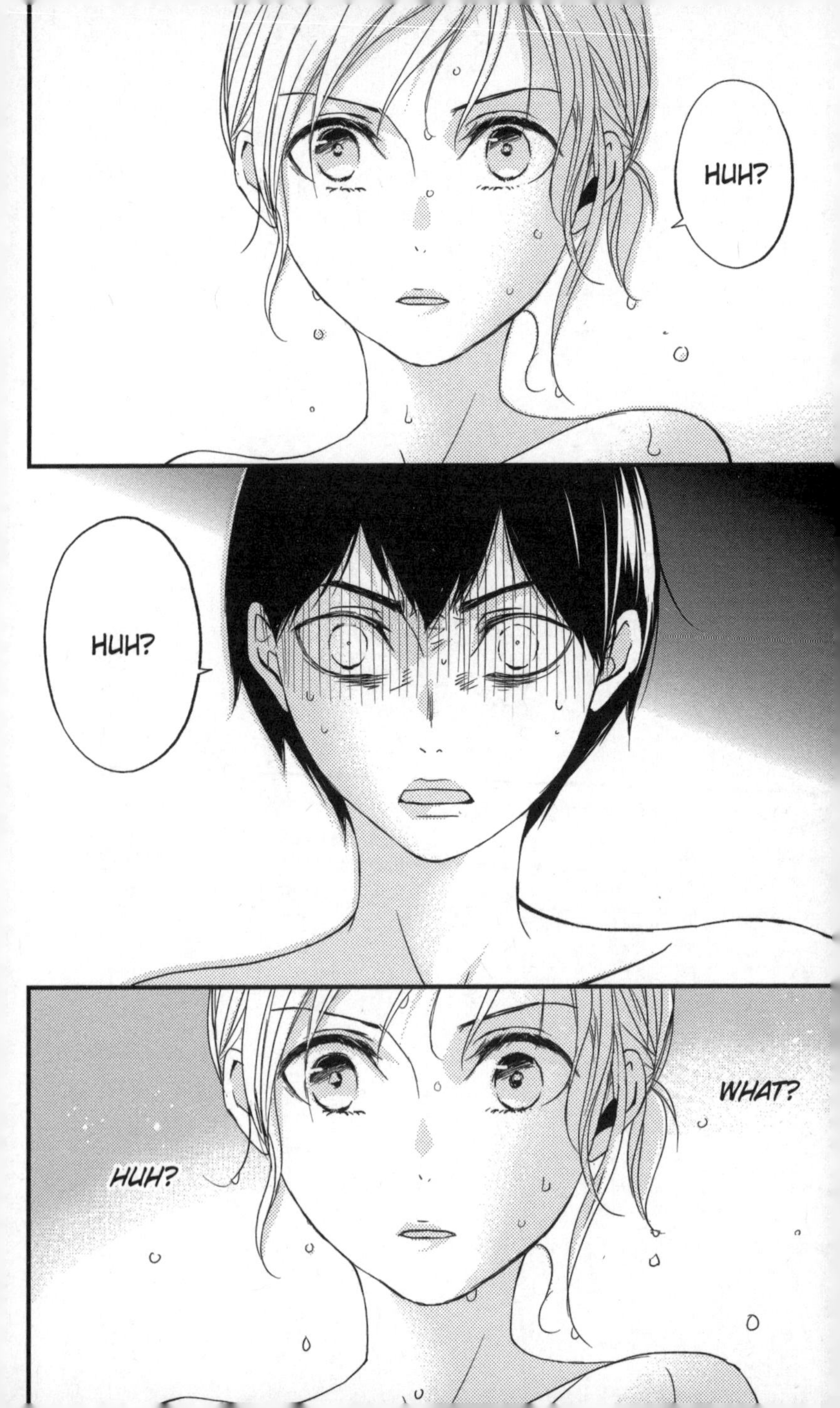
HUH?
HUH?
WHAT?
HUH?

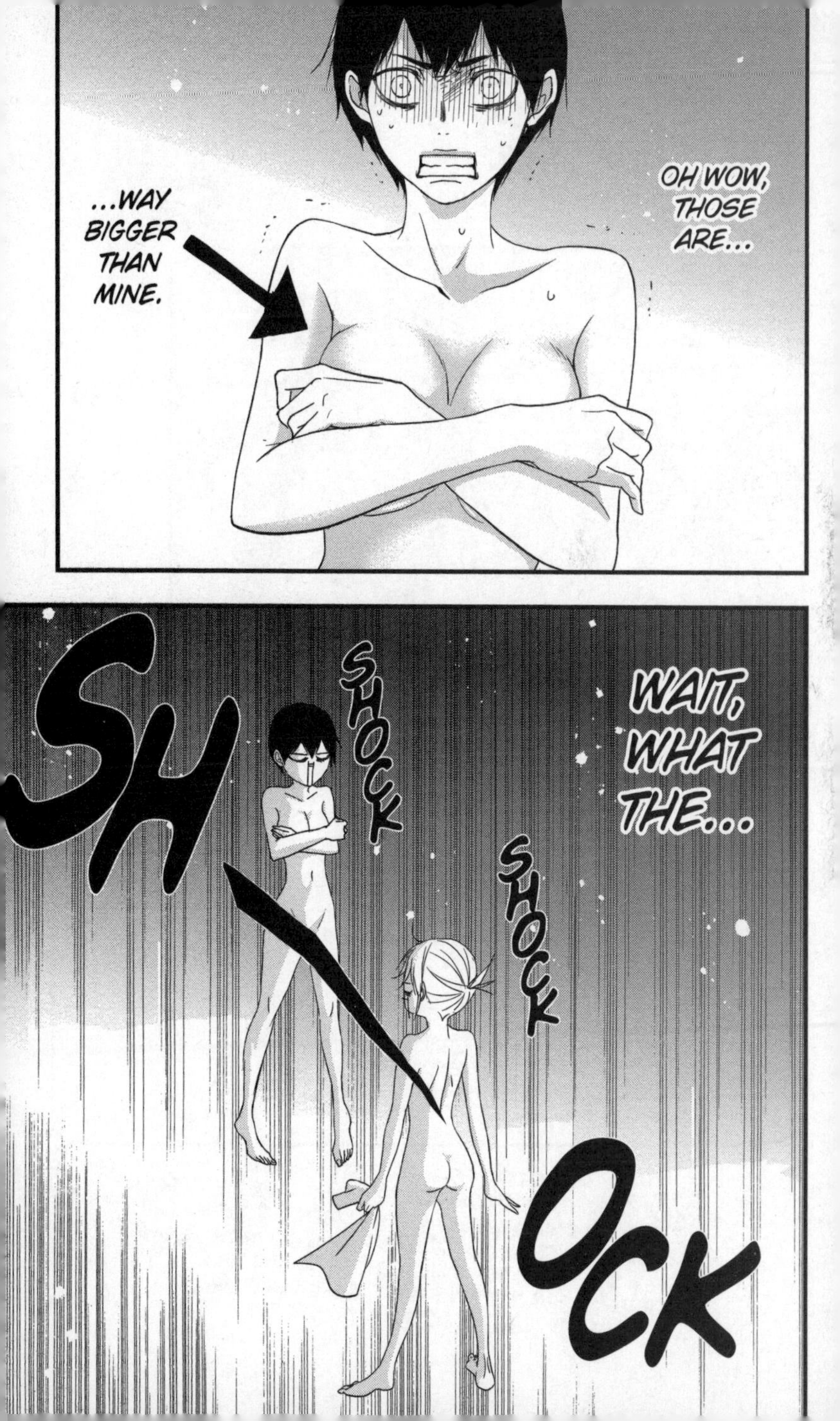
OH WOW, THOSE ARE...
...WAY BIGGER THAN MINE.
WAIT, WHAT THE...
SHOCK
SHOCK
SHOCK

MONTHLY BETSUCOMI SALE DATE NOTICE ON TWITTER

CHAPTER 52

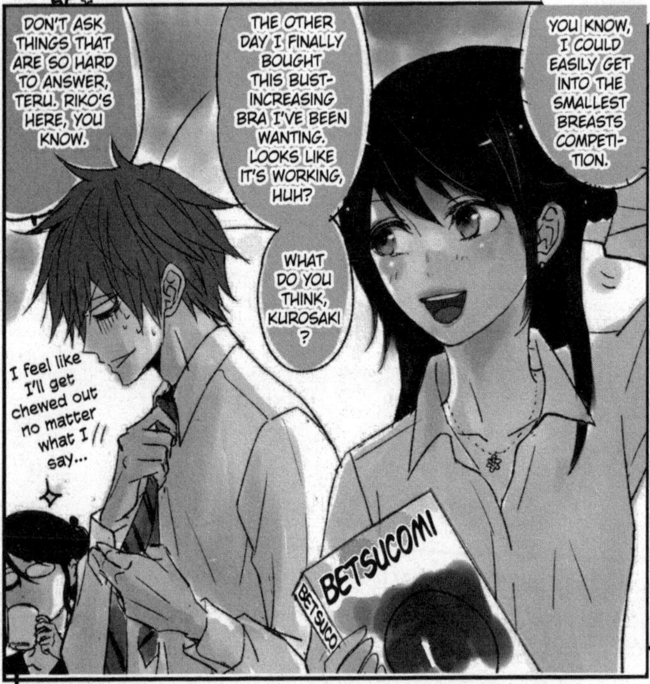

YOU KNOW, I COULD EASILY GET INTO THE SMALLEST BREASTS COMPETITION.
THE OTHER DAY I FINALLY BOUGHT THIS BUST-INCREASING BRA I'VE BEEN WANTING. LOOKS LIKE IT'S WORKING, HUH?
WHAT DO YOU THINK, KUROSAKI?
DON'T ASK THINGS THAT ARE SO HARD TO ANSWER, TERU. RIKO'S HERE, YOU KNOW.
I feel like I'll get chewed out no matter what I say...
BETSUCOMI
BETSUCO

LET'S SEE... WHAT'S UP IN *QUEEN'S QUALITY* THIS MONTH?

(1) BUCK-NAKED SHOWDOWN!
(2) IN THAT COMPETITION, THE TOP CONTENDERS WOULD BE HEROINES FROM MOTOMI'S MANGA.
(3) THE PIGGY MOSQUITO REPELLENT HOLDER IS GLARING.
THE EDITORIAL DEPARTMENT REFUSED TO LET ME SHOW THE GIRLS' NIPPLES. YOU CAN SEE HOW HARD I HAD TO WORK TO KEEP THEM COVERED IN CHAPTER 52!

FROM TIME TO TIME, I STILL LIKE TO DRAW CHARACTERS FROM *DENGEKI DAISY* FOR MY TWEETS. I GET A BIGGER REACTION THAN WHEN I DO *QUEEQUA* CHARACTERS. IT MAKES ME HAPPY THAT SO MANY PEOPLE SAY THEY STILL ENJOY THOSE CHARACTERS. THERE'S BEEN NOTHING SINCE THE BYAKKO ARC, BUT SOMEDAY, I HOPE TO DO A CROSSOVER AGAIN.

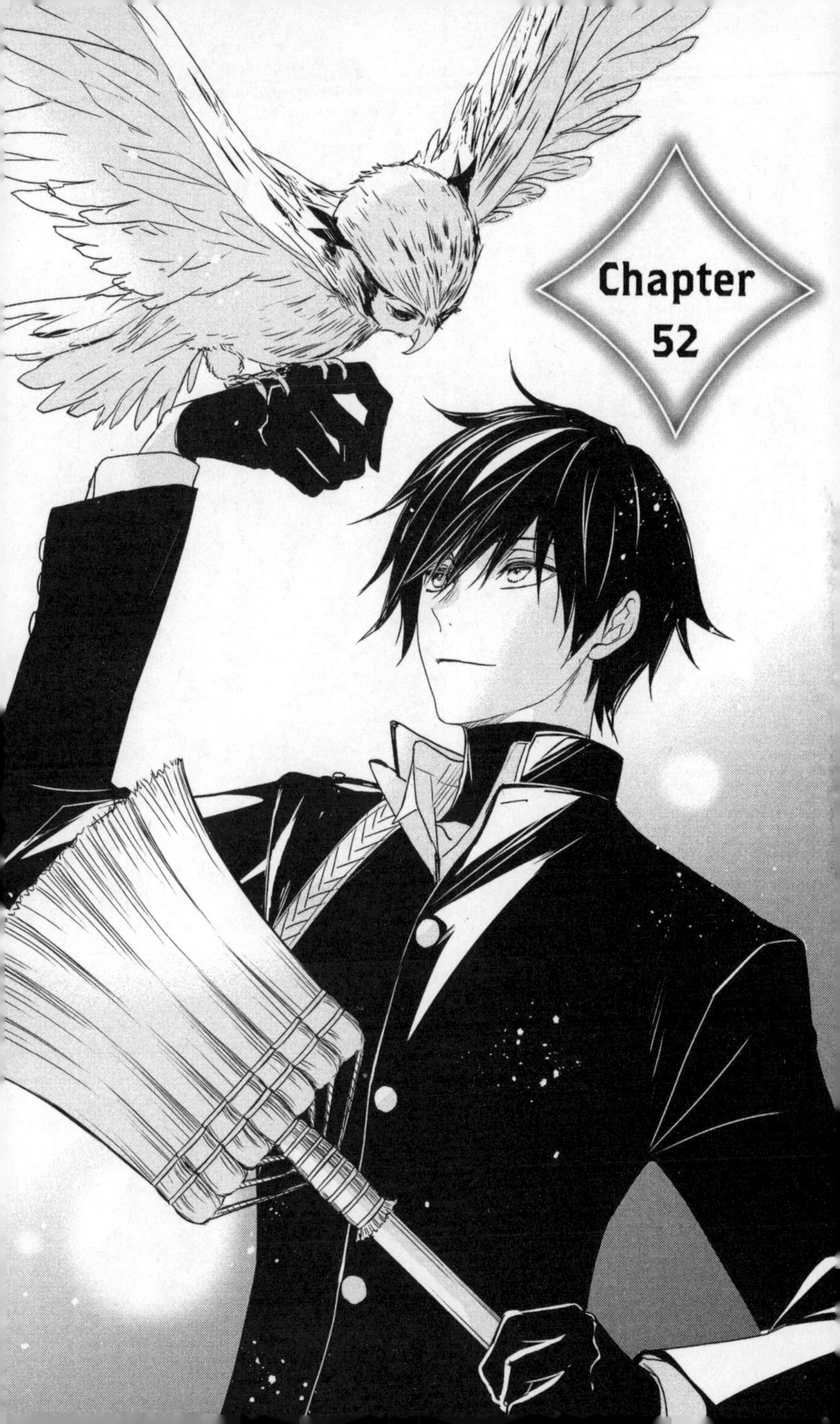
Chapter
52

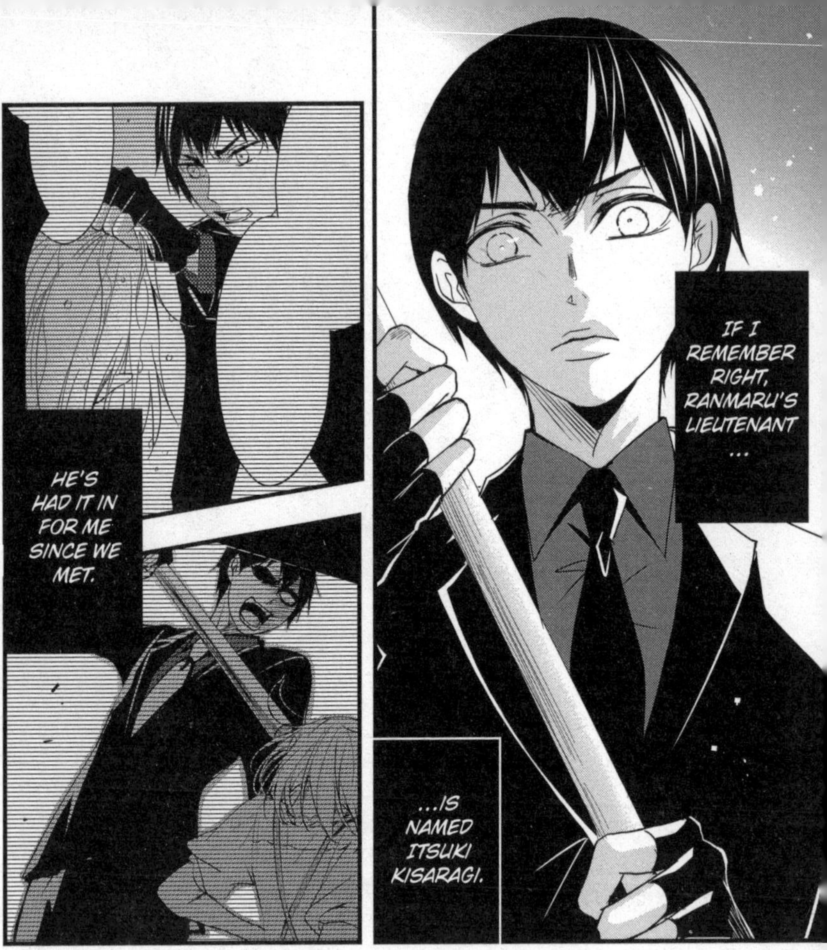
IF I REMEMBER RIGHT, RANMARU'S LIEUTENANT ...
...IS NAMED ITSUKI KISARAGI.
HE'S HAD IT IN FOR ME SINCE WE MET.

And so... Ever since volume 3, there've been hints that Itsuki is actually a girl, but it finally became clear. I think many people might have guessed from the shape of her body. I think she usually binds her breasts, but I wonder if she could really hide such huge boobs. If you've had any experience in this area, please let me know.

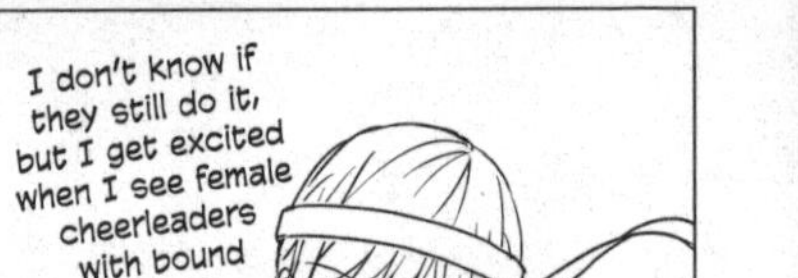
I don't know if they still do it, but I get excited when I see female cheerleaders with bound breasts.

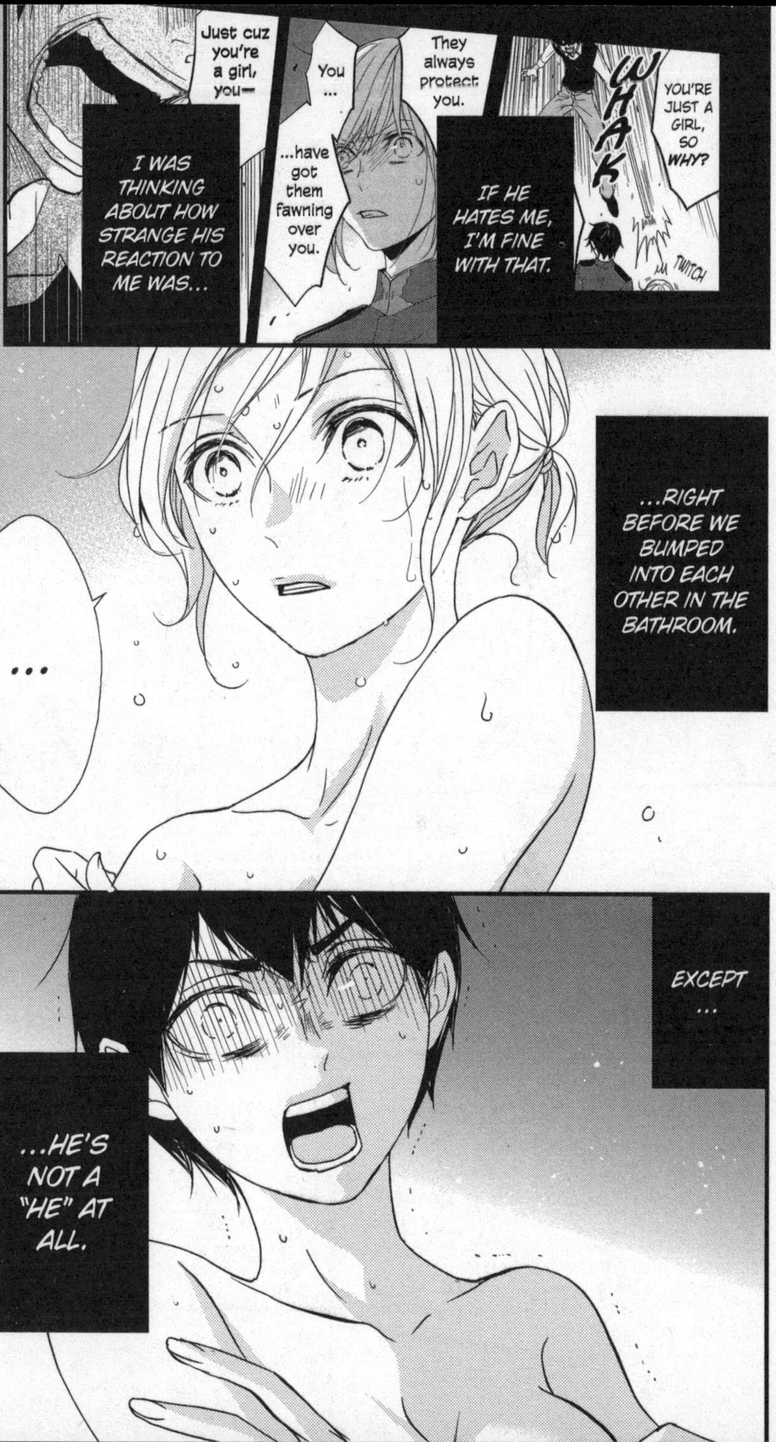
WHAK
YOU'RE JUST A GIRL, SO WHY?
TWITCH
IF HE HATES ME, I'M FINE WITH THAT.
They always protect you.
You ...
...have got them fawning over you.
Just cuz you're a girl, you—
I WAS THINKING ABOUT HOW STRANGE HIS REACTION TO ME WAS...
...RIGHT BEFORE WE BUMPED INTO EACH OTHER IN THE BATHROOM.
...
EXCEPT ...
...HE'S NOT A "HE" AT ALL.

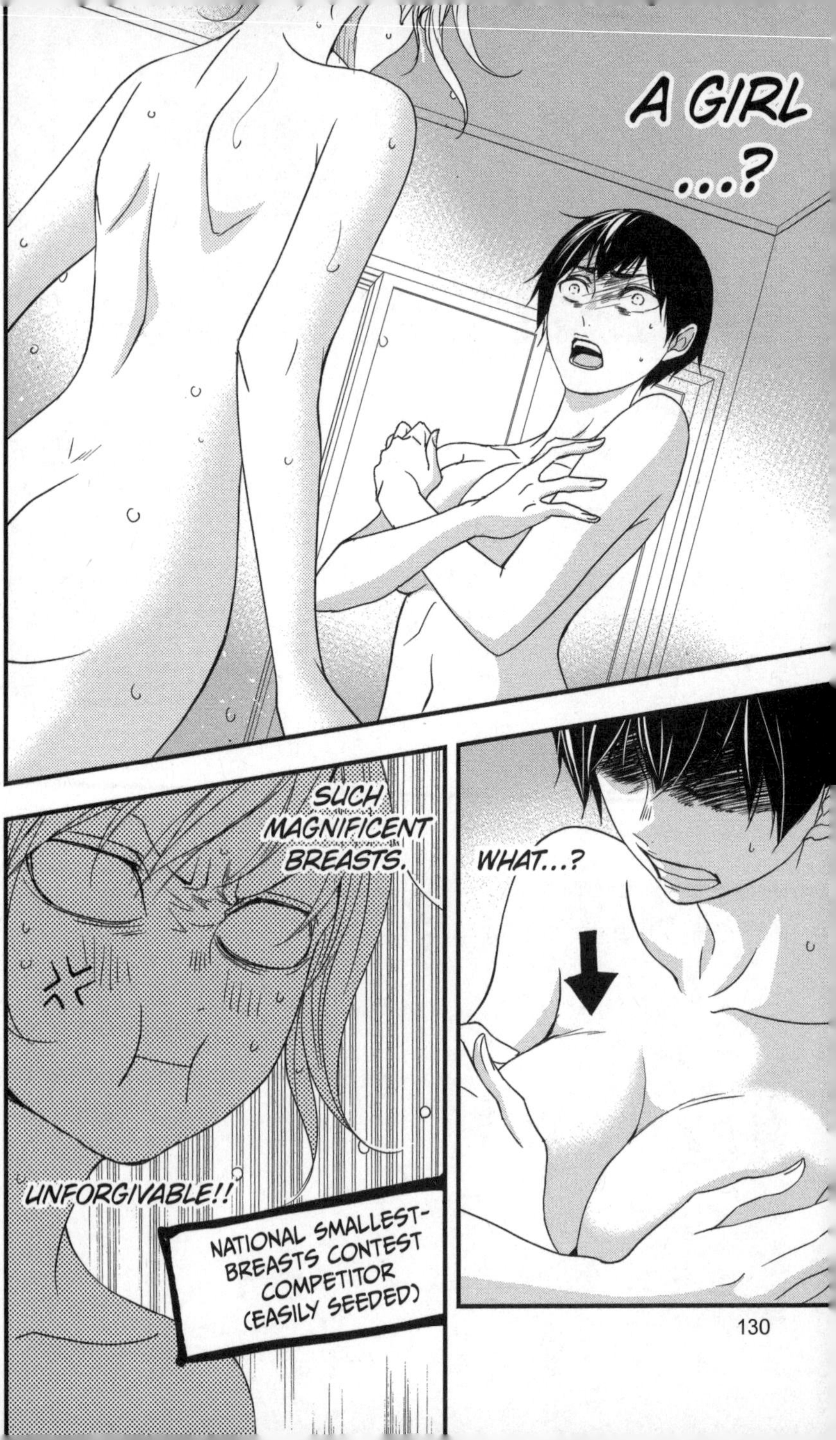
A GIRL ...?
WHAT...?
SUCH MAGNIFICENT BREASTS.
UNFORGIVABLE!!
NATIONAL SMALLEST-BREASTS CONTEST COMPETITOR (EASILY SEEDED)

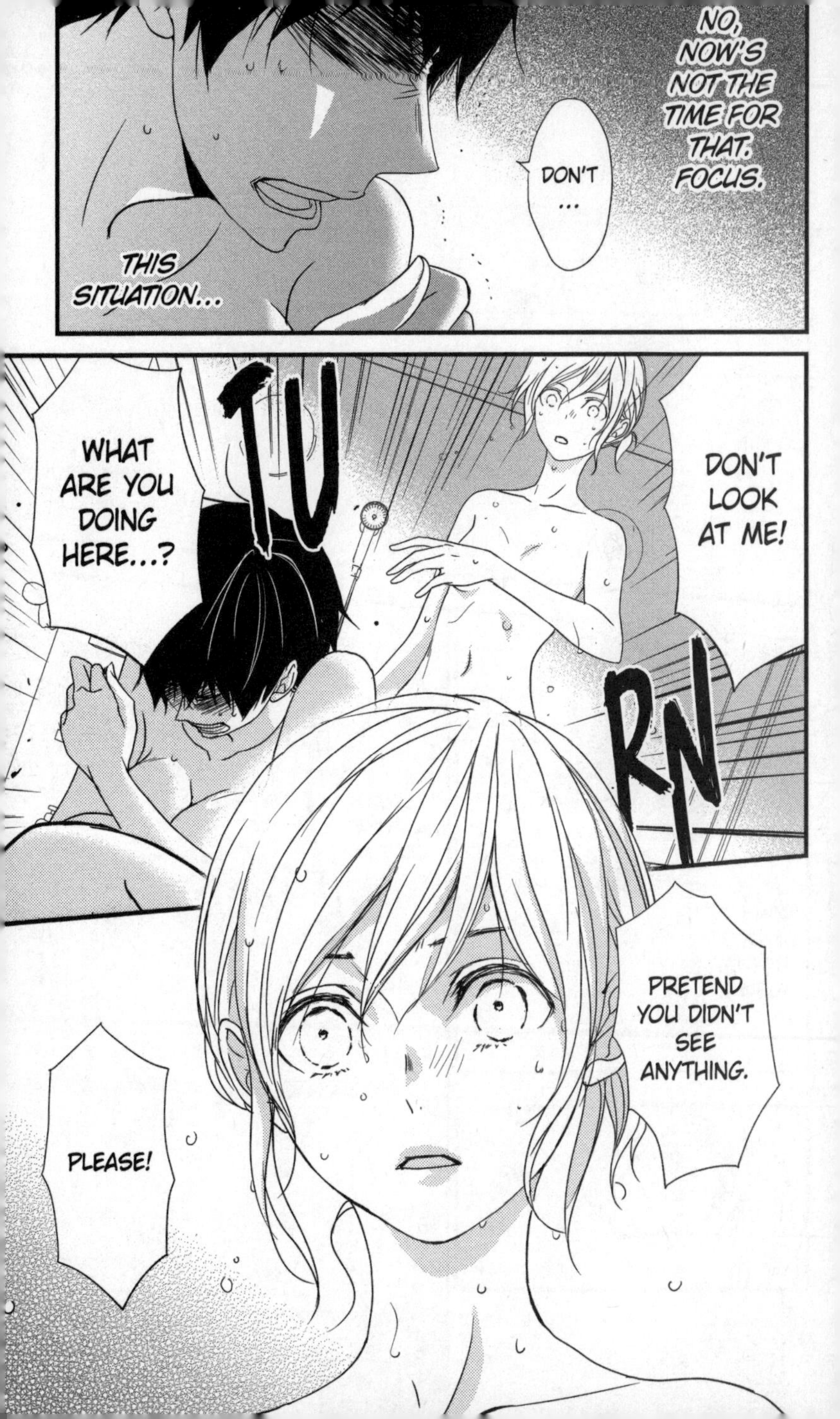
NO, NOW'S NOT THE TIME FOR THAT. FOCUS.
DON'T ...
THIS SITUATION...
DON'T LOOK AT ME!
TURN
WHAT ARE YOU DOING HERE...?
PRETEND YOU DIDN'T SEE ANYTHING.
PLEASE!

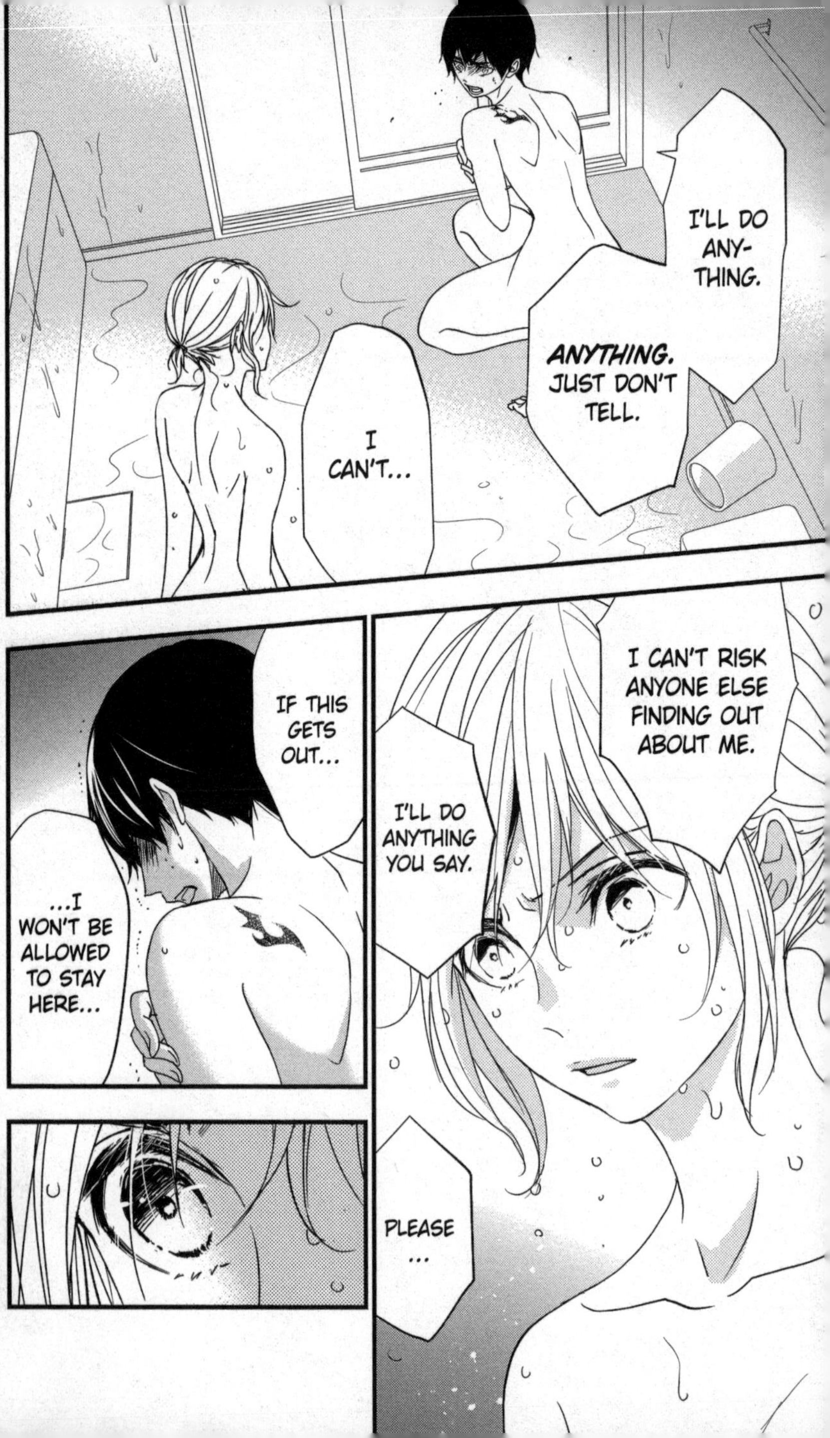
I'LL DO ANY-THING.
ANYTHING. JUST DON'T TELL.
I CAN'T...
I CAN'T RISK ANYONE ELSE FINDING OUT ABOUT ME.
I'LL DO ANYTHING YOU SAY.
PLEASE ...
IF THIS GETS OUT...
...I WON'T BE ALLOWED TO STAY HERE...

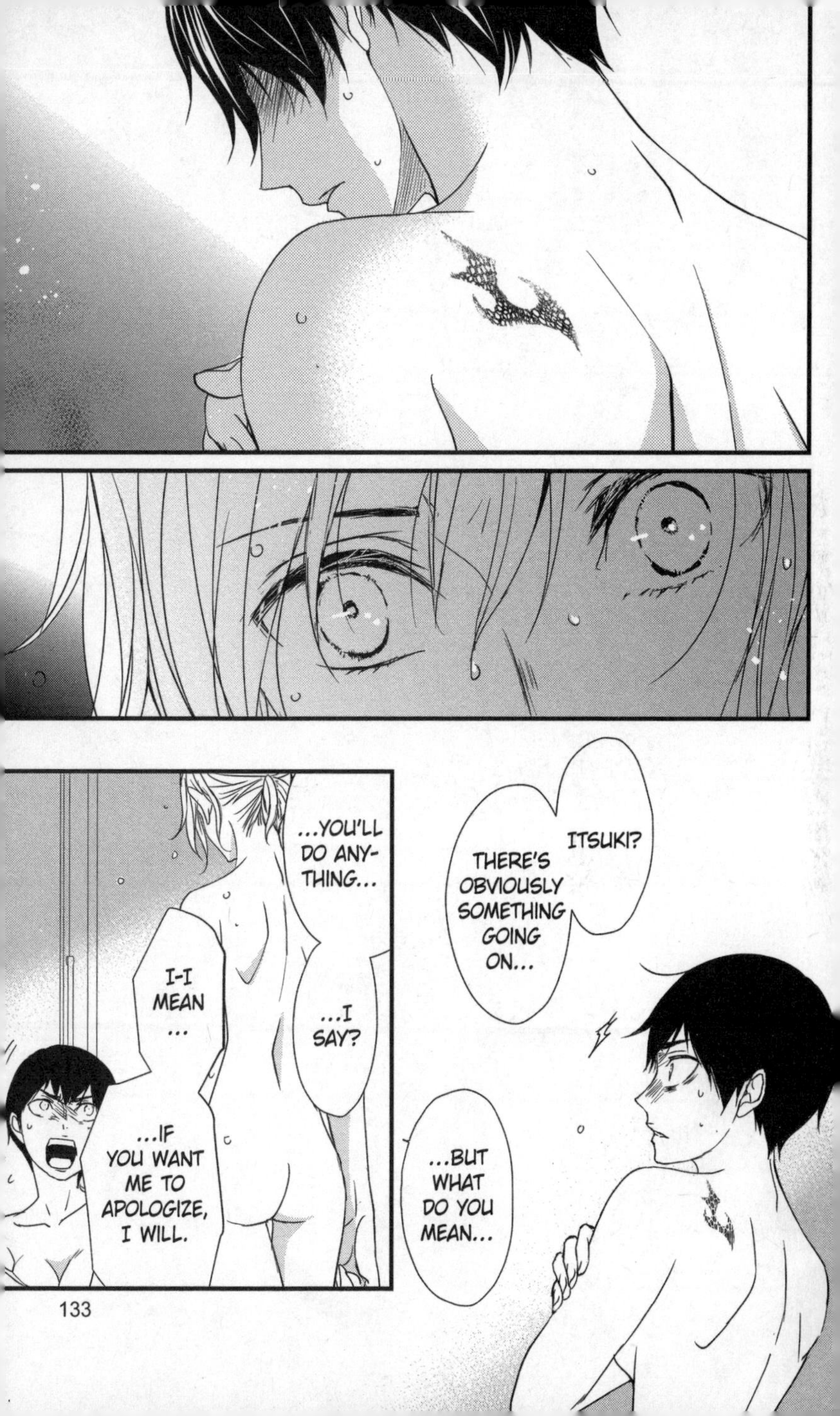
ITSUKI?
THERE'S OBVIOUSLY SOMETHING GOING ON...
...BUT WHAT DO YOU MEAN...
...YOU'LL DO ANYTHING...
...I SAY?
I-I MEAN...
...IF YOU WANT ME TO APOLOGIZE, I WILL.

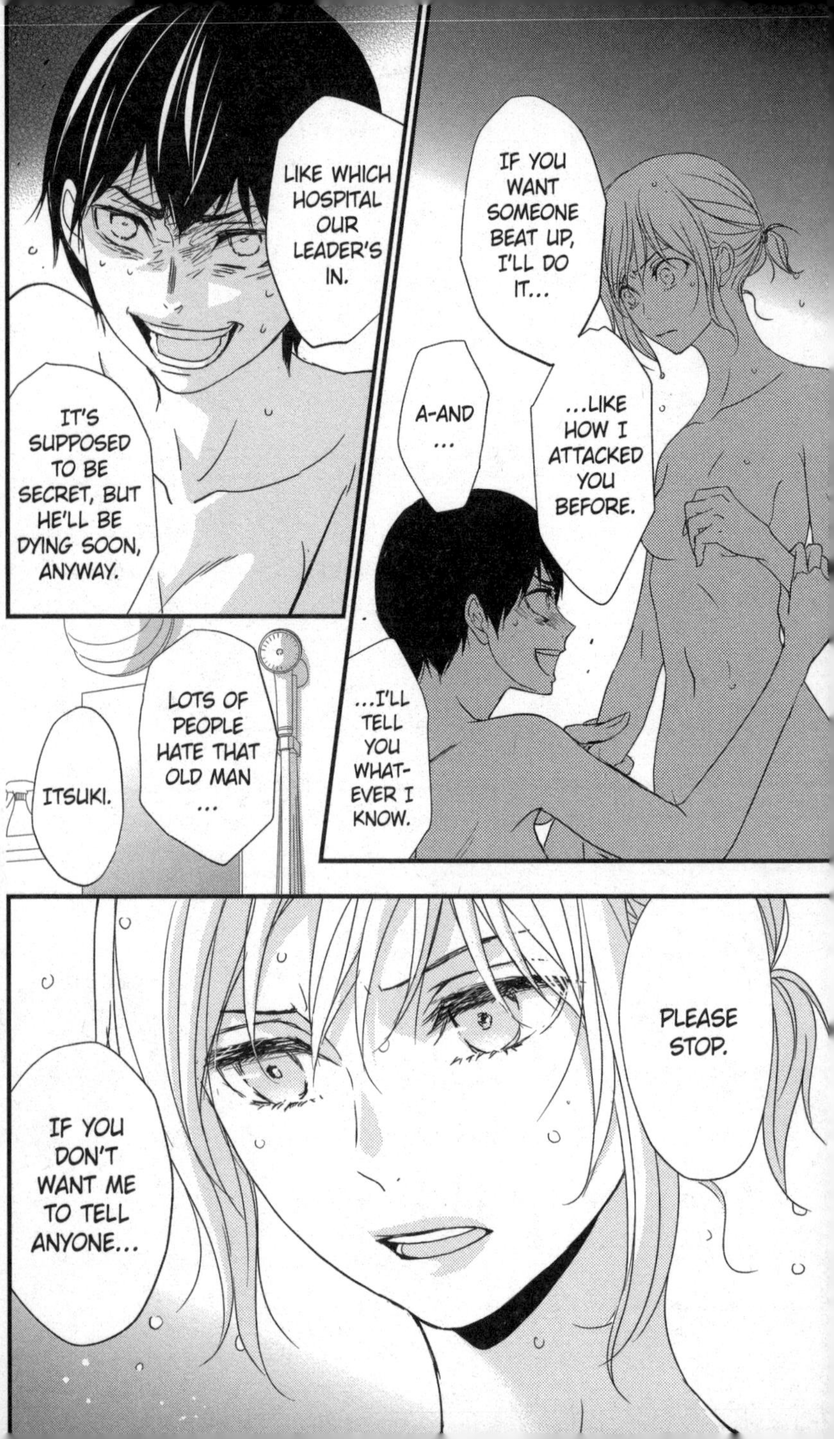
IF YOU WANT SOMEONE BEAT UP, I'LL DO IT...
...LIKE HOW I ATTACKED YOU BEFORE.
A-AND ...
...I'LL TELL YOU WHAT-EVER I KNOW.
LIKE WHICH HOSPITAL OUR LEADER'S IN.
IT'S SUPPOSED TO BE SECRET, BUT HE'LL BE DYING SOON, ANYWAY.
LOTS OF PEOPLE HATE THAT OLD MAN ...
ITSUKI.
PLEASE STOP.
IF YOU DON'T WANT ME TO TELL ANYONE...

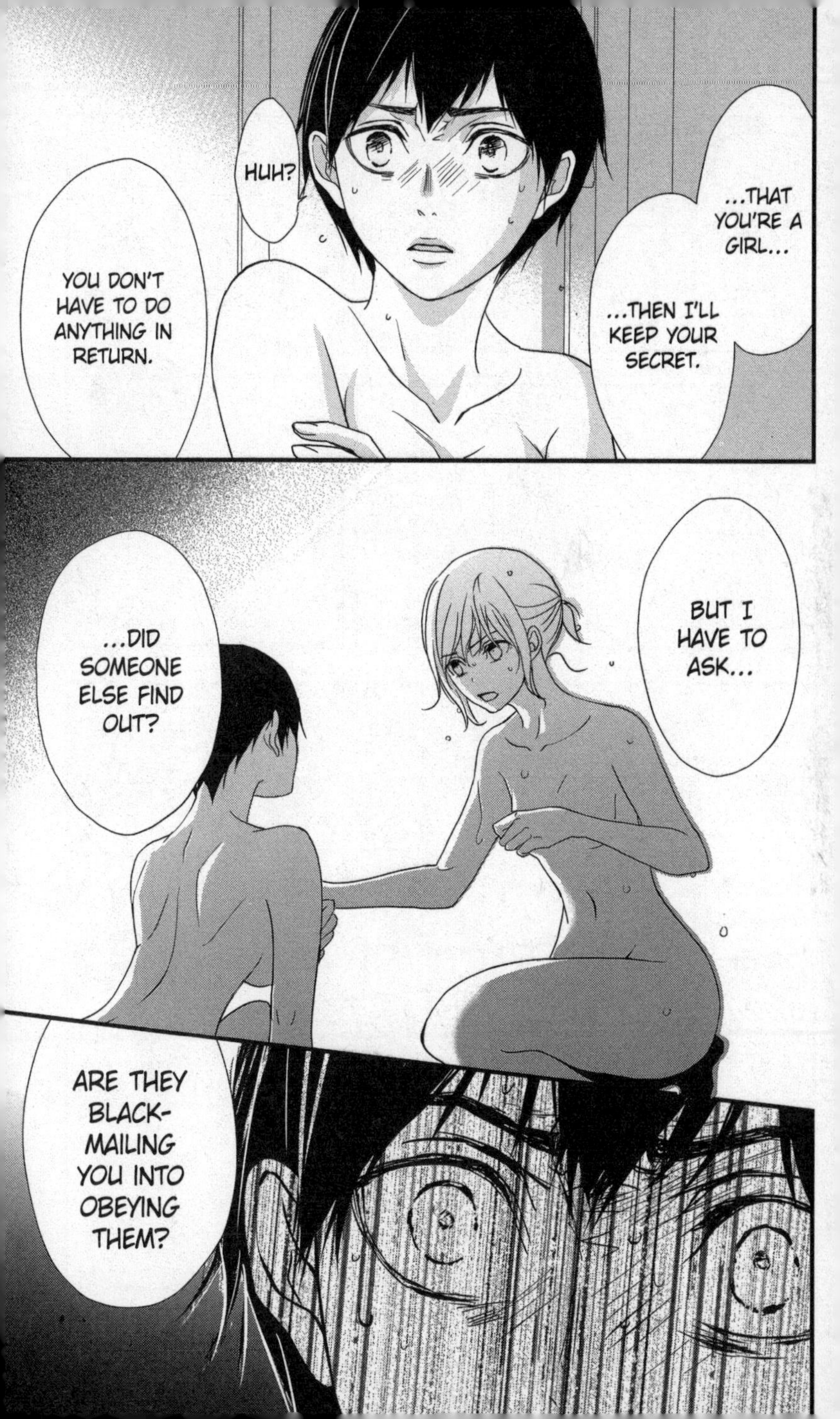
...THAT YOU'RE A GIRL...
...THEN I'LL KEEP YOUR SECRET.
HUH?
YOU DON'T HAVE TO DO ANYTHING IN RETURN.
BUT I HAVE TO ASK...
...DID SOMEONE ELSE FIND OUT?
ARE THEY BLACK-MAILING YOU INTO OBEYING THEM?

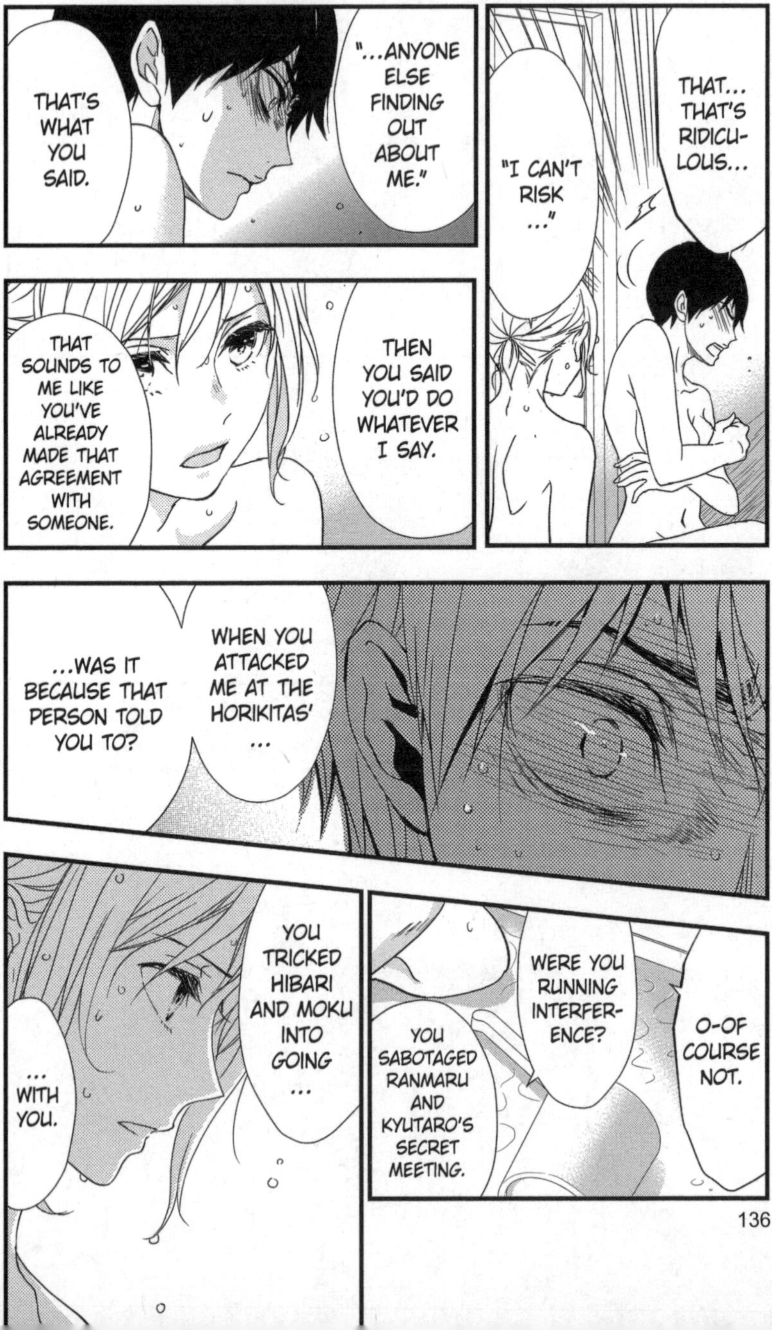
THAT... THAT'S RIDICU-LOUS...
"I CAN'T RISK ..."
"...ANYONE ELSE FINDING OUT ABOUT ME."
THAT'S WHAT YOU SAID.
THEN YOU SAID YOU'D DO WHATEVER I SAY.
THAT SOUNDS TO ME LIKE YOU'VE ALREADY MADE THAT AGREEMENT WITH SOMEONE.
WHEN YOU ATTACKED ME AT THE HORIKITAS' ...
...WAS IT BECAUSE THAT PERSON TOLD YOU TO?
O-OF COURSE NOT.
WERE YOU RUNNING INTERFER-ENCE?
YOU SABOTAGED RANMARU AND KYUTARO'S SECRET MEETING.
YOU TRICKED HIBARI AND MOKU INTO GOING ...
... WITH YOU.

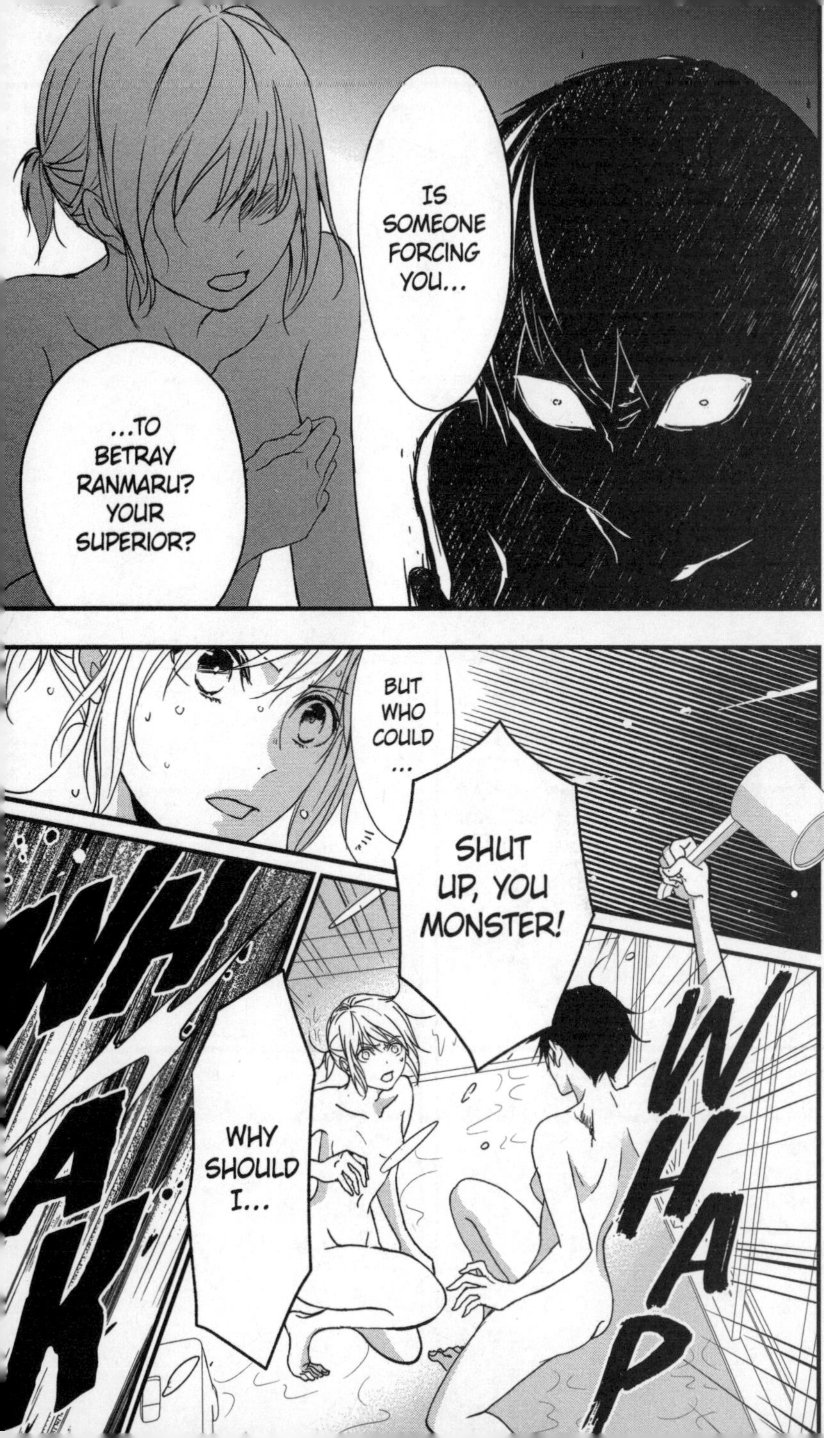
IS SOMEONE FORCING YOU...
...TO BETRAY RANMARU? YOUR SUPERIOR?
BUT WHO COULD ...
SHUT UP, YOU MONSTER!
WHAP
WHY SHOULD I...
WHAK

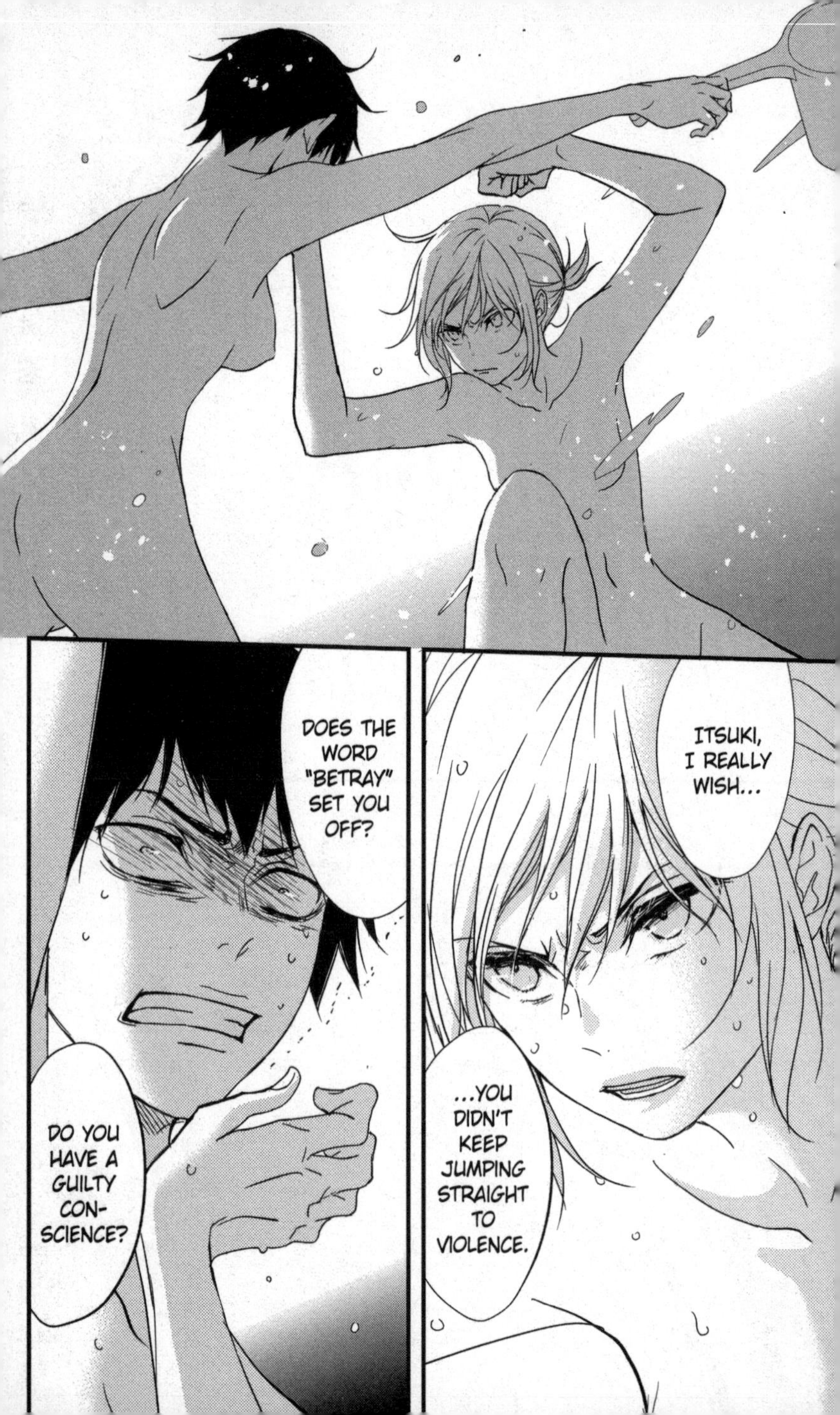
ITSUKI, I REALLY WISH...
...YOU DIDN'T KEEP JUMPING STRAIGHT TO VIOLENCE.
DOES THE WORD "BETRAY" SET YOU OFF?
DO YOU HAVE A GUILTY CON-SCIENCE?

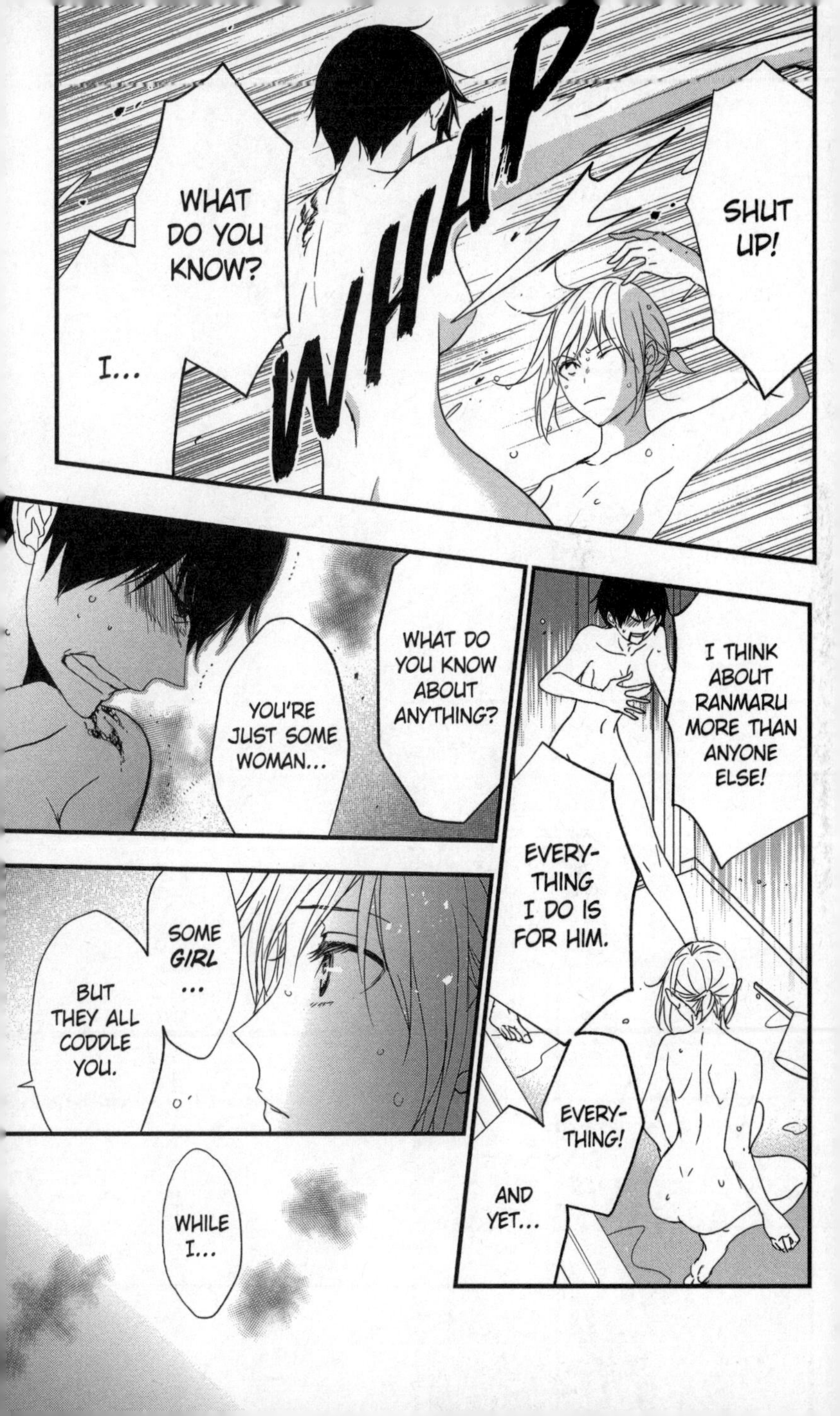
SHUT UP!
WHAP
WHAT DO YOU KNOW?
I...
I THINK ABOUT RANMARU MORE THAN ANYONE ELSE!
EVERYTHING I DO IS FOR HIM.
EVERYTHING!
AND YET...
WHAT DO YOU KNOW ABOUT ANYTHING?
YOU'RE JUST SOME WOMAN...
SOME GIRL...
BUT THEY ALL CODDLE YOU.
WHILE I...

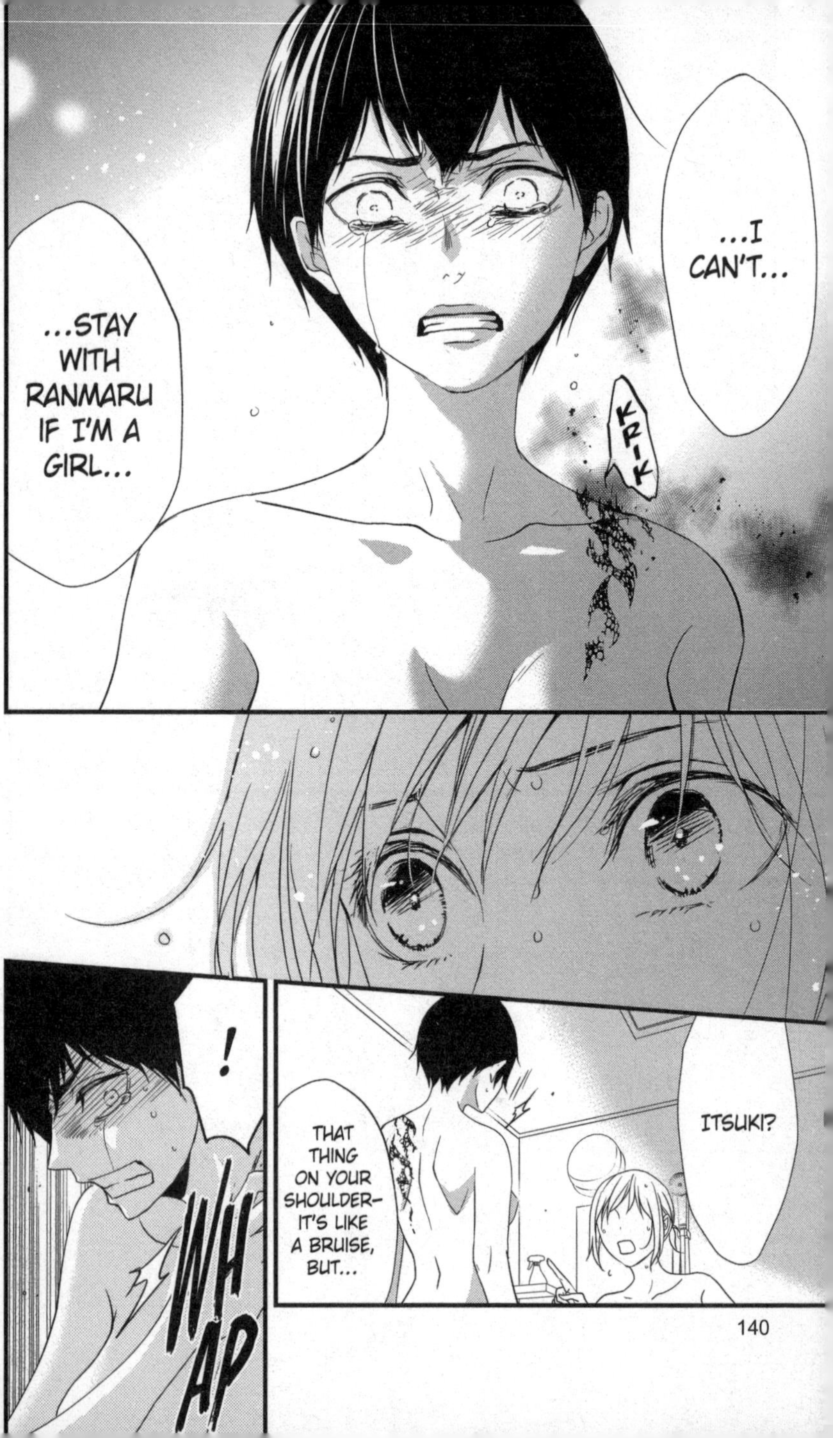
...I CAN'T...
KRIK
...STAY WITH RANMARU IF I'M A GIRL...
ITSUKI?
THAT THING ON YOUR SHOULDER- IT'S LIKE A BRUISE, BUT...
!
WHAP

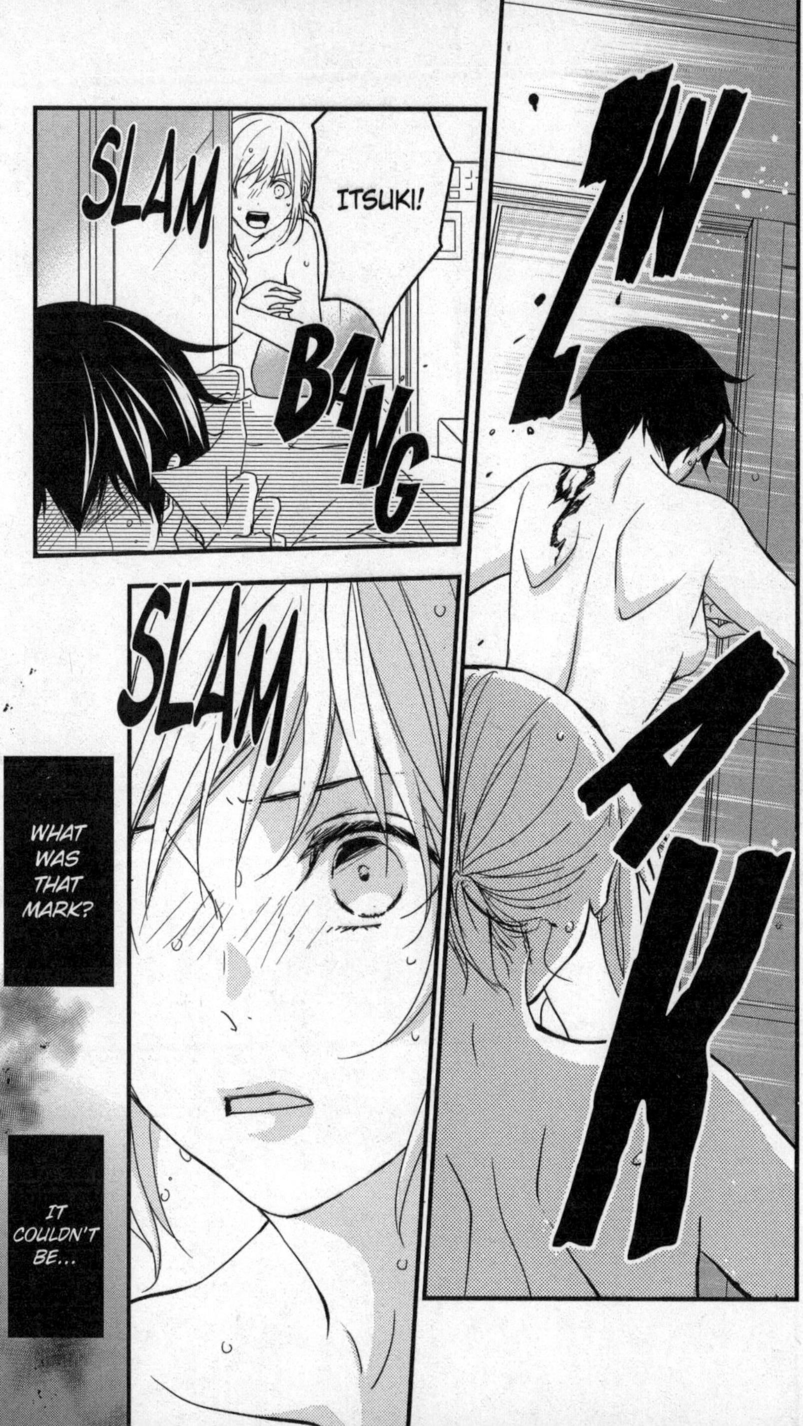
ZWAK
ITSUKI!
BANG
SLAM
SLAM
WHAT WAS THAT MARK?
IT COULDN'T BE...

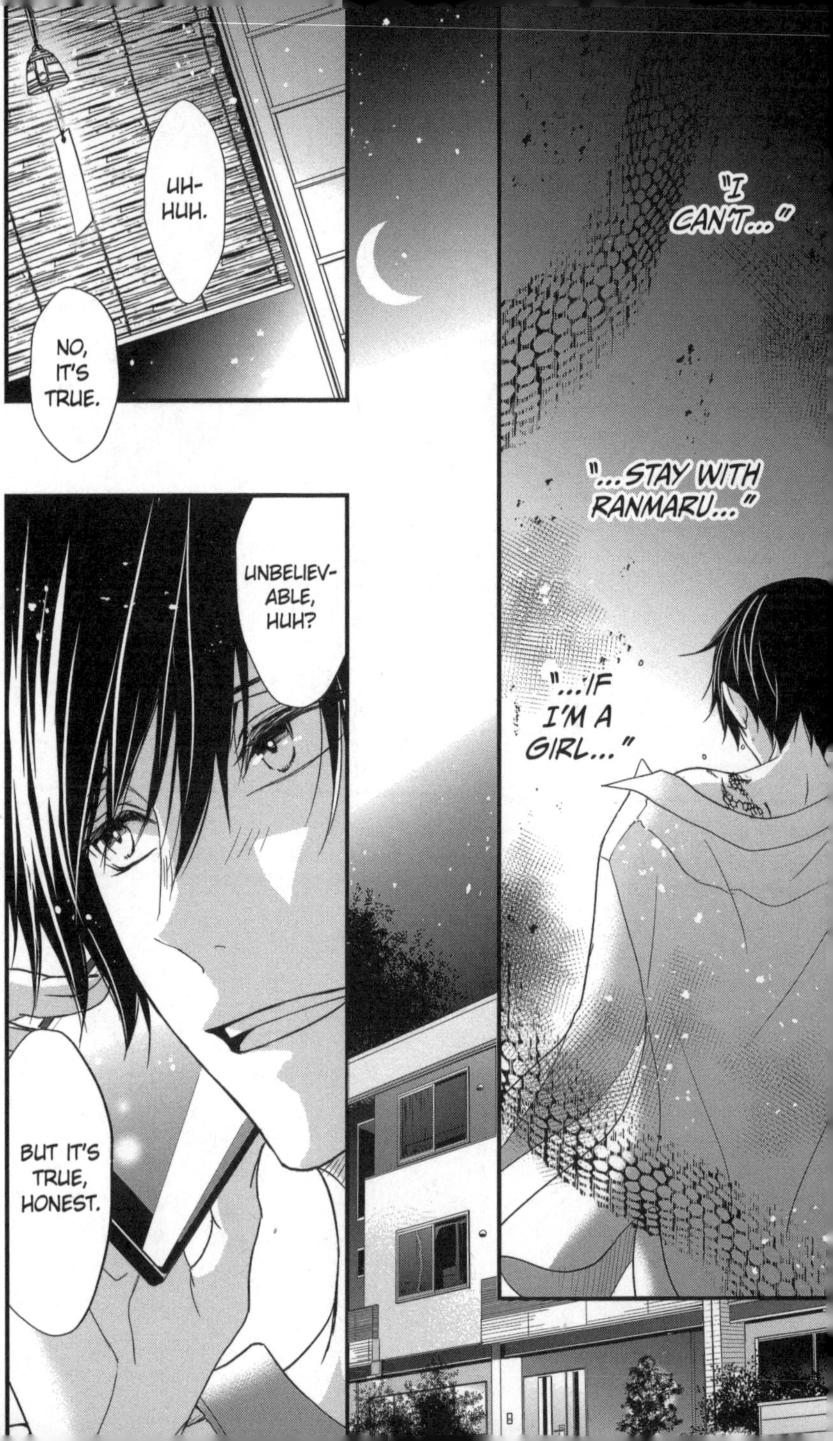
"I CAN'T..."
"...STAY WITH RANMARU..."
"...IF I'M A GIRL..."
UH-HUH.
NO, IT'S TRUE.
UNBELIEV-ABLE, HUH?
BUT IT'S TRUE, HONEST.

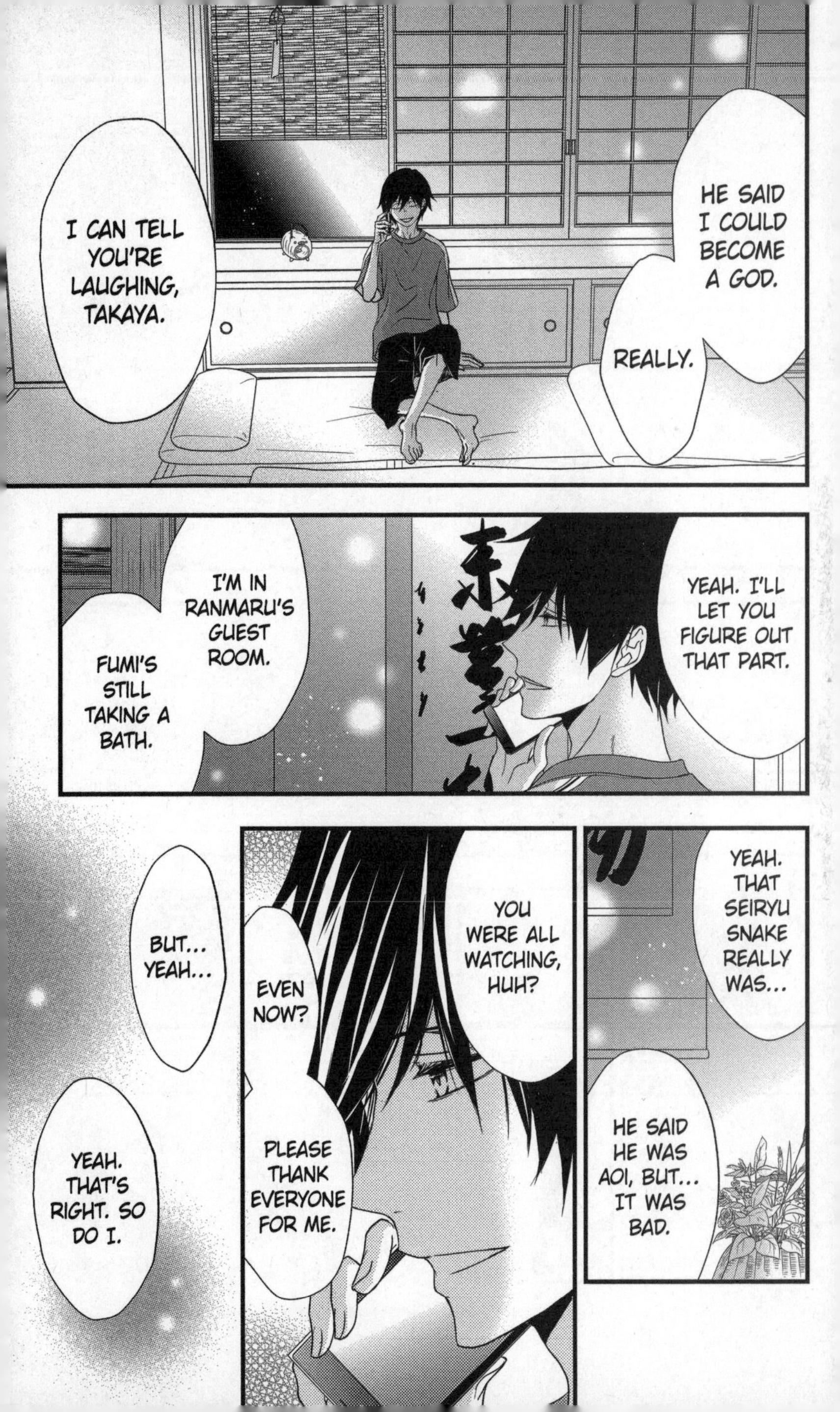
HE SAID I COULD BECOME A GOD.
REALLY.
I CAN TELL YOU'RE LAUGHING, TAKAYA.
YEAH. I'LL LET YOU FIGURE OUT THAT PART.
I'M IN RANMARU'S GUEST ROOM.
FUMI'S STILL TAKING A BATH.
YEAH. THAT SEIRYU SNAKE REALLY WAS...
HE SAID HE WAS AOI, BUT... IT WAS BAD.
YOU WERE ALL WATCHING, HUH?
EVEN NOW?
PLEASE THANK EVERYONE FOR ME.
BUT... YEAH...
YEAH. THAT'S RIGHT. SO DO I.

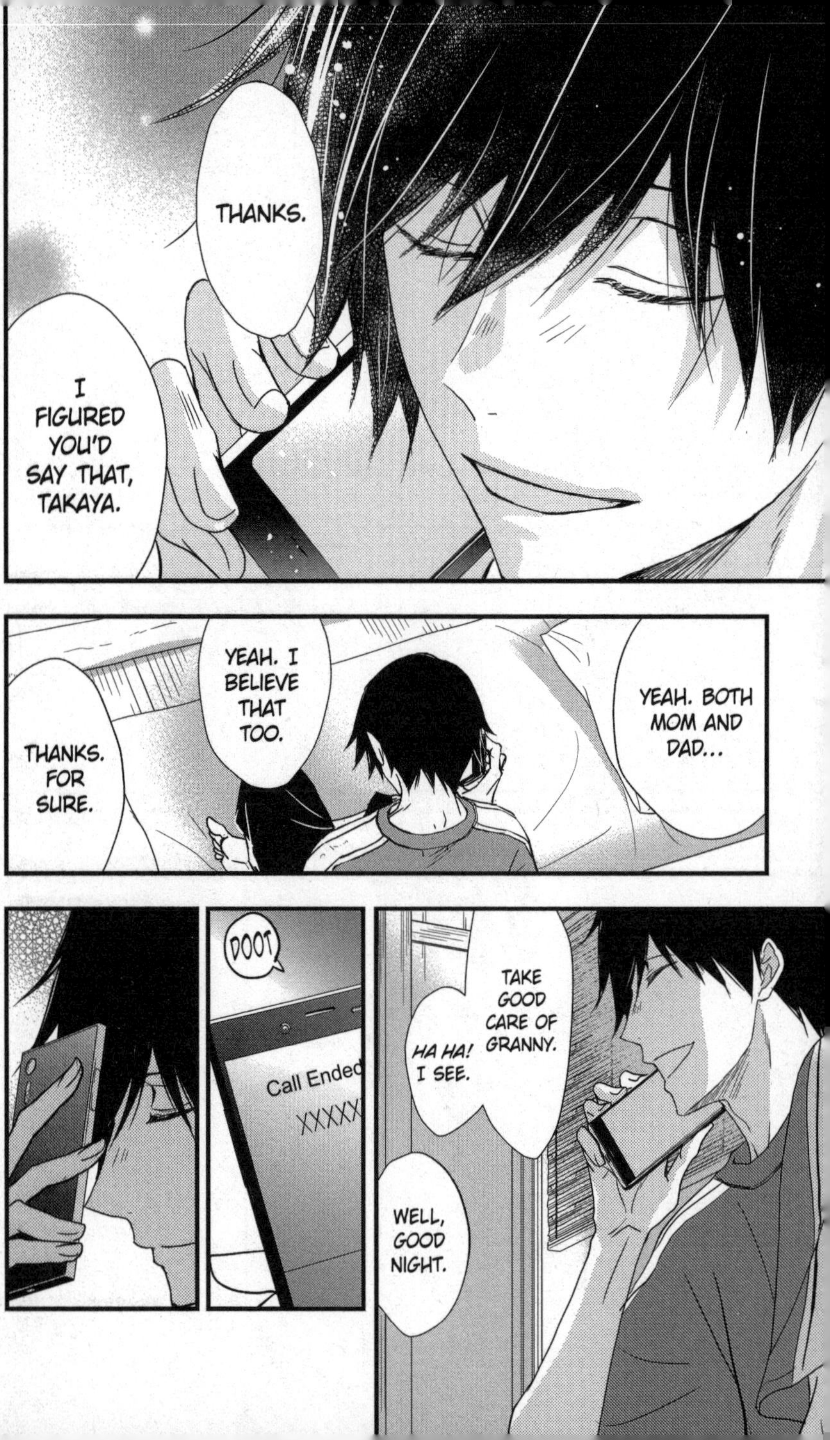
THANKS.
I FIGURED YOU'D SAY THAT, TAKAYA.
YEAH. BOTH MOM AND DAD...
YEAH. I BELIEVE THAT TOO.
THANKS. FOR SURE.
TAKE GOOD CARE OF GRANNY.
HA HA! I SEE.
WELL, GOOD NIGHT.
DOOT
Call Ended
XXXXX

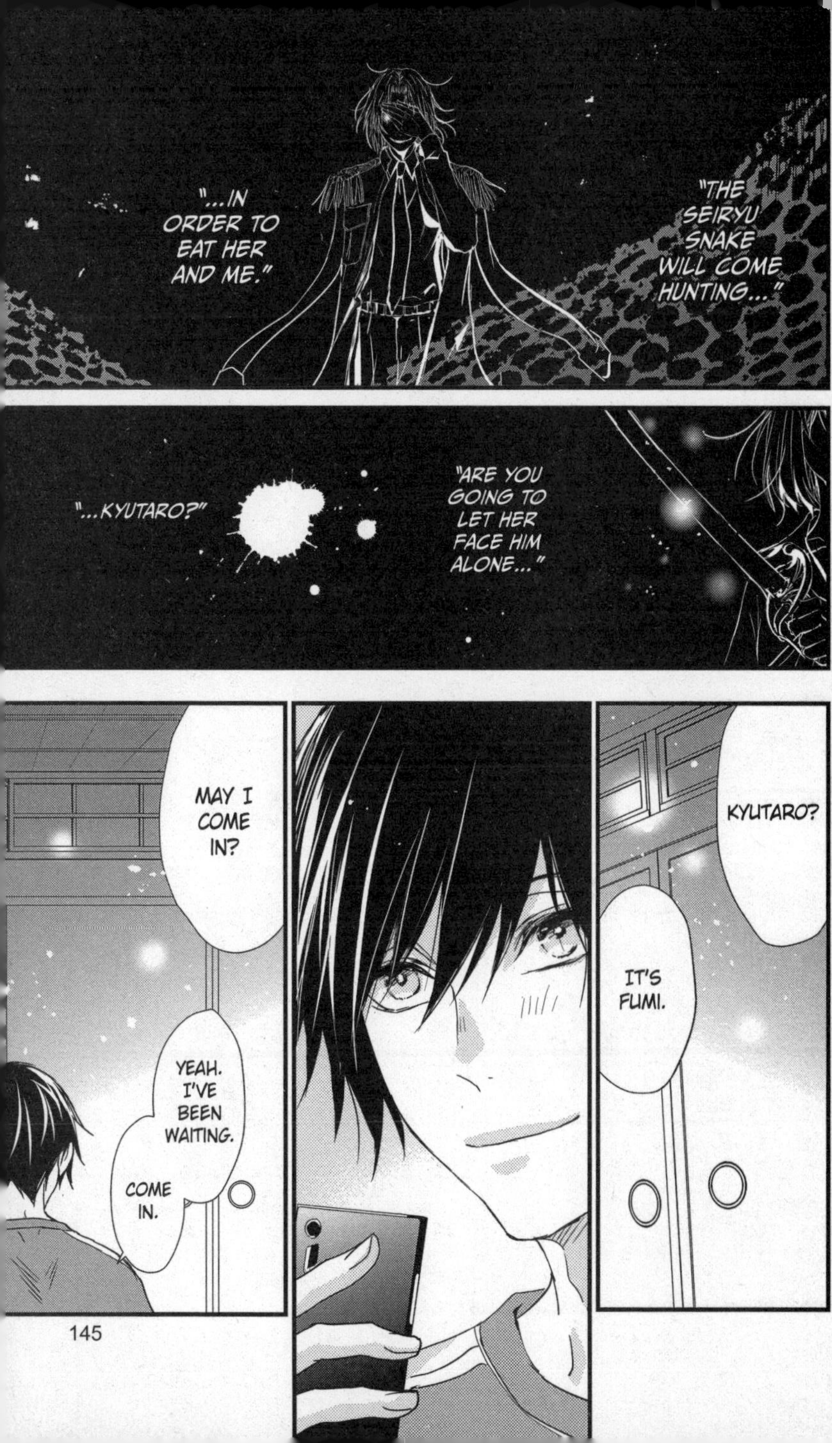
"THE SEIRYU SNAKE WILL COME HUNTING..."
"...IN ORDER TO EAT HER AND ME."
"ARE YOU GOING TO LET HER FACE HIM ALONE..."
"...KYUTARO?"
KYUTARO?
IT'S FUMI.
MAY I COME IN?
YEAH. I'VE BEEN WAITING.
COME IN.

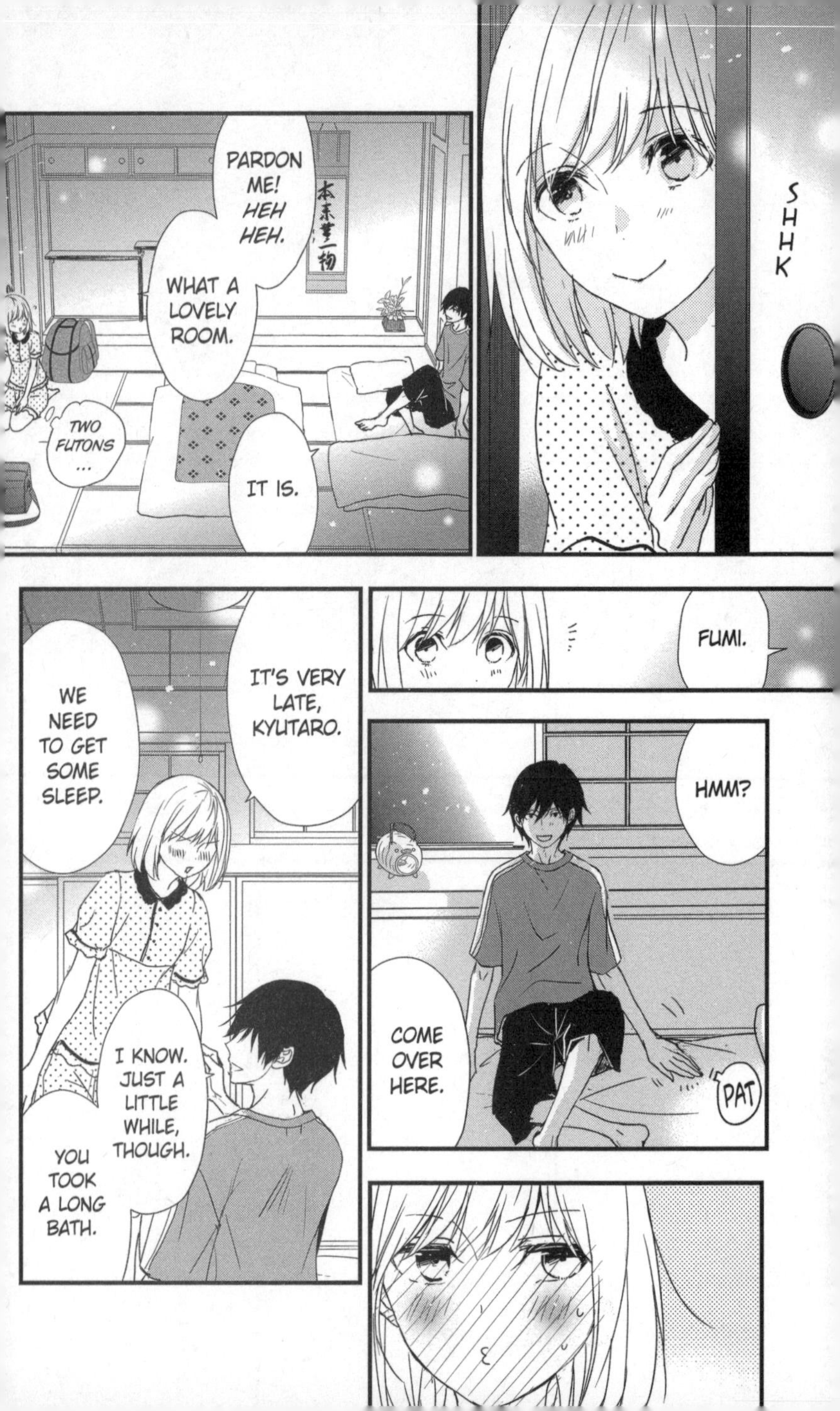
SHHK
PARDON ME! HEH HEH.
WHAT A LOVELY ROOM.
IT IS.
TWO FUTONS ...
FUMI.
HMM?
COME OVER HERE.
PAT
IT'S VERY LATE, KYUTARO.
WE NEED TO GET SOME SLEEP.
I KNOW. JUST A LITTLE WHILE, THOUGH.
YOU TOOK A LONG BATH.

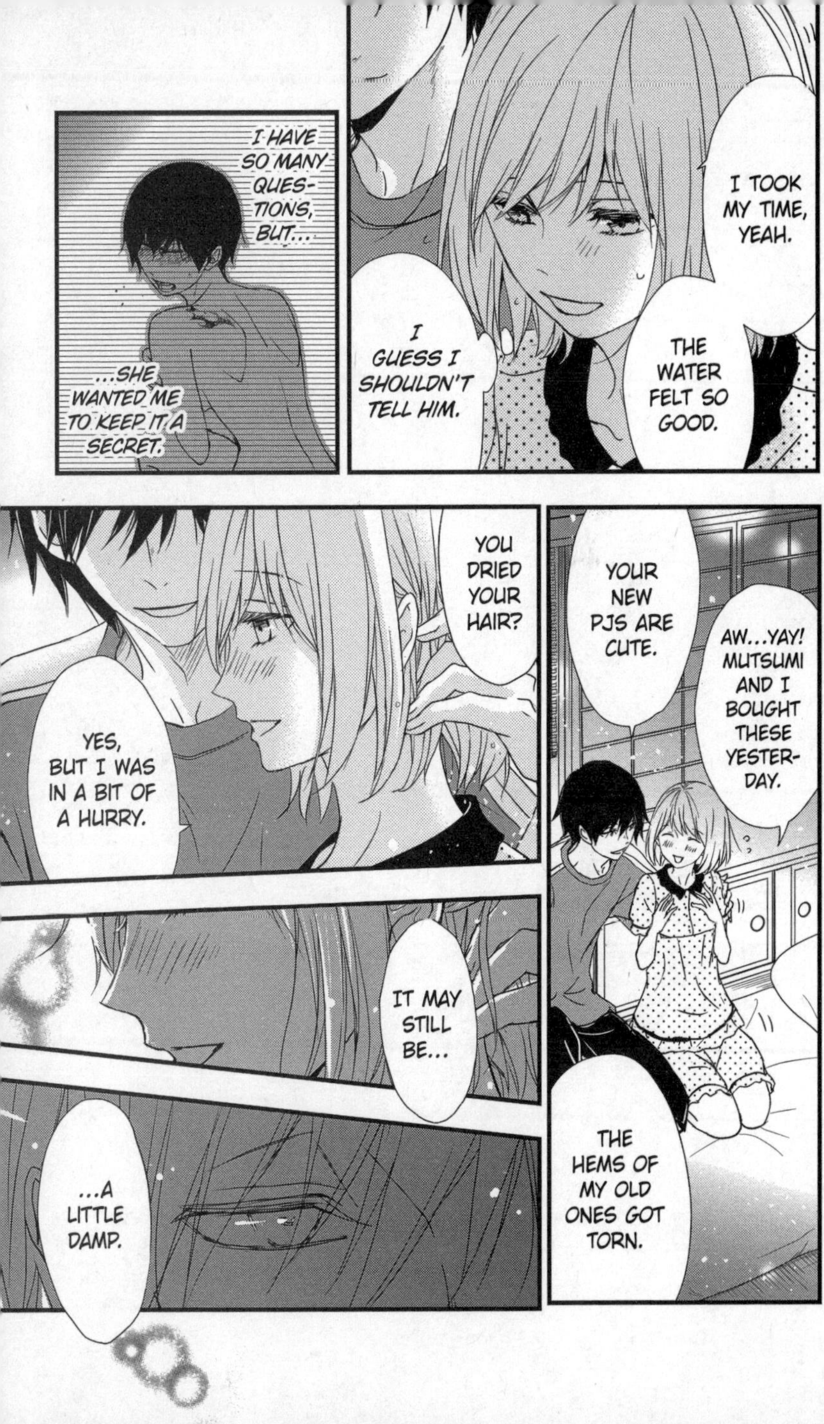
I TOOK MY TIME, YEAH.
THE WATER FELT SO GOOD.
I GUESS I SHOULDN'T TELL HIM.
I HAVE SO MANY QUES-TIONS, BUT...
...SHE WANTED ME TO KEEP IT A SECRET.
YOUR NEW PJS ARE CUTE.
AW...YAY! MUTSUMI AND I BOUGHT THESE YESTER-DAY.
THE HEMS OF MY OLD ONES GOT TORN.
YOU DRIED YOUR HAIR?
YES, BUT I WAS IN A BIT OF A HURRY.
IT MAY STILL BE...
...A LITTLE DAMP.

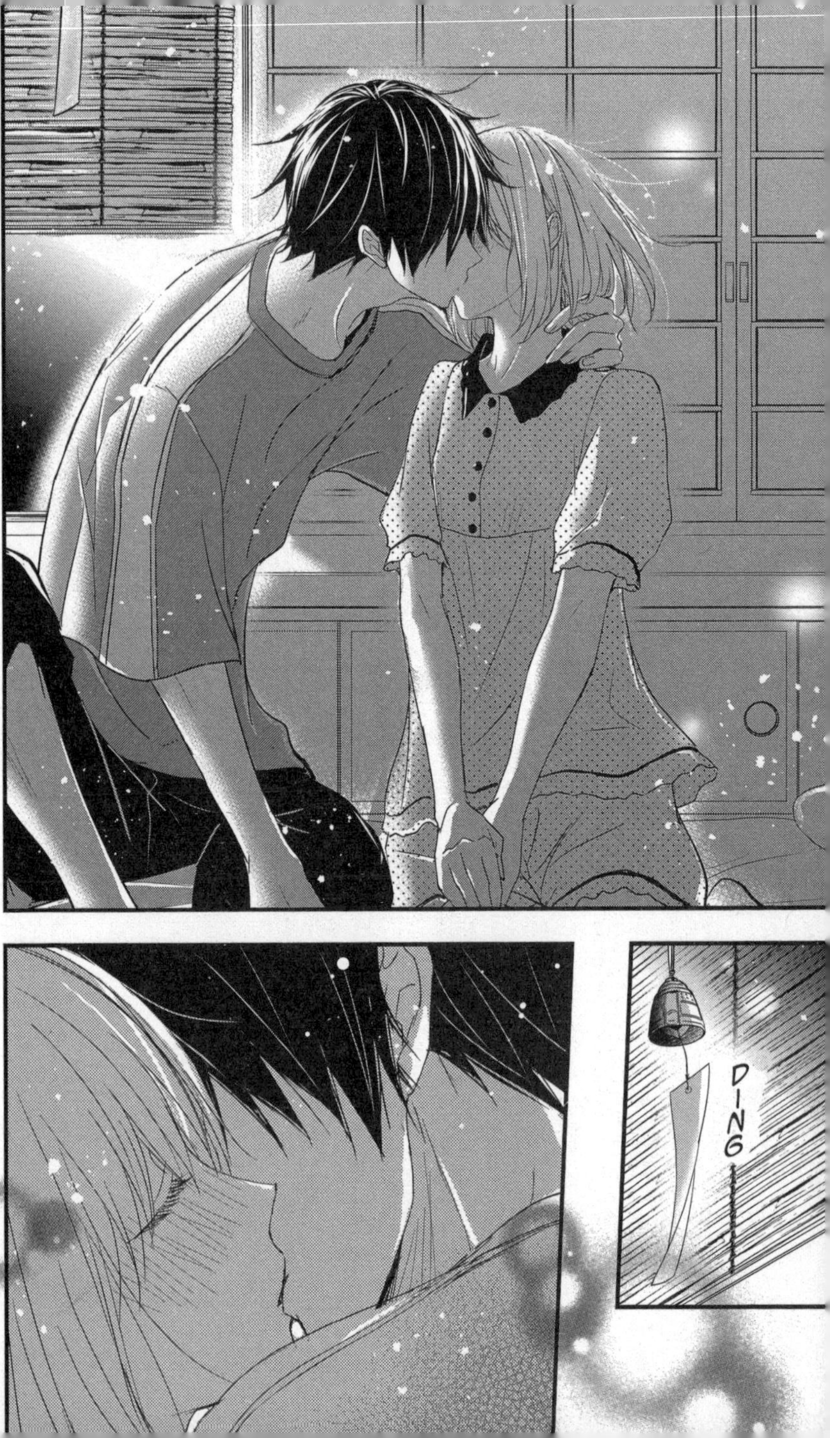
DING

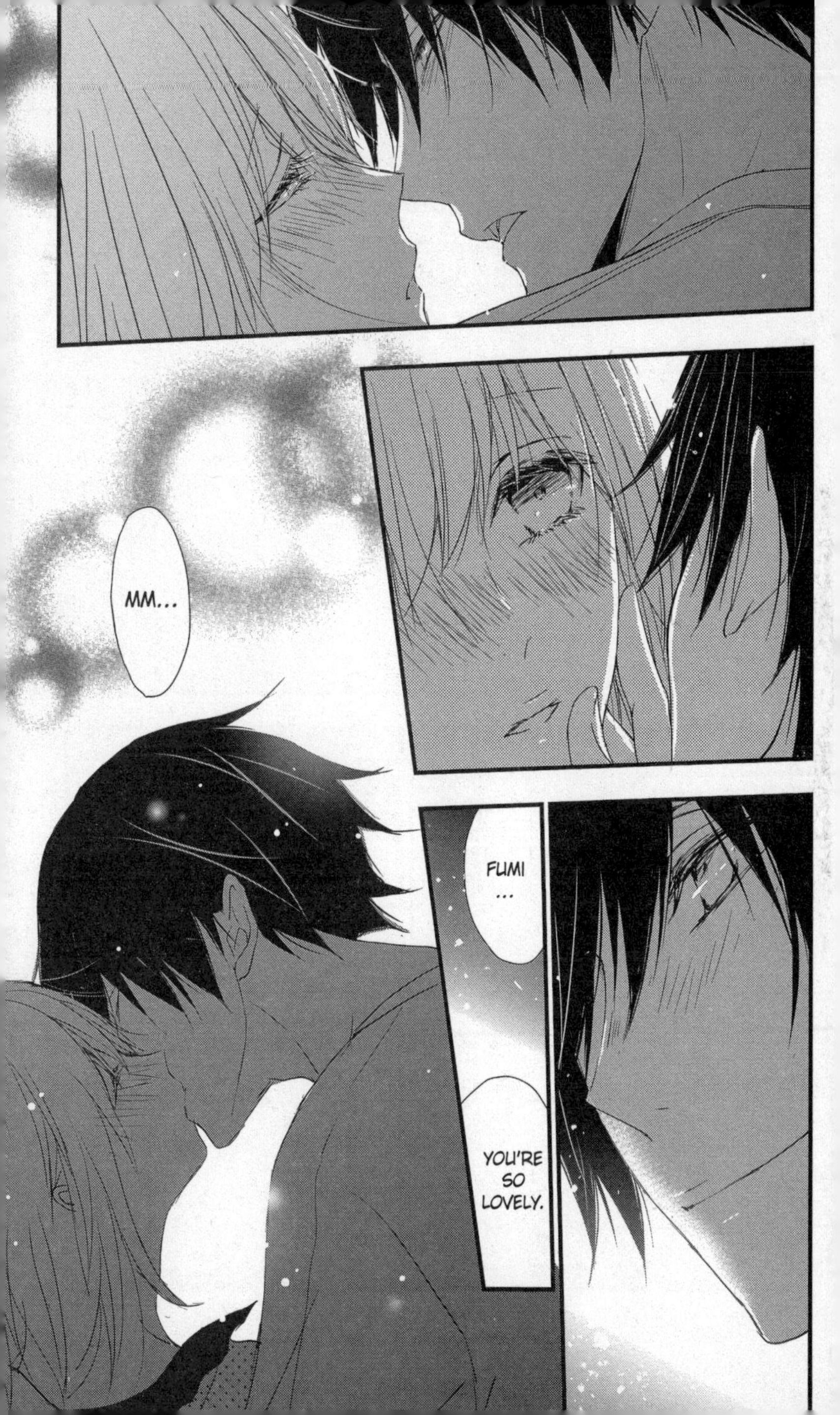
MM...
FUMI ...
YOU'RE SO LOVELY.

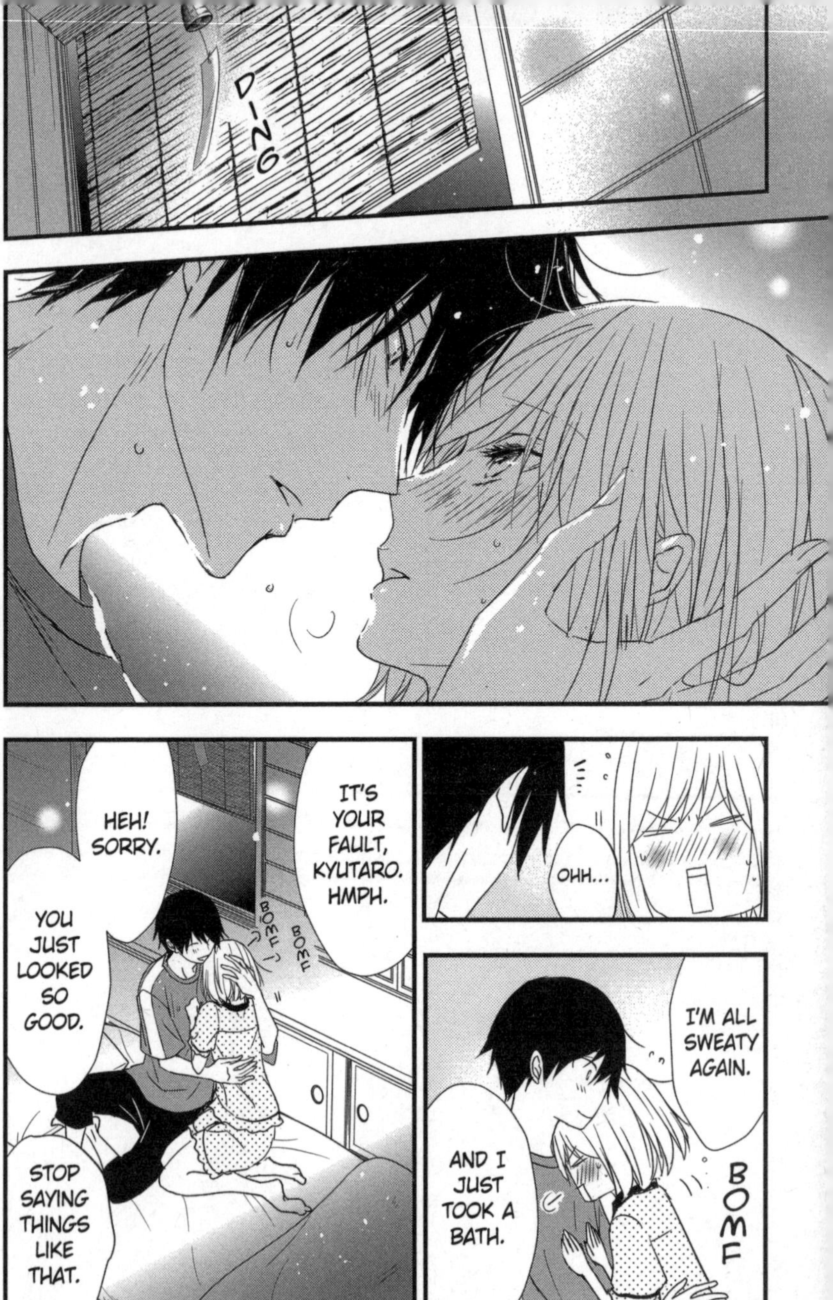
DING
OHH...
I'M ALL SWEATY AGAIN.
AND I JUST TOOK A BATH.
BOMF
IT'S YOUR FAULT, KYUTARO. HMPH.
HEH! SORRY.
YOU JUST LOOKED SO GOOD.
BOMF BOMF
STOP SAYING THINGS LIKE THAT.

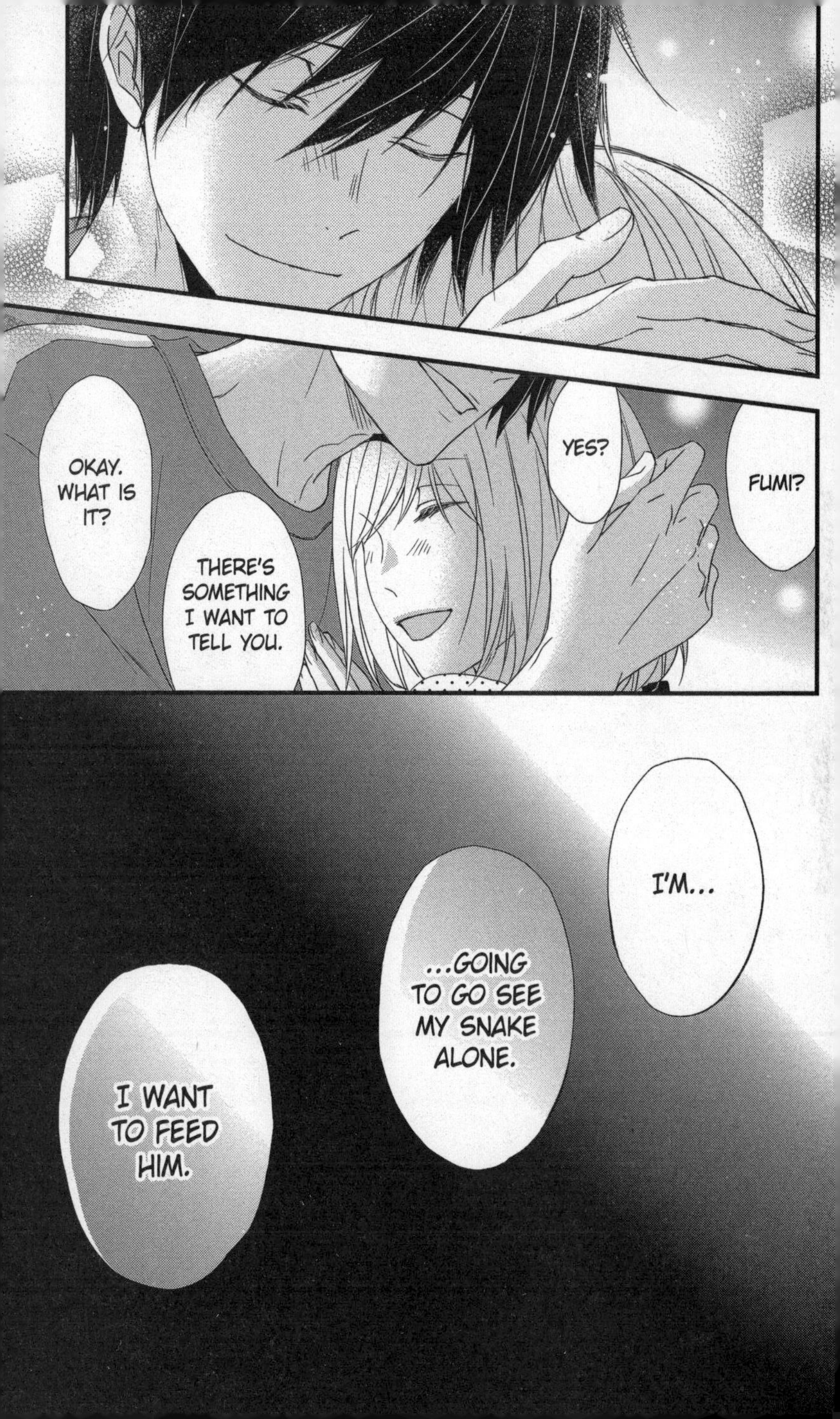
FUMI?
YES?
THERE'S SOMETHING I WANT TO TELL YOU.
OKAY. WHAT IS IT?
I'M...
...GOING TO GO SEE MY SNAKE ALONE.
I WANT TO FEED HIM.

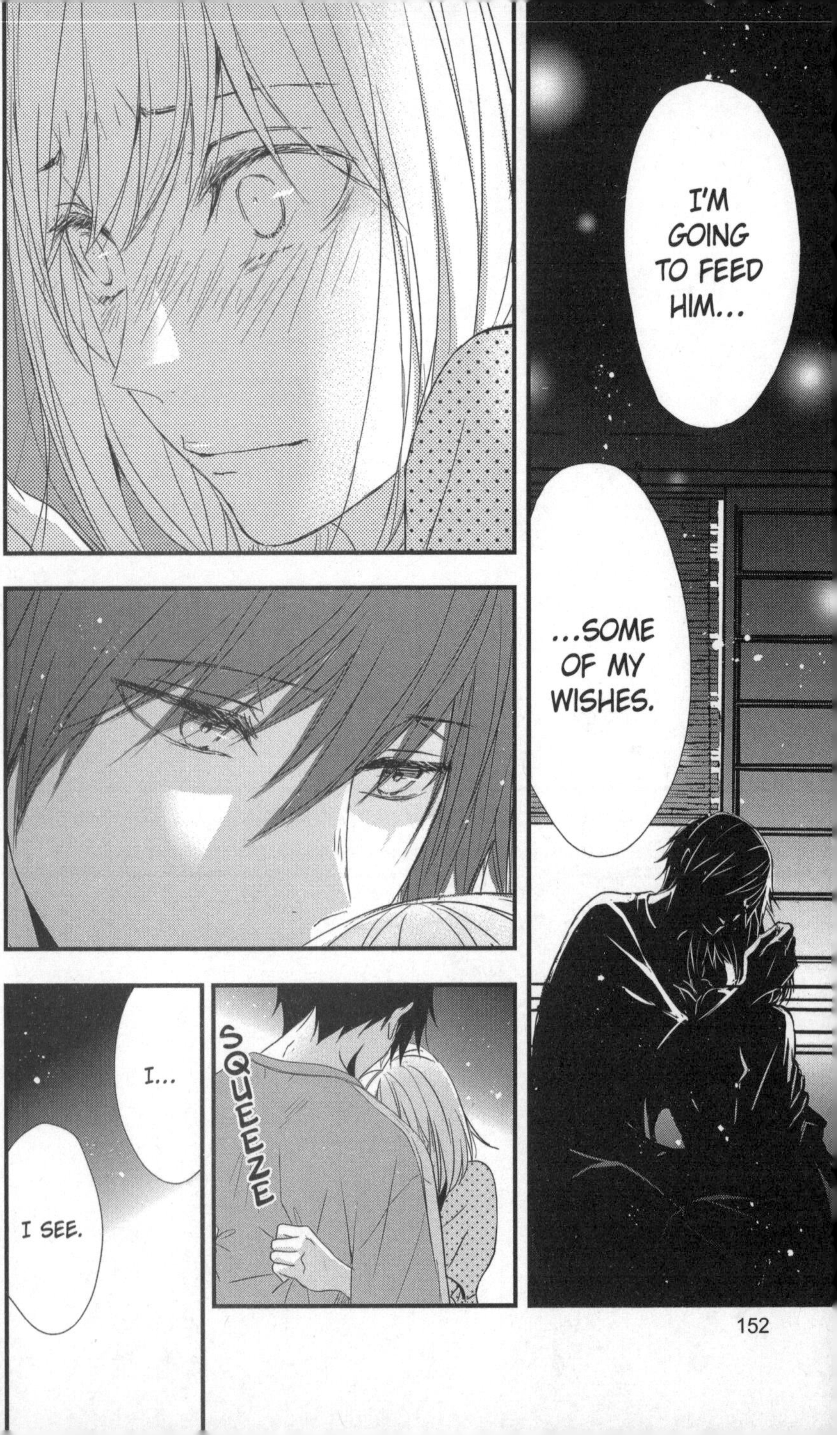
I'M GOING TO FEED HIM...
...SOME OF MY WISHES.
SQUEEZE
I...
I SEE.

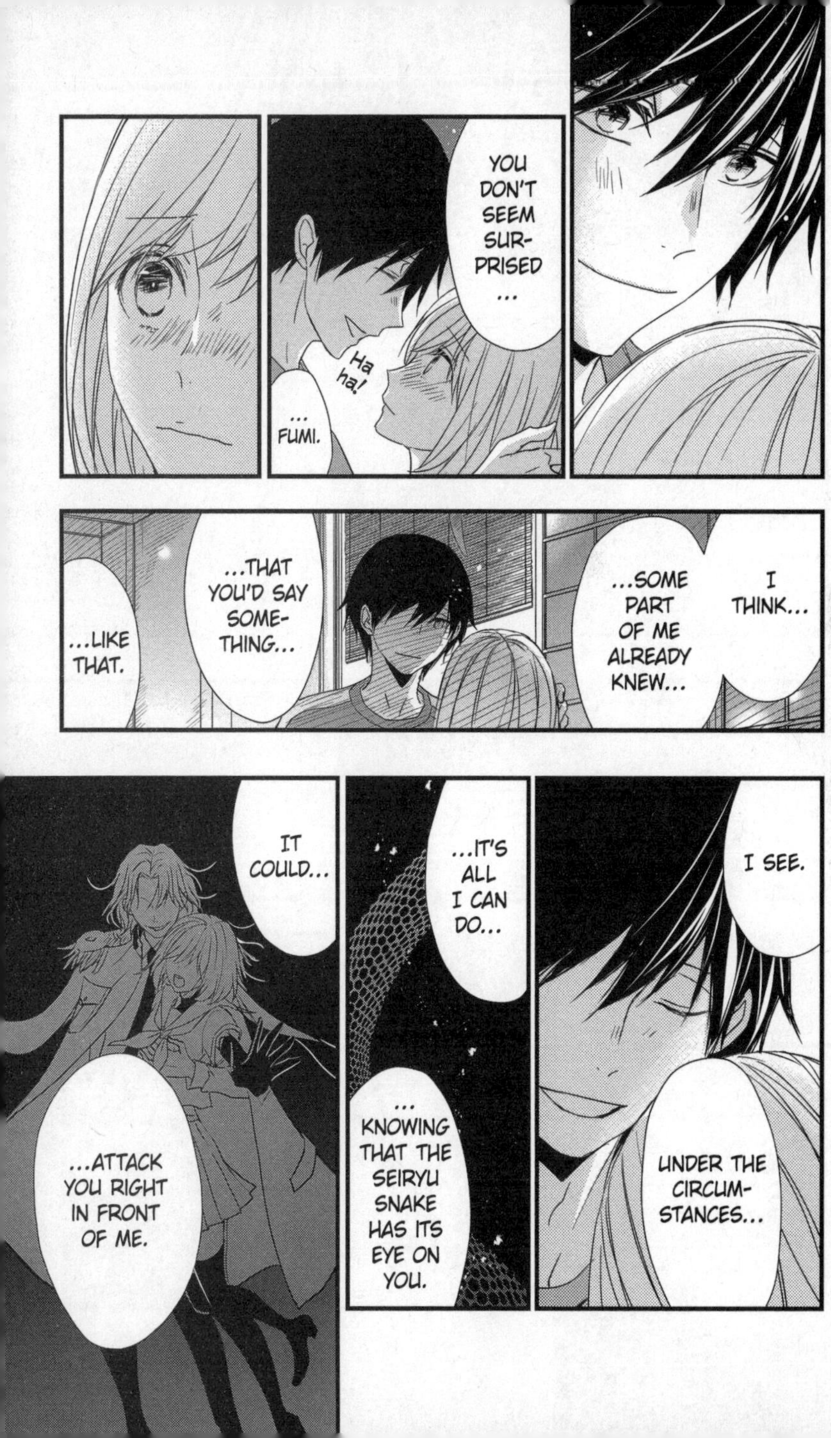
YOU DON'T SEEM SURPRISED...
Ha ha!
...FUMI.
I THINK...
...SOME PART OF ME ALREADY KNEW...
...THAT YOU'D SAY SOMETHING...
...LIKE THAT.
I SEE.
UNDER THE CIRCUMSTANCES...
...IT'S ALL I CAN DO...
...KNOWING THAT THE SEIRYU SNAKE HAS ITS EYE ON YOU.
IT COULD...
...ATTACK YOU RIGHT IN FRONT OF ME.

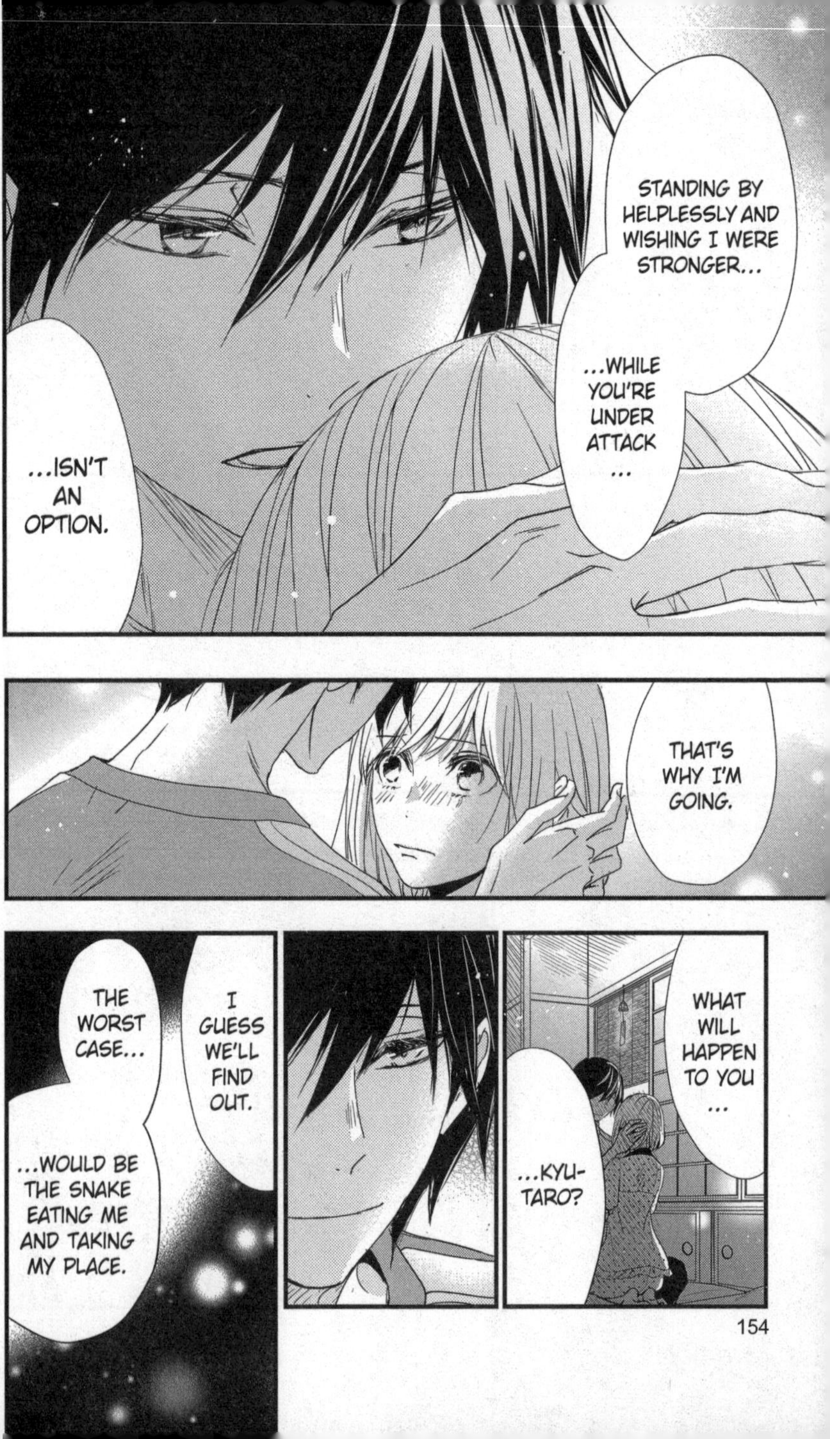
STANDING BY HELPLESSLY AND WISHING I WERE STRONGER...
...WHILE YOU'RE UNDER ATTACK...
...ISN'T AN OPTION.
THAT'S WHY I'M GOING.
WHAT WILL HAPPEN TO YOU...
...KYU-TARO?
I GUESS WE'LL FIND OUT.
THE WORST CASE...
...WOULD BE THE SNAKE EATING ME AND TAKING MY PLACE.

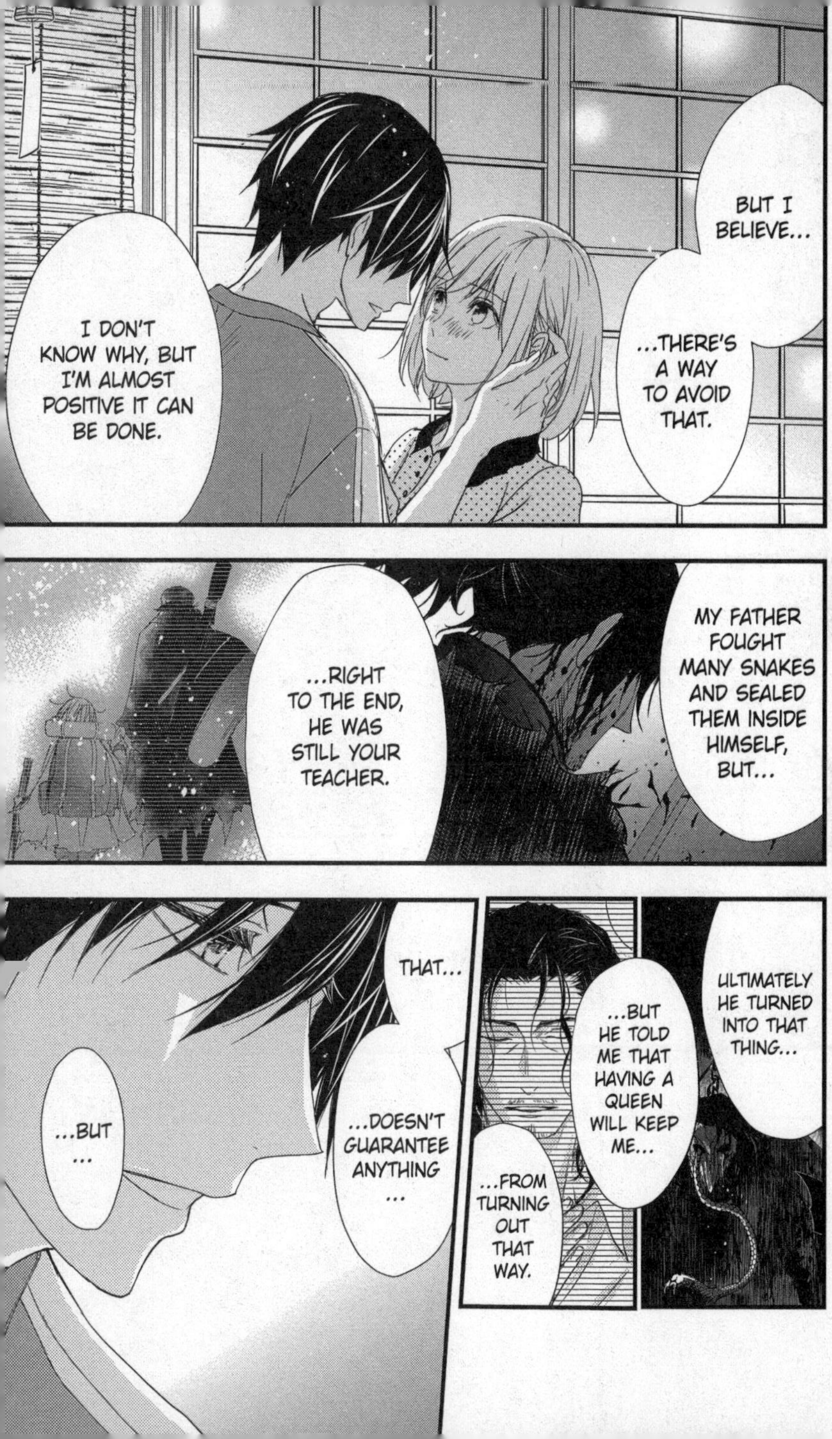
BUT I BELIEVE...
...THERE'S A WAY TO AVOID THAT.
I DON'T KNOW WHY, BUT I'M ALMOST POSITIVE IT CAN BE DONE.
MY FATHER FOUGHT MANY SNAKES AND SEALED THEM INSIDE HIMSELF, BUT...
...RIGHT TO THE END, HE WAS STILL YOUR TEACHER.
ULTIMATELY HE TURNED INTO THAT THING...
...BUT HE TOLD ME THAT HAVING A QUEEN WILL KEEP ME...
...FROM TURNING OUT THAT WAY.
THAT...
...DOESN'T GUARANTEE ANYTHING...
...BUT...

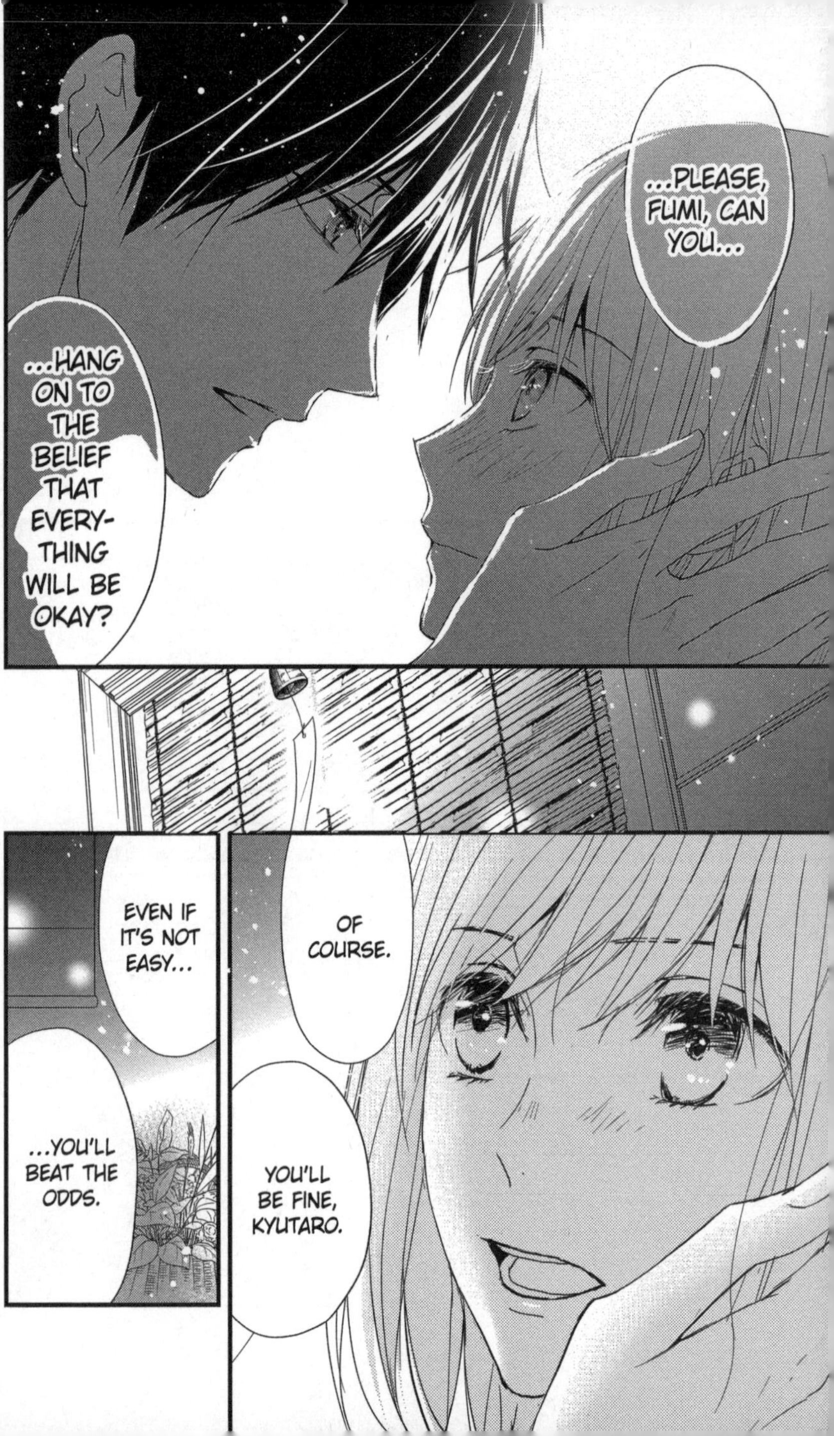
...PLEASE, FUMI, CAN YOU...
...HANG ON TO THE BELIEF THAT EVERY-THING WILL BE OKAY?
OF COURSE.
YOU'LL BE FINE, KYUTARO.
EVEN IF IT'S NOT EASY...
...YOU'LL BEAT THE ODDS.

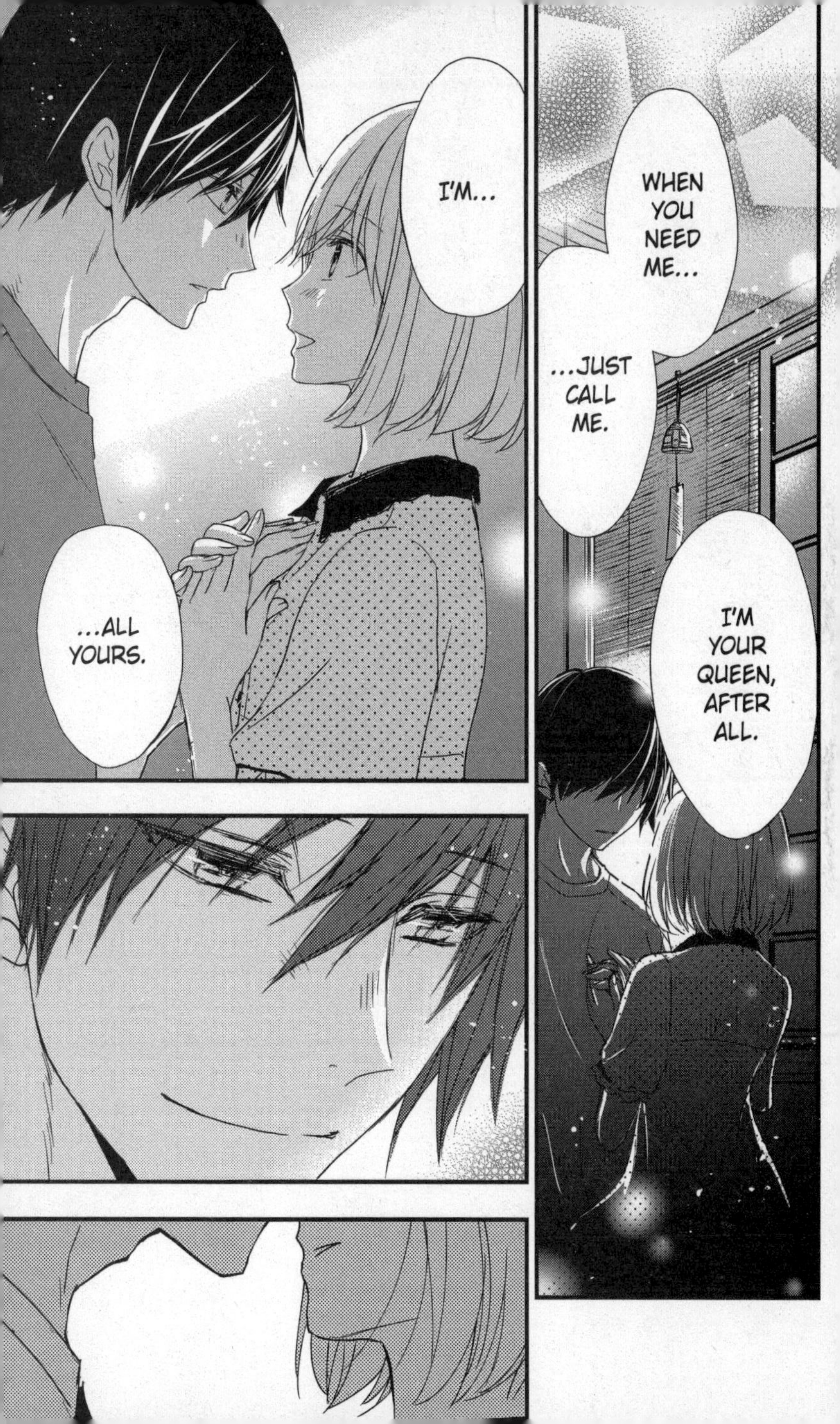
WHEN YOU NEED ME...
...JUST CALL ME.
I'M YOUR QUEEN, AFTER ALL.
I'M...
...ALL YOURS.

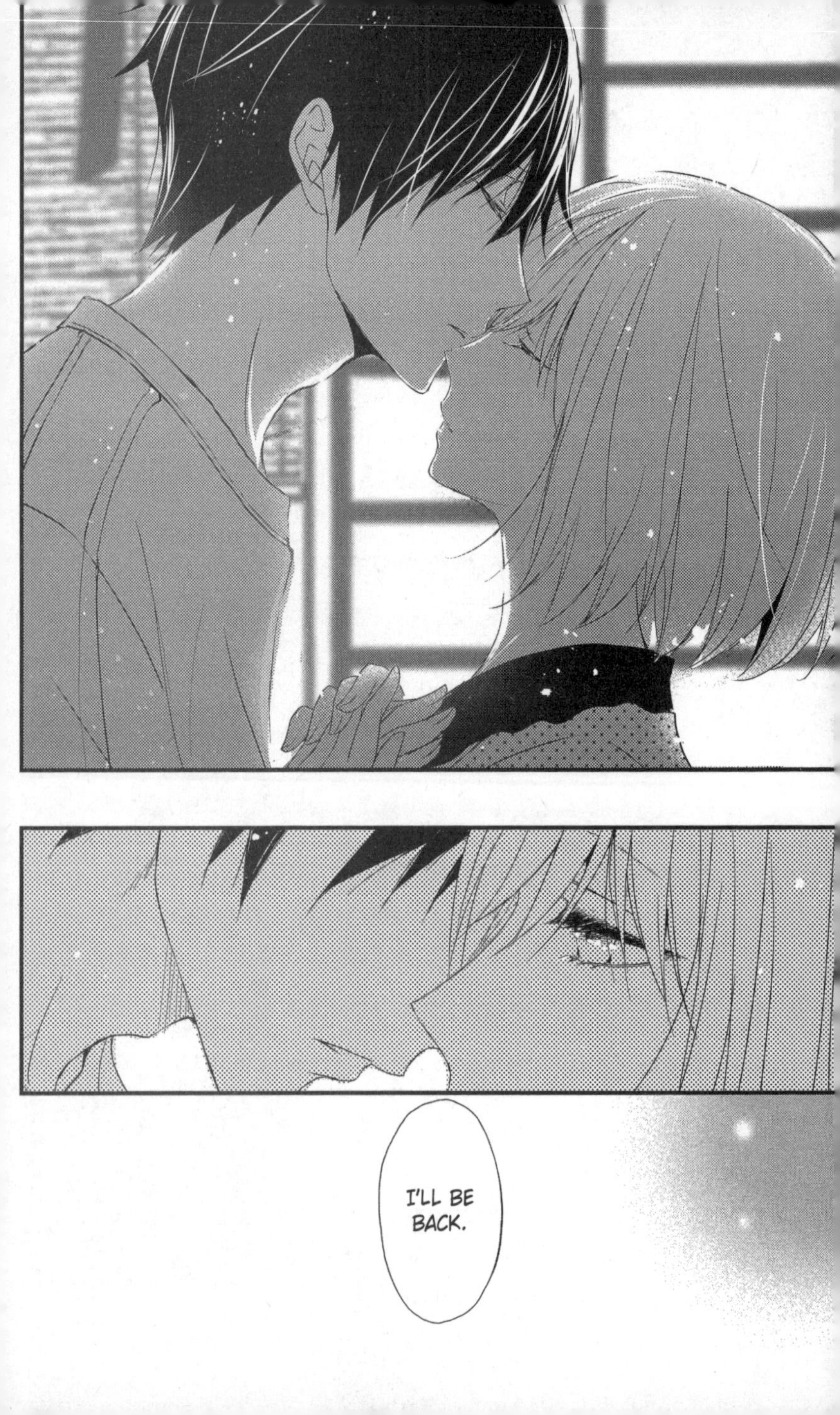
I'LL BE BACK.

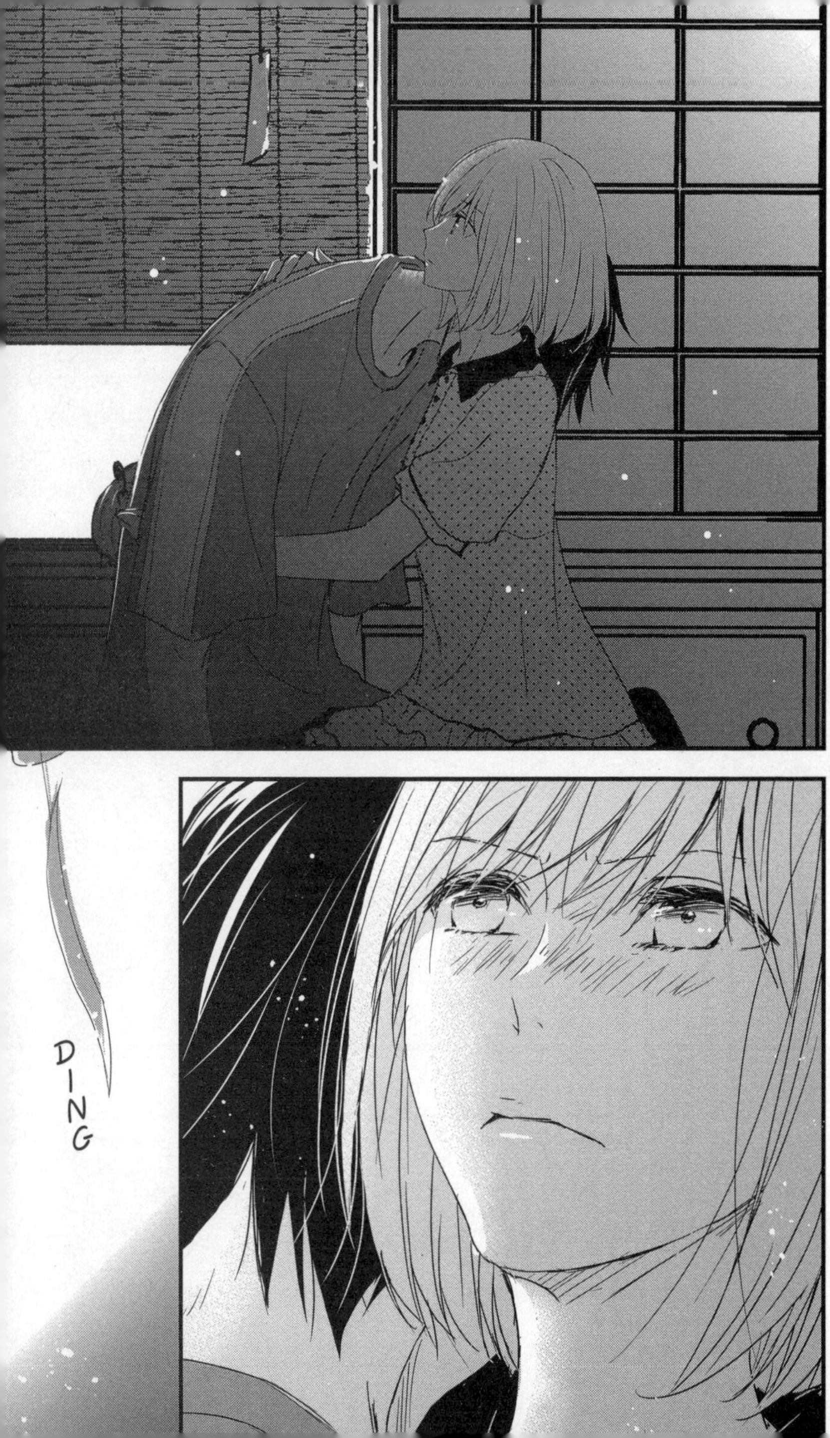
DING

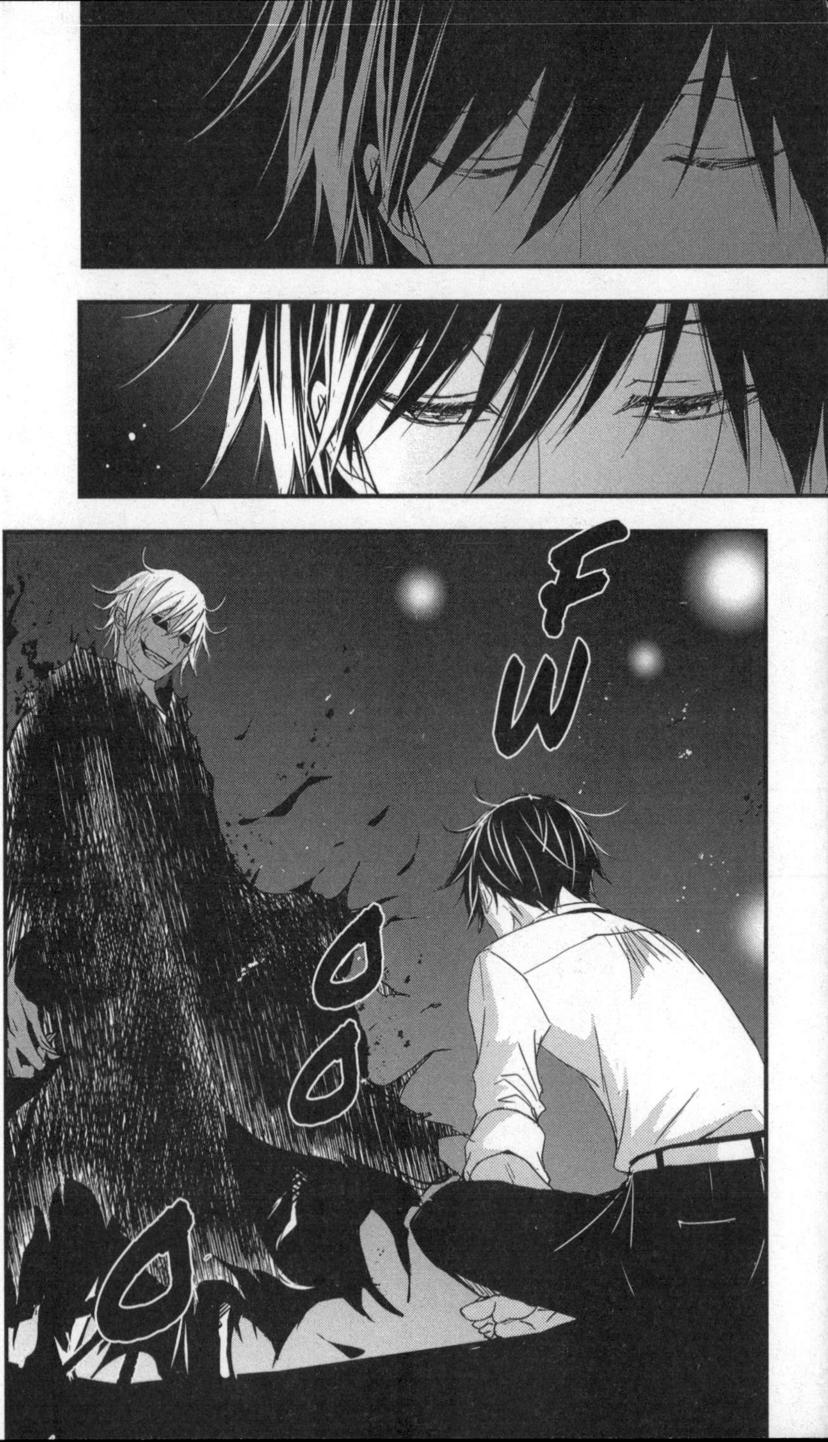
FWOOO

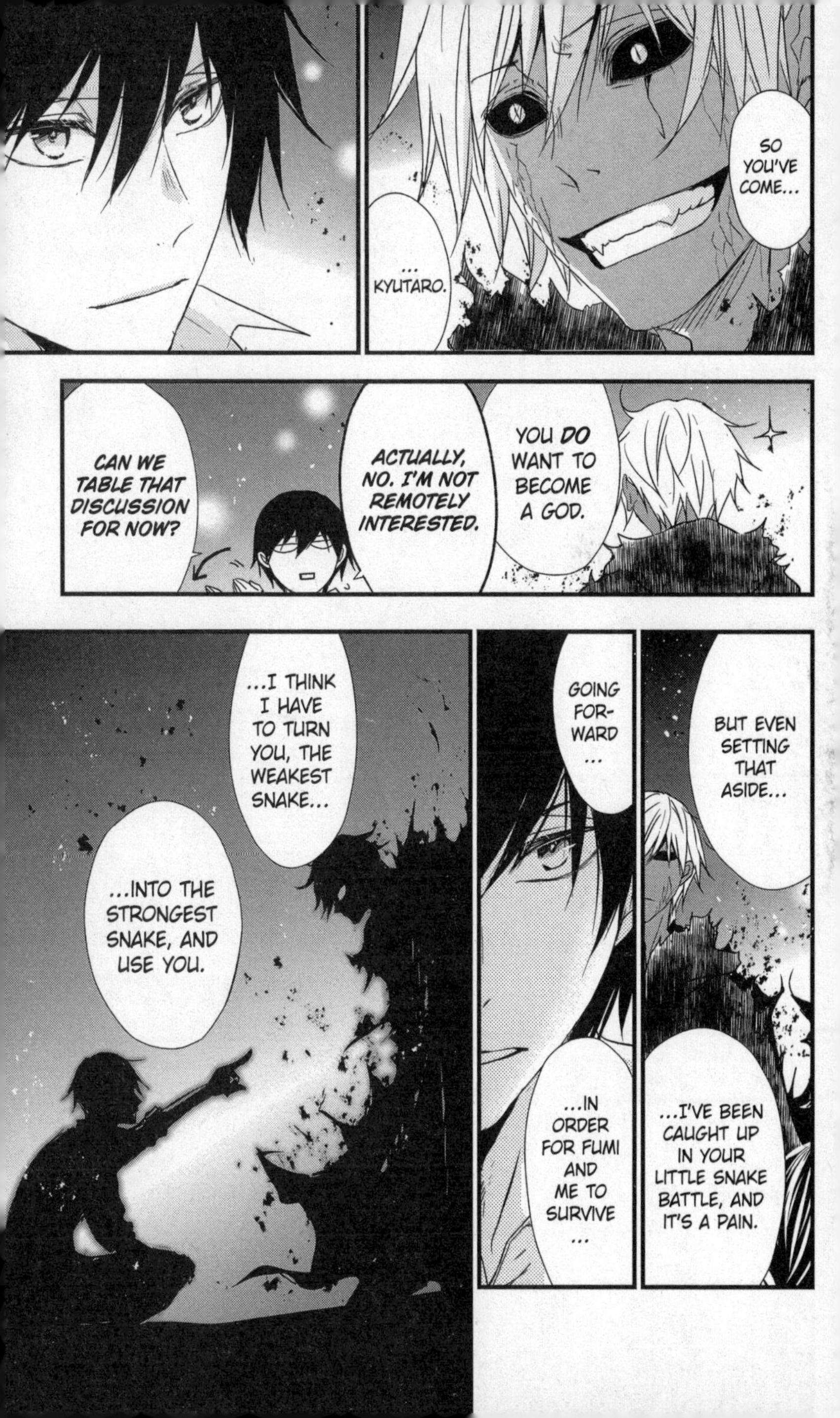
SO YOU'VE COME...
...KYUTARO.
YOU *DO* WANT TO BECOME A GOD.
ACTUALLY, NO. I'M NOT REMOTELY INTERESTED.
CAN WE TABLE THAT DISCUSSION FOR NOW?
BUT EVEN SETTING THAT ASIDE...
...I'VE BEEN CAUGHT UP IN YOUR LITTLE SNAKE BATTLE, AND IT'S A PAIN.
GOING FOR-WARD...
...IN ORDER FOR FUMI AND ME TO SURVIVE...
...I THINK I HAVE TO TURN YOU, THE WEAKEST SNAKE...
...INTO THE STRONGEST SNAKE, AND USE YOU.

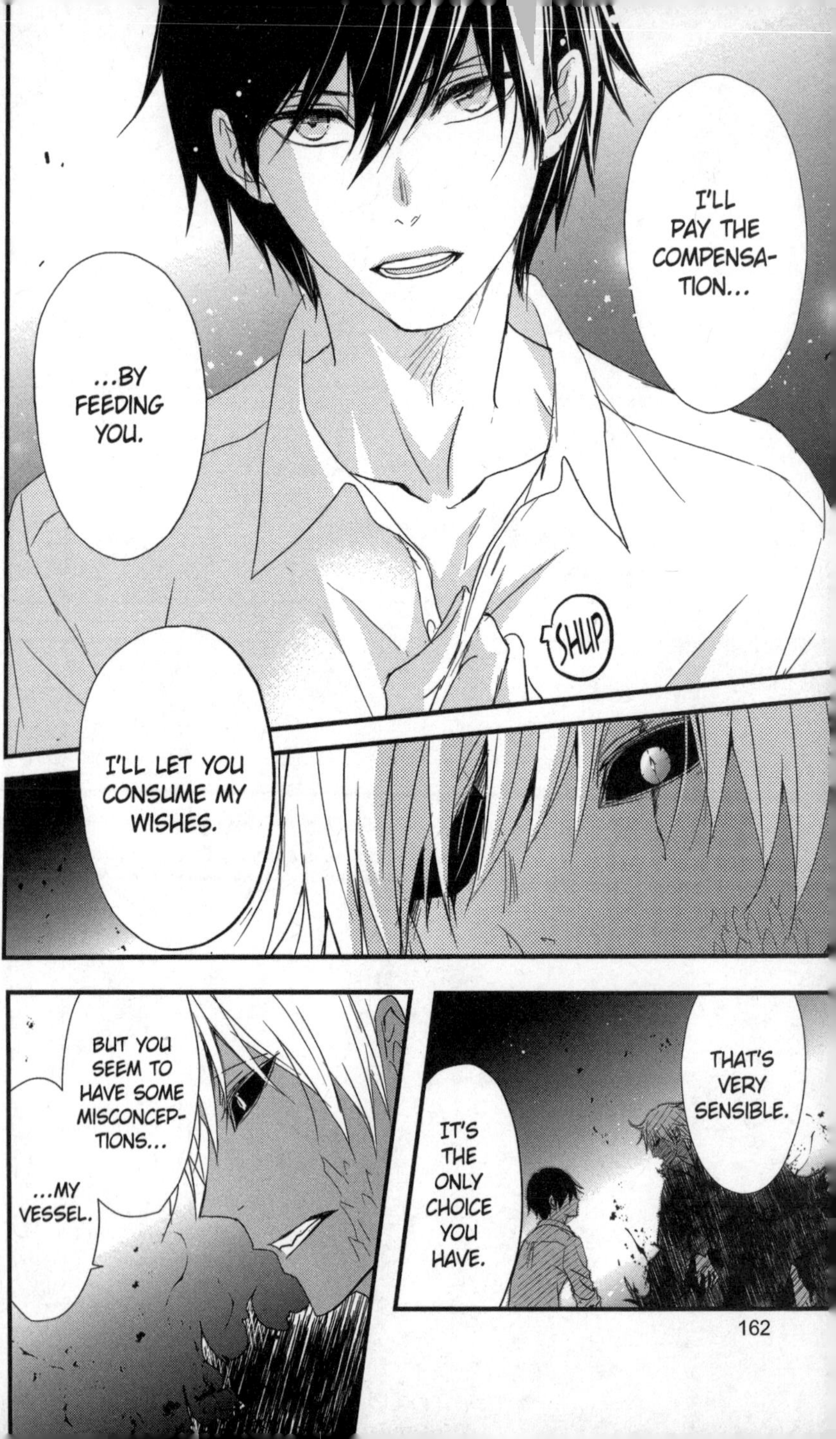

I'LL PAY THE COMPENSATION...
...BY FEEDING YOU.
SHUP
I'LL LET YOU CONSUME MY WISHES.
THAT'S VERY SENSIBLE.
IT'S THE ONLY CHOICE YOU HAVE.
BUT YOU SEEM TO HAVE SOME MISCONCEPTIONS...
...MY VESSEL.

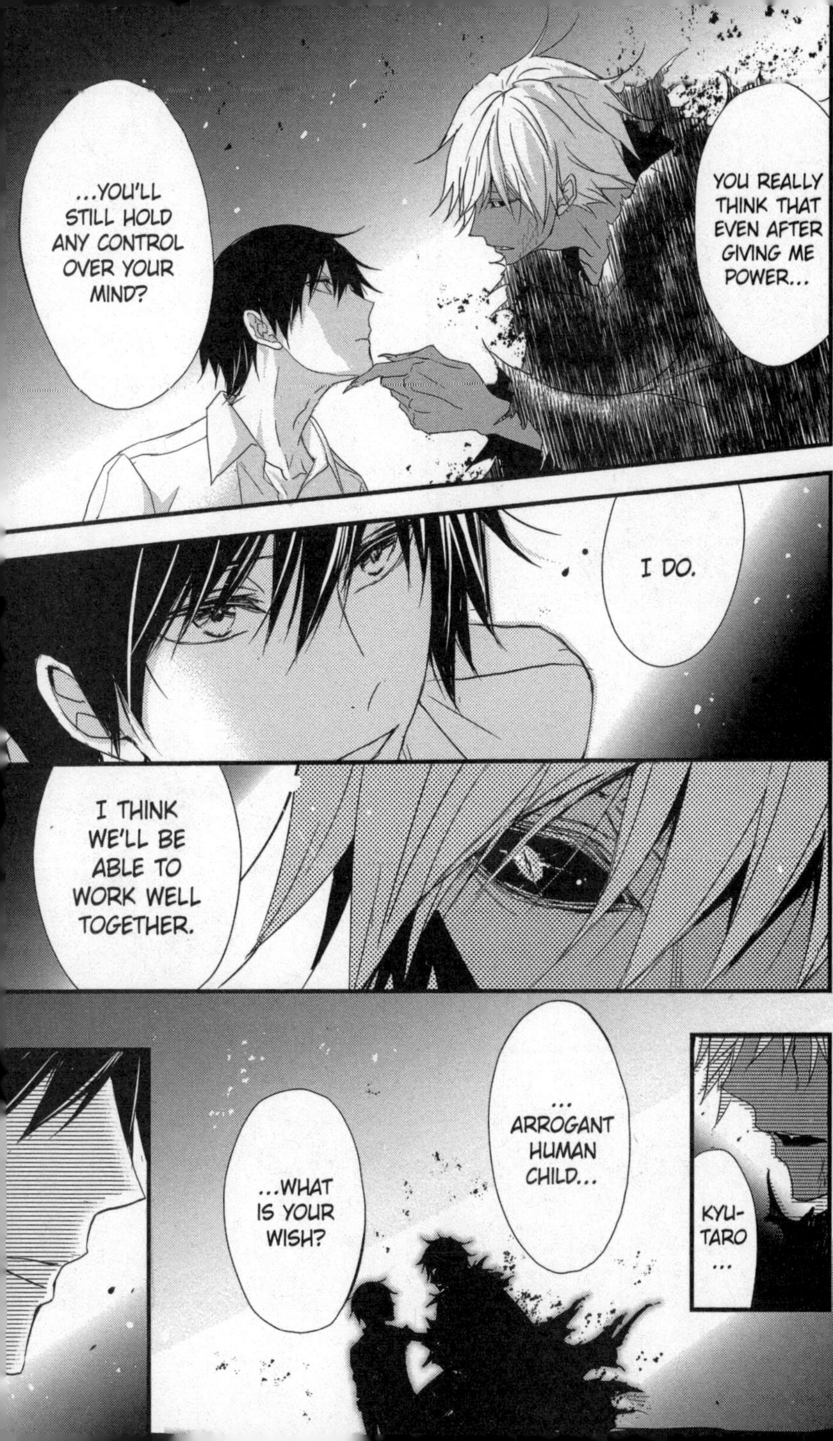
YOU REALLY THINK THAT EVEN AFTER GIVING ME POWER...
...YOU'LL STILL HOLD ANY CONTROL OVER YOUR MIND?
I DO.
I THINK WE'LL BE ABLE TO WORK WELL TOGETHER.
KYU-TARO ...
... ARROGANT HUMAN CHILD...
...WHAT IS YOUR WISH?

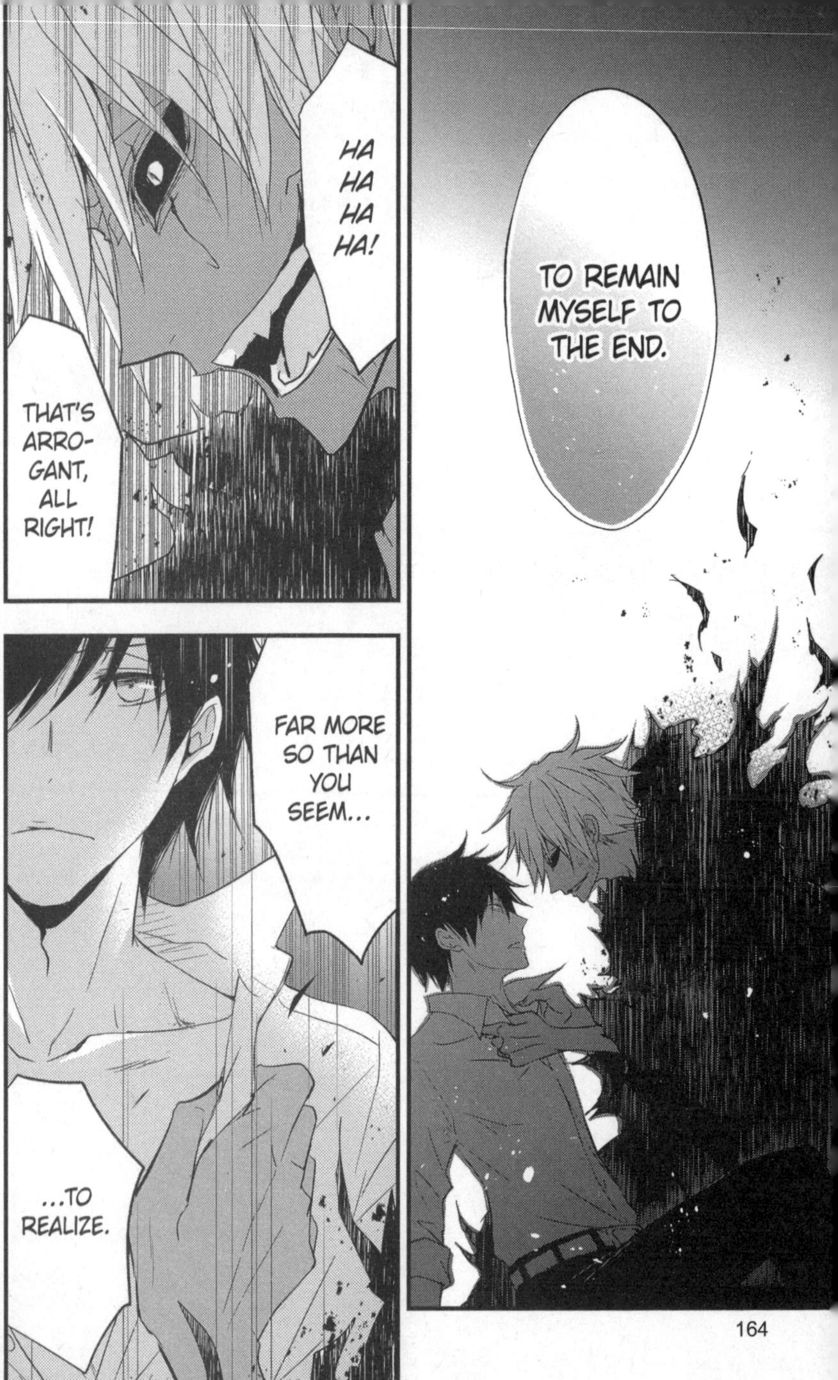
TO REMAIN MYSELF TO THE END.
HA HA HA HA!
THAT'S ARRO-GANT, ALL RIGHT!
FAR MORE SO THAN YOU SEEM...
...TO REALIZE.

WELL, SAVOR THAT FOOLISH- NESS...

I DO KNOW THAT IT'S ARROGANT.

...AS YOUR CONSCIOUS- NESS SLIPS AWAY.

BUT I STILL WANT TO REMAIN AS I AM.

I WANT TO MAKE IT BACK...

...TO YOUR SIDE.

Queen's Quality ⑪ The End

This is volume 11 of *Queen's Quality*. I worked on it under the watchful eye of my boss (my Java sparrow). I hope you like it!

—Kyousuke Motomi

Author Bio

Born on August 1, Kyousuke Motomi debuted in *Deluxe Betsucomi* with *Hetakuso Kyupiddo* (No Good Cupid) in 2002. She is the creator of *Dengeki Daisy*, *Beast Master* and *QQ Sweeper*, all available in North America from VIZ Media. Motomi enjoys sleeping, tea ceremonies and reading Haruki Murakami.

Queen's Quality

Vol. 11
Shojo Beat Edition

STORY AND ART BY
KYOUSUKE MOTOMI

QUEEN'S QUALITY Vol. 11
by Kyousuke MOTOMI
© 2016 Kyousuke MOTOMI
All rights reserved.
Original Japanese edition published by SHOGAKUKAN.
English translation rights in the United States of America, Canada, the United
Kingdom, Ireland, Australia and New Zealand arranged with SHOGAKUKAN.

ORIGINAL DESIGN/Chie SATO+Bay Bridge Studio

English Adaptation/Ysabet Reinhardt MacFarlane
Translation/JN Productions
Touch-Up Art & Lettering/Rina Mapa
Design/Julian [JR] Robinson
Editor/Amy Yu

The stories, characters and incidents mentioned in this publication are
entirely fictional.

Printed in the U.S.A.

Published by VIZ Media, LLC
P.O. Box 77010
San Francisco, CA 94107

10 9 8 7 6 5 4 3 2 1
First printing, March 2021

viz.com

shojobeat.com

This is the Last Page!

It's true: In keeping with the original Japanese comic format, this book reads from right to left—so action, sound effects and word balloons are completely reversed. This preserves the orientation of the original artwork—plus, it's fun! Check out the diagram shown here to get the hang of things, and then turn to the other side of the book to get started!

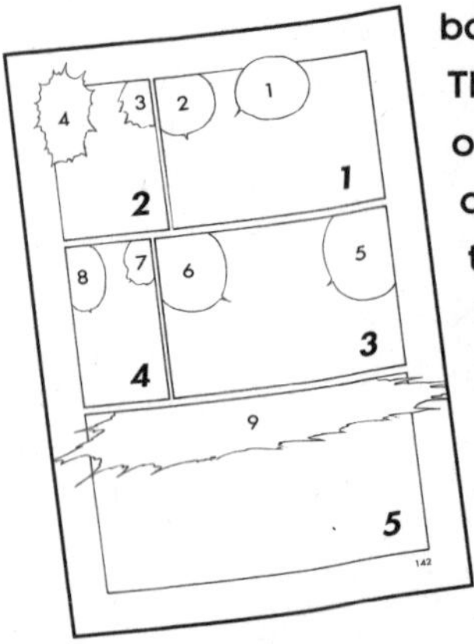
1
2
3
4
1
2
5
6
7
8
3
4
9
5
142

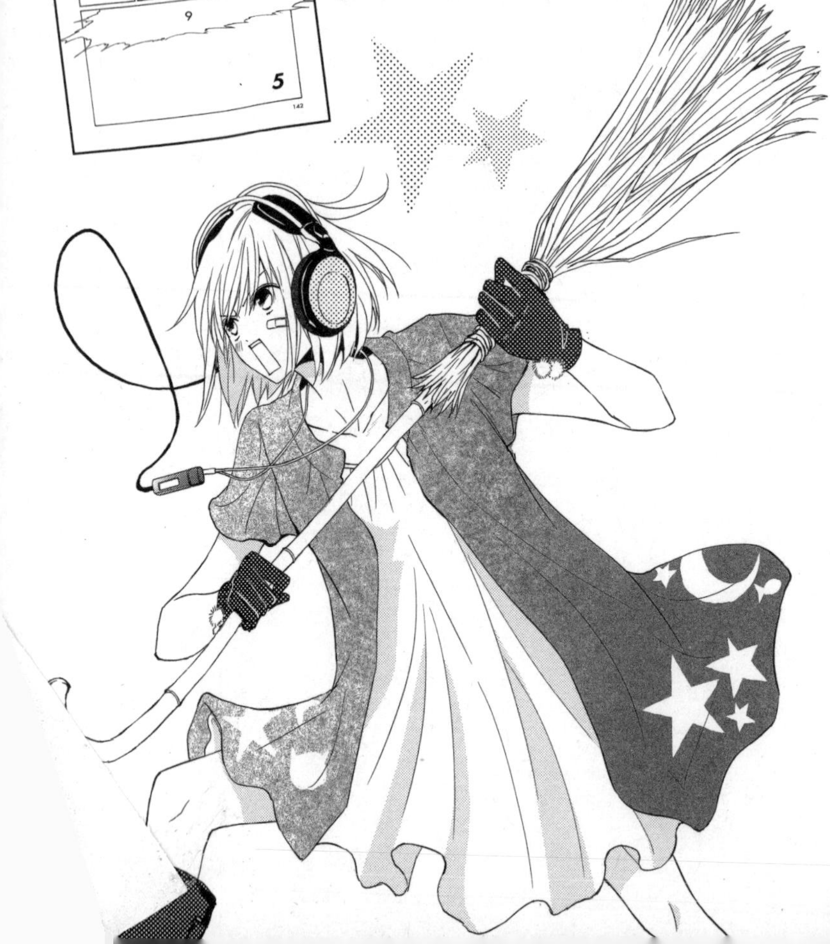